CLASSICAL ANTIQUITY IN HEAVY METAL MUSIC

IMAGINES – Classical Receptions in the Visual Performing Arts

Series Editors: Filippo Carlà-Uhink and Martin Lindner

Other titles in this series:

ART NOUVEAU AND THE CLASSICAL TRADITION
by Richard Warren

THE ANCIENT MEDITERRANEAN SEA IN MODERN VISUAL AND PERFORMING ARTS
edited by Rosario Rovira Guardiola

CLASSICAL ANTIQUITY IN HEAVY METAL MUSIC

edited by K. F. B. Fletcher and Osman Umurhan

BLOOMSBURY ACADEMIC
LONDON • NEW YORK • OXFORD • NEW DELHI • SYDNEY

BLOOMSBURY ACADEMIC
Bloomsbury Publishing Plc
50 Bedford Square, London, WC1B 3DP, UK
1385 Broadway, New York, NY 10018, USA
29 Earlsfort Terrace, Dublin 2, Ireland

BLOOMSBURY, BLOOMSBURY ACADEMIC and the Diana logo
are trademarks of Bloomsbury Publishing Plc

First published in Great Britain 2020
Paperback edition first published 2021

Copyright © K. F. B. Fletcher, Osman Umurhan and Contributors, 2020

K. F. B. Fletcher and Osman Umurhan have asserted their right under the Copyright,
Designs and Patents Act, 1988, to be identified as Authors of this work.

For legal purposes the Acknowledgements on p. x–xi constitute
an extension of this copyright page.

Cover design: Terry Woodley
Cover image © Antikenmuseum der Universität Heidelberg. Photograph: Hubert Vögele

All rights reserved. No part of this publication may be reproduced or
transmitted in any form or by any means, electronic or mechanical,
including photocopying, recording, or any information storage or retrieval
system, without prior permission in writing from the publishers.

Bloomsbury Publishing Plc does not have any control over, or responsibility for,
any third-party websites referred to or in this book. All internet addresses given
in this book were correct at the time of going to press. The author and publisher
regret any inconvenience caused if addresses have changed or sites have
ceased to exist, but can accept no responsibility for any such changes.

A catalogue record for this book is available from the British Library.

Library of Congress Cataloging-in-Publication Data
Names: Fletcher, K. F. B. | Umurhan, Osman, 1976-
Title: Classical antiquity in heavy metal music / edited by K. F. B. Fletcher and Osman Umurhan.
Description: London: New York, NY: Bloomsbury Academic, [2019] |
Series: Imagines : classical receptions in the visual performing arts |
Includes bibliographical references and index.
Identifiers: LCCN 2019014057 | ISBN 9781350075351 (hb) | ISBN 9781350075375 (epub)
Subjects: LCSH: Heavy metal (Music)–History and criticism. | Classical antiquities in music.
Classification: LCC ML3534 .C573 2019 | DDC 781.66–dc23
LC record available at https://lccn.loc.gov/2019014057

ISBN: HB: 978-1-3500-7535-1
PB: 978-1-3501-9138-9
ePDF: 978-1-3500-7536-8
eBook: 978-1-3500-7537-5

Series: IMAGINES—Classical Receptions in the Visual and Performing Arts

Typeset by RefineCatch Limited, Bungay, Suffolk

To find out more about our authors and books visit
www.bloomsbury.com and sign up for our newsletters.

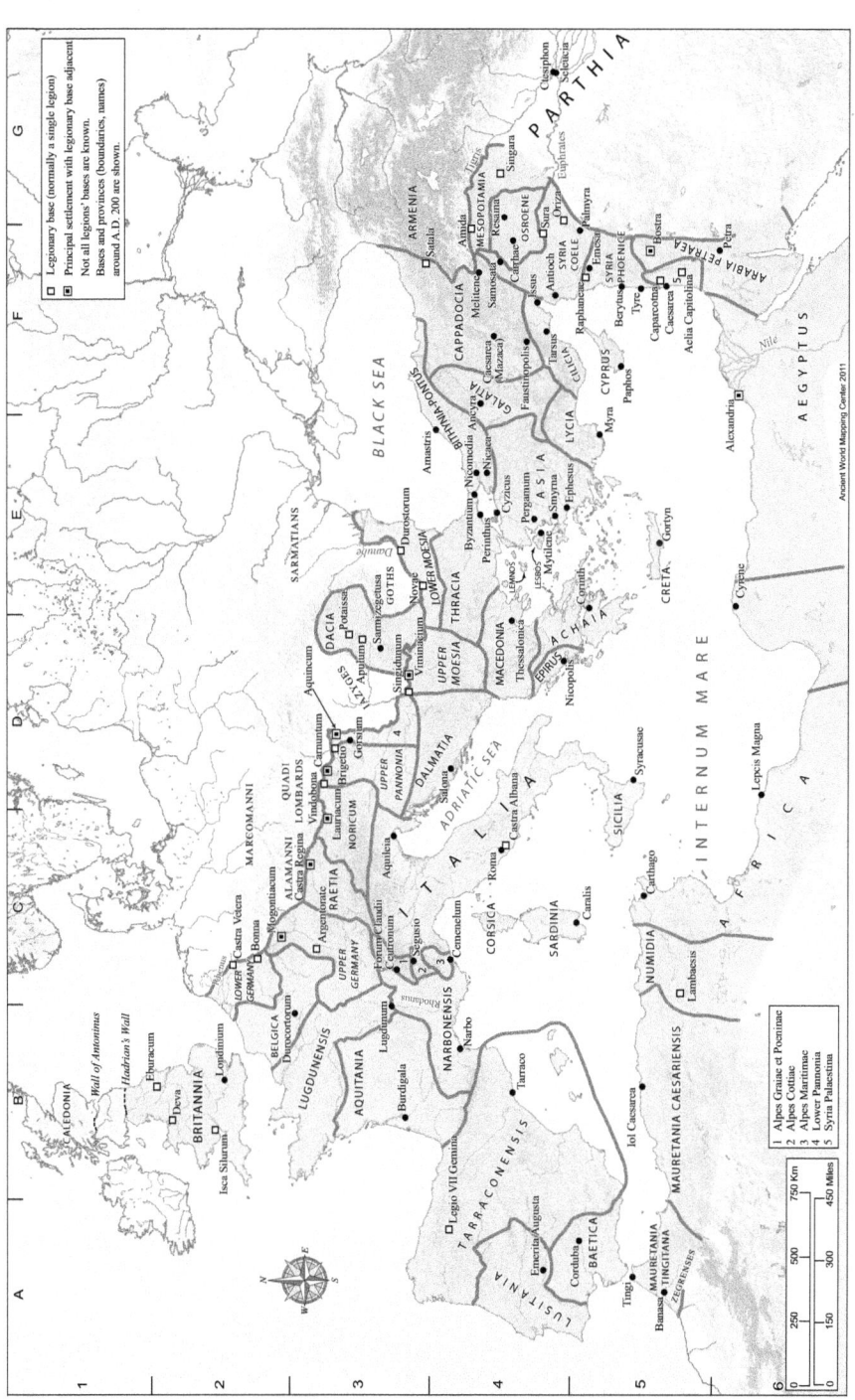

Figure 0.1 The Roman Empire, 200 CE. Ancient World Mapping Center © 2018 (awmc.unc.edu). Used by permission.

CONTENTS

List of Figures		viii
List of Contributors		ix
Acknowledgments		x
	Introduction: Where Metal and Classics Meet K. F. B. Fletcher and Osman Umurhan	1
1	Vergil's *Aeneid* and Nationalism in Italian Metal K. F. B. Fletcher	23
2	Eternal Defiance: Celtic Identity and the Classical Past in Heavy Metal Matthew Taylor	53
3	Screaming Ancient Greek Hymns: The Case of Kawir and the Greek Black Metal Scene Christodoulos Apergis	77
4	Cassandra's Plight: Gender, Genre, and Historical Concepts of Femininity in Gothic and Power Metal Linnea Åshede and Anna Foka	97
5	Heavy Metal Dido: Heimdall's "Ballad of the Queen" Lissa Crofton-Sleigh	115
6	A Metal *Monstrum*: Ex Deo's Caligula Iker Magro-Martínez	131
7	Occult and Pulp Visions of Greece and Rome in Heavy Metal Jared Secord	155
8	"When the Land Was Milk and Honey and Magic Was Strong and True": Edward Said, Ancient Egypt, and Heavy Metal Leire Olabarria	173
9	Coda: Some Trends in Metal's Use of Classical Antiquity Osman Umurhan	201
Bibliography		217
Index		247

FIGURES

0.1	The Roman Empire, 200 CE. Ancient World Mapping Center © 2018 (awmc.unc.edu). Used by permission	v
3.1	Kawir, *ΑΜΥΗΤΟΝ ΜΗ ΕΙΣΙΕΝΑΙ* (2016; Album cover)	82
4.1	Liv Kristine, vocalist. Theatre of Tragedy	104
5.1	Alexander Runciman, *Dido on the Seashore with a Sword in her Hand* [Verso: *Woman and Child*]. National Galleries of Scotland	119
6.1	Ex Deo, *Caligvla* (2012; Album cover)	137
8.1	Nile, *Ithyphallic* (2007; Album cover)	179
9.1	Ade, *Carthago Delenda Est* (2016; Album cover)	205

CONTRIBUTORS

Christodoulos Apergis
Doctoral candidate in Classics, University of Athens (Greece)

Linnea Åshede
Sub-editor of SKBL.se, University of Gothenburg (Sweden)

Lissa Crofton-Sleigh
Lecturer of Classics, Santa Clara University (USA)

K. F. B. Fletcher
Associate Professor of Classics, Louisiana State University (USA)

Anna Foka
Associate Professor in Information Technology and the Humanities and Project Manager of DH Uppsala (Sweden)

Iker Magro-Martínez
Doctoral candidate in Classics, UPV-EHU/University of the Basque Country (Spain)

Leire Olabarria
Lecturer of Egyptology, University of Birmingham (UK)

Jared Secord
Academic Development Specialist, University of Calgary (Canada)

Matthew Taylor
Adjunct Assistant Professor of Writing, Beloit College (USA)

Osman Umurhan
Associate Professor of Classics, University of New Mexico (USA)

ACKNOWLEDGMENTS

Over the course of this project, we have racked up an enormous list of debts, which we can only hope to partially repay here.

The first people who deserve our thanks are the contributors, not only for their contributions, but also for their patience and good humor. We thank our contributors for turning us on to new bands, and helping us see this material in new ways. As is inevitable with such a long-running project, some people who were involved in earlier stages do not appear in the final version, but we would like to thank them, too, for sharing their knowledge and enthusiasm with us.

This project began as a conference panel at the 2014 annual meeting of the Classical Association of the Middle West and South, and we would like to thank the original panel members, Matthew Taylor, Andrew Reinhardt, and especially Nick Fletcher, from whose knowledge of metal we have frequently benefited, and who constantly provided news of metal releases. We would also like to thank all of the people in attendance at that panel for their questions and their enthusiasm, which led us to believe that the topic would be worth considering at greater length.

At Bloomsbury, we would like to thank our editor, Alice Wright, for her early interest in the project, and doggedness in seeing it through to its conclusion, as well as for finding interested readers to give us helpful feedback in the project's earlier stages. The editorial staff, Emma Payne, Lily MacMahon, and Merv Honeywood, patiently provided technical assistance and answered countless questions at every step of the process. We would also like to thank the editors of the *Imagines* series, Filippo Carlà-Uhink and Martin Lindner, for embracing the book as part of their series and especially for their detailed comments on the manuscript.

We also express immense gratitude to *Encyclopaedia Metallum: The Metal Archives* for its single most extensive online archive of metal material—bands, discography, track listings, lyrics, reviews, and discussions—without which it would have been much more difficult to write this volume. The website darklyrics.com was also an invaluable resource.

Osman Umurhan would like to thank the following: his older brother Orkan, who first slapped Iron Maiden's newly released *The Number of the Beast* album on his six-year-old little brother's orange-and-tan-colored Fisher-Price record player; his parents, Taner and Aishe, for condoning their eldest son's choice as they gazed with great amusement upon their youngest son headbanging—even if a bit too dangerously!—to the player's tinny sound of galloping rhythms. Osman is also grateful to Dr. E. Victor Wolfenstein for turning him on at age 15 to Lord Tennyson's "The Charge of the Light Brigade," an act of kindness that would determine his future academic ventures with metal. Osman thanks Kris Fletcher, with whom discussions about metal and Classics first

Acknowledgments

began at a graduate student conference in 2004 and would forge a friendship sealed by the bond of metal. He also offers heartfelt thanks to Lorenzo F. Garcia Jr. and Monica Cyrino for their tireless support, ear, and advice throughout several years of work on this project; and to Susan and Una for allowing him to keep and play his turntable, although he still needs to sneak in new LPs through the back door. Up the Irons!

Kris Fletcher would like to give special thanks to Osman Umurhan, without whose enthusiasm he never would have gotten involved in such a project, let alone finished it (what a long, strange trip it's been since we bonded over the *Powerslave* cassette in my car!). He would also like to acknowledge the Eric Voegelin Interdisciplinary Faculty Seminar at Louisiana State University, the Louisiana Classical Association, and the Department of Classics at the University of Mississippi for giving him the opportunity to present some of his work on heavy metal and Classics at earlier stages of this project. His colleagues at LSU were ever supportive, especially Paolo Chirumbolo and Willie Major. For their help and support he also thanks: Nate French, Tom Kollai, Sean Harding, David Kutzko, Katherine McLoone, Robert Chenault, Nathan Bethell, Scott Smith, Ruth Scodel, Garrett and Tabby Bradley, Chase and Kristin Bishop, and Terry Taylor. Finally, Kris would also like to thank his family—Frank, Adam, Hattie, Madeira, Sage, Nick, Abbey, Claudia, Sandra, and especially his mother, Charlene, who was endlessly supportive but unfortunately did not live to see the finished project.

INTRODUCTION: WHERE METAL AND CLASSICS MEET

K. F. B. Fletcher and Osman Umurhan

Why an entire book devoted to the reception of Classical antiquity in heavy metal music? The short answer is simply because there is an extraordinary amount of it, a fact that might surprise those who only think of heavy metal as marginal and lowbrow.[1] But to say that there are hundreds of metal songs and albums devoted to Classical subjects—although true—does not necessarily make the proper impact. Rather, consider the fact that there are few standard undergraduate Classical Studies courses for which one could not come up with an accompanying heavy metal playlist.

For example, one could teach the Epic Tradition by assembling songs—or even whole albums—to accompany all the usual texts used in such courses. To limit ourselves to only one example for each text, one could include: Homer's *Iliad* (e.g., Manowar's song, "Achilles, Agony and Ecstasy in Eight Parts"), Homer's *Odyssey* (Symphony X, "Odyssey"), Hesiod's *Theogony* (Saltatio Mortis, "Prometheus"), Hesiod's *Works and Days* (Son of Aurelius, "Pandora's Burden"), Apollonius of Rhodes' *Argonautica* (Sacred Blood's album, *Argonautica*), Vergil's *Aeneid*, (Stormlord, *Hesperia*), and Ovid's *Metamorphoses* (Septicflesh, "Narcissus"). A Greek myth class could cover much of the same material, but also include Heracles (Bleeding Gods, *Dodekathlon*). Such examples could easily be multiplied many times over, since dozens of songs are based on some of the more famous texts from Classical antiquity. One could assign at least a song a day and not run out of material over the course of a semester.

If one preferred history, however, one could teach a course on Greek history that included songs—or albums—about the Minoans (Giant Squid, *Minoans*), the Athenian tyrannicides Harmodius and Aristogeiton (Thy Catafalque, "Deathless Souls Roam"), the Persian Wars (Holy Martyr, *Hellenic Warrior Spirit*), and Alexander the Great (Iron Maiden, "Alexander the Great").

A course on Roman history would have even more material.[2] One could cover early topics and figures such as Romulus and the founding of Rome (High on Fire, "Romulus and Remus"), the Etruscans (VerSacrum, *Tyrrenika*), Horatius at the bridge (Evil Scarecrow, "Horatius"), and the Punic Wars (Protean, "Hannibal"). The section on the late Republic and early Principate could treat Spartacus' slave revolt (Ade, *Spartacus*), Julius Caesar's campaigns in Gaul (Eluveitie, *Helvetios*), Cleopatra (White Skull, "Cleopathra" [sic]), the fall of Julius Caesar and rise of Augustus (ShadowIcon, *Empire in Ruins*), and the disaster in Teutoberg Forest (Rebellion, *Arminius—Furor Teutonicus*).

The Julio-Claudian emperors provide ample material for such a course, especially Tiberius (Ex Deo, "The Tiberius Cliff (Exile to Capri)"), Caligula (Sodom, "Caligula"), and Nero (Illusion Suite, "Nero"), about whom metal bands often write. But this period could also include famous events such as Boudicca's revolt (Goat of Mendes, "Boudicca's Triumph") and the Siege of Masada (Grave Digger, "Messada"). If one wanted to move past the Principate, one could cover the rise of Magnus Maximus (Macsen Wledig) in Britain (SuidAkrA, *Eternal Defiance*), the fall of Rome (Civil War, "Rome is Falling"), and even the rise of the Varangian Guard in the Byzantine period (Turisas, "The March of the Varangian Guard").

In short, there are heavy metal songs and albums drawing upon just about every time period and genre of Classical antiquity. And although the above is only a small sample of such material, there has been little acknowledgment of its existence by Classicists.[3] Furthermore, while this phenomenon has become increasingly popular in the new millennium, it goes back to metal's origins and is a defining characteristic of the genre. The purpose of this book is to explore the reasons for this link between heavy metal and the Classics, and what it can tell us about both Classics and heavy metal. While the bands mentioned above come from all over the world, of particular interest here is what we call "Mediterranean metal," music about classical subjects made by bands from countries with a Classical past, primarily as a part of the Roman Empire (see Figure 0.1).

This book owes its origin to a panel at the 2014 annual meeting of the Classical Association of the Middle West and South. When we first assembled that panel, it was with only a few other Classicists that we already knew were fans of heavy metal. The panel was well attended, and comments from the surprisingly large crowd made us realize that there was more interest in the subject than we would have imagined—and that there were more bands out there writing about such things than we knew.

As a result of the panel's success, we decided to send out an open call for papers. The subsequent proposals covered a wide variety of topics, with varying degrees of connection with the ancient world. We have tried to pick papers that reflect an array of approaches to the ancient world, across a variety of subgenres, by bands from a range of countries. But this is in no way an attempt to tell the story of metal and Classics in any systematic or encyclopedic way. We hope, however, that these case studies will provide some sense of the material that is out there and offer some ways of considering what it tells us about both heavy metal and about the ancient world. As will be clear, much work remains to be done—especially since every passing year sees the release of additional relevant songs and albums.

Although we hope that this book will be of interest—and accessible—to fans more generally, it is written primarily for two audiences: scholars of Classics and of Metal Studies. Even though the two groups overlap more than even we would have believed possible when we began this project, they will come to this material from two very different perspectives. It is our aim to speak profitably to both groups, which means that, at times, the background given will be unnecessary for one audience. We encourage readers to skip these sections.

The rest of this introduction provides a background that either one or both these audiences will find useful for reading the papers that follow. We aim to explain what we mean by both "Classics" and "heavy metal," and also to situate these papers within broader scholarly conversations about Classical reception and Metal Studies, two recently flourishing fields that both began in the early 1990s. We end by providing an overview of the book's chapters as a way of making some general observations about Classics in heavy metal.

Classics and Classical Studies

Classics is the study of the ancient Greek and Roman world.[4] While it was traditionally thought of as "Classical philology," the detailed study of texts written in ancient Greek and Latin (and sometimes Hebrew), "Classics" and the increasingly popular "Classical Studies" (which generally implies less emphasis on Greek and Latin) have come to encompass the study of the ancient world in its entirety, including art, architecture, daily life, etc.[5] The heart of the discipline, however, remains the ancient texts that provide the majority of our information about the ancient world. Since the contributors to this current volume are primarily Classicists, they tend to come to the material from a literary perspective, and thus focus more on the lyrics of these songs than is often the case in Metal Studies.

Although such boundaries are always in flux (and continue to expand), the temporal limits of Classics generally range from the composition of Homer's epic poems in the eighth century BCE to the Greek and Latin literature of the second century CE. While numerous metal bands show an interest in both earlier and later periods of the ancient world, the contributions here stay largely within these traditional parameters, because they encompass the most famous figures, events, and works of literature that we associate with ancient Greece and Rome.

Reception Studies

Because the term is used differently by various academic fields, it is worth introducing Reception Studies as it is generally practiced in Classics, and by the contributors in this volume. Building upon the work of scholars such as Hans Robert Jauss and Wolfgang Iser, who sought to contextualize the reading of texts by later readers, Classicists such as Charles Martindale, Richard Thomas, Lorna Hardwick, and others began to examine the ways in which all of our knowledge of and approaches to material from the ancient world are mediated by countless other authors, readers, scholars, etc.[6] This approach goes beyond earlier, more linear, notions of influence and the Classical tradition, since Reception Studies considers not just, for example, how our knowledge of Homer's *Odyssey* affects our reading of Vergil's *Aeneid*, but also how our knowledge of the *Aeneid* influences our reading of the *Odyssey*. Similarly, our reading of the *Aeneid*—and of Vergil himself—will forever be influenced by the existence of Dante's *Divine Comedy*, in which Vergil serves as a guide for the later Italian poet. A reading of Tennyson's poem "Ulysses," influenced by Dante, in turn effectively changes the ending of Homer's poem by suggesting Odysseus' unhappiness with the sedentary life in Ithaca. While earlier approaches to the Classical tradition would have highlighted a linear influence from Homer to Vergil to Dante to Tennyson, Reception Studies focuses on how the meaning of the earlier text can change once a reader reads these chronologically later accounts, and thus highlights the fluidity of a text's meaning. At the same time, Reception Studies also tries to address how changes within society affect the ever-shifting meaning of a text.

As this applies to heavy metal, then, Reception Studies is not just about identifying songs and albums that use material from the ancient world, and showing from which texts (ancient or modern) they draw their information, but also includes understanding how these albums and songs offer readings of these ancient texts that influence how their listeners view and understand Greece and Rome. These bands do not simply draw on ancient material; they play a part in transforming those texts and participating in the ongoing conversation about the meaning of such texts as Homer's *Odyssey*, or figures such as "Julius Caesar," or even ideas such as "Rome."

Its current popularity, however, makes it easy to avoid asking—let alone answering—the fundamental question: what is the point of Reception Studies?[7] Perhaps its most obvious appeal is that it allows Classicists to highlight the continuing influence and appeal of Greek and Roman material. The danger here is what we might think of as the transitive property of relevance, which states that one thing is worth studying because it was important to someone else who is obviously worth studying. For example, one might argue that the Roman historian Tacitus is worth studying because he was important to John Adams, who as a Founding Father is the very epitome of importance (from an American perspective, at least). While Reception Studies can serve as a reminder of a text's continued vitality, it should not be a validation of its significance.

Whether they admit it or not, another appeal of Reception Studies for Classicists is that it allows them to pursue material that is technically outside their field. Like many fans of television shows, movies, comics, and science fiction, for example, they want to talk about the material they love; Reception Studies gives them an acceptable, professional framework within which to do so.[8] The challenges here are twofold: that scholars are teaching and writing about material which they do not know as well as their academic specialty; and that scholars are teaching pop culture, not because they have anything to say about reception per se, but simply to draw in more students.

But part of a modern Classicist's job is to serve as a mediator between the original material and its contemporary use.[9] This is not as simple as penning a quick editorial cataloguing mistakes any time a new movie or television show comes out. Rather, it means helping explain to a contemporary audience the material behind contemporary manifestations, what that material might mean, and how we know it. In short, to be a Classicist now must include some sort of Reception Studies. To some extent, this can even be the most public-facing aspect of a career in Classics.

Although most of the contributors to this volume are Classicists by training and fans of metal on a personal level, we have made every effort to engage with metal music not just as an appendage to Classics, but also on its own terms and within its own scholarly framework.[10] It is certainly possible—even likely—that our position as fans makes us biased. But who, other than fans, would pursue this material in this way? Similarly, we do not decry people who write about Aristophanes, say, or Ovid as being fans—though most (if not all) of them are clearly fans of these authors. It is impossible to separate our fandom from this project; indeed, the latter would not exist without the former.

Even proponents of Reception Studies, however, may balk at a book on Classical reception in heavy metal, since the music has generally been written off as violent, stupid, lowbrow, low class, or even Satanic.[11] Such a subject may seem a bridge too far, or a clear indication that the field has reached saturation and is on its way to its demise. But the recent upswing in the amount of this material further suggests the need for such a study. At a time when Classics is especially embattled in terms of its diminishing role in the future of education, it seems ironic that there should be such a blossoming of interest in it within this genre of music. Can Classics be arid and out of touch if it is vitally alive within this music? Can heavy metal music be lowbrow if it is full of references to Classical myth and history? The seeming clash between the common stereotypes of metal and its association with Classics demands attention.

Reception in music

If the tone of this introduction seems defensive, it is because this project was motivated in part by our desire as fans of heavy metal to defend it from its detractors, or at least give people a better understanding of some of the material out there. And, while heavy metal has long been stereotyped, within the context of Classical reception the view is doubly negative. Although Classical Reception Studies has come to embrace an increasingly wide range of material—from cinema to comic books to children's books—there remains a classist tinge to Classical Reception Studies in dealing with music.

Simply put: when people talk about Classical reception in music, what they almost universally mean is Classical music, especially opera.[12] But if one of the aims of Reception Studies is understanding the appeal of Classics to our contemporaries, then opera offers a very limited perspective. Opera is now associated primarily with the upper class and is generally considered difficult for the average person to access, at least in terms of performance (however, good quality recordings of operas are more readily available than ever before). Similarly, while new operas continue to be written, most would agree that its golden age is long behind us.[13] Therefore, while studying opera's use of Classics is valuable, it tells us little about Classics' popularity—in either sense of the term—today.[14]

The emphasis on opera to the almost complete exclusion of metal raises the question of whether certain types of reception are considered more worthwhile than others. In some sense, this question lays bare contesting views of the purpose of Reception Studies. One of the leading scholars of Classical reception, Charles Martindale (2013: 176), represents the most extreme end of the spectrum. In considering the place of reception within the academic study of Classics when it manifests in something like a "Classics in Film" course, he claims:

One suspects that film is often chosen, not without considerable condescension, out of a somewhat desperate desire for "relevance" or modernity—proof that Classics is somehow still "alive." Classics is more alive to my thinking in Joyce's *Ulysses* or the poetry of Seamus Heaney than in *Gladiator* (2000: Ridley Scott). And does *Gladiator* or *Alexander* (2004: Oliver Stone) initiate us into a serious or profound dialogue with antiquity? (Of course, a film *could* achieve this—*Agora* (2009: Alejandro Amenábar) comes closer.) To avoid misunderstanding I say again that what is wrong with *Gladiator* in terms of its suitability for a Classics syllabus is not that it is a popular film but that it does not present a thoroughly imagined classical world.

But Martindale never defines what he means by "a thoroughly imagined classical world," and it is hard not to read this passage as an out-moded, classist separation of high art from popular fare. Furthermore, on some levels, his assertion is groundless, since *Gladiator* attempts to put the ancient world on the screen in a way that engages spectators enough to feel that they are watching something from the ancient world.

It is hard, therefore, not to read this as a classist assertion. And what of popularity? Surely more people have seen *Gladiator* than have read *Ulysses*—at least in its entirety. While *Ulysses* is often considered the best novel ever written, that statement is often made in the same breath as the claim that it is almost never read all the way through.[15] *Gladiator*, on the other hand, grossed almost half a billion dollars worldwide in theaters, and continues to find an audience on cable television on weekend afternoons, meaning that millions of people have seen the movie.[16] It also helped inspire numerous subsequent films set in the ancient world, thereby revitalizing a whole genre. Furthermore, *Gladiator* drove numerous students to take Classics courses when it debuted, and so something about its presentation of the ancient world fired students' imaginations.[17]

Accordingly, one of the aims of this book is to show that even a popular, modern musical genre, often written off as lowbrow by its critics, participates in the ongoing conversation about the meaning of antiquity in sophisticated ways.[18] To study the reception of Vergil, for example, should not restrict us to Dante or—in music—Berlioz. Rather, we can learn something about Vergil through Stormlord as well as Berlioz, Heimdall as well as Purcell.

Heavy metal and its history

Like any genre, the origins of heavy metal ("metal" for short) are contested, as are its boundaries, but what follows should suffice as a starting point for those unfamiliar with the music.[19] Individual papers will explore certain subgenres more closely, and raise issues about how to draw genre distinctions, as well as explore how different subgenres and their respective concerns influence their choice and use of material from the Classical world.

Heavy metal is an originally British music form that began to develop in the late 1960s. The bands most associated with its origins are Led Zeppelin and especially Black

Sabbath, both of which formed in the last couple of years of the 1960s. Other bands also came into existence in Britain at the same time, including Cream (1966), Deep Purple (1968), and Judas Priest (1969, although they did not release an album until 1974). All these bands contributed to the distorted electric-guitar driven, blues-based blueprint for metal, but because Led Zeppelin released what many consider their most metal album, *Led Zeppelin II*, in 1969 and Black Sabbath released its first two albums, *Black Sabbath* and *Paranoid*, in 1970, this two-year period is often considered the beginning of metal. These groups set the template for much of what was to follow, including an interest in the fantastic, the occult, myth, and history. Appropriately enough, the story of Classics in metal begins with these groups and the two most famous heroes from Homer, the earliest Greek writer: in 1967, Cream released the song "Tales of Brave Ulysses" (*Disraeli Gears*), followed in 1976 by Led Zeppelin's "Achilles Last Stand" [sic] (*Presence*).[20]

The name "heavy metal" comes from the metallic sound of the distorted electric guitar that defines metal, but also alludes to its geographical origins.[21] Black Sabbath came from the industrial town of Birmingham, and they—and others—have often connected the nature of their music with the gritty, blue-collar nature of post-War England.[22] Rob Halford, the lead singer of Judas Priest, makes this connection explicit in his solo song "Made in Hell":

From memories of '68 when the wizard shook the world
Metal came from foundries where the Midlands sound unfurled
The Bullring was a lonely place of concrete towers and steel
The coal mines and the industries were all I had to feel . . .[23]

"The wizard" is an allusion to a song of the same name on Black Sabbath's first album, and the Bullring is a place in central Birmingham, home to both Black Sabbath and Judas Priest. This song connects the sound of a type of music with the region from which it arose, emphasizing the literal metal ("foundries," "steel") that gave rise to the figurative metal.[24] In America, this kind of connection between metal and heavy industry was also apparent in Detroit, which produced hard rock/early metal bands such as Alice Cooper, Grand Funk Railroad, the MC5, and The Stooges. As metal spread in its early years, it maintained its blue-collar, industrial roots.

In this initial phase, metal stuck close to its blues-based, rock 'n' roll origins, and bands generally avoided the term "heavy metal," which was often used in the rock press in a derogatory sense. Such critics predicted a swift end for the genre, and in the mid-1970s, it looked as if they might be right, as metal seemed to be dying.[25] In the late 1970s, however, it returned with a vengeance in a movement referred to as the New Wave of British Heavy Metal (NWOBHM), which ushered in a new group of bands that set the tone for future development. The most famous of these bands are Iron Maiden and Def Leppard, though the latter has completely distanced itself from its metal roots over the years. Bands such as Saxon, Venom, and Diamond Head had less long-lasting commercial success, but all exercised great influence on the development of subsequent subgenres.

This phase of metal's history is important not only because it revivified metal in the face of the New Wave/punk movement, but also because it pushed metal to the next level, moving it away from its blues roots.[26] Bands began to embrace the term "heavy metal," and to craft its definitive image, from the stage look of leather and spikes of Judas Priest to the now-famous mascot of Iron Maiden ("Eddie"). As Waksman (2009: 7–8) stresses, genre is not just about music.

Iron Maiden deserve to be singled out because they are perhaps more responsible for the wide variety of subjects in heavy metal songs than almost any other band. While groups such as Led Zeppelin and Black Sabbath had treated fantasy, the occult, and even antiquity to some extent, Iron Maiden took such tendencies to the next degree. In 1983, the band released their album *Piece of Mind*, the first to feature what is considered their classic lineup, and which exemplifies the range of material considered suitable for heavy metal songs. This kind of sanctioning of topics and themes is especially important because metal is in many ways a very conservative genre.[27] Once a band of Iron Maiden's stature writes a song about something, other bands will follow.

Piece of Mind includes one of Iron Maiden's signature songs, "The Trooper," based on Tennyson's poem "The Charge of the Light Brigade," in turn about the Crimean War.[28] The album's first single (and their first ever released in the US) was "The Flight of Icarus," an odd retelling of the Icarus myth, and another song, "To Tame a Land," is a seven-and-a-half minute epic based on Frank Herbert's science-fiction novel, *Dune*. Other songs on the album are based on other eras of history, short stories, and movies (as multiple chapters will show, bands' views of antiquity have often been shaped in part by movies).[29] To some extent, albums such as *Piece of Mind* defined the nature of heavy metal songs, and Iron Maiden have been followed in this regard throughout metal's history.[30] NWOBHM both reinvigorated heavy metal and further defined its core tendencies.

Thrash metal is a primarily American outgrowth of NWOBHM characterized by its speed and aggressiveness. It completely changed the face of metal by making it faster and heavier, and even less closely related to the blues. Most famous of the thrash bands are Metallica, Megadeth, and Slayer, all of which have sold millions of albums worldwide. Unlike their NWOBHM predecessors, these bands did not generally write about fantasy novels or historical figures—Anthrax's "Medusa" (*Spreading the Disease*, 1985) is an exception—but were more explicitly political, with common themes being the distrust of established government and the unnecessary tragedy of war. While metal was always rebellious, thrash metal marked a move toward darker, violent, and more asocial subjects—a tendency shared in part by its musical descendants, the subgenres that are often lumped together under the term "extreme metal," which includes most notably death metal and black metal, but also less prevalent subgenres.[31]

Death metal gets its name from its focus on the dark and macabre. Musically, it is characterized by its speed and complexity, sometimes being likened to jazz in its affinity for odd time signatures and numerous key changes. Vocally, it differs from metal's originally clean-toned vocals by its use of unpitched growling, a style sometimes referred to as "Cookie Monster vocals."[32] The origins of death metal are primarily connected with Tampa, Florida and Stockholm, then Gothenburg, Sweden.[33]

Black metal gets its name from the 1982 album *Black Metal* by the NWOBHM band Venom.[34] Although black metal overlaps to some extent with death metal in its subject matter, stylistically it is radically different. While death metal is characterized by its technique and polish, black metal generally favors the opposite aesthetic, choosing poor production values and sloppy playing, often reveling in the simplicity of song structure and guitar parts, and demonstrating an overlap with certain punk rock sensibilities.[35] Black metal also tends more to the atmospheric, in part through the use of synthesizers; an album beginning with the sound of wind and church bells is common enough to be considered a trope. Black metal is also visually different, as its practitioners have taken the traditional look of NWOBHM—with its leather, spikes, and bullet belts—and pushed it further, most obviously through the use of so-called "corpse paint," white and black make-up applied to the face to make it look more skeletal and/or like a corpse.[36]

Black metal plays an important role in Mediterranean metal because it gave rise to Viking metal, which was a key catalyst for the development of the focus on the ancient world (below). Black metal has proven to be one of the most popular subgenres of metal and has had great influence on the global scene; there are now black metal bands spread throughout the world. This popularity is reflected in black metal's position as the darling of Metal Studies.

The 1980s also saw the development of what is variously called "hair metal," "glam metal," or—even more dismissively—"lite metal." Associated primarily with the Sunset Strip in West Hollywood, California, this subgenre includes bands such as Poison and Warrant, who followed in the wake of bands such as Van Halen and Mötley Crüe who combined traditional metal with 1970s glam rock (such as the New York Dolls), putting an emphasis on stagecraft and over-the-top dress and performance. Almost no references to the ancient world are to be found in the discography of these bands, as they tend to focus on sex, drugs, and rock 'n' roll. Such bands evince almost no interest in history or literature, so are largely unimportant for the following chapters. Their historical importance for metal, however, lies in widening its commercial appeal, in large part by attracting more female fans.

As the 1990s dawned, metal was a dominant commercial force on radio and MTV, but there was a backlash against hair metal, which had become ubiquitous and formulaic. As so-called grunge bands such as Nirvana, Soundgarden, and Pearl Jam gained in popularity, metal took a commercial backseat, a situation mirrored (and exacerbated) by the departure of the vocalists from both Iron Maiden and Judas Priest, longtime torchbearers for all things metal. Furthermore, many metal acts disbanded entirely. An exception to these trends was Metallica, who released their self-titled album (also known as the *Black Album*) in 1991, which has become metal's bestselling album by a long margin and—along with the groove metal of Pantera—helped pave the way for metal's next major commercial stage, "nu metal" (also known as "nü metal" and "rap metal"). The American bands Korn, Limp Bizkit, and others mixed heavy guitars with rapping and even DJs (Linkin Park later became the epitome of such bands) who appealed to an audience that was also embracing hip-hop.

In Europe, however, traditional metal remained more viable, and this period saw the advent of power metal. Inspired by bands such as Iron Maiden and Judas Priest, as well as the German band Helloween, power metal bands offered songs with the traditional heavy guitars and speed, but with even more catchy melodies and heavily harmonized choruses. This subgenre is often derided for being too "pop," a charge that is not without merit, considering its practitioners' being raised on European pop acts such as ABBA.[37] Like traditional metal, power metal draws on historical and literary topics as part of a general focus on larger-than-life, epic characters, and narratives. Although metal had always had a connection with fantasy, it was during this period that bands such as Germany's Blind Guardian pioneered what is variously called "Hobbit" or "Tolkien metal" as a nod to the influence of J. R. R. Tolkien on their lyrics.

As the new millennium dawned, metal returned to its roots with the so-called New Wave of American Heavy Metal, which produced bands such as Avenged Sevenfold and Trivium, who play traditional metal, but faster and heavier, and with updated production quality. Black metal continues to thrive and spread around the world, and traditional acts such as Iron Maiden and Metallica still tour the world with a high profile. Despite continued predictions of metal's demise, the music continues to adapt and thrive.

The rise of Mediterranean metal

From its origins, metal has shown an interest in material from history and mythology—so much so, in fact, that this interest can be considered a defining characteristic of heavy metal.[38] But this interest has intensified among a subset of bands, especially from the area once covered by the Roman Empire, which is to say most of modern Europe (see Figure 0.1). While the term has its limitations, "Mediterranean metal" is a useful shorthand for the bands that come from this area and draw repeatedly upon ancient material.[39] This is not to imply that bands from these areas—especially Italy and Greece—are the only ones drawing on the ancient world. Rather, this term reflects the fact that bands from these areas (neither a traditionally robust source of metal) do so at a higher rate than other bands and—as subsequent chapters will show—in a different manner.

Mediterranean metal is the logical outcome of another key development within the history of metal, the birth of Viking metal.[40] Like Classical material, the Vikings had appeared sporadically in metal from its very beginning. Interest in the Vikings is evident in metal's origins. Led Zeppelin's "Immigrant Song" (1970) was written by the band while in Iceland, thereby paving the way for later bands and sanctioning the use of such material (things came full circle when this song was used in multiple scenes in the 2017 blockbuster film, *Thor: Ragnarok*). The band claimed to have been influenced by the landscape, and the Northern European landscape became one of the primary inspirations for Viking metal.[41] The influential American band Manowar also embraced the Viking theme, beginning with "Gates of Valhalla," on 1983's *Into Glory Ride*, the cover of which album shows the band dressed as barbarians and wielding weapons; the band continued to embrace Vikings and Norse myth as part of their general focus on military glory and manliness. The 1985 song "I am a Viking" by Yngwie Malmsteen's Rising Force was notable for being by a Swedish musician, thereby paving the way for other Scandinavian artists to make such a connection between their heritage and the subject matter of their songs.[42]

But 1990 is considered a watershed moment in the history of Viking metal (and thus metal generally) because the Swedish black metal band Bathory released *Hammerheart*, a concept album about the Vikings. The band already exercised incalculable influence on the formation and development of Scandinavian black metal, but this, their fifth studio album, is considered the beginning of Viking metal. Although Bathory had written songs about Vikings before, *Hammerheart* was a departure in sound and subject matter; all the songs were devoted to Viking history and culture, and the cover art is Sir Frank Dicksee's *The Funeral of a Viking* (1893).

In the wake of this well-received album, more bands began to write songs and albums about the Vikings, first in Scandinavian countries, then elsewhere in the world, mostly in countries that could still claim at least a tenuous connection to them. Norway's Enslaved, who debuted with *Vikingligr Veldi* ("Viking Warrior Aristocracy") in 1994, is in many ways the first true Viking metal band, because of their consistent focus on such material from the beginning of their career.[43] Bathory and Enslaved were, in turn, followed by numerous bands such as Burzum (Norway), Emperor (Norway), Falkenbach (Germany), Amon Amarth (Sweden), and Týr (Faroe Islands). While most of these bands are considered extreme metal (i.e., black metal, death metal, doom metal, grindcore, etc.), the designation "Viking metal" refers not to the style of the music but to the contents of the lyrics and—to a lesser extent—to the appearance of bands on stage and the album artwork.[44] The same is true for Mediterranean metal, and we use the designation on the basis of subject matter rather than musical style.[45]

There are numerous reasons for the rise of Viking metal and its connection primarily with Scandinavian countries, which produce a staggering number of metal bands.[46] One popular explanation—mentioned above—is geographical: some scholars suggest that the long, dark winters and dramatic landscapes make such music inevitable.[47] Others have also suggested that the music is a response to the social democracies and economic prosperity of Scandinavian countries.[48] Because people have good opportunities for education, health care, and leisure, they are able to rebel against the system with relative freedom and in relative comfort.

The focus on Vikings by these bands is also a reaction against Christianity.[49] Extreme metal traditionally has a Satanic element, although many argue that its Satanism is more of an anti-authoritarian philosophy than a religious position *per se*.[50] Within the context of Viking metal, the Vikings are viewed as being true Scandinavians, while later, Christian, invaders are seen as interlopers who threaten native culture. In this regard, there is a connection between Vikings and paganism, as both are viewed as pre-dating Christianity and thus being of greater value.[51] This religious and political element is also fundamental to the rise and spread of Mediterranean metal.

But Viking metal eventually spread to countries with no real connection with the Vikings or Norse religion. For example, the Italian epic metal band Wotan gets its name from the Germanic name for the Norse god Odin and released a demo in 2000 called

Under the Sign of Odin's Crows. Their debut album, *Carmina Barbarica*, has numerous songs about Norse myth (but also includes songs about the battle of Thermopylae and the Gallic chieftain Vercingetorix, who fought against Julius Caesar). This kind of cultural appropriation sparked outrage because this material was considered by some to be the property only of Scandinavians.[52] Such criticism reflects the notion that bands are performing national identity through their music, the logical conclusion being that if a Scandinavian band should be writing about Vikings, then a Greek band should be writing about Greek mythology, and an Italian band should be writing about the Romans.

This kind of localized thinking— especially the pagan sentiments of extreme metal— developed hand in hand with the larger spread of metal throughout the world. For example, the black metal band Rotting Christ helped put Greece on the metal map in the late '80s and early '90s, sharing many of the same anti-Christian sentiments as bands from other parts of Europe.[53] This approach is one of the factors that ultimately led to the proliferation of metal songs and albums about pre-Christian history in these countries, and what the rise of Mediterranean metal in the midst of these developments tells us about Classics merits inquiry.

There is another similarity between Viking and Mediterranean metal. Von Helden (2017: 173) argues that "metal culture willingly absorbs Norse themes, since they are compatible to metal aesthetics." The same is true of aspects of the Classical world and explains the early interest in figures such as Achilles, Alexander the Great, and Julius Caesar, all larger-than-life men of military prowess. But there are also key differences between the two. In her treatment of Norwegian metal, von Helden (2017: 151) notes that the bands she spoke to did not read the original sources for their material; as we will see repeatedly in the following chapters, this is often not the case with metal bands, many of whom draw on or even quote Greek and Roman literary sources. In part because of this greater engagement with the sources, Mediterranean metal shows a much wider range of historical and mythological subject matter than does Viking metal. It is also more inclusive. To quote from von Helden (2017: 173) once more: "The representations of mythology do not take up female actors, which is remarkable, since there are many female characters of importance." As the chapters by Crofton-Sleigh, Åshede and Foka, and Umurhan show, metal bands increasingly sing about female characters from Greek and Roman myth and history. Mediterranean metal to some extent has taken the idea of Viking metal to the next level.[54]

Metal Studies as emerging field

The rise of Metal Studies as an academic discipline also encourages such an investigation. In part because heavy metal is itself relatively new, Metal Studies is a young discipline. While key studies came out relatively early (e.g. Walser 1993a, Weinstein 2000), there was no critical mass until the first decade of the new millennium, and it was only in 2015 that the field got its own journal, *Metal Studies*—a clear sign of a level of academic maturity and respectability.[55]

Apart from the general lack of respect for metal as an artistic medium, an additional institutional obstacle is that Metal Studies does not fit neatly into any one department.[56] Rather, like Classical Studies, it is defined not by methodology but by subject matter, and is a combination of numerous fields, including musicology, cultural studies, psychology, political science, and others. As Weinstein (2016: 23) says, "Metal studies is not a paradigmatic science but a study of a content area. It is properly called a study—the application of multiple disciplines, multiple methods, and multiple theoretical paradigms to a particular content." With no obvious home department, Metal Studies must fight even harder for academic legitimacy.

One discipline conspicuously missing from most of Metal Studies, however, is any form of literary studies. In fact, much Metal Studies downplays the significance of the songs' lyrics, either dismissing them or failing to address them with any sophistication. For example, in Weinstein's seminal *Heavy Metal: The Music and its Culture*, she claims that (2000: 26), "Many fans and critics would agree that in heavy metal the lyrics are less relevant as words than as sound." This is a claim that has been echoed by countless subsequent studies, and while it may be true, saying that the lyrics are less important than the sound does not mean that the lyrics are unimportant. Such a generalization also does not apply equally to all subgenres, let alone bands.

It is to this often-neglected area of Metal Studies that we can most hope to add. It is our hope that this focus on the lyrics can contribute to the growth of Metal Studies at large by showing that at least for some bands the lyrics are essential, especially within certain subgenres that place much more emphasis on the content of their songs than others.

Key themes and organization

While some readers will undoubtedly skip to the chapters with titles that interest them, we have arranged them in such a way that, when read in sequence, some of the larger trends in metal's use of Greco-Roman antiquity should become clear. As the intersection of Classics and metal is a relatively new area of study, it would be difficult—if not impossible—to provide a comprehensive overview of the phenomenon or of approaches to the subject, but it is our hope that, together, these case studies provide some sense of metal's wide-ranging and ever-growing use of the ancient world, and show just how many different ways these bands have of viewing and reinterpreting this material.

The first three chapters all explore different aspects of how various bands present the (putative) ancient heritage of their countries.[57] These come first because nationalism is arguably the most obvious and important factor in the rise of Mediterranean metal. Numerous bands draw on their countries' ancient past to comment on and explore their modern identity, a trend that is a part of the larger resurgence of nineteenth-century-style nationalism at the beginning of the twenty-first century, and one which draws attention to the longstanding use of Classics to advance nationalist agendas.[58]

Again, terminology presents a challenge. We refer to bands' use of the history of the regions from which they come as "nationalistic," though we know that for some readers this term can only have negative connotations—not all of which are applicable to all the bands discussed here. At the same time, the term "patriotic" would strike many as naïve and would seem to separate this phenomenon from larger political and cultural developments in recent years. But we have not tried to impose any terminology—let alone any political perspective—on our contributors, and the authors approach this link between band and country in different ways.

K. F. B. Fletcher uses two concept albums based on Vergil's *Aeneid* released in 2013 by Italian bands to explore some of the motivations for, and difficulties with, approaching ancient Rome for Italian metal musicians. Although Heimdall's and Stormlord's treatments of the poem differ in terms of structure and the choice of which languages they use, they are similar in focusing on Rome's greatness and the high price paid by Aeneas and others to set in motion the Roman Empire. They are also similar in making no explicit connection between Aeneas, the Roman Empire, and modern Italy, and not attempting to lay claim to the glory of Rome—let alone making any claims of European dominance. Accordingly, Fletcher argues that we can consider these Italian bands' turn to the *Aeneid* as nationalistic in the sense that they are Italian and talking about the Roman national epic, but contrasts their use of Rome with that of other, more aggressively nationalistic Italian metal bands, to show that they fall on one end of the spectrum of (ab)uses of history and myth that are a product of this "nationalistic turn" in metal in recent years. While some bands invoke the ancient world as part of a right-wing political agenda, bands such as Heimdall and Stormlord use the *Aeneid* to speak both to an Italian audience and to the larger global metal audience, putting a local inflection on a global medium without advancing a nationalistic cause.

The next chapter demonstrates that this nationalistic use of antiquity is also available to the descendants of Rome's enemies, such as the Helvetians, whose territory was in modern Switzerland and whose history is the subject of multiple songs and albums by the Swiss folk metal band Eluveitie. Matthew Taylor shows how Eluveitie offers a postcolonial reading of Julius Caesar's *Gallic Wars*, reading between the lines of the conqueror's narrative to find the voice of the Celtic resistance. Taylor also examines SuidAkrA's album *Eternal Defiance*, which tells the story of the Roman emperor Magnus Maximus, known in Welsh legend as Macsen Wledig. Even in drawing on historical sources, both of these bands are influenced by modern constructions of ancient Celtic identity; Taylor offers an important reminder that even the original sources for historical events have been shaped by the needs of their writers and audiences. These bands offer a startlingly different view of the Roman Empire than that provided by the *Aeneid* albums discussed by Fletcher, which suggests that the view of Rome is conditioned in part by nationality, and that such metal albums are yet one more instance within a long tradition of political readings of Roman history.

Christodoulos Apergis' analysis of the hymns written and performed by the Greek black metal band Kawir—named after the mythical Kabeiroi—argues that the characteristic anti-Christian element of black metal shapes Kawir's use of ancient Greek hymns. This band has not only set to music numerous ancient Greek hymns (written by authors such as Callimachus and Proclus as well as anonymous "Homeric" and "Orphic" hymns), but also composed their own, following closely many of the tropes of the ancient ones. This is not just an abstract exercise for Kawir, however, since the band is part of a pagan revival movement in Greece (and other places) that promotes the worship of the Olympian pantheon. Kawir's use of this ancient material therefore reflects the connection between national and religious identities—although Apergis argues that, unlike other far-right Greek metal bands that use these hymns, Kawir's religious concerns do not make them political. Although there is a certain irony in Kawir setting to music hymns that may never have been performed in antiquity, in this case the use of ancient material is vital and shows how much more than a literary exercise the use of Classics by metal can be.

The next two chapters explore issues of gender by considering some of the ways that heavy metal portrays women from antiquity. Classics and heavy metal have both been traditionally focused on men and notions of masculinity. But as Classical scholarship has continued to reorient itself to focus on previously ignored voices, so too has recent work on metal shown that the situation within the genre and its scenes is not as simple as some would have it.[59] Furthermore, the presence of women in the genre has been increasing, with more and more women visible as members of bands—especially as vocalists—in a variety of subgenres. In this sense, metal's increasing focus on women in antiquity reflects both Classics' changing priorities and mirrors metal's development more generally and provides some clues as to how we might read these changes.

Lissa Crofton-Sleigh returns to Heimdall's *Aeneid* to explore its presentation of Dido, the doomed queen of Carthage. By focusing on the album's fifth track, "Ballad of the Queen," Crofton-Sleigh argues that the use of instruments other than the electric guitar can be gendered as feminine and shows how the use of the heavy metal ballad form introduces a female voice into an album—and narrative—that is otherwise dominated by male voices. Dido has always attracted sympathy for her position as victim of Aeneas and his fate, and Heimdall continue this tradition by presenting her song as one of mourning. As with the *Aeneid* itself, Dido's presence in Aeneas' journey creates a feminine, personal space that contrasts with the masculine, imperial narrative of the proto-Roman hero.

Linnea Åshede and Anna Foka explore metal's presentation of gender by using gothic metal (a subgenre defined by its mournful nature and generally slower tempi, as well as its combination of male and female vocals) and power metal (defined by its speed and heavily melodic choruses). They use songs about Cassandra, the Trojan prophetess whom no one ever believed, by Theatre of Tragedy (one of whose two vocalists is a woman) and Blind Guardian as exemplars of these two subgenres, respectively, to contrast the ways in which gender can be approached in metal—and to show how these bands move past simplistic, traditional notions of the role of women in metal. Since antiquity, Cassandra has been a useful figure for exploring issues of male control and the suppression of female speech, and Åshede and Foka show that she continues to play a similar role in heavy metal.

Like Åshede and Foka, Iker Magro-Martínez focuses on one figure from antiquity, in this case a Roman historical personage, the Roman Emperor Gaius, better known as Caligula (ruled 37–41 CE). He argues that many metal bands are attracted to figures such as Caligula because of their general interest in and fascination with all things evil.

By focusing especially on songs from the 2012 album *Caligvla* by the Italian-Canadian band Ex Deo, he shows that the metal depiction of Caligula fits with the longstanding portrayal of him as a monster, and more closely mirrors the representation of Caligula in literature and movies than the scholarly treatments of him, providing an example of how the ancient world's influence on metal is often mediated—in this case, especially by the infamous 1979 *Penthouse*-produced film, *Caligula*. To some extent, then, Caligula is less interesting to metal bands as an historical figure than he is as the epitome of debauched, capricious tyranny, and so metal bands use him evocatively, rather than out of any desire to provide an historically accurate and up-to-date biography.

Jared Secord, too, focuses on some of the ways in which metal bands' view of the Greco-Roman past is often filtered through other genres and media; in the case of the bands he treats, these filters are pulp writing or mysticism. He argues that bands such as the Swiss death metal band Celtic Frost and the Swedish symphonic metal band Therion draw on less familiar aspects of Greco-Roman antiquity as part of a broader interest in the occult. For such bands—which he labels "esoteric metal" because of their interests—most of Classical literature and history is too familiar, and not exotic enough for their purposes. He shows that they draw on occult and magical aspects of antiquity, and argues that while these bands are bookish, they read indiscriminately, often drawing heavily on works not taken seriously by Classicists and historians. He also discusses the case of the British symphonic black metal band Bal-Sagoth, which draws on the ancient world as filtered through the works of H. P. Lovecraft and Robert E. Howard (author of the *Conan* books), blending aspects of the ancient world with an eclectic mix of fantasy and horror writing, thereby creating their own "antediluvian" world about which they write songs. For these bands, then, the mainstream Classical world is too familiar, and too safe, so they must look elsewhere in antiquity for material.

Leire Olabarria also discusses the appeal for metal bands of the occult and esoteric aspects of antiquity and offers the volume's lone consideration of Egypt, examining the portrayal of Egypt primarily by the American death metal band Nile, whose music consistently draws on Egyptian history and mythology. As she shows, the view of Egypt in metal is always mediated through both popular depictions of Egypt and scholarship of varying respectability—even when written by Egyptian metal musicians. There are, therefore, two Egypts, the scholarly one and the popular one, and there is often a tension between the two of them. Unlike most of the bands in this book, Nile is not writing about the history of their home region, and Olabarria connects Nile's focus on Egypt as mystical and violent with Edward Said's classic formulation of "Orientalism," the way the West has continuously constructed an essentialized version of the East as "Other."

In the coda, Osman Umurhan takes stock of some prominent trends in metal's engagement with Classical antiquity that emerge from the volume's various scholarly treatments. One significant trend is metal's increasing circulation across national borders, continents, and socio-economic classes, due in large part to technological advances generated by globalization. As metal spreads and reaches a larger, more international, and increasingly diverse audience, its practitioners' engagement with the Classical past continues to assume new shapes and forms increasingly informed by local needs.

Introduction

Umurhan argues that since metal continues to refashion Greece and Rome, it behooves Classicists to be sensitive to the ways and means by which Classical antiquity acquires new meaning and relevance in media outside academia.

Conclusion

Heavy metal music serves as a microcosm for examining the modern reception of the Classical world, as it demonstrates many of the ways that antiquity has been used in the late twentieth and twenty-first centuries. The initial strain of Classics-based metal focused primarily on famous individual figures such as Achilles and Icarus, using them because they speak to some of metal's fundamental concerns, such as powerful masculinity and rebellion against authority.[60] As the prevalence of Classics within metal has grown, and Mediterranean metal in particular has flourished, more recondite subjects have become acceptable as topics for songs, and nationalism has played an increased role in how many bands have viewed the Classical past. While bands do not only write songs about the history of their own lands, this kind of focus is increasingly common, and stresses the connection between modern nation and putative national ancestors. In this sense, heavy metal follows conservative trends, reacting in the face of increasing globalization; the irony is that the global spread of metal has allowed this nationalistic gesture to be replayed throughout the world as metal takes on new local inflections.

One of the things that we hope this volume demonstrates is the polyvalence of the ancient Greek and Roman worlds. "Greece" and "Rome" are not monolithic, homogeneous entities, but fluid notions, different aspects of which appeal to different musicians in different subgenres at different times. And, as is arguably true of all reception, these artists tend to find the version of antiquity they go looking for and can make antiquity seem more or less familiar as they see fit.

We must also remember the presence of the audience. In the case of most of these songs and albums, the use of antiquity is evocative; the average listener does not know—or care—if a Latin phrase is wrong, or a date is off.[61] These lyrics, coupled with appropriate music, can still have the intended effect of conjuring up an image of the ancient Mediterranean world.

As views of the Classical world have changed in recent times, though, so too has metal's use of Classics. Recent scholars of Classical Studies have increasingly focused on reading between the lines of canonical works (and reading long-ignored works) to help recover other voices from the ancient world, including those of women, slaves, and foreigners. Metal bands, too, have (unknowingly or not) also embraced this trend, and begun to include more female characters from the ancient world, offering perspectives that were often considered lacking in metal's early history.

This evolving relationship between Classics and heavy metal reveals the value of reception, since it shows that neither exists in a vacuum, and that both are participating in a larger conversation about the meaning of antiquity. The meaning of the ancient world is not static, but changes little by little, with each new album, and every new song.

Notes

1. This stereotype persists, even if it is not as strong as it was in the 1980s, motivating and fueled in turn by such things as the 1985 hearings on obscenity in music led by the Parents Music Resource Center (PMRC) and the 1986 documentary *Heavy Metal Parking Lot*.
2. Cf. Lindner and Wieland (2018: 33), who note that in the case of heavy metal band names, those drawing on Greek material come mostly from myth, while those somehow related to Rome are mostly historical.
3. For Classics and heavy metal, see Pendergast (1988), Puca (1997), Campbell (2009), Cavallini (2009), Liverani (2009), Umurhan (2012), Djurslev (2015), Fletcher (2015), Fletcher (2019), and McParland (2018: 72–80). Lindner and Wieland (2018) show that approximately 2,000 metal bands have names connected with the Greco-Roman world. For an overview of work done on Classics in popular music, see Stoffel (2015: 125–26).
4. For an overview of Classics and its history, see Beard and Henderson (1995).
5. This shift is evident in the oldest professional society for Classics in America changing its name from the American Philological Association (founded 1869) to the Society for Classical Studies in 2013.
6. Fundamental and introductory works include—but are by no means limited to—Martindale (1993), Hardwick (2003), Martindale and Thomas (2006), and Hardwick and Stray (2008). For a recent attempt to rethink some of the basic assumptions of reception, see the papers in Butler (2016). For a discussion of Butler (2016), see Umurhan (this volume).
7. One reflection of this popularity is the proliferation of journals devoted to Classical reception, including the *International Journal of the Classical Tradition* (first issue: 1995), *New Voices in Classical Reception Studies* (2006), and *Classical Receptions Journal* (2009).
8. For a recent interest in comics by Classicists, see the variety of case studies in Kovacs and Marshall (2011, 2016), as well as those on science fiction in Rogers and Stevens (2014, 2019).
9. For a similar claim applied to Medievalists, see Dobschenzki (2015: 11).
10. Cf. Savigny and Schaap (2018) for the challenges of fans writing about heavy metal from an academic perspective. See Kovacs and Marshall (2011: 6) on the overlap between Classicists and fans of comic books.
11. One of the most infamous condemnations of heavy metal is Arnett (1996). For other traditional attacks on metal, see Weinstein (2000: 237–75).
12. For discussion of the general lack of scholarly interest in popular music by Classicists, see Stoffel (2015).
13. For example, in his introduction to opera, Plotkin (1994: 28) calls the nineteenth century "the golden age of opera" and says, "It is safe to say that the overwhelming majority of works presented on the world's stages appeared in just 140 years, between 1786 (*Le Nozze di Figaro*) and 1926 (*Turandot*, Puccini's last opera)."
14. See, for example, Fitzgerald (2014: 341): "it is arguable that the most exciting development in the reception of the *Aeneid* over the last half century has been the gradual entry of Berlioz's *Les Troyens* into the operatic repertoire." "Most exciting" to whom?
15. E.g., "What's somewhat surprising given all of the book's adulations, however, is how shockingly common it is for even people who own *Ulysses* to have never read it, at least not in its entirety" (Wolff-Mann 2016).
16. The numbers for *Gladiator* at the box office can be found at "Box Office Mojo: Gladiator" (2019).

17. The phrase "the *Gladiator* effect" is used variously—by Classicists and others—to mean both the wave of books and movies set in the ancient world following the success of *Gladiator* and the surge in popularity of college-level classes focusing on Roman history and gladiators specifically.
18. Frith (1996) argues passionately for the value of popular music and the study of it.
19. For more detailed histories of the genre, see Christe (2003) and Wiederhorn and Turman (2013). For a lighter approach to metal's history, see O'Neill (2018).
20. For more on Achilles in metal, see Puca (1997) and Cavallini (2009).
21. On the name, see Weinstein (2014a) and the response by Brown (2015).
22. E.g., Harrison (2010).
23. From the song "Made in Hell" from the Halford album *Resurrection* (2000).
24. Cf. the connection between the drive of rock 'n' roll with the sound of a train on the railroad tracks in Chuck Berry's "Johnny B. Goode": "He used to carry his guitar in a gunny sack / Go sit beneath the tree by the railroad track / Oh, the engineers would see him sitting in the shade / Strumming with the rhythm that the drivers made."
25. In the 1980 *Rolling Stone Illustrated History of Rock and Roll*, the famed rock critic Lester Bangs wrote the following entry for "heavy metal": "As its detractors have always claimed, heavy-metal rock is nothing more than a bunch of noise; it is not music, it's distortion—and that is precisely why its adherents find it appealing. Of all contemporary rock, it is the genre most closely identified with violence and aggression, rapine and carnage. Heavy metal orchestrates technological nihilism, which may be one reason it seemed to run dry in the mid-Seventies" (332). For more on Bangs and his generally dim view of early heavy metal, see Weinstein (2014a). For the early critical reception of heavy metal in *Rolling Stone*, see Brown (2015: 251–58).
26. For a brief overview of metal's move away from the blues, see Heritage (2016: 52–3), who discusses this transition to help explain metal's use of "neo-classical" elements.
27. See Weinstein (2000: 89), Wallach, Berger, Greene (2011b: 27), and Hjelm, Kahn-Harris, and LeVine (2013b: 10): "What binds metal together though is a relatively stable canon of artists—Iron Maiden, Judas Priest, Black Sabbath and Slayer being particularly revered—and a core of themes and preoccupations that are pursued across metal sub-genres."
28. "The Trooper" remains a staple of their concerts, and in 2013 the band released a beer of the same name in conjunction with Robinsons Brewery in Stockport, England.
29. E.g., Cavallini (2009: 120) argues that Jag Panzer's song "Achilles" (*Casting the Stones*, 2014) follows Petersen's *Troy*.
30. This is not to suggest that such themes suddenly appeared fully formed on this album; their previous album, *Killers* (1981), contained instrumentals called "The Ides of March" and "Genghis Khan."
31. For an introduction to extreme metal and especially its scene, see Kahn-Harris (2007).
32. For an introduction to metal vocals, see Mesiä and Ribaldini (2015).
33. For the history of Swedish death metal, see Ekeroth (2006). Phillipov (2014) discusses death metal and its subject matter and the problems—and possibilities—raised by its analysis.
34. For an exhaustive history of black metal, see Patterson (2013).
35. Thrash is itself often considered a mix of metal and punk. For the longstanding connection here, see Waksman (2009).
36. This face paint has its own pedigree, too, coming from King Diamond, the singer for the Danish band Mercyful Fate, which is often grouped with NWOBHM bands. On numerous

37. occasions, King Diamond has said that he was inspired by the face paint used by the members of KISS.
37. This overlap between pop and metal is also apparent in the fact that the Swedish songwriters/producers Max Martin and Shellback both started out as heavy metal performers before writing and producing hit songs for artists such as Britney Spears, Kelly Clarkson, Taylor Swift, the Backstreet Boys, and other chart-topping acts.
38. McParland (2018) addresses the subject of myth in metal, but in a careless, mistake-filled manner.
39. But cf. Lindner and Wieland (2018: 36–7), who note that when it comes to band names, "immediate local, regional or national connections are the exception to the rule."
40. For treatments of Viking metal, see Trafford and Pluskowski (2007), von Helden (2010a) and (2010b), Ashby and Schofield (2015), and von Helden (2017).
41. For the influence of the Norwegian landscape see, e.g., Moynihan and Søderlind (2003: 203), who note that "nearly every single Black Metal band has had themselves photographed amongst snow and trees." See further von Helden (2017: 59–69), who argues that the depiction of the landscape in Norwegian metal is usually as part of a mythical context. For the importance of the Northern England landscape as an influence on Northern English black metal bands, see Spracklen, Lucas, and Deeks (2014: 56–60).
42. Von Helden (2010b: 33) traces the origins of Nordic metal to the release in 1984 of the compilation album *Scandinavian Metal Attack*.
43. Their debut album is written primarily in Icelandic, but they have also used Norwegian and Old Norse for their lyrics (in addition to English).
44. Von Helden (2010a: 257).
45. Again, the term is not perfect, but "Classics metal" would be too close to classic metal, which refers to bands such as Iron Maiden and Judas Priest, who play what is considered a traditional form of metal. "Greco-Roman metal" would imply that these bands only write about Greeks and Romans, or from Greek and Roman perspectives, which is not the case.
46. On the determinants of metal production by country, see Maguire (2015), who identifies multiple factors, including "Scandinavian Legal History." For more on the spread of metal, see Mayer and Timberlake (2014), who argue that the internet has been essential to the spread of metal and that, "all else equal, countries with higher per capita income do not produce significantly more metal; however, more democratic and economically integrated countries do" (41).
47. See n. 41.
48. E.g., Trafford and Pluskowski (2007: 71) offer possible reasons for changes in Scandinavian metal in the late 1980s and early 1990s, including a response to changing European concerns post-1989, as well as the financial stability of these countries, which gives rise to a revolt against the respectability of a middle-class life. Ekeroth (2006: 6–7) suggests that part of the reason for metal's predominance in Sweden is because "Sweden is generally made up of extremely small and boring towns." He also notes the instruments, rehearsal rooms, and even recording facilities made available for free or at very low cost by Swedish cities. Gardenour Walter (2015: 17) connects the rise of black metal in Norway with the "exceptionally stable economy and a static bourgeois culture, as well as the traditional Lutheran conservatism."
49. For the religious and mythical aspects of Norwegian metal music, see von Helden (2017: 69–95).
50. For a brief overview of the approaches to Satanism by metal musicians and scholars, see Hagen (2011: 190–91). For a fuller discussion, see Moynihan and Søderlind (2003: 215–70),

whose treatment of the violence of the early black metal scene in Norway served as the basis for the 2018 film, *Lords of Chaos* (directed by Jonas Åkerlund, the former drummer of Bathory who is now famous for directing music videos for Metallica, Madonna, Taylor Swift, and many others).

51. A good example of this slippage between pagans and Vikings is the title of the song "Swedish Pagans" about Vikings by the Swedish band Sabaton. For the influence of heathenism on black metal, see Granholm (2011a). For the connection between Satanism and paganism more broadly, see Gardell (2003: 284–323).
52. See, for example, the remarks of Emperor's Mortiis quoted by Crofton-Sleigh (this volume). Gardenour Walter (2015: 19) also notes that the use of Satanism and other anti-Christian elements make less sense when black metal moves "into non-Christian and post-colonial contexts."
53. For an overview of Rotting Christ's history and their part in the early Greek metal scene, see Patterson (2013: 85–92).
54. The same thing is happening in other parts of the world, too. For example, see Dairianathan (2009) and (2011) on Vedic metal, metal by Indian bands based on the sacred ancient *Vedas*.
55. For valuable overviews of the development of Metal Studies, see Brown (2011) and Weinstein (2016b).
56. For a discussion of some of the challenges facing metal studies, see Savigny and Schaap (2018).
57. The connection between place and music has become an increasingly popular topic of discussion. See the chapters in Biddle and Knights (2007) for an example of some trends in this area.
58. For discussion of Classics and twenty-first-century nationalism, see Zuckerberg (2018).
59. For recent work on heavy metal and gender, see the papers in Heesch and Scott (2016).
60. Cavallini (2009: 116) suggests that because war is a common theme in metal it was inevitable that metal bands would be interested in Achilles.
61. As Stoffel (2015: 131) suggests, pop music uses "Codes" to reach a wide audience, and antiquity is only one such set of signs.

CHAPTER 1
VERGIL'S *AENEID* AND NATIONALISM IN ITALIAN METAL
K. F. B. Fletcher

In 2013, three Italian bands—Stormlord, Heimdall, and Hesperia—released concept albums based on Vergil's epic poem, the *Aeneid*. And this was not even the first time the *Aeneid* had been the focus of an entire metal album; Hesperia had already released *Aeneidos Metalli Apotheosis Pt. I* in 2003, with Parts II, III, and IV following in 2008, 2013, and 2015, respectively. But 2013 was a watershed moment because of this simultaneity, and because Heimdall and Stormlord are more established acts on an international level than Hesperia, a one-man band whose early albums were not distributed widely, which never performs live, and only writes in Italian and Latin, thereby limiting its audience (for more on language choice, see below). Accordingly, I will focus primarily on the albums by Stormlord and Heimdall, named *Hesperia* and *Aeneid*, respectively.

These albums reflect a growing trend in the use of Classical mythology as part of a reflection on and construction of national identity by Greek and Italian bands. In hindsight, the use of Vergil's epic poem by Italian metal bands may seem inevitable because it is often considered the "national epic" of the Roman Empire, and exerted a strong influence on subsequent Italian literature.[1] That three bands chose to tackle this foundational text in the same year suggests that Mediterranean metal has reached a certain degree of maturity. At the same time, the use of the *Aeneid* by modern bands testifies to its continued relevance to modern issues, and shows that the poem continues to be even more vital than many of its most ardent supporters realize.

After exploring the reasons for bands to choose the *Aeneid*, I will discuss the two bands' motivations and show how their careers reflect general trends in heavy metal, with a move from sporadic use of Classical material to more sustained use by bands from the Mediterranean. Then I will examine the albums themselves—focusing both on their general content and on more specific issues, such as their treatment of the prologue, their choice of language—to give a sense of the range of approaches metal bands have to using a Classical text and to provide background for the rest of the discussion. Although the albums differ in some, more superficial ways, they offer similar readings of the poem, treating it as a story of heroic sacrifice for greater glory. What is perhaps surprising, however, is that neither band makes an explicit connection between Aeneas and modern Italy as part of an attempt, as Italians, to share in the glory of the Roman Empire. The avoidance of any such political move stands in marked contrast to the aggressive nationalism of some other Italian metal bands' use of Rome—as well as other modern readings of the *Aeneid*. The differences between what these two bands and others are doing should serve as a warning against interpreting all Mediterranean metal the same way. For bands such as Heimdall and Stormlord, at least, the use of Roman literature and myth is a way to speak simultaneously to an Italian audience and the global metal world.

Why Vergil? The *Aeneid* and its reception

"Our classic, the classic of all Europe, is Virgil."

—T. S. Eliot[2]

Although the story of Aeneas' journey to Italy is not now as well known to the general public in most of the non-Italian world as other epic sagas from the ancient world (especially Homer), it is the most famous Roman legend.[3] For an Italian band looking for mythological/legendary material from Rome's past, the only other comparable candidate would be the story of Romulus and Remus, twin brothers and sons of the war god Mars, who fight over who will found the city that becomes Rome, with Romulus killing Remus in the process. While this story is perhaps now better known than that of Aeneas, it presents several problems for would-be adapters: it is short, it involves the founder of Rome killing his brother, and there is no canonical literary version.[4] All in all, it would be difficult to devote an entire album to it (this perception might soon change, however, due to the release in early 2019 of an Italian film called *Il primo re*—"The First King"—about Romulus and Remus).[5] By contrast, the story of Aeneas found its canonical form in Vergil's *Aeneid*, one of the central works of Western literature essentially since the moment of its publication.[6] For the Romans (and their putative descendants), one of the most obvious places to find their mythological history is in Vergil's *Aeneid*.[7]

The poem tells the story of the Trojan Aeneas' journey after the Trojan War from Troy to Italy, where he founds Lavinium, the city from which spring Alba Longa and ultimately Rome. The poem does not, then, technically tell the story of the foundation of Rome, but rather of the Roman race, a broader topic and one that is more inclusive, focusing as it does on the blend of Italians, Greeks, and Trojans that make up what will become Rome.[8]

The poem falls into two halves of six books each. The first half is dominated by the journey to Italy and includes a stop at the newly founded colony of Carthage (Rome's enemy in the three Punic Wars and the home of Hannibal) and a journey to the Underworld for Aeneas to see his father. Books 2 and 3 are narrated to the Carthaginians by Aeneas and recount the fall of Troy and the bulk of the journey, respectively. The queen of Carthage, Dido, falls in love with Aeneas, and kills herself when he leaves, cursing his descendants and setting the Punic Wars in motion centuries later.

The second half of the poem takes place in Italy and recounts the war between Aeneas and Turnus for Lavinia, the daughter of the local king, Latinus. The poem ends with Aeneas killing Turnus after a resolution between the god Jupiter (who knows what is fated to pass) and his wife Juno (who loves the Carthaginians and also favors the Italians over the Trojans) that the Trojans will give up their language and customs and blend with the Latins to become Italian (*Aeneid* 12.793–840).

Vergil's *Aeneid* and Nationalism in Italian Metal

Publius Vergilius Maro (70–19 BCE) began writing the *Aeneid* around 29 BCE, at the end of three-quarters of a century's worth of civil strife, first between the Romans and their Italian allies in the so-called Social Wars, and then a series of civil wars, first between Julius Caesar and Pompey the Great and then between Caesar's adopted son Octavian and Marcus Antonius (better known now as Marc Antony).[9] The poem heralds the beginning of a new era in Roman history, and lauds the peace brought by Octavian, who in 27 became Augustus Caesar, the first Roman emperor.

As far as we can tell, the poem was an instant classic, studied and quoted throughout the Roman Empire soon after its publication. Accordingly, ever since its release, it has been central to Western educational curricula, and has always had a special resonance in Italy.[10] Perhaps most famously, Dante chooses Vergil for his guide through the Inferno and Purgatory in the *Divine Comedy*, exclaiming upon his first encounter with him that Vergil is his poetic master and the source of his style (*Divine Comedy* 1.79–87). The poem has also exerted influence in the realm of music, from Medieval music to opera to Bob Dylan.[11] In short, it is impossible to overstate the influence of Vergil—and especially the *Aeneid*—on Western literature; as the Eliot quotation at the beginning of this section shows, for many, the *Aeneid* is the definitive piece of Roman literature, and Vergil the quintessential Roman poet.[12] Given the enduring popularity of the poem, it was inevitable that it would eventually find its way into metal. The only surprising thing is that it took so long to do so.

Because it has always been a staple of Italian education, the poem recommends itself perhaps especially to Italians. As a poem about the foundation of a nation and the unification of Italy, it fit especially with the new emphasis on Classics—especially the Roman Empire under Augustus—under the Fascists and lent itself to obvious nationalistic readings.[13] Its emphasis on Italian unity means that the poem can be—and often has been—read as offering a vision of Italy's creation as a unified nation destined for glory.[14] For Italian bands, then, the *Aeneid* is an obvious source for a discussion of Italian history, and possibly a way to explore the nature of Italian identity.

In no small part because of the links between Fascists and Rome, Mussolini and Augustus, the reception of the *Aeneid* is complicated in the second half of the twentieth century.[15] To frame it in broad terms, scholars tend to classify readings of the *Aeneid* as falling somewhere on a spectrum between "optimistic" and "pessimistic."[16] The former is predominant in the tradition, and views Vergil as sincerely praising Augustus through his ancestor Aeneas. Such a reading tends to be sympathetic to Aeneas and justifies his actions through their ultimate benefit to Rome, which culminates in the new Golden Age under Augustus. The pessimistic approach to the *Aeneid*—associated with multiple scholars connected with Harvard who are therefore sometimes referred to as the "Harvard pessimists"—gained popularity in the middle of the twentieth century, and picked up steam in the last half of the century, especially in America.[17] This reading of the *Aeneid* highlights ambiguities in the poem and argues that Vergil undercuts his ostensible message, thereby criticizing the Augustan regime, or at least expressing his doubts about the cost of the current political environment. While scholars often disavow the polarizing terms of this debate, it continues to inform most interpretations of the poem.

I offer this radically simplified overview of the way modern scholars talk about interpretations and uses of the *Aeneid* not to suggest that these bands are—or should be—aware of trends in Vergilian scholarship, but rather to stress that they had a choice in how to read the *Aeneid*. These two types of readings have always existed outside of academia and being aware of them can help us consider how nationalistic (or not) these treatments of the poem are. While, on the analogy of Viking metal, we might expect Italian bands to highlight their connection to the glories of the Roman Empire, Heimdall and Stormlord offer no such reading, and do not attempt to minimize what can be viewed as Aeneas' negative characteristics or deeds. Although these bands unsurprisingly fall more on the optimistic end of the spectrum, there is no simplistic whitewashing of the *Aeneid* or its hero here. Metal's turn to local topics may be nationalistic in origin, but not all bands approach such material in the same way, or with the same intent.

The "nationalistic turn" in heavy metal

Although various bands had written the occasional song about the Classical world, Classics did not become a common topic until another group from history became ubiquitous in metal: the Vikings.[18] In 1990, the Swedish black metal band Bathory released their album *Hammerheart*, thereby giving birth to the subgenre of Viking metal.[19] Defined not by musical style but by the contents of its lyrics, Viking metal became increasingly popular, especially in countries with historical connections with the Vikings. By the end of the decade, there were countless Viking metal bands in Sweden, Norway, and Finland.

The reasons for this fascination with the Vikings are clear and expressed already by Bathory's front man Quorthon in the liner notes for their album, *Blood on Ice*, in which he explains why he moved away from Satanic material (the traditional *métier* of black metal) and began writing about the Vikings. It is worth quoting at length because it touches on so many of the driving forces behind Mediterranean metal:[20]

> So what was the "soul" of *Blood on Ice*? It actually started with the decline of enthusiasm for yet another full-length album packed with screams of satan etc., and all this due to the fact that I came to the personal conclusion that this whole satanic bit was a fake: A hoax created by another hoax—the Christian church, the very institution and way of life that we wanted to give a nice big fat ball breaker of a kick, by picking up the satanic and occult topics in our lyrics, in the first place. It's not easy coming out of school and starting a band at the age of fifteen and lacking the sort of experiences that great metal lyrics seemed to be made of, such as striding a Harley going down the highway doing 120 and fondling a babe's tits while drinking from a bottle of whiskey, like all the big bands seemed to do it. And what the hell ... you gotta write songs about something, right!?
>
> ... Since I am an avid fan of history, the natural step would be to find something in history that could replace a thing like the dark (not necessarily always the evil) side

Vergil's *Aeneid* and Nationalism in Italian Metal

of life (and death). And what could be more simple and natural than to pick up on the Viking era. Great era, and great material for metal lyrics. *Being Swedish and all, having a personal relation to, and linked by blood to, that era at the same time as it was a, if not a well-known, so at least an internationally infamous moment in history, I sensed that here I just might have something.* Especially well suited was it since it was an era that reached its peak just before the Christian circus came around northern Europe and Sweden in the tenth century, establishing itself as the dictatorial way of life and death.

And so that satan and hell type of soup was changed for proud and strong nordsmen, shiny blades of broadswords, dragon ships and a party-'til-you-puke type of living up there in the great halls ... an image of my ancestors and that era not too far away from the romanticised and, to a great extent, utterly wrong image most people have of that period in time through countless Hollywood productions etc.[21]

Two ideas here proved essential for subsequent developments in metal. The first is the idea that there is a link "by blood," and a sense of having a longstanding connection with the history of one's country. The second is that because the Vikings are well known around the world, they have the potential, as the subject matter for songs, to resonate with audiences at home and abroad. The focus on the Vikings thus allowed these Scandinavian bands to perform their internationally recognized identity as Scandinavians, while also engaging in the traditional extreme metal attack on Christianity.[22] While early attacks on Christianity began in the guise of Satanism, they quickly came to be part of a larger pagan agenda, bent on recovering the glory days of these countries before Christianity invaded.[23]

But the trend reached beyond these countries, and bands all over the world began making Viking metal. The disconnect was obvious to some, and gave rise to Mediterranean metal, written by bands from around the Mediterranean, especially Greece and Italy—including Heimdall and Stormlord.

Introducing the bands

Although they play different styles, both bands are Italian and both had a tradition of occasionally using mythological subjects before turning to these ambitious album-length projects.[24] Heimdall was founded in 1994 and plays traditional power metal, a style characterized in part by its clean-tone vocal melodies, harmonized choruses, and general bombast. To some extent their career reflects the general move from Norse mythology to local topics in Mediterranean metal: their name is that of a Norse god, and they began writing songs about Norse mythology, only turning to Roman legend with their *Aeneid* album.

When asked about their name in a 2003 interview, guitarist and lyricist Fabio Calluori responded, "When we started in 1994 we wanted a name that sounded epic and powerful as the music that we play. I very much like history, the ancient legends/tales and the mythology—of course, also the Nordic one, and I think that they are patrimony of all people."[25] Their use of the name of a Norse god for their band reflects the belief that a band from any country could use Norse myth, and Norse mythology was an easy choice for source material in the early 1990s, when Viking metal was becoming popular.[26] It is only recently that other local material has been deemed appropriate for such extended adaptation and use, in part because bands from Scandinavian countries decried the use of Viking material by non-Scandinavian bands.[27]

That interview, however, predates their *Aeneid* album and Calluori's later interviews reflect a slightly different view. When asked in one interview about his motivations for writing about the poem, Calluori replied:

> I felt the need to write something important and impressive, something very ambitious that could distinguish Heimdall in the metal scene and hence the idea to narrate the story of one of the greatest epic poem. Greek and Roman themes have been previously treated by various bands but no one—at least from what I know—spoke of the origins of our Latin-Roman culture through an entire concept album. It's something that characterizes us.[28]

While not as aggressive as Quorthon's references to "blood," the phrase "our Latin-Roman culture" reflects the same sense of possession. Myths might belong to all peoples, but a poem such as the *Aeneid* has a more specific connection.[29]

Stormlord turned to Classical material as a reaction to the widespread use of Norse material by metal bands. Founded in 1991, Stormlord hail from Rome, and often refer to their music as "extreme epic metal," though we might also call it symphonic death metal, a blend of traditional death metal (growling vocals, detuned guitars) with largely synthesized orchestral effects. Like many metal bands, Stormlord show an interest in literature and history, with songs inspired by Lovecraft, Coleridge, and Dante. Well before their concept album on the *Aeneid*, Stormlord was also drawing on the Italian past; 2008's *Mare Nostrum*, for instance, is named after one of the Roman names for the Mediterranean ("Our Sea") and the title track is about Rome's wars against Carthage. They also have a particular interest in the Samnites, one of the Italian peoples who fought with the Romans in the fourth and third centuries BCE, about whom they write in "Under the Samnites' Spears" (*At the Gates of Utopia*, 2001) and "The Oath of the Legion" (*The Gorgon Cult*, 2004). Both songs exalt the might of the Samnites and show that Stormlord's interest in Italian history is not limited to the Romans.[30]

An interview with bassist and primary lyricist Francesco Bucci for the website *Metal Rules* shows Stormlord's longstanding interest in Rome and the importance of having a local connection with the material:

> We took inspiration from the huge mythology of our land. As you know, the Roman and Greek legends are really beautiful and amazing, but in this time there's the trend to talk about the Scandinavian myths. We live in Rome and we don't feel

able to speak about legends that are not from our country. Often we also speak about historical events and about the glory of the Roman Empire, which used to rule all over the known World for Hundreds of years! We are proud of our past and that's why we choose these subjects. I think it's more interesting to write down something in which you believe deeply than to tell stories about Vikings who lived in a land thousands of miles away from your land.[31]

Even more so than Calluori's later interviews, Bucci's remarks make explicit the drive behind both Viking and Mediterranean metal at their most extreme: the sense that some material belongs to you by birth, and some does not; that these are legends from "our country" and therefore this qualifies as "our past." This line of thinking implies that being Italian gives you a privileged access to the Roman Empire that those born outside of its former borders do not have. Although the bands treat the poem very differently when adapting it to a musical form, they approach it with a similar underlying philosophy.

Comparison of the albums

Before returning to the question of what it might mean for an Italian band to write about Vergil's *Aeneid* in the early twenty-first century, I want to examine how these two albums draw on and respond to the inherent focus on Italian identity in the *Aeneid*, adapting it for their own purposes as part of the ongoing development of Mediterranean metal. This will provide context for the discussion at the end of the chapter, but also offer two examples of the ways in which metal bands can engage at length with Classical literature.

I will focus here on three aspects of these albums: (1) the material they choose to include and exclude, and how they arrange it; (2) their treatment of the famous *Aeneid* prologue; and (3) their choice of which language(s) to use. In all these cases, Heimdall offer what can be considered a more straightforwardly faithful approach to the poem, trying to convey its plot and main themes as clearly and comprehensively as possible. This approach gives the impression of telling a story, without obvious commentary on the poem's possible relevance to questions of Italian identity. In contrast, Stormlord offer a more impressionistic approach to the poem, and are more ambitious in using multiple languages to different ends, and more clearly focusing on Italy itself. Nevertheless, both bands focus on the difficulties faced, and the personal sacrifices made, by Aeneas to make Rome possible, and emphasize its fated greatness.[32]

Selection and arrangement of material

The overall arrangement of the albums and their material reveals the different focus of the two bands. Heimdall take a straightforward approach, offering thirteen tracks, one as a prologue (Track 1, "Prologue") and then twelve other songs, one for each of the twelve books of Vergil's poem. They draw attention to this correspondence by listing each book number and then the track after it, even putting both the first two tracks under the heading of "Book I" on the back of the CD case so that it only has twelve entries. Although each of these tracks offers only select parts from the corresponding book and thus does not exactly reproduce the entire plot in detail, the plan of one song per book reflects a certain view of fidelity and a desire for a type of completeness.

The choice of material for each song reveals a differing valuation of the books, in many ways reflecting traditional views of the relative worth of the individual books. One manifestation of this weighing is the relative length of songs, which range from 1:15 (tr. 1) to 5:03 (tr. 8). Perhaps the clearest choice is the decision to make Track 6, "Funeral Song," a short instrumental. This track is dedicated to Book 5 of the *Aeneid*, in which the Trojans land in Sicily and celebrate the one-year anniversary of Aeneas' father's death with a series of games. This book also contains the Trojan women's burning of some of their ships, which necessitates leaving behind the Trojan women and the elderly. But by framing this book as a "Funeral Song," and offering a brief, dirge-like instrumental in A minor for this track (complete with the sounds of a crackling fire and the tolling of a bell), Heimdall focus on the death of Aeneas' father Anchises, thereby emphasizing Aeneas' personal losses on the journey to Italy.[33] To call this a funeral is, technically, incorrect, since Anchises has been dead for a year, but this choice emphasizes the hardships of the journey, and does not allow it to be tempered by the joy of the games, which many see as a primary characteristic of the book.[34] There is no room for the temporary joys of competition—even if, in the poem, the games take up 500 of the book's 871 lines (104–603).[35]

By only offering eight tracks, however, Stormlord immediately disrupt any one-to-one correspondence between album and text. Their songs differ even more widely in duration than do Heimdall's, from 1:08 (tr. 6) to 9:41 (tr. 8), further frustrating any such equivalence.[36] They also differ from Heimdall by not choosing song titles with an obvious connection to the book about which they are writing. Rather, the names of some of these tracks—"Motherland" (tr. 2), "Hesperia" (tr. 4), and "Onward to Roma" (tr. 5)—reflect their overriding interest in Aeneas' journey from one place to another, which is also evident in their choice of album title; while Heimdall again show a more straightforward notion of fidelity by preserving the poem's title as their album title, Stormlord use "Hesperia," a Greek name for Italy meaning simply, "the Western land." Vergil uses the term frequently in the *Aeneid*; it is the first name for Italy that Aeneas hears when the ghost of his wife tells him to leave Troy and seek Hesperia (2.781). While Heimdall advertise clearly their connection with Vergil's poem, Stormlord emphasize instead their focus on Italy's legendary past. Only by listening to the lyrics and/or reading the liner notes would most people learn that this album is based on the *Aeneid*.

Other choices further reinforce these differences in approach. In addition to their lyrics, Heimdall include notes on the story in the album's liner notes (sometimes quoting from the poem in English), so that listeners can fill in the gaps left by the lyrics. Again, there is the sense that they are following the poem faithfully, trying to present the story in an accurate and linear fashion. For example, although they never refer to Aeneas' Italian nemesis Turnus by name in the songs, his name appears throughout the liner notes. Someone who read all Heimdall's lyrics and liner notes would accordingly have a fair understanding of the basic plot of the *Aeneid*.

The same cannot be said of *Hesperia*. Stormlord focus primarily on the first half of the poem, which details Aeneas' trip from Troy to Italy, with much of the action happening at Carthage, where the queen, Dido, falls in love with Aeneas.[37] Focusing on the first half of the poem downplays the war between Aeneas and Turnus (whom they never mention), which Vergil portrays as a sort of civil war.[38] They also never mention Lavinia, Aeneas' future bride and the ostensible reason he fights Turnus, who was previously set to marry her (as with Turnus, Heimdall mention her only in the liner notes). But Lavinia is the eponym of Lavinium, the city Aeneas founds, and so is not directly connected with Rome. By removing Turnus and Lavinia, Stormlord focus more on Aeneas' connection with Rome and the sacrifices he must make on his way to Italy, presenting him as a largely sympathetic character, and offering a more optimistic reading of the poem. The omission of the final battle between Aeneas and Turnus obviates any need to confront the morality of Aeneas' killing of his defeated foe (see below).[39]

The focus on the poem's first half echoes a longstanding preference. Since antiquity, the parts of the poem that have received most attention come from the first half.[40] Dido has proven to be Vergil's most enduring creation, and her story takes place in the first half.[41] The allure of the first half is such that even in academia, a common charge leveled against studies of the *Aeneid* is that they neglect the poem's second half.[42] There are many reasons for the longstanding preference for the poem's first half: it deals with characters and places familiar from other literature, including both of Homer's poems; people generally know the beginnings of works the best; the personal, emotional aspects of Aeneas' relationships especially with Dido, but also with his wife, Anchises, and other Trojans such as Helenus and Andromache; an aesthetic opinion that the first half is superior. And since Aeneas is clearly the main character of the first half, which revolves around his emotions in dealing with the fall of Troy, the loss of his father, and his abortive relationship with Dido, focusing on it privileges the narrative of the personal hardships he must endure to found the Roman race, rather than the war in Italy and the damage done there by the Trojans which are the focus of the second half.[43]

The Prologue

The beginning of the *Aeneid* is extraordinarily well known and was quoted early and often, including in ancient graffiti.[44] The poem's prologue (Book 1, verses 1–33) lays out the main themes of the work, and announces Vergil's purpose: telling the story of the origin of the Roman race. Both bands devote a great deal of time to this prologue, and although they choose to quote different sections, both focus somewhat misleadingly on the poem's status as an origin story for Rome.

The first track on the Heimdall album is simply called "Prologue," and consists of a whispered recitation of the first seven lines of the poem, from the most famous English translation of the poem, that of John Dryden (1697):[45]

> Arms, and the man I sing, who, forc'd by fate
> And haughty Juno's unrelenting hate,

> Expell'd and exil'd, left the Trojan shore.
> Long labors, both by sea and land, he'd borne,
> And in the doubtful war, before he won
> The Latian realm, and built the destin'd town;
> His banish'd gods restor'd to rites divine,
> And settled sure succession in his line,
> From whence the race of Alban fathers come,
> And the long glories of majestic Rome.[46]

The choice to speak, rather than sing, these lines of poetry over swelling orchestral music emphasizes their pre-existing status as poetry, and is another mark of Heimdall's general fidelity. This choice also marks out the prologue from the rest of the album, emphasizing the song's function as a prelude to the album.

By choosing to end with line 7 of the prologue, Heimdall emphasizes the connection between the poem and the ultimate foundation of Rome; "Rome" is the final word of Dryden's translation of that verse, as *Romae* ("of Rome") is the final word in Latin.[47] The excision of the rest of the prologue puts a focus on the big picture to the exclusion of the broader thematic issues of the poem and its plot, and Heimdall's "Prologue" recasts the *Aeneid* prologue through omission, emphasizing the foundational aspect of the poem and Aeneas' connection with the city of Rome at the beginning of the album.

The prologue is the subject of two of the thirteen tracks on Heimdall's album, as the second track, "Forced by Fate," also covers that material. While this song is ostensibly devoted to all of Book 1, it draws almost exclusively from the prologue. This longer track includes more details from the *Aeneid* prologue, and its title is a modification of Dryden's translation ("forc'd by fate") of the description of Aeneas as "a fugitive because of fate" (*fato profugus*, 1.2).[48] This track, however, addresses larger plot issues, summarizes parts of the poem (e.g., the main stops on the Trojans' journey to Italy), and highlights the general suffering the Trojans will undergo to reach what Heimdall refer to as "the promised land." It thus acts as more of an introduction to the rest of the album than the previous track.[49] This song also introduces a refrain—"For the will of fate—from the ashes/Of the land afire/Through many tears—hear/A new birth will rise"—to drive home the point that the focus of the album is Rome's rise from Troy's destruction and Aeneas' personal losses.

This chorus picks up on many key words and images from the first half of the *Aeneid*. The reference to fire recalls the importance of fire in both Books 2 (the burning of Troy) and especially 4 (the fire of Dido's love and then her death on the pyre).[50] The "will of fate" is a central theme, too, and appears multiple times in the first 33 lines (1: *fato*; 18: *fata*; 22: *Parcas*; 32: *fatis*). Finally, the reference to tears alludes to the pervasive grief of the poem's first half but, more specifically, may also recall one of the most famous lines of the first book. As Aeneas and his companion Achates view images of the Trojan War in Juno's temple in Carthage, Aeneas declares, *sunt lacrimae rerum* (*Aen.* 1.462), a perennially debated line that means either "there are tears for things" or "there are tears of things."[51] Heimdall's first two tracks thus offer an introduction to the high stakes of the story as well as its main themes, especially the price paid for the new empire.

Stormlord's approach to the prologue is less direct. Their first track, "Aeneas," acts as a prologue by playing with dynamic, beginning softly and fading in before building to a crescendo, with the lyrics beginning only at 1:22. But they differ from Heimdall by retaining the original Latin, making Vergil's material less accessible to the general metal audience (for more on language choices, see below). While they, too, have modified the prologue through omission, they go further than Heimdall not only by quoting more lines (1.1–17, 19–20, 22, 5–7, 33), but also by repeating lines 5–7, *multa quoque et bello passus, dum conderet urbem/inferretque deos Latio; genus unde Latinum/Albanique patres atque altae moenia Romae* ("He also suffered many things even in war, until he could found the city/and bring the gods to Latium, from where come the Latin race/and the Alban fathers and the walls of high Rome"). The repetition of these three lines turns them into a chorus of sorts and helps reimagine the poem as a song. It also reflects a reading of the *Aeneid* as primarily a foundation story of Rome, much as does Heimdall's choice to end "Prologue" with those lines—even though the "city" referred to in line 5 is technically Lavinium, as Aeneas is long dead before the foundation of Rome by Romulus.

Stormlord's idiosyncratic quotation of the prologue further emphasizes what they consider the most relevant aspect of the story, especially their quotation of the phrase *sic volvere Parcas* ("that the Parcae [i.e. the Fates] were unrolling in such a way," 1.22). Taking this phrase—which they also use as the title for track 6 on the album—out of its grammatical context (it is part of an indirect statement) emphasizes the role of fate in the story and the idea that Rome is destined for greatness. Their willingness to reshape the text to their ends means that unlike Heimdall they include line 33, the last line of the long prologue and arguably the most programmatic line of the proem: *tantae molis erat Romanam condere gentem* ("so difficult was it to found the Roman race," 1.33). Ending with 33 emphasizes the connection with Rome and elides Lavinium (and Alba Longa) even more than Vergil already does, but also focuses on the difficulties faced by Aeneas to accomplish his goals.[52]

Language

The bands' treatments of the prologue also exemplify their differing approaches to language in their adaptations of the *Aeneid*; their choice of what languages to use and when to reflect the kinds of choices faced by metal bands from non-English-speaking countries. Heimdall's choice of the most venerable of English translations of the *Aeneid* to some extent marks its audience as Anglophone, perhaps as a nod to the fact that English was the first—and continues to be the primary—language of heavy metal. Heimdall also use only English in both lyrics and liner notes, revealing their conception of their audience primarily as the international metal audience.

Stormlord are more ambitious in mixing English, Latin, and Italian—all languages they have used on previous albums. Their choice reflects not only their differing aims, but also the importance of language and the blending of languages in the *Aeneid* itself. While the choice to use untranslated Latin is arguably equally alienating to all fans, the choice of Italian is a clear signal of audience as well as a declaration of the poem's special connection with Italians. They do, however, make concessions to the general, international metal audience by including the English translation of almost all the Latin and Italian in the liner notes (see below).

Stormlord's setting the original Latin to music in the prologue means doing away with the original meter of the poem, essentially rewriting it as a song. Vergil wrote his poem in the meter of ancient epic, dactylic hexameter. Unlike English meter, Latin meter is quantitative (i.e. based on the length of syllables rather than the stress). Each line, composed of six metrical feet, generally has one caesura, or main pause, usually in the third foot, but sometimes in the fourth. Stormlord has used these caesurae as places to pause (e.g. 1, 3, 5, 7), treating them almost as if they were the ends of lines of a song. And they have done this intentionally. Bucci said in a 2013 interview that:

> Our desire to create a bridge between past and present is the reason why the lyrics of the opening song, "Aeneas," are nothing more than the original words taken from the proem of the *Aeneid*. These lyrics are sung in Latin following the original metrical accent (dactylic hexameter), an experiment never tried before in Metal music, for which we have collaborated with some professional Latin teachers.[53]

Similarly, the use by vocalist Cristiano Borchi of two different singing styles (one is the deeper, more traditionally death metal-sounding style, and the other is the screaming style more common in black metal) serves to punctuate the line endings of the original poem, as for example at the end of lines 4–9.[54] Thus, although Stormlord alter the presentation of the lines to fit their music, the use of the caesura as a place to pause and of heavier vocals at line-end helps to convey some sense of the original meter.

Stormlord use Latin in two songs (1, 5) and Italian in three (2, 4, 8), and if we think of the album as broken down into two roughly equal sides of four tracks each, then the Latin appears in the first song on each side, declaring an initial connection with the original poem; the Latin gives each track the feel of a prologue for the side.[55] Italian then appears in the final song on each side, suggesting the historical movement from Latin to Italian; as Latin provides an opening effect, Italian has a closural effect. Track 2, "Motherland" is an outlier in this pattern, as it is the only song with Latin or Italian that does not have a matching partner, and in which the Italian is not translated in the liner notes (see below on this song).

Stormlord use Italian in places that touch directly upon the Roman future in tracks 2 and 8. The title track is all in Italian, and is addressed by Aeneas to Italy, with a refrain of "Tu sei Hesperia" ("You are Hesperia"). By adopting this persona, the band can sing a song to Italy, and their choice of Italian strengthens this connection. This is an Italian song in every sense of the word: sung to ancient Italy in Italian by one of the most famous figures from its legendary past. It is a bittersweet song (the music matches the tone of the lyrics in this regard), as Aeneas addresses the fact that his desire for Italy trumps his desire for Dido, whom he has left behind. It is also a song of patriotic personal sacrifice, reflecting the cost of Italy, as Aeneas laments that despite the divine nature of the mission, he cannot forget the longing or lust ("brama") to forget his destiny and escape. In this song, Hesperia inflames Aeneas, in pointed contrast to Dido's pyre, on which she kills herself.[56] Aeneas must carry on because "canti di onori venturi/da Roma declamano il nome 'Hesperia'" ("songs of distant honours/From Rome they declaim the name 'Hesperia'").

Besides their quotation of the prologue, Stormlord's only use of Latin comes in track 5, "Onward to Roma," even the title of which shows linguistic mixing. As in this title, Stormlord only use "Roma" and never "Rome" in their lyrics, thereby subtly privileging the Latin—and Italian—name of the city over the English one (possibly to show the connection between the two languages). (Their use of "Rome" in their translations in the CD booklet make the consciousness of this choice clear.) The title connects Aeneas to Rome in a way he does not connect himself in the poem, since Lavinium is his fated city. The rousing chorus "Onward to Roma" collapses this distinction between Lavinium and Rome.

As with their use of Italian, so their use of Latin has a significant connection with place. They quote lines 781-784 from Book 6, the part of Anchises' prophecy to Aeneas in the Underworld that refers to Romulus, founder of Rome:

> en huius, nate, auspiciis incluta Roma
> imperium terris, animos aequabit Olympo,
> septemque una sibi muro circumdabit arces,
> felix prole virum . . .

In the CD booklet, they provide the following translation for the Latin (along with the citation), and the way they have the lines separated reflects the way they separate the Latin, too:

> "Behold, o son!
> By his auspices shall that glorious Rome extend
> Her empire to earth's ends, her ambitions to the skies,
> And shall embrace seven hills with a single city's wall,
> Blessed in a brood of heroes."

Although they do not credit the source, this appears to be a slightly modified version of Fairclough's Loeb translation. As Anchises tells Aeneas of the greatness to come to their line, he mentions the city of Rome by name, which Aeneas hears here for the first time in the poem.[57] In this anthemic song, Stormlord have chosen to quote the Latin of the main description of Rome in the poem as a nod to the city and its history.

Immediately after the Latin they quote another famous part of Anchises' prophecy, this time in English: "Be thy charge, Roman,/To rule the nations in thine empire,/To crown peace with justice,/To spare the vanquished and to crush the proud" (*Aeneid* 6.851-3).[58] These are some of the most (in)famous lines from the poem because they ostensibly sum up the Roman mission and because the apostrophe directly links the Roman reader with Aeneas; Anchises is speaking across the ages to all Romans.[59] By quoting this apostrophe, Stormlord momentarily treat their audience as if they were Roman—and the choice of English for these lines may serve as an invitation of sorts, a (temporary) opening up of Roman identity to all listeners, at the same time ensuring that this definition of what it means to be Roman reaches the widest swath of their metal-listening audience.

Stormlord's blending of languages mirrors the blending of cultures and languages that make up Italy as Vergil describes it, which is particularly clear at the end of the poem, when Jupiter and Juno reach an agreement before Aeneas kills Turnus and ends the war. Juno asks that the Latins neither be subsumed nor become Trojan. Jupiter responds (*Aen.* 12.834–839):

> "The Ausonians [Italians] will keep their paternal speech and customs, and as it is now, so will their name be; mixed in body alone the Trojans will subside. I will add the manner and rites of worship and I will make them all Latins, of one speech. The mixed race that will rise from this blood you will see surpass men, surpass gods in dutifulness..."[60]

These lines provide one of the best examples of the theme of mixing that runs throughout the poem.

Stormlord, in turn, emphasize through their use of three languages that both the *Aeneid* and *Hesperia* are in part about navigating identity. As the *Aeneid* balances the constituent elements of the Roman Empire, so Stormlord grapple with the elements of their identity. To use English, Latin, and Italian is what it means to be an Italian metal band in the twenty-first century.[61]

The connection between Italy and the Roman Empire in Heimdall and Stormlord

These two bands' treatments of the *Aeneid* differ in obvious, significant ways. Beyond their stylistic choices because of the their respective subgenres (the difference between power metal and death metal vocals, for instance, will be immediately clear, even to people who know nothing about metal), there are major differences in structure and language: while Heimdall allot one song per book in an attempt to go through the poem in order, Stormlord follow no such sequence, and largely ignore much of the poem; similarly, while Stormlord use English, Latin, and Italian, Heimdall only use English, maintaining a consistency throughout.

But there are more similarities than differences between the two albums, as they largely share a very common reading of the *Aeneid*, one which is largely optimistic, but does not shy away from the darker aspects of Aeneas' journey. Neither band attempts to whitewash what many readers have viewed as Aeneas' failings, therefore neither offers simplistic praise of the founder of the Roman race. In this final section, I will show the ways in which both bands acknowledge negative aspects of Aeneas' story and then argue—in part by contrasting the approach to Rome taken by other Italian metal bands—that they avoid any kind of simplistic nationalistic reading of the *Aeneid* and the connection between Rome and Italy.

The two main ways in which these bands acknowledge a more pessimistic reading of the *Aeneid* is in how they view Aeneas' decision to leave Dido, and how they treat the wars waged by Aeneas, especially in Italy. As Crofton-Sleigh shows in her contribution to this volume, Heimdall privilege Dido's perspective by making hers the voice of their song for Book 4, "The Ballad of the Queen," as she addresses the absent Aeneas, saying she "was so foolish to hear your words." Rather than focusing on Aeneas and his justifications for leaving Carthage, Heimdall emphasize Dido's belief that she has been betrayed and show the effects of his decision in a mournful ballad that she sings right before committing suicide.

Stormlord likewise do not shy away from the ways in which this episode can be read as casting a negative light on Aeneas. They make Dido the focus of one song, "Bearer of Fate" (track 3), in which Aeneas repeatedly laments that "She's my love, I must leave her" and that he is "dying a bit inside" as she mourns. Although most of the lines are from Aeneas' perspective, the guest vocalist Elisabetta Marchetti sings the following lines twice: "Venus, release this life / Hades, please, receive my soul," providing a literal female voice in the song. But perhaps the most striking lines are: "I feel your sorrow, I wasn't strong enough / To be your lover and not the bearer of fate." This is a pointed reversal of the optimistic reading of the Dido episode, that Aeneas' willingness to leave Dido at the command of the gods reflects his dutifulness. Both bands thus embrace, rather than minimize, the tragedy of the episode, in part by giving Dido a voice in their narratives.

Similarly, both acknowledge the price paid by people fighting in the Trojans' wars; although metal traditionally praises martial valor, neither band only—or even primarily—focuses on the glorious aspects of battle. Heimdall's penultimate song, that devoted to Book 11, focuses on the death of Aeneas' young ally Pallas, who was killed by Turnus. It is a short (1:37), very sad song, and the music is largely piano-based, and in a minor key. The final lines are "Away in the sky thy spirit flies/While these tears say goodbye" ("Away"). Even though only 224 of Book 11's 915 lines are on the funerals of Pallas and all the other warriors on both sides, and there are much more famous episodes in the book (especially the story of Camilla, the Italian warrior maiden), Heimdall's focus on this funeral adds a mournful tone before the story's climax.

Similarly, in treating the final fight between Turnus and Aeneas, they do not shy away from Aeneas' decision to kill Turnus after the latter has submitted and begged for mercy (*Aen.* 12.930–8). Critics have seen Aeneas' killing of Turnus while boiling with rage (*fervidus*, 12.951) as counter to Anchises' command to spare the defeated. Not only do Heimdall not minimize what many have considered a very dark way to end the poem, they have arguably emphasized it by making the last line of their album be "Aeneas slays the foe blinded by anger" ("The Last Act").

Stormlord's final song is called "Those Upon the Pyre," and focuses on all of the losses the Trojans have suffered to get where they are, claiming at one point that "We belong to those upon the pyre/All for them, all for those laid on the fire." The song starts out slowly and resembles a funeral march with its overall quiet dynamic and use of the snare drum. Although the song does not maintain its funereal sound—before the lyrics start it becomes heavy, and mid-tempo—the mood is set to match the focus in the lyrics on the price paid by the Trojans to get where they are.

Neither band, therefore, avoids the negative aspects of Aeneas' journey, or minimizes the price paid to found the Roman race. At the same time, neither band makes any explicit attempt to link Rome and modern Italy. There are thus no simple expressions in these albums declaring Rome the greatest empire of all time, let alone making a connection between being Italian and having a share in this glory. Such a connection may be—and likely is—implicit, in part by the simple fact that these are Italian bands writing about the Romans, but is far different from some of the aggressive statements made by some of their peers.

Perhaps the clearest evidence that neither band is pushing a blindly nationalistic agenda is their general avoidance of references to Italy. While Heimdall mention Italy by name a handful of times in the story sections they put between songs in the liner notes, they never mention it in any of the song lyrics. Because they quote the proem, they should, in theory, mention it, since it appears in line 2 (*Italiam . . . venit*, "he came to Italy), but because they quote Dryden's translation, which omits "Italy," they, too, omit it.

Because Stormlord quote this proem in Latin, they mention Italy by name twice in their first song, first in line 2, and then in line 13, in which *Italiam* is said to be opposite Carthage. The only other time Stormlord refer to Italy is in the second song, "Motherland": the elder Trojan Nautes speaks to Aeneas, telling him—in Italian—that the fates pushed him *sino a lambire le italiche coste* ("as far as to touch the Italian coasts").

Similarly, both bands talk about Aeneas' connection to Rome and the greatness of his destiny, but neither makes any claim that they are the heirs to this destiny. While the interviews quoted above reveal the way they perceive themselves as having a connection with this material, their use of it is very different from that of other bands. Heimdall's liner notes are explicit in linking Aeneas with Rome, but their actual lyrics do not stress this point. In the song for Book 6, "Underworld," Anchises says to Aeneas: "You'll see the kings of the world,/Of the empires to come" and Aeneas later asks, "How many tears will be poured for/The kingdom to come?" Anchises focuses on the glory, but Aeneas returns to the theme of tears that runs through the album. Similarly, in the final song, the chorus declares, "Master of the thunder/Their future in your hands/Master of the thunder/It's the birth of the empire" ("The Last Act"), which contrasts with the focus on Aeneas' anger at the end of the song. In both cases, then, Heimdall connect Aeneas' journey with something larger, but temper it with darker aspects and make no simplistic claims of inherited Italian glory.

Stormlord perhaps come closer to making such a connection between Troy, Rome, and modern Italy at a few points on *Hesperia*. In the second song, "Motherland," the Trojans who carry on from Sicily after the burning of the ships refer to themselves as "the chosen ones/of Ilium." As at *Aeneid* 5.709–18, the Trojan elder Nautes tells Aeneas that he must continue on his fated journey, and says that:

Soffrendo l'ira celeste	Suffering the celestial anger,
Nel Lazio porrai nuovi dei	Into Latium you will bring new gods
Ed il sangue latino dei padri	And the Latin blood of the fathers
Che sopra quei colli ergeran Roma ...	That on top of those hills will build Rome ...

I have given my translation of these lines alongside the Italian, since this is the one piece they do not translate in their liner notes. The reference to the fathers and the hills recalls *Aeneid* 1.6–7: "from where come the Latin race and the Alban fathers and the walls of high Rome." The reference to "sangue latino" may raise red flags for some, but it is close to a part of Vergil's prologue.

An Italian section in the album's final song, "Those Upon the Pyre," may also suggest to some a nationalistic reading (their translation is given to the side):

"La progenie di Iulo cantiamo,	"The offspring of Iulo we sing,
Che estendera il dominio sino alle terre	That will lead the kingdom to the lands
Distese oltre le stelle,	Laid beyond the stars,
Dove eterno Atlante la celeste volta regge."	Where Atlas carries the heavens eternally."

Iulus is Aeneas' son (also called Ascanius), from whom the Julian clan (*gens Iulia*) was said to have descended, the most famous member of which was Julius Caesar, adopted father of Augustus.

Although "progenie di Iulo" more obviously refers to Augustus, it could also refer to all Italians, and the end of this song may hint at such a reading; after the Italian lines quoted above, the final lines of the song are:

Far away from home we roam,
Covered with the long,
Heavy shades of the forefathers,
We feel of centuries the weight
Our destinies, every single one of them now belongs
To those upon the pyre
All for those laid on the fire

When the rays of a future sun
Will shine over a thousand domes,
When all these old wounds will hurt no more,
When the warbringer will rest,
In the flame you will find us all,
You'll find us all into the pyre ...

The reference to the weight of destiny and forefathers suggests a continuity, and the "domes" may be more appropriate for modern Rome than Augustan Rome, but this is far from an explicit connection between Aeneas and modern Italians. In fact, one could read these lines solely within the context of the poem. In Book 8, Aeneas' mother Venus brings her son a suit of arms made by Vulcan, the god of the forge. Vergil provides a lengthy ecphrasis of the shield (*Aen.* 8.626–728), detailing numerous historical events depicted on it, including Octavian's victory at Actium in 31 BCE, which essentially made him the sole power in Rome. After this long ecphrasis, Vergil says that Aeneas, though he does not know what the images mean, rejoices in them, "lifting up on his shoulder both the fame and fates of his descendants" (*attollens umero famamque et fata nepotum*, *Aen.* 8.731).

It is likewise possible to read another reference in such a way. In the penultimate song on *Hesperia*, "My Lost Empire," Aeneas laments the fall of Troy. But he looks ahead:

> Too deep for words
> The pain brought by this bitter story
> Whose remembrance
> Still blinds my eyes with salty tears
> This dying domain was a cradle of flesh
> Where from blood and fire the eagle rose . . .
>
> And when the world will fear your name
> It will bow to my lost empire
> And to those who gave their lives
> For you to claim the crown
> For you to shine . . .

"Your name" almost certainly refers to Rome, and while the "eagle" recalls the prominence of the Roman eagle in Fascist imagery, it is also the symbol of the Roman military. Similarly, the reference to "blood" can be read as an appeal to nativism, but the context here suggests that it refers to the wars the Trojans have fought. Likewise, the idea that Rome's ultimate victory over Greece will be revenge for the Trojan War is already in the *Aeneid*, both when Jupiter consoles Venus (*Aen.* 1.283–5) and when Aeneas visits his father in the Underworld (*Aen.* 6.836–40). Therefore, although some may be inclined to view such a song as nationalistic, a comparison with other Italian metal bands will show the kind of explicit connection between Rome and Italy that Stormlord and Heimdall are not making.

Nationalism in other Italian metal

As I mentioned above, another Italian metal band has written about Vergil's *Aeneid*. In fact, the pagan black metal band Hesperia has written four albums on the topic—the third of which came out in the same year as the Stormlord and Heimdall albums. I have not talked about these albums for two major reasons. The first is that this band does not have the kind of international reputation that even Heimdall and Stormlord have

Vergil's *Aeneid* and Nationalism in Italian Metal

(neither is a household name in metal). It is also the project of one person, who refers to himself as Hesperus, and as far as I can tell, he does not perform live, let alone tour. But Hesperia's four-album project devoted to the *Aeneid* is the most ambitious attempt to treat the *Aeneid* in metal by far, as well as the most explicitly Italian.[62]

The focus on Italy is perhaps most immediately apparent in the title of Hesperia's 2013 *Aeneid* album: *Spiritvs Italicvs—Aeneidos Metalli Apotheosis Pars III* ("Italian Spirit—The Apotheosis of the Metal Aeneid Part III"). Furthermore, three of the song titles on the album include the same phrase, *Spiritvs Italicvs*. If there were any doubt about the nature of the approach, the album's cover removes all doubts; it is a photograph of Hesperus, in the corpse paint that black-metal musicians often wear, holding an Italian flag in the castle at Pievefavera, which was built over Roman Faveria.[63] The entire photograph is black and white (or rather, the sepia tones of an old black-and-white photo) except for the Italian flag. Around the edge of the photo is a gold border containing numerous symbols of ancient Rome, including the legionary eagle—which within the context has a clear Fascistic meaning.

The band's official YouTube channel supports such an interpretation. On the page for the video of "Metallvm Italicvm I," from their final *Aeneid* album, *Metallvm Italicvm*, there is a statement attributed to Hesperus in 2014, declaring:

> The album is also a MANIFESTO of the spiritual/cultural/musical genre called METALLVM ITALICVM (it: Metallo Italico; eng: Italic Metal):
>
> - Against the italian "esterofilia" & the Decay of the Ancient Italic Glory & Spirit
> - Against the homogenisation of music & art
> - For the creation of the cultural & spiritual music genre: METALLVM ITALICVM
> - For the Return of the Italic "IMPERIAL" scene through Metallum and Arts
> - For the Return of Hesperia & the ITALIC Golden age Metallvm Italicvm is a strong attack to the false emperors of nowdays.[64]

The condemnation of "esterofilia" ("an (excessive) love for foreign things") is xenophobic at best, and more likely racist. The worries about "homogenisation" can be construed as another dog-whistle term, suggesting that essential differences between countries and/or races are being eroded by immigration and the forces of globalization. This language—though still somewhat coded—is vastly more nationalistic than anything in the albums by Heimdall or Stormlord.

Other Italian metal bands are even more explicit in using Italy's past to talk about the present. The traditional metal band Centvrion writes frequently about the Roman Empire in a nostalgic, wistful way.[65] Their 2002 album, *Non Plvs Vltra*, contains a song called "Roma Capvt Mundi," a Latin phrase which means "Rome, Head [or Capital] of the World," and has been used since antiquity to highlight Rome's position in the Empire and then later in the Catholic world.[66] This song calls for Rome to rise up to rule the world once more and the second half expresses a clearly nationalistic sentiment:

> Rome you'll be the queen of all skies
> I feel myself part of the light
> I need to feed on your might . . .
> I'm dying for disrupt the chains
> for the tomorrow of elected people that dream the victory
> (bound to the empire of purity)
> High fly eagle supremacy of divine race
> perpetual vision bless my life for dominate
> clear horizon of our flag
> You're the bringer of the gold dawn
> amazing universe of power
> take my breath away by your lighting
> and our blood will shine bright high over the world . . .

The reference to "elected people" is likely meant to be equivalent to the Italian phrase "popolo eletto," which would be more familiar in English as "chosen people," a sense reinforced by the phrase "supremacy of divine race" and the disquieting references to "purity" and "blood," which provide clear evidence of a dangerous right-wing nationalism that recalls all too clearly the Second World War. Finally, "gold dawn" may be a nod to Golden Dawn, a far-right political party in Greece.[67] This nationalistic—even Fascistic—approach to Rome's ancient history is radically different than that found in Stormlord and Heimdall, neither of which advances any such political aims (however vague).

One final example will cement the point that, while Stormlord's and Heimdall's use of the *Aeneid* can be considered nationalistic in one sense, their turn to the ancient world is not connected with the retrograde right-wing uses of antiquity that have unfortunately become increasingly common at the beginning of the twenty-first century.[68] The traditional/power metal band Holy Martyr call the final song on their *Still at War* album (2007) "Ave atque Vale," using the famous final phrase of the Roman poet Catullus' (*ca.* 84–54 BCE) poem to his dead brother (101), meaning "hail and farewell."[69] This song is a lament for Europe, with the chorus exclaiming:

> Where is my Europe? Now disappeared
> Star full of brightness in the dark of the night
> One land, once might, I'm searching my Europe
> No more shall rise, the flag of the empire.

Later in the song, they declare:

> Land of the Fathers, Land of the Culture
> Guide of the world since the dawn of time
> I see no future, no more tradition
> Europe is falling, condemned to die.

The fact that the rest of the album is a mix of songs about the Roman Empire, ancient Greece, and the Vikings reflects the similarities behind Viking and Mediterranean metal but also, suggests how we are to read the reference to "the empire." Here, Rome clearly stands for a simplified version of "Western Civilization," which is equated with Europe, and reflects the idea that the Roman Empire was synonymous with Europe.[70] The nationalistic ideas are obvious here, as Holy Martyr draw a direct line between themselves and their ancestors in a Europe that they view as having given culture to the world.

In contrast with such extreme examples, then, what Heimdall and Stormlord do is very different. We can describe their use of Roman mythology as "patriotic" or even "nationalistic" in the sense that they admit, as Italians, to feeling some connection between them and ancient Rome. But their albums advance no simplistic notion that the greatness of Rome accrues to all Italians, let alone a political agenda.

Conclusion: Nationalisms in Mediterranean metal

It would be easy to dismiss the question of how nationalistic a particular Italian metal band's use of Vergil is if it were not for the fact that the *Aeneid* continues to appear in larger political debates in Italy, perhaps most visibly within the context of the refugee crisis.[71] Since the current refugee crisis began in Italy—like in other parts of Europe—in 2013, numerous writers in Italy and elsewhere have pointed out that Aeneas was himself a refugee, citing Vergil's designation of him as *profugus* in 1.2.[72] For example, Turin's *La Stampa* published an article titled, "Profughi come Enea" ("Refugees Like Aeneas"), with the subtitle, "Scappava dalla guerra per cercare un destino migliore, lezione di storia sul mito fondante della nostra civiltà" ("He was escaping from the war to search for a better fate, a lesson from history on the founding myth of our civilization").[73] This argument gained additional prominence when, in late 2018, the United Nations refugee agency UNHCR released a book in Italy titled, *Anche Superman era un rifugiato. Storie vere di coraggio per un mondo migliore* (*Superman Was a Refugee, Too. True Stories of Courage for a Better World*).[74] Like earlier assertions that Aeneas was a refugee, the inclusion of Aeneas in this book was met with scorn by many on the right, including numerous pieces in *Il Primato Nazionale*,[75] the paper for the far-right, neo-Fascist Italian political party CasaPound.[76] This party's view of Vergil is perhaps clearest in a post on Vergil's birthday (October 15) in 2017, entitled "Mai dubitare del risveglio italiano: leggere Virgilio per ritrovare noi stessi" ("Never doubt the Italian reawakening: reading Vergil to discover ourselves"), in which they claim:

> It is to this magnificent example of struggle and victory that we today have to turn to in order *to find again a way that will definitively remove the attempts to debase and obscure any desire to redeem the Italian people*. Against those who want us to be children of nothing, without a past and, inevitably, without any future but to be gradually replaced by others and others, it is now necessary to rediscover our most ancient and most sacred memory.[77]

They end the piece by saying that "we" should entrust ourselves to Vergil, just as Dante did, creating a direct line between Aeneas, Vergil, Dante, and modern Italians in a way that bands such as Stormlord and Heimdall do not.

The ways in which we read the *Aeneid* is thus not some arcane matter, restricted only to the Ivory Tower, but part of a long history of the poem's use by numerous regimes throughout Western history as part of a justification of domination, and the straight line drawn between Augustan Rome and modern Italy is a fiction meant to serve political and cultural ends.[78] The debate over the meaning of Vergil's Aeneas in contemporary political debates therefore reflects the continued vitality of such Classical texts, and reminds us of the ways in which different countries can perceive of themselves as having different relationships with the ancient world. The continued relevance of the *Aeneid* means that we cannot write off as a coincidence the appearance in the same year of three Italian metal albums based on it or try to explain it only by referring to trends in metal.

The growth of what we might think of as "Mediterranean metal"—bands from the Mediterranean that write songs about the Greco-Roman legendary and historical past—is at least in part a response to a variety of political and cultural trends. First and foremost, the focus on national identity is a common phenomenon in countries belonging to the European Union, seemingly an attempt to maintain some core identity in the face of globalization and so many borders (concrete and metaphorical) coming down.[79] As events in 2016 in both Europe and the United States have made clear, nationalism continues to regain prominence—and has real consequences in terms of increasingly right-wing politicians and parties gaining power.

Despite the temptation to connect these two events—the resurgence of nationalism and the advent of Mediterranean metal— it is impossible to tell how many bands embrace Greco-Roman antiquity in the way that Centvrion and Holy Martyr do, in part because such bands are generally less well known, and attain (even) less commercial success than most metal bands. But the majority of Mediterranean metal bands seem not to approach this material in such a simplistic way, and some are clearly aware of the dangers of talking about this material. For instance, the German power metal band Rebellion released an album in 2012 called *Arminius: Furor Teutonicus*, which is about the man sometimes known as "Herman the German," a Cheruscian chieftain who served as an auxiliary in the Roman army before eventually leading the German tribes against the Romans, giving them one of their worst defeats in the Battle of Teutoberg Forest in 9 CE. This album charts Arminius' rise in the Roman army and in Roman society before his growing disgust with Rome leads him back home.[80] In an interview discussing the album, bass player and lyricist Tomi Göttlich talked about the potential problems with the subject matter when asked about his motivations for writing about German history:[81]

> When I thought about doing Arminius, the first thing was "No, you can't do that." Because Hitler did all that, and it started in the time of Bismarck, so it was when Germany as a nation, the German Reich was founded, and the German people started to dig out some national pride, and we all know where that led to.

So here in Germany, people are very careful with wearing Thor's hammers and all those symbols, and persons of history who have been used or misused by Nazi dictatorship, so we're kind of careful with that. But on the other hand, I think it's a part of at least the history of the country where I live, or it happened close to where I lived. I would not call it the history of Germany, simply because so much has happened in those 2,000 years that I do not think there's too much that we still share or have in common with the old Germanic tribes. But of course, it happened here, and there are also some connections that do lead up to our time. So I thought, I don't want to leave all this to the Nazis, to the right-wing fascists. I think it doesn't belong to them. So if I write about it, I sort of take it a bit away from them, claim my part in it or my ownership of it, if you want, in a certain way. So this was also a motivation.

Göttlich's statements reflect both the appeal of this material while also showing an awareness of how fraught the use of antiquity is.[82] Geographical proximity to such sites promotes the idea of some kind of connection with this material, even in the face of an awareness of the extent to which "Germany" and "German history" are shifting constructs (it is worth noting that Göttlich is not a full-time musician, but is also a high-school History and English teacher). If Rebellion have a political agenda—a prospect with which Göttlich seems uncomfortable—it is to counter the right-wing appropriations of such history.

But the trends that culminate in three Italian metal bands writing whole albums based on Vergil's *Aeneid* in the same year are not just political. As the Introduction to this volume shows, grand, epic themes have always been a part of metal, so it is not surprising to find epic poetry adapted to metal. Like the growth of Mediterranean metal generally, it is a reflection of its larger growth in the wake of Viking metal, as a result of which bands increasingly write about their own areas. And this is part of the push and pull of being a heavy metal artist in the early twenty-first century, participating in a truly global medium, yet wanting to speak to local fans. As I mentioned above, language is one part of this issue, as every metal band from a non-English-speaking country is faced with the choice of singing in their native tongue, thereby appealing to their local audience, or singing in English, thus privileging the global metal audience. The choice to use material perceived as being local is therefore a way to have the best of both worlds, and address multiple audiences at once. The Greek power metal band Sacred Blood, who have written albums about Thermopylae, Alexander the Great, and the Argonauts, make this idea explicit. When asked in an interview about whether their motivation for choosing their subject matter was in part a matter of education, their lyricist, Marios Koutsoukos, said:

> Exactly. It's a matter of identity, you know. When you have a Greek metal band, metal is like an international medium. It unites people from all around the world, but when you listen to a Greek metal band, I would like to listen about Greek themes. So as to have an inspiration or motivation to look further and research a story or mythology that I didn't know that well before. And in the same manner,

you listen to an Italian band, you want to know about the history of Italy. There's a Chinese band, a Mongol band, with some themes from the Mongolian Steppe, which is the greatest thing about metal. You can have all this diversity and at the same time, this educational character, which gives metal an edge compared to other forms of music, other mediums of expression.[83]

Koutsoukos echoes the claims made throughout this book, that metal differs from other contemporary musical genres in its consistent use of literature and mythology. At the same time, this response exemplifies metal's "glocalizing" tendencies, or simultaneous negotiation of local and global concerns.[84] For a Greek band to use Greek material allows them to speak to their Greek audience, but also share what Greekness means to them with the rest of the world.

As metal spreads around the world and local scenes coalesce, bands from those scenes begin to develop their own identities and voices, in part by drawing upon local lore—and these uses fall along a wide spectrum in terms of their politics. What starts as a sort of mimicry, then, with Greek and Italian bands writing songs about Norse myth, develops into an assertion of a certain degree of independence. Mediterranean metal still belongs to the global metal community, but is also a beast unto itself.[85]

Notes

1. This influence is most obvious in the Middle Ages, on which see the classic work of Comparetti (1997: esp. 189–94). For Vergil's enormous influence on Italian literature in the Renaissance, see Kallendorf (1989) and (1999) and Wilson-Okamura (2010).
2. Eliot (1945: 31). Note that "Virgil" is an alternative spelling of "Vergil" (from the original Latin *Vergilius*). On the spelling of the name and its changes, see Wilson-Okamura (2010: 15–44).
3. Within Italy, it is better known than elsewhere because it still occupies a position within the middle- and high-school curriculum.
4. The account at Livy 1.4.1–1.7.3 is perhaps the most famous but is only about four pages long.
5. The founding of Rome has, however, been the subject of individual songs, such as Ex Deo's "Romulus" (*Romulus*, 2009). For more on Ex Deo, see Magro-Martínez (this volume).
6. The bibliography on the reception of the *Aeneid* is immense. The best recent places to start are Ziolkowski and Putnam (2008), Farrell and Putnam (2014), and Hardie (2014), who notes that, "To write a comprehensive literary and cultural history of the reception of Virgil would be little less than to write a literary and cultural history of western Europe and its former overseas possessions" (2).
7. For a brief survey of Vergil's enormous influence on Italian literature, see Pertile (2014), with references.
8. On the ways in which the *Aeneid* reflects and meditates upon Roman identity and Roman nation-building, see Toll (1997), Syed (2005), Reed (2007), and Fletcher (2014). The poem is only one part of the larger ongoing process that gave rise to the idea of "Italy" during the Roman Republic and Principate, on which now see Carlà-Uhink (2017a).
9. For a good recent overview of the period, see Alston (2015). The classic account of the period is Syme (1939).

10. For example, the first-century teacher of rhetoric, Quintilian, says that students should begin by reading Homer in Greek and Vergil in Latin (*Institutio oratoria* 1.8.5; 10.1.85–6). Cf. Hardie (2014: 7): "On the death of Vergil in 19 BC the *Aeneid* instantly became a school text" (with references).

11. For the reception of Vergil in music see Strunk (1930), Draheim (1983), Thomas (2007: 30–5), Fitzgerald (2014), and Wilson ("n.d.").

12. Eliot's reading of Vergil is not without its problems. For discussion, see Ziolkowski (1993: 119–28).

13. For the interrelation between Classics and Fascism, see Canfora (1977). For Fascist readings of Vergil, see Thomas (2001: 222–77).

14. Although it gained prominence under Fascism, it long predates that movement. For instance, discussing Vergil's influence on Dante and his contemporaries, Comparetti (1997: 204–5) says that "Dante therefore is not an admirer of Vergil merely because of the great fame which tradition allotted to him ... The perfection of Vergil's work he feels as only a true poet may; and he is proud as an Italian of this miracle of art, for Latin and Italian are equally the national language of Italy ..."

15. For a recent overview of such connections, see the papers in Roche and Demetriou (2017).

16. For useful overviews of the changing political readings of the Aeneid, see Harrison (1990), Stahl (1998), and Perkell (1999). For the limited nature of these now somewhat-outmoded terms, see Kennedy (1992).

17. As Thomas (2001) and Kallendorff (2007) show, however, the pessimistic reading is not solely a product of the twentieth century.

18. For a lengthier discussion of this development, see Fletcher and Umurhan (this volume).

19. Like all origin stories, this is an oversimplification of a movement that was already in the air. For more on Viking Metal and its origins, see Trafford and Pluskowski (2007) and Ashby and Schofield (2015).

20. The album was recorded in 1989 but not released until 1996, since—as he explains elsewhere in the liner notes—Quorthon worried both that the recording quality was too poor and that people would view the new Viking material unfavorably. He also refers to the influence of Conan the Barbarian comics (see Secord, this volume) and the operas of Richard Wagner.

21. *Blood on Ice* liner notes (my emphasis, everything else *sic*). Quorthon's reference to the overlap with the depiction of Vikings in movies is a reminder that many of the bands that draw on the ancient world are also influenced by cinematic depictions. For example, see Magro-Martínez (this volume) on the influence of the movie *Caligula* (1979) on Ex Deo's depiction of the emperors Tiberius and Caligula.

22. For more on black metal's opposition to Christianity, see Apergis (this volume).

23. For some sense of these changes, see Moynihan and Søderlind (2003).

24. In some sense, these bands can be viewed as following the so-called "Vergilian career," working their way up to the most serious subjects. This career model is mapped out in the ancient biographies of Vergil but is complicated by authors such as Putnam (2010).

25. J. P. (2002). Not all would agree with Calluori's claim that the Vikings are the "patrimony of all people;" many non-Scandinavian bands attempting to play Viking metal have been met with mockery and/or scorn (see below).

26. According to the *Encyclopaedia Metallum* (www.metal-archives.com), this name has also been used for bands in Chile, Colombia, Portugal, and Spain.

27. See, e.g., the statement made by Emperor's Mortiis quoted by Crofton-Sleigh (this volume).
28. Pardo (2013). Note that Calluori's statement here suggests that even another Italian metal artist was unaware of Hesperia's 2003 and 2008 albums based on the *Aeneid*.
29. In another contemporaneous interview (Abate 2013), Calluori talks about his choice of the *Aeneid*: not only is it famous, he says, but "poi è quello che comunque parla della nascita della cultura latina, quindi, ci interessa più direttamente come storia" ("because it's that which speaks of the birth of Latin culture, therefore it interests us more directly as history").
30. This provides a valuable reminder that while the Romans were the most obvious historical entity for Italians to draw on, they were not the only ones (see De Francesco (2015) for the ways in which the Fascists cemented the Romans' central position). In metal, Rome predominates, but bands occasionally talk about other ancient Italic peoples, such as Stormlord and the Samnites, or VerSacrum's 2009 album, *Tyrrenika*, which is about the Etruscans.
31. "Ice Maiden" (2000).
32. I will use the terms "Rome" (of the empire) and "Italy" to some extent as synonyms, a use which I think is fair not only for these bands but also for Vergil and his contemporaries; see Richardson (2008). For the ways in which the Romans used the names "Rome" and "Italy," see also Carlà-Uhink (2017a: 97–111).
33. Their choice recalls the earlier general view that Book 5 is one of the weaker parts of the poem and perhaps even unfinished. For these earlier criticisms of Book 5, see Kehoe (1989).
34. It is worth noting that even some Vergilian scholars incorrectly refer to these as "funeral games." For the importance of joy in Book 5, see Miniconi (1962: 568) and Fletcher (2014: 165–66). For the importance of the games, see Cairns (1989: 215–48) and Feldherr (1995).
35. Cf. Crofton-Sleigh (this volume) for how track 5 focuses on the end of Dido's relationship with Aeneas rather than the earlier, happier parts of Book 4.
36. By contrast, the books in the *Aeneid* range in length from 705 lines (Book 4) to 952 lines (Book 12).
37. For more on the presentation in music of the relationship between Dido and Aeneas, see Crofton-Sleigh (this volume).
38. Pogorzelski (2009).
39. This scene is central to many "pessimistic" approaches to the poem, especially in the work of Michael Putnam, most recently Putnam (2013).
40. Cf. Gransden (1996: xvi): "The first half of the *Aeneid* contains the poem's three most popular and influential books: II (the fall of Troy), IV (the tragedy of Dido) and VI (the descent into the underworld)." Wilson-Okamura (2010: 215–27) notes that in the Middle Ages, people focused almost exclusively on the poem's first six books, but that in the Renaissance, there was greater interest in the whole poem (though the first half still predominated). On the favoring of different books at different times (though with a preference for the first half generally),
see Kallendorf (2010: 239–40).
41. Both Strunk (1930) and Draheim (1983) show that Dido is Vergil's most influential creation in terms of music. Cf. the catalogue in Kailuweit (2005: 351–424).
42. See e.g., O'Hara (2006) on Syed (2005). This preference for the first half is evident in schools, too. On the Advanced Placement syllabus for high-school Latin in the States, for instance, only Latin from Books 1, 2, 4, and 6 is assigned. Even in Italy, where I am told it is more common to read the entire poem in translation than in the States, the parts of the poem read in Latin primarily come from the first half.

43. Perkell (1999: 19) argues that the pessimistic reading of the poem stems in part from a great focus on its second half.
44. For the early reception of the Aeneid, see the texts collected at Ziolkowski and Putnam (2008: 5–14). For an introduction to *Aeneid*-based graffiti at Pompeii, see Franklin (1997).
45. On the quality and influence of Dryden's translation, see Burrow (1993: 28–31) and Scully (2018).
46. These are the lines as printed in the CD booklet, but Dryden writes "he bore" rather than "he'd borne" in line 4.
47. All quotations of Vergil come from Mynors' Oxford Classical Text.
48. As we will see below, this term *profugus* is a bone of contention for some modern Italian interpretations of the *Aeneid*. Except where otherwise noted, all translations are my own.
49. As mentioned above, the two tracks are listed together as one entry on the back of the CD.
50. Most famously treated by Knox (1950).
51. For a recent discussion of this line and the problems of interpreting it, see Wharton (2008), with additional bibliography.
52. It is a testament to Vergil's craft that, even though Aeneas technically has nothing to do with the foundation of the city of Rome itself, readers (especially my undergraduates) usually consider the *Aeneid* to be about Aeneas' foundation of Rome.
53. Holopainen (2013).
54. G/Ab Svenym Volgar dei Xacrestani, frontman of Deviate Damaen, is a guest vocalist on this track, but does a spoken/chanted version of *Aen.* 1.12–17 (3:08–3:47).
55. Although to date *Hesperia* has only been released on CD, the influence of sides on LPs and cassettes continues to affect the arrangement of digital music.
56. This section possibly recalls Aeneas' confrontation with Dido before leaving Carthage, in which he tells her that Italy, not she, is his *amor* (*Aen.* 4.347).
57. Because the *Aeneid* is in many ways a poem about fathers and sons, it is fitting that the bassist and lyricist Francesco Bucci dedicated the album to his recently deceased father.
58. "tu regere imperio populos, Romane, memento/(hae tibi erunt artes), pacique imponere morem, / parcere subiectis et debellare superbos." They do not translate the phrase *hae tibi erunt artes* ("these will be your arts") at the beginning of line 852.
59. On the importance of these lines, see Zetzel (1989) and Syed (2004: 72–3).
60. "*sermonem Ausonii patrium moresque tenebunt,/utque est nomen erit; commixti corpore tantum / subsident Teucri. morem ritusque sacrorum /adiciam faciamque omnis uno ore Latinos. / hinc genus Ausonio mixtum quod sanguine surget, / supra homines, supra ire deos pietate videbis....*"
61. As Osman Umurhan reminds me, this recalls the famous saying attributed to Ennius, one of the forefathers of Latin literature. According to Aulus Gellius (*NA* 17.17.1), "Quintus Ennius used to say that he had three hearts because he knew how to speak Greek and Oscan and Latin."
62. In a 2015 interview, Hesperus explains the arrangement of the albums: "The 4 albums about Eneide are in chronological order: Eneide is divided in 12 books (chapters). '*Aeneidos pars I*' talks about books 1–2, '*In Honorem Herois*' about books 3-4-5, '*Spiritvs Italicvs*' about books 6-7-8-9, '*Metallvm Italicvm*' about books 10-11-12" (Dimitris 2015).
63. This according to Hesperia Home Page (2015).
64. HesperiaOfficial (2015). See also Hesperia Home Page (2015) for the same statement.
65. On the spelling of Latin words with "v" rather than "u," see Magro-Martínez (this volume).

66. The earliest use of the phrase seems to be in the first-century CE Latin poet Lucan, who uses *caput mundi* at *Bellum Civile* 2.136 and *ipsa, caput mundi . . . Roma* at 2.655–656. On the larger issue of how the Romans viewed themselves as the center of the world, see Carlà-Uhink (2017b).
67. For more on Golden Dawn and Greek nationalism, see Apergis (this volume).
68. On this trend and suggestions for how Classicists can—and should—respond to such uses, see Zuckerberg (2018).
69. Vergil uses a variation of this phrase at *Aen.* 11.97–98, when Aeneas speaks at the funeral of Pallas.
70. Although such claims about Europe are often tied with notions of white supremacy, it is worth noting that Holy Martyr's 2011 album, *Invincible*, is about Japanese history, and focuses especially on the samurai.
71. The timing of these albums relative to the refugee crisis can lead to idle speculation about how—if at all—they would have differed had they been released a year or two later.
72. E.g., see the remarks by Giusti (2018) about what it means to be an Italian Classicist in the early twenty-first century. Non-Italian Classicists such as Beard (2015) and Knox (2017) were also among those who weighed in to make this point.
73. Porliod (2017).
74. Scego (2018).
75. E.g., "Enea non era un 'profugo', il suo era un ritorno all'origine" (Mocci 2016); "Enea è un rifugiato? Il suo avo Dardano ci risponde con un categorico 'No'" (Scarsini 2018); and "Enea non è un eroe "pro migranti". Insegniamo l'Eneide ai semicolti" (Bartolucci 2019). Cf. the piece in *Giovani A Destra* ("Youths on the Right"): "Enea non era un migrante e, soprattutto, non era turco" (Ciampa 2018).
76. For an introduction to CasaPound, see Jones (2018). The party was named partly in honor of Ezra Pound who, despite his Fascist sympathies, was not a fan of Vergil; see Ziolkowski (1993: 191–2) and s.v. "Pound, Ezra."
77. Staff Writer (2017): "È a questo magnifico esempio di lotta e di vittoria cui noi oggi dobbiamo rivolgerci per poter *ritrovare una via che allontani definitivamente i tentativi di svilire e ottenebrare qualsiasi volontà di riscatto del popolo italiano*. Contro chi ci vorrebbe figli del nulla, senza passato e, per forza di cose, senza alcun futuro se non quello di essere sostituiti progressivamente da altro e da altri, occorre ora più che mai riscoprire la nostra memoria più antica e più sacra" (original emphasis).
78. For an attempt to sketch out the influence of the story of Aeneas on subsequent conceptions of empire, see Waswo (1997).
79. For discussion of this phenomenon and its larger context, see the chapters in Checkel and Katzenstein (2009). For more on globalization and the future of metal, see Umurhan (this volume).
80. An album such as *Arminius* is part of the reason why the term "Mediterranean metal" is in some ways better than "Greco-Roman metal," since the latter implies that it only comes from Greece or Italy or is only from the perspective of the Greeks or Romans. In *Arminius*, however, the Romans are clearly negative figures—as they are in the Swiss band Eluveitie's *Helvetios*, on which see Taylor (this volume).
81. Dr. Metal (2013). Like many bands that can be considered Mediterranean metal, Rebellion do not just write about Classical antiquity: they have three albums based on Viking history, as well as albums based on Shakespeare's *Macbeth* and *King Lear*.

82. For a similar awareness of how such subject matter might be (mis)construed, see Magro-Martínez's discussion of Ex Deo in this volume.

83. This is from a transcription of an interview conducted on March 19, 2014 with Dr. Metal (2014), who graciously provided me with a copy. Just before this section, the guitarist Polydeykis, said: "When we started Sacred Blood, we decided that we want to deal with themes and myths and history of things in Greece. As strange as it may seem in modern Greece, it's not widely known or it is known only until a certain aspect. It is not widely known to all its aspects and details. So in the heavy metal music, most bands make songs about Norse mythology, fantastic literature. Not many bands deal with ancient Greece and this kind of history and mythology that in my opinion and all members of Sacred Blood opinion, are very fascinating, and I think metal fans should give a chance to ancient Greek mythology, to enter their hearts through metal music. I think they will cherish it and they will be very much fond of it."

84. On the idea of glocalization and its application to metal, see Weinstein (2011) 54–5, with references. For metal's spread throughout the world and its responses to globalization, see Wallach, Berger, and Greene (2011a). See also Fletcher (2019).

85. I would like to thank Paolo Chirumbolo, Nick Fletcher, Scott Randall, and Matthew Taylor for their help with various aspects of this chapter. I owe an enormous debt of gratitude to both Filippo Carlà-Uhink for enormously helpful comments on an earlier draft of this piece and Osman Umurhan for reading numerous versions.

CHAPTER 2
ETERNAL DEFIANCE: CELTIC IDENTITY AND THE CLASSICAL PAST IN HEAVY METAL
Matthew Taylor

This chapter argues that heavy metal music can engage in the same kind of "imaginative historiography" shown by Maria Wyke (1997) to be a fundamental element of Classically themed cinema. It examines the imaginative re-appropriation of traditional Roman history in the service of constructing non-Roman cultural identities in the present day, and focuses more specifically on those metal artists who engage with the Classical past in order to establish and legitimate supposedly Celtic identities. Far from being mere symptoms of so-called "Celtomania," I argue that these bands present a subaltern vision of history which, if not originally political in its intent, certainly offers a provocative, even postcolonial, reading of Rome's history.[1] Moreover, their work provides a productive opportunity to appreciate how Classical sources are often read in the service of European identity politics, and thus to situate heavy metal within such political and cultural narratives.

The bands I discuss in this chapter are usually classified as folk metal, a form of metal hybridized by "the integration of folk music, mythological and/or cosmological stories, vocal performances in non-English languages, a focus on historical events or historical figures and lyrics or images that identify with a specific nation or group of people."[2] Whether folk metal is to be understood as a development of thrash, black, or death metal,[3] it represents a subgenre of metal that bridges other subgenres, and thus is deeply implicated in the practices of taxonomy and erudition that Keith Kahn-Harris has shown are a distinct element of metal culture.[4] Indeed, there is even some argument about whether folk metal should be considered metal at all.[5] The potentially precarious situation of folk metal within metal reflects the status of folk traditions more broadly, not just in folk music's relationship to Classical "art" music, but also in the opposition between oral traditions and the authority of canonical historiography. "Folk" can be employed in all of these contexts as a "connotative concept" to resist the ordering of knowledge, culture, and identity by institutional systems[6]—including the discipline of Classics, which in its textual and philological focus is often naturally at odds with folk traditions.

For many bands, such folk invocations, whether musical or lyrical, are a means of identifying with a national past that is distinctly their own.[7] Peter A. Marjenin has characterized this as "a mechanism for the preservation of folk music and culture in resistance to Europeanization and Americanization," albeit one that still participates in a global culture defined by such influences (in this case, metal itself).[8] Aaron Mulvany invokes the Bakhtinian concept of the "chronotope" to describe this compositional practice, which he argues creates a strong connection between time and space to imagine a place where things were different; in the bands' reliance on myth or imagination, this often entails the conjuring of "imaginary places" that cannot properly be said to have existed.[9] Some bands, however, engage more directly with authoritative historical traditions, pulling material from the same sources as historians, but reconfiguring them into new narratives of national and cultural resistance. They could be said to trade in imagined, rather than imaginary, places: ones with more substance in an historical sense, but where events transpired differently. Such is the case with Eluveitie and SuidAkrA, the subjects of this chapter, who adapt and subvert Classical traditions to produce pre-European, Celtic identity formations through the integration of heavy metal and folk music.

We are Helvetios

Eluveitie hail from Switzerland and take their name from the ancient Helvetians, the Celtic tribe whose migrations from that region are recounted in the opening chapters (1.1–30) of Julius Caesar's *Bellum Gallicum* (*Gallic War*, hereafter *BGall*). Formed in 2002 by front man Christian "Chrigel" Glanzmann, the band promote their identification with their ancient forbears through a brand of metal that leans particularly on Celtic instruments and melodies for its folk elements. They also pepper their otherwise English lyrics with ancient Gaulish, sometimes even composing whole songs in that language.[10]

Eluveitie's music is closest in form to melodic death metal, specifically bands like At the Gates and In Flames from Gothenburg in Sweden. Developing from the Swedish death metal scene of the early 1990s, melodic death metal tempered the aural ferocity and structural complexity of death metal with a clearer production, more traditional verse/chorus patterns, and a greater focus on melody.[11] Where In Flames would layer electric guitars in harmonized melodic lines over a foundation of aggressive and energetic riffing, Eluveitie supplement a similar bedrock of metallic guitar work with melodies from instruments such as the fiddle and the hurdy-gurdy, aiming to promote "a direct affiliation to the instrument's geographical location and culture."[12]

Eluveitie are quite catholic in their approach to Celtic affiliation, borrowing liberally from Irish, Scottish, and Breton music traditions, and thus incorporating instruments like the uilleann pipes, patterns such as the Scottish round, and styles like the Gwerz lament. Eluveitie's pan-Celtic approach mirrors trends in Celtic identity politics generally—and Iron Age archaeology more specifically—in which until the late twentieth century it was still common to posit the spread of a common Celtic "La Tène" culture emanating from the area of ancient Switzerland to encompass much of northern and western Europe.[13] The conceit of a coherent La Tène culture has in some cases become the basis for a European cultural identity specifically distinct from Greece and Rome, which, in such discourses, is often separated from Europe and categorized as "Mediterranean" culture. In their instrumentation and composition, then, Eluveitie directly reflect Celtic identity politics in the modern world, which seek to excavate a lost community by uniting scattered elements of Celtic culture from across Europe.

While their musical identity may be based on an amalgam of Celtic music fused to a metallic core, the lyrical trappings of Eluveitie's output are filtered through the traditions of Classical scholarship. The archaeologist Andrew Fitzpatrick has observed that the "creation of a 'Celtic Europe'... reflects the depth of the debt to Classical Studies in the study of the European Iron Age," referring to the critical role played by Greco-Roman literary and material evidence in the search for ancient Celts.[14] A similar debt is exhibited in the words Eluveitie use to express themselves. The name of the band itself is taken directly from an inscription on a clay vase found in 1985 during excavations at Castellazzo della Garolda in Mantua in Northern Italy;[15] the word appears incised on the inside of the bowl, written from right to left in Etruscan script. Whether this is a simple ethnic identifier or, as recent commentators have suggested, brands the artifact as the product of a Helvetian potter, it is believed to constitute the earliest existing written testimony to the Helvetian people, dating to around 300 BCE.[16] Sparse archaeological evidence from the Swiss plateau does show settlement of the area consistent with La Tène material culture, but does not yield direct testimony to the Helvetians specifically, who are otherwise only known to us from Greek and Roman authors.[17]

Before the discovery of the vase, the earliest reference to the Helvetians was found in Posidonius, a Greek philosopher who supposedly travelled among the Gauls in the early first century BCE; his account of those travels, now lost, is transmitted piecemeal in quotations by later authors. The geographer Strabo, writing in Greek in the time of the Roman emperor Augustus, cites Posidonius for the information that the Helvetians were "men who were rich in gold but peaceful," until enticed into a life of larceny by their greedy observation of the predations of their neighbors the Cimbri.[18] This loose smattering of evidence—a vase, a citation in Strabo, and a few archaeological sites—constitute all we have to complement and complicate the main source for the ancient Helvetians: the war diaries of the Roman statesman, general, and dictator Julius Caesar.

Eluveitie rely on Caesar extensively as a source for their lyrics, going so far as to base an entire album on his account of history. Yet, this process of adaptation is also one of contestation, as Eluveitie rework Caesar's narrative to serve the reputation of the Helvetians, rather than that of an aristocratic Roman conqueror. This reconfiguration is all the richer because the original text serves the ideological aims of two distinct parties: Rome as an imperial, colonizing power and Caesar as a self-aggrandizing politician. Before examining how Eluveitie adapt Caesar, therefore, it is necessary to investigate the rhetorical strategies intrinsic to Caesar's representation of the Helvetians and other Celtic peoples.

Meet the enemy

Following his consulship of 59 BCE, the ambitious Caesar was assigned the Roman provinces of Gallia Cisalpina, Gallia Transalpina, and Illyricum (territories loosely conforming to northern Italy, the very south of France, and Croatia/Bosnia and Herzegovina). Having already established himself as a force to be reckoned with in

Roman politics, Caesar needed both a profound military victory and a huge supply of money to ensure his star kept rising, and he found both in the conquest of what remained of Gaul (what the Romans then called Gallia Comata, or "Long-haired Gaul"), an area of land encompassing much of modern France and Belgium.

It was traditional for Roman generals to keep accounts of their actions—*commentarii* in Latin—that could be rendered to the Senate as proof of good conduct and argument for the award of honors. The Latin work known to us as *Bellum Gallicum* (*BGall*) is written in the form of such *commentarii*, offering an account of Caesar's actions in Gaul year-by-year and charting the course of his interventions beyond the Alps and the trajectory of the final conquest of the Gallic people. It provides a sustained justification for his war with the Gauls and the strategies and procurements necessary to prosecute it. It is famously composed as a third-person narrative, contributing the illusion of dispassionate objectivity to what is, at its heart, an account of personal achievement.

The pretext for Caesar's initial intervention in Further Gaul was the unexpected migration of the Helvetians from their home on the Swiss plateau. The first thirty chapters of *BGall* recount the details of this migration, Caesar's response, and the crushing defeat of the Helvetians at Roman hands. From start to finish, Caesar offers an implicit argument for the necessity of military intervention in the affair, constructing the Helvetians as formidable warriors, but also as perfidious and rapacious nomads who represent an urgent threat to Roman interests in the area.

The Helvetians are first introduced during Caesar's geographic survey of Gaul and its three parts, in which he claims "they outstrip all the other Gauls in *virtus*, because they engage in battle with the Germans almost every day, either trying to keep them from their own borders or bringing war into theirs" (1.1.4). The Helvetians are thus implicated in Caesar's general picture of Gallic and Germanic character, where distance from the civilizing force of Roman culture and proximity to bellicose barbarians makes people into more ferocious fighters. Caesar is participating here in the broader Greco-Roman ethnographical tradition, which both demarcated space using the people who occupied it and explained the national character of those peoples by the influence of the space upon them. The *BGall* demonstrates how ethnography served the Roman ideology of *imperium sine fine* ("empire without end/border"), since it uses native peoples both to mark the borders of territory and to promote Rome's crossing of those borders.[19] *Virtus*, most simply translated as "manly virtue" or "courage," is generally understood to be a distinctly Roman value, denoting both ferocity and steadfastness in battle. Describing the Helvetians in this way grants them a measure of respect in Roman terms, but is also a decidedly imperial act, since it constitutes them firmly in those terms and thus as the subject of Roman discourse.[20] According to Caesar, it was precisely their *virtus*, together with a concern over population growth, that inspired the Helvetians to leave the confines of their homeland (1.2.1–5). They spent two years cultivating supplies for the migration, then in 58 BCE set forth toward the Roman province of Gallia Transalpina, having burned all their homes and their surplus crops (1.4.1–5.4).

From the beginning, Caesar carefully layers his narrative with warrants for his interruption of this migration. He has already claimed that the Helvetians are fierce warriors, intent on settling within Gaul, and that they have left themselves no home to which they might return. He continues to develop his *casus belli* when he explains why he refused their formal request to pass peacefully through Roman territory:

> because Caesar yet held in his memory that [in 107 BCE] the consul Lucius Cassius had been killed by the Helvetians, and his army beaten and sent under the yoke ... nor did he believe that men with hostile spirit, given free rein to journey through the province, would hold themselves back from injury and malfeasance.
>
> Caesar, BGall 1.7.4–5

The Helvetians therefore tried to bypass Roman holdings and reach the land of the Santones (modern Saintonge) on the west coast of France, which bordered Gallia Transalpina. Caesar argues this was a further rationale for war, claiming "that it would be of great danger to the province to have such warlike men, hostile to the Roman people, living next to lands that were unprotected and abounded in grain" (1.10.2). His reasoning was supposedly confirmed by formal complaints from Gallic allies of the Romans about the Helvetians ravaging their lands, and so he resolved to stop them by force (1.11.4–5).

Catching up with the Helvetians as they were crossing the river Saône, Caesar fell upon the rear section of their column by night and defeated them soundly (1.12.1–3). He then recounts an attempt by the Helvetians at parlay, which serves as a further opportunity to figure their threat in terms of *virtus*. The Helvetians minimize Caesar's night-attack as a minor victory and claim they "had been taught by their fathers and ancestors to fight with *virtus* rather than win by trickery and traps" (1.13.4). Caesar claims these envoys were led by one Divico, the architect of Rome's earlier defeat in 107 BCE, a chronological improbability that demonstrates Caesar's rhetorical aims in maximizing the Helvetians' affronts to Roman power. Caesar's retort to the Helvetians argues that Cassius' army had been ambushed—and thus beaten by trickery, not *virtus*—and adds their recent crimes against the allied Gauls to the list of charges. He claims he offered to make peace if the Helvetians would surrender hostages to guarantee their promises, to which Divico responded that "their ancestors had taught them to receive hostages, not to give them—of this fact the Roman people were witness" (1.14.7) before walking away from negotiations. Caesar thus has the Helvetians make competing claims to *virtus* and present divergent interpretations of recent history, demonstrating the contestable nature of events even as he arranges them to meet his own rhetorical goals.

According to Caesar, the final confrontation with the Helvetians came shortly thereafter near the Aeduan town of Bibracte, an occasion where both sides demonstrated their *virtus*. The Romans won the day, but Caesar claims the fighting was fierce and that, although the battle lasted the whole afternoon, "no one saw a Helvetian turn and flee" (1.26.2). Following their surrender, Caesar records that of the 368,000 Helvetian men, women, and children who left the Swiss plateau, only 111,000 returned home (1.29.1–3).

The Helvetians had provided a convenient threat for Caesar in 58 BCE, leaving him with a foothold in Gaul, a stake in Gallic politics, and control of a large army. They also serve a convenient role in his rhetoric, establishing programmatically most of the tropes that he subsequently uses to characterize the Gauls as a people and justify their ultimate conquest. Yes, they are fierce, strong, and resolute, but they are also—according to Caesar—proud, ungrateful, and untrustworthy. They bring conflict to Roman territory and foment revolt among Rome's allies, representing their intentions as peaceful even as they ravage the lands through which they pass. They are naturally warlike, hostile to Rome, and therefore present a clear and present danger to her interests. As Andrew Riggsby has shown, this is the logic of the whole *BGall*, which extends to the Gauls the compliment of great *virtus*, but only to figure them as a threat to Rome, and one which therefore needs subduing; it also works to make of them one people, such that they can be conceptualized as a nation that *can* be subdued, and such that when Caesar makes the claim *omni Gallia pacata* (2.35.1: "Gaul was completely pacified") it has real meaning—both symbolic and strategic.[21]

An enemy stereotype

Faced with the fact that Caesar is the richest literary source for the ancient Helvetians, Eluveitie's lyrical choices are often torn between relying on the Roman general to reconstruct their past and castigating him for his misrepresentation of their people. This latter theme begins in earnest on the single "Thousandfold" from 2010's *Everything Remains (As It Never Was)*. While the song is primarily a celebration of Gallic unity in the face of Roman aggression, it also contains a strong critique of Caesar's *commentarii*, claiming that by constructing an "enemy stereotype" to serve his political needs, Caesar did more damage with his narrative than he did with his army:

> Sprinkled by the trappings
> Of words that make the outlines
> Blur on the showplace of made history
> The folk is willed
> To parrot the dished up tale
> The lure of a higher meaning
>
> Cheat, you had to create
> An enemy stereotype
> To receive your absolution
> A frothy poor excuse for your foray
> To disengage from the deeps
> of your encumbrance
>
> *Chorus*:
> Behold
> All our gold
> Thousandfold
> Bereave me!

Declined
Truths ensign
Forever mine!
Bereave me!

March in with ten legions
Whilst the crucial weapon's not the *pilum*
But the feather held in your hand
Penned in blood
Your tall tales rule the forum
Altering it into the battlefield.

      Eluveitie, *"Thousandfold,"* Everything Remains (As It Never Was*), 2010*

The critique is clear and consistent, acknowledging the great mark left by Caesar's account on the discursive construction that is "made history." The lyrics draw attention to Caesar's implicit argument—his "higher meaning"—and reduce the representation of the Helvetians in *BGall* to an "enemy stereotype" that afforded him "absolution" and "excuse." In "Thousandfold," therefore, Eluveitie can be said to accuse *BGall* of being what Mary Louise Pratt (2008: 8–9) calls an "anti-conquest narrative," a text which employs "strategies of representation" to turn resistance to colonization into proof that the colonized need colonizing. There are certainly hallmarks of such a narrative in the original text, such as Caesar's repeated claims to have "pacified" Gaul, which paints Rome as the bringer of *peace* and the Gauls, by extension, as untrustworthy troublemakers.

 The video for this track situates the band in a bucolic representation of a Gallic homestead, complete with actors in antiquarian garb; it offers a vision of the Helvetians as peaceful farmers, while the chorus reminds us that they were supposedly rich in gold (*per* Posidonius), and thus presumably had no need of plunder, predation, or pacification. By recasting the Gallic War as a struggle for freedom and a pre-colonial way of life—embodied in the idyllic imagery of the video—Eluveitie claim to redress the wrongs done to Gaul's memory. The connection to *BGall* is also made explicit in the video by frequent overlays of the opening lines to the second chapter of Book 1 about the Helvetians, which appear on a parchment as though they are being written by Caesar's hand. This juxtaposition suggests a critique of the privilege of written history to fix memory and meaning, a privilege that folk traditions—both oral and musical—could be said to challenge.

 Eluveitie would significantly expand on all the aspects of criticism deployed in "Thousandfold" on their next release, *Helvetios* (2012), a concept album that presents a narrative of Caesar's conquests from the perspective of the Helvetians and other Gauls, emphasizing the bravery and freedom of the native peoples while characterizing the Romans as rapacious, immoral, and untrustworthy. This counter-narrative presents a Gallic perspective on Rome's history as the basis for a modern, anticolonial, Celtic identity.

The band make repeated claims to speak for their dead ancestors and thus preserve the memory of the Helvetian people, inventing a folk tradition to establish a chronotope that, in turn, provides the basis for Swiss heritage in the modern day. On "Uxellodunon," the final musical track on *Helvetios*, the chorus promises that "[w]e will never forget, the things we've seen, the deaths we died, the tears we cried, we will never regret we defied." Similarly, the spoken-word tracks "Prologue" and "Epilogue" frame the album as the culmination of an oral tradition of song that preserves the true fate and memory of the ancient Helvetian people:

> When I reminisce about all those years of tribulation, I mostly remember our songs. We died, and our blood seeped away on the battlefields; but our songs survived, together with those of us that returned. And as they too will die one day, our songs will live on, and will be sung by our children, and by our children's children. This is how we will be remembered. This is who we were.
>
> Eluveitie, "Epilogue," Helvetios, 2012

In another example of Eluveitie's synthetic, La Tène approach to Celtic culture, these words are spoken in a Scottish brogue, presumably adopted as a clear way to communicate "Celtic-ness" to an Anglophone audience. Eluveitie do not actually have access to the oral tradition celebrated here and must rely on Caesar for much of the album's material, but the claims made by these tracks are still true in a certain sense: by inventing a musical tradition in the twenty-first century that tells tales of this people from a perspective of *their* national interest (rather than Rome's), Eluveitie could be said to constitute a divergent folk tradition from the scraps of evidence that remain in the more historical record. This is not so different from the practice Saidiya Hartman (2008) has named "critical fabulation," a type of narrative composition that works with the historical archive but rearranges and imagines to contest the violence (both corporal and epistemic) of history. The idea that this tradition will be reclaimed from and by song has its own significance, since, as Riggsby (2006: 63) has noted, the Gallic class of bards, attested in other ancient sources, were written out of Caesar's account entirely.

Helvetios draws its lyrical strength from the themes of unity and defiance to be found in retelling the Gallic War as a tale of resistance, so Helvetian identity tends to be subsumed within a broader Gallic identity. The Helvetians do receive special attention, however, in a sequence of songs beginning with track two, "Helvetios," and followed by four songs that explore the character of their people, describe the beauty of their homes, and record their decision to burn their villages and set out west. The appeals to natural freedom and national unity found herein are perhaps what we would expect from the romanticization of a "barbarian" past, which challenges the modernizing influence of conquest and civilization with a discourse of enlightened simplicity:

> 'Cause we're born free!
> 'Cause we're born wild!
> 'Cause we are indomitable and bold!

'Cause we are fire! (*brave*)
'Cause we are wave! (*strong*)
'Cause we are rock! (*tribe*)
We are one—we are Helvetios!

Eluveitie, "Helvetios," Helvetios, 2012

This chorus uses tropes of "hard primitivism" to supply both the empowering elements of metal and the bucolic romance of folk. Yet it also presents a picture of the barbarian with which we should be familiar from Roman texts like Caesar's *BGall*. Even the chorus of "Helvetios," in its appeals to a national character formed by the natural environment, is an echo of Greco-Roman ethnographic epistemology.[22]

Helvetios' themes of *virtus* and righteous anger are well suited to metal, which tends in its music, lyrics, and imagery toward bombastic celebrations of power and masculinity;[23] several songs on the album are triumphant in tone or call Caesar out directly. Eluveitie's account of the engagement at the river Saône, entitled "Meet the Enemy," follows Caesar's, but is markedly different in its emphasis. Eluveitie stress the fact that Caesar attacked the rear of their column under the cover of night ("At somber nightfall the defenseless were bestially run down / Saône stained with Helvetic blood"), an accusation to which they return at the opening of a later track, "Havoc"; what for Caesar was the avenging of public and private injury is here cast as the hollow slaughter of innocents. The rest of "Meet the Enemy" alludes to the ensuing diplomacy between Divico and Caesar, branding the Roman general a "liar." Whereas in the *BGall* Caesar casts his enemies as stubborn and refutes their version of events, here only the Helvetians are given a voice, and they instead seem steadfast and defiant. In the interlude before the final chorus, Anna Murphy, then Eluveitie's female vocalist and hurdy-gurdy player, spits a composite of the Helvetian boasts from *BGall*: "It is not us to go under the yoke / Of that fact the Roman people are witness / We will not bow!" While the words themselves have not been substantially altered, they are recontextualized within the driving fury of "Meet the Enemy" as a puissant rallying cry of Helvetian pride.

With the tenth track of the album, "Havoc," *Helvetios* turn from the Helvetians specifically to the Gauls more generally, mirroring the expansion of Caesar's ambitions from his initial interventions to the conquest of an entire nation. The message of "Havoc" is one of Rome's relentless rapacity, the dark mirror image of Caesar's vision of empire as a beneficent pacifying force ("Imperial needs are met / At bloody cost of free tribes / Invasion, raid and war atrocity / In the name of S.P.Q.R.").[24] Eluveitie again lay bare the naked aggression of Roman foreign policy, and emphasize the abridgment of natural freedom to counter Roman representative strategies that would argue that these people cannot exercise freedom responsibly. Caesar's voice is heard in "Havoc," but he speaks in Latin, bellowing "*Gallia est pacata!*" ("Gaul has been pacified!"). This choice serves to separate the listener from the Roman and identify her instead with the English-speaking Gallic voice of the song. This implicit identification with the Helvetians and Gauls occurs all over *Helvetios*, where lyrics usually adopt a first-person perspective or seem to address the listener directly;[25] it perhaps reaches its peak in "The Uprising," where in a spoken interlude someone—presumably Vercingetorix, the chieftain under whom the Gauls united in 53 BCE—addresses his fellow Gauls, encouraging them to see the opportunity before them: "A country of our own / A free Gaul!"

Eluveitie, therefore, do not necessarily present an entirely contradictory picture of their Helvetians; rather, they take the characterization offered by Roman sources and celebrate it. Obstinacy and recalcitrance become defiance and a will to freedom, and the lack of faith Caesar observed in the Gauls becomes instead a refusal to submit to Rome's yoke. In the manner in which Eluveitie reflect Rome's picture of the Gauls back at them, their music should perhaps be characterized as postcolonial, in that Eluveitie's Helvetian identity occupies a liminal space between a native or true identity and the identity constructed for them by their colonizers.[26] By taking ownership of the identity created for them by Caesar and his *commentarii*, Eluveitie seek to reconfigure the dominant narrative of Roman history by resisting its strategies of representation. Mary Pratt (2008: 7) has used the term "transculturation" to describe "how subordinated or marginal groups select and invent from materials transmitted to them by a dominant or metropolitan culture." This is precisely what Eluveitie do on *Helvetios*.

Our barren sacrifice

Eluveitie's themes of transculturation culminate in the song "Alesia," the fourteenth track on *Helvetios*. The siege of Alesia, for which Caesar is again our primary source, is often adduced as the pinnacle of his Gallic campaigns and a perfect demonstration of his logistical mastery and tactical flair. Indeed, it has been described as "one of the most extraordinary military engagements in the history of warfare," and represents the climax of a narrative theme in *BGall* where Rome defeats her enemies by her superior technology as much as by her *virtus*.[27] Driving Vercingetorix and his army to take refuge in the Gallic hill-fort of Alesia, Caesar began encircling it with fortifications fourteen miles in length (a siege practice the Romans called *circumvallatio*). When Gaul poured out reinforcements to lift the siege, Caesar built a second, outward-facing set of fortifications, effectively trapping his own army in the narrow confines between. Through a mixture of lethal engineering, personal leadership, and Roman discipline, Caesar held out long enough that the reinforcements dissipated, and Vercingetorix surrendered. In the hands of a pro-Roman heavy metal band such as Ex Deo, this story is told as one of triumph and glory, including the un-ironic alignment of territorial and sexual conquest.[28]

Eluveitie, however, strip Alesia of all heroism and triumph and cast its fall as a day of tragedy, suffering, and sacrifice:

> *(Murphy:)* The grass was as green as it always was that sinister day
> The blackbirds sang their songs as they always did that black-letter day
> We passed the great gate for the very last time
> I did not look back, I knew we'd stay

(Glanzmann:) I knew they would not let us go
(Both:) Leave the death strip
(Glanzmann:) I saw the gleam in their eyes of fear and enslavement
(Both:) The crushing weight

(Murphy:) Beloveth ground take me home

(Both:) Alesia, Alisanos
Wake me when I'm gone
Ianotouta, eternity
Proclaim our barren sacrifice

Eluveitie, "Alesia," Helvetios, 2012

Glanzmann's customary growling vocals are counterpoised by Murphy's singing, which speaks for the women and children cast out of the besieged city and left to starve to death within Caesar's circumvallation. While Murphy does not growl like Glanzmann, she uses her voice to similarly dramatic effect, alternately soaring and cracking in a manner suited to both the material and the milieu of metal.[29] This shift in focus makes the suffering of the Gallic women the central element of this Alesia narrative, and reminds us squarely of the cost of Roman glory. This stands in stark contrast to Caesar's own account of the siege, which gives extremely short shrift to the fate of the women and children, who presumably endured many days of misery and hunger, trapped as they were between the walls and works at Alesia.[30] It also presents an interesting counterpoint to traditional metal lyrics, which have been characterized as cultivating a "misogynist fantasy of a world without women."[31]

Eluveitie's reorientation of Alesia mirrors developments in the archaeology of the site. The original excavations that found the ancient hill-fort in the nineteenth century were driven by Napoleon III's interest in aligning the memory of his uncle Bonaparte more closely with his hero Julius Caesar.[32] There followed, however, a shift in the priorities of French archaeology to a more anticolonial stance; this included the recuperation of Vercingetorix as a French folk hero, with a statue being erected in his honor at Alesia in 1865.[33] A similar anticolonialism can be observed in Eluveitie's juxtaposition of the Latinate word "Alesia" with "Alesanos," the name of a Gallic deity worshipped in the surrounding area. In both cases, Alesia has been reconfigured from the location of Caesar's triumph to a site for the commemoration of Gallic defiance and loss.

Of course, Eluveitie's lyrical constructions are not just anticolonial but also *post-colonial*, in that they still depend on the colonizer for much of their transculturated narrative and identity. Eluveitie cannot escape the debt they owe to Caesar. Even as they name him a "liar" in "Meet the Enemy," they also accept his claim that the ancient Helvetians had intended to migrate to Santones in "Santonian Shores"—a fact for which he is the only authority. Likewise, Eluveitie seem unaware of the irony of proclaiming a "free Gallia" in the songs "Havoc" and "The Uprising," even though the peoples of whom they sing only became "Gallia" before and under the might of Rome. Again, as Riggsby has argued, the homogenization of such a vast assemblage of peoples under the name of "Gallia" is a Roman imperial strategy, one that makes their subjugation both possible and necessary, akin to what Gayatri Spivak has called "the production" of the colonial subject.[34] In *BGall*, it is the unification of the Gauls into one vast army—which can be defeated decisively at Alesia—that ultimately leads to their final pacification. Much like Vercingetorix, Eluveitie find themselves caught in the double-bind of the colonial subject, whose unification and resistance serves the ideological and strategic imperatives of the colonial power.

On torrid sand

A similarly postcolonial project can be found in the work of SuidAkrA, a folk metal band from Germany who adapt both the music and the heritage of so-called insular Celts. While there remains an open question as to how "Celtic" Germany ever was, front man Arkadius Antonik frequently invokes the conceits of La Tène cultural theory to justify his immersive use of Scottish, Irish, and Welsh folk traditions.[35] Suggestively, the geographical disconnect between German and Irish–Scottish–Welsh Celticism could be said to reflect and underline the historical disconnect between ancient Celts and their modern inheritors, realizing the rupture in time through the more obvious rupture in space.[36] SuidAkrA mix metal and folk music in a similar manner to Eluveitie, layering bagpipes and patterns like Irish jigs over a foundation of melodic death metal in the Gothenburg style.[37] Much like Eluveitie's *Helvetios*, SuidAkrA's 2006 album *Caledonia* tells the tale of the Roman invasion of Scotland from the perspective of the natives. The cover of this album already evokes several concepts familiar from our discussion of Eluveitie, depicting a humanoid figure seemingly composed of Celtic labyrinth patterns emerging from the soil of Scotland to challenge a Roman centurion bearing a legionary eagle.

Caledonia explores the Roman invasion of Scotland and the Celtic resistance and, while it is ultimately more triumphant in tone than *Helvetios*, it similarly imagines the experience of Roman imperialism from the perspective of its provincial subjects. Although at least one track on *Caledonia*, "Dawning Tempest," takes up the perspective of a Roman soldier, it is to emphasize how inhospitable the land is to the legions and the ferociousness of the foe that they face—a Roman trope turned to the service of Celtic pride. Like the early tracks on *Helvetios*, *Caledonia* emphasizes the comparative attunement of its Caledonians to their natural surroundings, demonstrating once more the folk metal tropes of a connection to nature and the rejection of civilizing culture. The video for the song "The IXth Legion" cuts back and forth between the footage of the band playing in the forest, wearing warpaint with a piper by their side, and playing in modern dress in a dilapidated warehouse. This cross-cutting reflects the transhistorical nature of both SuidAkrA and Eluveitie's identity politics, which seek to root a modern, Celtic, identity in a politicized representation of the past.

Since *Caledonia* is so similar to *Helvetios* in the way it constructs a postcolonial vision of Roman history, I do not wish to retread the details of that vision in great detail. Like

Eluveitie, SuidAkrA employ Celtic instruments—in this case, "highland bagpipes" played by collaborator Axel Römer—on songs intended to invoke Caledonian identity, such as "Highland Hills" and "The IXth Legion." The third track, "The Ember Deid (Part II)," is sung in Scots dialect, which, although not the language spoken by the ancient inhabitants of Scotland, has a connection to Scottish nationalism which serves the album's folk conceits. The lyrics of *Caledonia* hit the same marks as *Helvetios*, with "Evoke the Demon" mirroring "The Uprising" as a call to arms against the Roman invaders and "On Torrid Sands" offering the same defiant anticolonial rhetoric ("We who are about to die / Won't salute you and no *victis* honor / To the fallen ones"). As with the "Prologue" and "Epilogue" on *Helvetios*, SuidAkrA refer to a tradition of memory distinct from written history, this time preserved by the "standing stones" mentioned in both "Highland Hills" and "The IXth Legion."

Perhaps most importantly, the culture that SuidAkrA names their enemy again provides the best sources for the ancient peoples with whom they identify. Just as Eluveitie champion the cause of a "free Gaul," a colonial construction brought forth in the face of Roman imperialism, so SuidAkrA brand their Celtic chronotope with a Roman marker: Caledonia, a name given to the region by Roman writers.[38] Further, the primary source for SuidAkrA's *Caledonia* must be Tacitus' *Agricola*, a late-first century CE account of the conquest of Britain by the eponymous Roman general, Gnaeus Julius Agricola. Tacitus composed the account not just as a Roman deeply implicated in imperial culture and politics, but as the son-in-law of Agricola, and so, like Caesar, he must be understood to write with certain rhetorical goals—although perhaps more complex ones. Significantly, SuidAkrA paraphrase the famous speech Tacitus attributes to the Caledonian chieftain Calgacus in the liner notes to the album. This speech has long been understood to represent a powerful moment of reflexive Roman self-critique, and it is the source of the famous aphorism *ubi solitudinem faciunt, pacem appellant* (commonly glossed as "they make a desert and call it peace"), referring to the harsh cost of Roman imperialism.[39] Both *Helvetios* and *Caledonia* could be said to elaborate on this sentiment, laying bare the dark underbelly of empire that Tacitus could only gesture toward through the character of Calgacus. Where he used a barbarian chieftain as the mouthpiece for Roman anxieties about empire, SuidAkrA and Eluveitie expand this conceit into a sustained critique by making the barbarian the focus and hero of the narrative. Conversely, just as Caesar and Tacitus construct the Gauls and Caledonians as fierce warriors to enhance the achievement of Roman *virtus*, so on *Caledonia*, SuidAkrA emphasize the martial vigor of "The IXth Legion" (a Roman army whose disappearance in Britain owes more to folklore than history),[40] once more turning an imperial trope to the advantage of the colonial subject.

The head of a Roman emperor

The muddling of identity—modern Germano-Celtic, ancient insular Celt, and Roman imperial subject—becomes even more rich and confused on SuidAkrA's *Eternal Defiance* (2013), a concept album based on the history and folklore surrounding the Roman emperor Magnus Maximus. The title of the album suggests postcolonial conceits similar to *Helvetios* and *Caledonia*, since it appears to subvert the Roman imperial slogan VICTORIA AETERNA ("eternal victory") into a motto of colonial resistance.[41] But the traditions which SuidAkrA adapt for their album concept are much more complicated than subject versus colonial power and are worth examining in more detail.

The historical Maximus was a Spanish-born Roman citizen and military commander who led an uprising in ancient Britain and Gaul to become emperor of the Roman West in 383–388 CE; he is chiefly known to us from a near-contemporary speech commemorating his subsequent downfall and from scattered references in later Greco-Roman writers.[42] Maximus was later taken up in Welsh folklore, mythologized as the hero Macsen Wledig, where he became a figure of Celtic pride and wellspring of an emerging British identity. On *Eternal Defiance*, SuidAkrA weave together strands from both traditions to tell a romantic story of Romano-Celtic triumph and tragedy, backed by a mature blend of melodic death metal, symphonic orchestration, and bagpipes.[43]

Among what Classical sources we have, the tradition regarding Maximus is subject to distortion based on the rhetorical aims of the author. The most direct source—the encomiastic speech delivered by Pacatus in honor of Theodosius I in 389 CE—is clearly biased in favor of its subject, and thus intent on blackening Maximus as a ravening, irreligious usurper.[44] Though Pacatus may be checked using other accounts, they are subject to their own interest, with the next best source, the later historian Zosimus, being "virulently anti-Theodosian."[45] So it is important to remember that, like Caesar's Helvetians, the supposedly historical subject of *Eternal Defiance* has already been shaped to fit the needs of writers and audiences in specific contexts.

It seems relatively certain that Maximus was born in Roman Spain and served in Britain as a military commander,[46] where he may have been instrumental in holding off a Pictish invasion.[47] In 383 CE, he was proclaimed emperor by his troops in Britain and led an army over into Gaul; Zosimus claims the native resolve and contumacy of the British troops was partly to blame, a familiar description of the non-Roman.[48] The Roman Empire was, at this time, split between east and west, with an emperor governing each half. Having defeated the western emperor Gratian in battle, Maximus was recognized by the eastern emperor, Theodosius, and granted legal control of the western empire.[49] After he sought to extend his dominion by invading Italy in 387 CE, Maximus' army was defeated by Theodosius at the Battle of Save in 388 CE and Maximus himself was captured and executed.[50]

The historical evidence for Maximus is scant, partly because he appears to have suffered the so-called *damnatio memoriae*—a process of semi-official memory sanction that saw his name struck from inscriptions and his images removed after his defeat and death.[51] *Damnatio memoriae* is something of a modern construct: scholars have recovered the remnants of certain practices and classified them under a neologistic marker that gives narrative shape to history. So, Maximus has endured recurrent distortions: recognized legally as emperor, then damned as a usurping tyrant, and later enshrined as the victim of *damnatio*. SuidAkrA take advantage of the sanctions as part of their fantastical version of Maximus' story with album closer "Damnatio Memoriae," a song which indulges the fantasy that he persisted after death as an immortal talking head. Like Eluveitie, SuidAkrA here produce a gap between Classical historical traditions and other forms of representation, opening a space for their imaginative reconstruction of Maximus even as they acknowledge their debt to Classical sources.

While his place in Roman history was significantly diminished with his defeat, Maximus would find new life in early British literature and identity politics.[52] He appears as "Maximian" in Geoffrey of Monmouth's twelfth-century work *Historia Regum Britanniae* or *History of the Kings of Britain* (*HRB*), "one of the most popular texts of the Middle Ages," which can itself be characterized as an attempt to excavate an authentic pre-Saxon, pre-Norman British identity from the past, analogous to the work of both Eluveitie and SuidAkrA in the present. *HRB* has been characterized as a work of "'synthetic pseudo-history,' which projects a national unity onto a legendary past," essentially using the form and logic of historiography as a vessel for nationalist fictions about Britain's history.[53] It follows the ninth-century *Historia Brittonum* (*History of the Britains*) in claiming that Britain was actually founded by a Roman called Brutus, whence came its name.[54] Geoffrey asserts that Maximian was himself a Roman senator, born to a Roman mother and British father (the uncle of the emperor Constantine) and so "bearing regal parentage from the blood of each" (5.10). The historical Maximus bears no genealogical connection to Constantine, nor was the latter British (although he was elevated to the position of western emperor there in 306 CE).[55] Here Geoffrey was participating in a tradition that increased the prestige of Britain and its kings by tying them genealogically to Roman emperors—first Constantine, and then Maximus.[56]

In *HRB*, the aging British King Octavius solicits Maximian to come to Britain from Rome to marry his daughter and become the next king. Maximian is persuaded by the promise of British troops to help resolve his pre-existing conflict with the emperor Gratian, and after five years of preparation (during which he defended Britain against insurgencies from Scotland) he crosses to Gaul and soundly defeats Gratian. Geoffrey compresses the sequence of Maximian's campaigns significantly, focusing more on the fate of Octavius' nephew, Conan Meriadoc, who founded Brittany ("a second Britain") with Maximian's blessing (5.14; seeming to follow the *Historiae Brittonum*, ch. 21). Instead of a decisive military defeat at the hands of Theodosius, Maximian is assassinated in Rome by Gratian's allies (5.16).

Maximus grows more fantastical in the collection of Welsh prose tales known as the *Mabinogion*, where he appears as "Macsen Wledig" in a story called "Breudwyt Macsen Wledig" ("The Dream of Macsen Wledig," hereafter *BMW*).[57] The name "Macsen" or "Maxen" seems to have developed from the abridgment of "Maximus" to "Maxim" in Welsh genealogical records, while the title "Wledig" is understood to indicate a form of military authority.[58] Macsen is already emperor of Rome at the beginning of the story, when he dreams of a beautiful woman, named Elen, trapped in a tower in Wales. The use of the name "Elen" suggests a further mingling of Roman history and British folklore, since it connects *BMW*'s heroine to St. Helena, the mother of the emperor Constantine, whom Geoffrey had claimed was also the daughter of a British king.[59] Macsen travels to Britain to marry Elen, grants sovereignty over Britain to her father as a wedding gift, and spends seven years there.⁶⁰ He then receives word that he has been usurped in Rome and leads an army of Britons to reclaim his throne. The brothers of Elen—including Conan, here Cynan—are instrumental in taking Rome and restoring Macsen to power, whereupon he empowers them to conquer further lands, leading to the founding of Brittany. Although it is a more romantic tale than Geoffrey's, *BMW* incorporates several similar elements, including the marriage to a British woman, a sojourn in Britain, and the subsequent conquest of the western Roman Empire. While both texts implicate Maximus more fully into British history through marriage and his relationship with Conan/Cynan, they also show more investment in establishing the legitimacy of his reign as emperor than the Roman sources, in which he is more clearly a usurper. So, again, we see the memory of Maximus inflected to serve competing interests of national and individual sovereignty.

The peculiar role of Maximus as a cultural nexus is demonstrated most concretely by an inscription on the Pillar of Eliseg, a Welsh monument dated to the ninth century CE. On the Pillar was inscribed a genealogy of the kings of Powys, who came to power after Rome abandoned Britain in the fifth century CE; it was composed in Latin but written in insular script.⁶¹ The text claims that Vortigern, the putative founder of the line, married one Sevira, "the daughter of king Maximus who killed the king of the Romans" (*Maximi/[re]gis qui occidit regem Romano/rum*). The goal here seems clear: to establish the authority of Vortigern's line by connecting it genealogically to Maximus. That it commemorates him as the slayer of the "king" of the Romans (the emperor Gratian) should not be surprising on a monument to Celtic pride, but it is remarkable that it does so in Latin and preserves Maximus' name in its Latinate form, not as Maxim or Macsen. The Pillar of Eliseg is thus itself an early example of transculturation, as it works to forge a Welsh identity in the terms of their former colonial oppressors. The kings of Powys thus drew capital both from violent resistance to imperial culture and their mastery of that culture.

The eagle and the dragon

The representative strategies of the Pillar foreshadow those of SuidAkrA, who combine details from Maximus' historical career with elements of Macsen's folk romance to produce a hybrid character embodying the pleasurable puissance of both Roman emperor and Celtic hero. After the musical overture of "Storming the Walls," *Eternal Defiance* begins its lyrical tale with track two, "Inner Sanctum," which describes an assault on a crusader fortress and the discovery of Macsen's head within. Although he is generally called Macsen, the identity of the album's hero is hybridized from the very beginning, with those who discover him unsure if they have found "The head of a Roman Emperor / Adored with a laurel crown? / Or the face of a Celtic king / With runic Ogham carved?" This song also exemplifies a tendency on the album to add elements from other Celtic myths to the story of Macsen. The album's repeated conceit that Macsen lived on after death as a talking head is not found in any of the primary sources for Macsen/Maximian, and likely represents a confusion with the Welsh myth of Brân the Blessed, which also appears in the *Mabinogion*.⁶² This is possibly confirmed by the song "Pair Dadeni," named for a mythical cauldron that supposedly granted immortality, which is also found in Brân's tale in the *Mabinogion* and similarly has no place in Macsen's traditional tale. Tellingly, SuidAkrA have Macsen baptized in this cauldron—which the song explicitly links to Brân—presumably leading to his immortality. This may be a deliberate addition of material to fill out events during Macsen's sojourn in Britain, which is thinly attested in both Classical and mythological sources. Intentional or not, the inclusion of these extremely fantastical elements grants further privilege to folk and pseudohistorical traditions, over the ascendant rationality of historiography and scholarly *Quellenforschung*—"our more pedantic science," in the words of one *Mabinogion* scholar.⁶³

On the third track, "Beneath the Red Eagle," SuidAkrA cleave to the Classical version of Macsen's origins, imagining him as a young man in Spain being called to serve in Rome's legions, and featuring guest vocalist Tina Stabel in the role of his mother. No longer the enemy or victim of imperial power, in "Beneath the Red Eagle" the Celtic colonial subject becomes the Roman himself, with the eagle transforming from its metonymic role as symbol of the oppressor in Eluveitie's "The Uprising" into a sign worth killing and dying for. The vocal exchange between Stabel and Antonik evokes the colonial reach of imperial ideology, with his mother entreating him to fight and die for Rome and Macsen affirming that he will ("Beneath the eagle [you/I] will march / To fight for Rome to slay or die / Under the eagle [you/I] will ride / To fight to the end and then fight again"). Similarly, the video for the following track, "March of Conquest," which chronicles Macsen's rise through the ranks of the Roman army, sees the band foregoing the woad and kilts of *Caledonia*'s "The IXth Legion" for a pastiche of Roman legionary armor—reflecting in their costume the transition from Caledonian resistance to postcolonial hybrid.⁶⁴

With track four, "Pair Dadeni," SuidAkrA's Macsen arrives in Britain and the band switches to folklore to continue his tale. Again, it seems that they borrow quite broadly from Welsh mythology to fill out this episode in Macsen's life, as the lyrics invent a journey to the castle Dinas Brân and his baptism by druids in Brân's cauldron, granting him immortality. The shift in source material for the lyrics is complemented by choices in instrumentation:

> Because of the fact that this song deals with Macsen's period in Britannia, we knew immediately that the bagpipes will be the most important thing and that's how we composed this song. It's based on the melody line of the bagpipes. This song manages to work without any orchestral arrangements and still sound very epic and bombastic.⁶⁵

As Antonik himself explains it, the bagpipes are an important factor in establishing a geographical folk element within the song, while the orchestral arrangements that marked "Beneath the Red Eagle" and "March of Conquest" retreat into the background.

This is further testimony to the pan-Celtic nature of SuidAkrA's music: a German band using Scottish instruments to conjure a Welsh hero. Moreover, Antonik invokes the idea of "Britannia," which, like Gallia and Caledonia, is an ethno-geographic concept of Roman origin. The lyrics of this song also mark the shift in Macsen's identity from Roman to Briton, as it opens with the verse "Marching on to Dinas Brân / The ravens called his name / Bearer of the Eagle Red / To Britain Macsen came" and ends, "Crowned King at Dinas Brân / The ravens called his name /Bearer of the Dragon Red / In Britain Macsen stayed." The metonymic work of the album continues, with the supplanting of the Roman eagle by the Welsh dragon marking Macsen's shift from Roman emperor to British king.

With the next two tracks, SuidAkrA move to a more direct adaptation of material from "The Dream of Macsen Wledig." The first, "Mindsong," is an acoustic ballad recounting Macsen's prophetic dream of Elen and his romantic union with her. By SuidAkrA's standards, the song is extremely stripped down and gives Stabel's performance as the bewitching voice of Elen pride of place, addressing Macsen directly as "emperor of Rome." "Rage for Revenge" continues the poem's version of Macsen's story, with the news reaching him that interests in Rome have deposed him as emperor; SuidAkrA thus participate in the British tradition of representing him as a rightful ruler of the Roman West who travels to Britain, contrary to the Roman tradition that resolutely acknowledges his usurpation of Gratian's position. SuidAkrA once more invoke the eagle/dragon symbolism to both unite and differentiate Macsen's cultural identities ("Under the Eagle Macsen left / To die or triumph over Gaul / Under the Dragon he'd return / Retaliate and conquer Rome"), this time marking the colonizing subject as the one who is changed by their journey to colonial realms. They follow *BMW* in laying the credit for his victory at Rome at the feet of "the sons of Eudav," juxtaposing their "dragon army" with Macsen finally assuming a fully Romanized identity: "Magnus Maximus sat on the Throne."[66] Interestingly, SuidAkrA render Macsen at his most British once he has achieved his final dominion as Roman emperor: "A Celtic army Macsen raised / To march and take the throne / To join him in his wrath for Rome / To aid him in his rage for revenge."

In *BMW*, this is where Macsen's story stops, but *Eternal Defiance* turns back to Roman history and his ignominious end recorded in sources such as Pacatus and Zosimus. "The Dragon's Head" addresses the Battle of the Save and Macsen's capture and execution at Aquileia, emphasizing both the conflict's tragic element of civil war ("It's Roman against Roman / A clash of West and East") and the failure of Macsen's prophetic sight (again, part of the apocryphal conceit of his afterlife as an oracular head). Its representation stands at odds with Pacatus' *Panegyric*, which instead emphasizes the righteous punishment of a usurper and the magnanimity of his rival (43.2–4), exposing once again the ideological aims of each text. SuidAkrA's song is of interest for how it marks the end of Macsen's imperial career as the beginning of his life in British tradition, with the final lyrics "Magnus Maximus / The Emperor is dead / Behold Penn Dragon / The Dragon's Head." Although this is in part a pun on the idea of Macsen's decapitation and fantastical afterlife, in a figurative manner it also establishes a truth about the part he has come to play in both literature and culture. After his death in 388 CE, Maximus became little more than a footnote in the career of Theodosius I, an emperor who casts a long shadow over Roman history. But as he passed from history into the realm of folk traditions, Macsen took on a greater power, as a source of legitimating authority and a means of shaping new cultural identities from the remains of Rome's empire.

Notably, *Eternal Defiance* includes no mention of the founding of Brittany, a core element of the myth of Macsen in British literature and a cornerstone in the foundation of post-Roman Celtic identity. One would expect SuidAkrA—a band committed to a vision of pan-European Celticism—to feature this element of the story, and they may have omitted it to sidestep the accompanying atrocities recounted by both Geoffrey and the *Mabinogion*.[67]

In his transformation from Maximus to Maximian to Macsen, the progressive manipulation of the memory of this historical figure renders him a powerful symbol of European hybridity and multiple, interacting contestations of identity—Roman, British, and Celtic. *Eternal Defiance* represents but a single transaction within a long tradition of political readings of Maximus, which range from historiography to folklore to heavy metal. Indeed, the only real innovation made by SuidAkrA is the recombination of this tradition into a cohesive story which bestrides all those that have come before. Just as the tradition surrounding Magnus Maximus reflects the increasing hybridization of Roman identity in the later Empire and beyond, *Eternal Defiance* embodies the ambivalent essence of Celtic identity and the bands who must recover it from Roman traditions.

Conclusion

Like many scholarly commentators on authors like Julius Caesar and Tacitus, both Eluveitie and SuidAkrA recognize in Roman sources the elements of the anti-conquest narrative that form Rome's implicit argument for the conquest and subjugation of ancient Europe. They engage in a critique of these sources akin to the work of Classical scholars, but are able to use the imaginative dimension of their creative projects to take that critique a step further, bending the analysis of imperialist discourse into a truly postcolonial, transculturated history of the peoples they consider their cultural ancestors.[68] As *Eternal Defiance* shows, this practice is only new in form. The ideological content of their songs is well-matched by their music, which similarly blends a dominant form of instrumentation and arrangement with elements that formerly had no place or voice in the genre.

To a certain extent, I would argue that this music is itself also postcolonial, in that it fuses the generic sounds and aesthetics of western heavy metal with instruments and tunes specific to Celtic musical traditions. The music itself, therefore, cannot escape the colonial history of Europe, which was shaped by the Roman Empire and its legacy through post-Classical reception and the promotion of hegemonic cultural forms, from literary texts to musical performance.[69] We can witness a similar process in the bands' choice to sing primarily in English. By appropriating a popular form of music and using it to sing their own songs, Eluveitie and SuidAkrA produce a rich form of postcolonial discourse, one which appeals to romantic ideals of freedom and resistance to challenge the historical portrait of Celtic peoples. While this, in turn, challenges the Roman version of Europe's history, it nevertheless confirms the central place of Rome and her traditions within the history of European cultural identity.

Notes

1. On Celtomania, see Cunliffe (1997: 13). For an argument against "Celtoskepticism," see Megaw and Megaw (1996).
2. Marjenin (2002: 2).
3. During et al. (2007: 101) argue for the importance of Skyclad's 1991 album *The Wayward Sons of Mother Earth*, which saw founder Martin Walkyier augmenting the up-tempo, technical sound of his previous work in thrash metal band Sabbat with violins and adaptations of Irish jigs. Mulvany (2000) largely ignores the existence of Skyclad, preferring the narrative of folk metal as an offshoot of early 1990s Scandinavian black metal. The bands discussed in this chapter specifically cite the influence of the death metal bands that emerged from Stockholm and Gothenburg in Sweden in the same period (see below). The Swedish band Bathory—progenitors of both black and so-called Viking metal—may be a common influence on all these bands; see Ekeroth, (2006: 27–34; 36–9) and Piotrowska (2015: 103–6). For the stylistic differences between death and black metal, see Fletcher and Umurhan (this volume) and Bogue (2004).
4. Kahn-Harris (2007: 122–23).
5. Marjenin (2014: 115).
6. Mulvany (2000: i–v). In this respect, folk may be more "metal" than metal itself.
7. Mulvany (2000: 94) argues this is not just a matter of "jingoistic nationalism," but Spracklen (2015) explores the role of hegemonic masculinity and monoracial identity politics in folk metal.
8. Marjenin (2014: 10; 101–12).
9. Mulvany (2000: 43), after Bakhtin (1981).
10. Modern knowledge of ancient Gaulish is based primarily on a small corpus of inscriptions. While Eluveitie's basic morphology seems to be generally correct, Glanzmann emphasized in an early interview that he made no claim to present accurate Gaulish (Eluveitie.ch 2004). On *Helvetios* (discussed below), the band credit Armin Kaar and Dominic Rivers for any Gaulish translations.
11. Ekeroth (2006: 267); see also Kahn-Harris (2007: 106). Glanzmann has described Eluveitie as a combination of "authentically played traditional Celtic folk music on one side and quite modern-styled melodic death metal in the Gothenburg vain [sic]" (Neilstein 2008). The influence of albums such as At the Gates' *Terminal Spirit Disease* (1994) and In Flames' *Subterranean* (1995) is obvious; Anders Björler of At the Gates has actually characterized early In Flames as "'happy' folk music" in comparison to his own band (quoted in Ekeroth (2006: 267)).
12. Marjenin (2014: 54).
13. Fitzpatrick (1996). See also Drinkwater (1983: 1–13) and Cunliffe (1997: 1–7).
14. Fitzpatrick (1996: 241).

15. During et al. (2007: 40).
16. For images of the vase and discussion of the inscription, see Vitali and Kaenel (2000); they cite an anecdote from Pliny the Elder's *Natural History* (12.2.5), which suggests a Helvetian artificer by the name of Helico was present in Rome prior to the Gallic invasion of 390 BCE. If the inscription brands the object as "Helvetian"—rather than recording the name of the artisan, as we find in Greco-Roman products—then we perhaps have evidence of an imperial practice still common in contemporary art circles and critiqued by Appiah (1991).
17. Vitali and Kaenel (2000: 116–17). Compare Riggsby (2006: 66) for La Tène sites in southern Germany.
18. Strabo *Geog.* 7.2.2; all translations are my own. The Helvetians (rendered as Ἐλουηττίοι in Strabo's Greek) receive passing mentions also at 4.3.3–4, 4.6.8, 4.6.11, and 7.1.5, where Strabo uses them as reference points against which to establish the locations of other peoples and places.
19. For a survey of Greco-Roman ethnography, see Rives (1999: 11–21). It was claimed that Jupiter had granted the Romans *imperium sine fine* (Verg. *Aen.* 1.279).
20. Riggsby (2006: 83–105) argues that *virtus* is reconfigured in *BGall* from an innate quality to something attained through experience. Rives (1999: 20) notes that bravery was "the topic of numerous anecdotes" about the Celts in Greco-Roman ethnography.
21. Riggsby (2006: 30).
22. On folk metal tropes, see Kahn-Harris (2007:10) and Marjenin (2014: 92–3). On Greco-Roman ethnography, see Rives (1999: 16).
23. Walser (1993a: 108–36) and Kahn-Harris (2007: 75–7).
24. "S.P.Q.R." stands for *Senatus Populusque Romanus*, the "Senate and People of Rome."
25. Both "Prologue" and "Epilogue" adopt the perspective of a Helvetian recalling his people's past, while four of the first five musical tracks use the first-person singular or plural in their description of the Helvetians and their migration. The choruses of several songs, including "Helvetios," "A Rose for Epona," "Alesia," and "Uxellodunon," also employ the first person; if a listener were to sing along with these tracks, she would thus take on the role of a Helvetian/Gaul.
26. For example, Appiah (1991: 347–49) discusses how the postcolonial subject cannot be cleanly separated from the influence of the colonizer, and often finds expression through colonial institutions and discursive frameworks.
27. Billows (2009: 160). The siege of Alesia is recounted in *BGall* 7.68–89. On technology in *BGall*, see Riggsby (2006: 97–100).
28. "Storm the Gates of Alesia" from 2009's *Romulus* includes the memorable chorus "Succumb to circumvallation / Penetrate the Gallic nation." For more on Ex Deo, see Umurhan (2012), Magro-Martínez (this volume), and Umurhan (this volume).
29. Walser (1993a: 45) and Kahn-Harris (2007: 32).
30. *BGall.* 7.78.3–5. Caesar makes no attempt to justify his decision, but the Imperial historian Cassius Dio (40.40) emphasizes the exigency of Caesar's supply to excuse this action.
31. Kahn-Harris (2007: 76), following Walser (1993a). For more on the changing place of women in metal, see Åshede and Foka (this volume) and Crofton-Sleigh (this volume).
32. Keppie (1984: 65–8). For comparison, see Rives (1999: 3) for political agendas in German archaeology during the Nazi period.
33. Fleury-Ilet (1996: 196–208). For more on France, Caesar, and Vercingetorix, see Wyke (2007: 41–65).

34. Spivak (1994: 77), who is specifically interested in the homogenization of subaltern identity by the discourse of imperial power.
35. Rose (2013).
36. Sites with evidence of La Tène culture have been found in southern Germany; see Vitali and Kaenel (2000: 116–17). Riggsby (2006: 50–9, 65) argues that Caesar and his fellow Romans are partially responsible for the strict ethnographic separation between the Celtic and Germanic peoples of their time. For a picture of the complicated question of Celtic and Germanic ethnicity, see Rives (1999: 7–11).
37. Antonik has specifically acknowledged the debt his music owes to early In Flames, including *Subterranean*, as well as early folk metal bands such as Finland's Amorphis and some black metal like Norway's Emperor (Rose 2013).
38. The earliest uses of "Caledonia" appear to come in Pliny's *Natural History* (4.30) and Lucan's *Bellum Civile* (6.68), both from the mid-first century CE. Both authors use it adjectivally to mark the furthest reaches of Roman exploration or British settlement, respectively. It has been suggested, based on Ptolemy's *Geography* (2.3), that the Romans named the whole region after a tribe called the Caledonii.
39. The speech appears in Tacitus *Agricola* 30–2. The liner notes present a pastiche of it before the lyrics to "Evoke the Demon," though notably omit "they make a desert and call it peace." The continuing currency of Calgacus' sentiment is demonstrated by its appearance in recent works as disparate as Morris (2014: 27–9) and Mitchell (2012: 63).
40. A tale popularized by Rosemary Sutcliff's novel *The Eagle of the Ninth* (1954). See Campbell (2010) for the story of how speculation about the legion's fate became historical orthodoxy.
41. Known chiefly from Roman coinage; see McCormick (1986: 4 n.13).
42. Pacatus, *Panegyric of Theodosius* (= *Pan. Lat.* 2) 26–45; Zosimus 4.34–46; Ambrose *Epistles* 24; Orosius 7.34.9–35.9; Sulpicius Severus, *Vita Martini* 20.1–9, *Dialogues* 3.11–13; Prosper Tiro *Chronica Minora* I 461–2. Some inscriptions, laws, and coinage also attest to his reign (Lunn-Rockliffe 2010: 320–21).
43. Antonik has acknowledged the presence of both traditions in the album's story (Rose 2013).
44. The Panegyric is transmitted as part of the corpus called *XII Panegyrici Latini*. The best edition is Nixon and Rodgers (1994); as they note, Pacatus' "verbose and platitudinous vaporing" was actually a feature of this genre of speech-writing, but his obvious bias "may disconcert the reader who approaches our speech to glean historical info" (444–45). See also Lunn-Rockliffe (2010: esp. 324).
45. Nixon and Rodgers (1994: 443).
46. Maximus' Spanish origins are largely based on an inscription from Tarraconensis; see *CIL* II 4911 (Siresa) with Matthews (1975: 174–75).
47. Claimed in the *Gallic Chronicle of 452* (*Chronica Minora* I 646), the only source. The *Chronicle* places this event in 384 CE, the year after his acclamation as emperor in Britain, but it has been argued that the order of events should be reversed (Birley 1981: 351). Nixon and Rodgers (1994: 477 n.78) note that such a victory may explain Maximus' later Welsh popularity. His title of "Wledig" in the Welsh tradition has been used as the basis for conjecturing that he had specific legal powers in Britain, as putative *dux Britanniae* (Stevens 1938: 89–91).
48. Zosimus 4.35. Salway (1997: 298) argues that this characterization may not have been undeserved.
49. See Lunn-Rockliffe (2010: 320–21) and, more briefly, Matthews (1975: 179).

50. For a nuanced historical account of Maximus' revolt, see Matthews (1975: 173–82, 223–25).
51. Thus, more accurately termed *abolitio memoriae*, although both are neologisms. For such procedures, see Hedrick (2000). Lunn-Rockliffe (2010: 321–24) provides a compelling summary of the evidence for sanctions against Maximus.
52. In the sixth-century CE text *De Excidio et Conquestu Britanniae* (*On the Destruction and Conquest of Britain*) by the British writer St. Gildas, Maximus is still remembered as a tyrant and usurper, and blamed for stripping Britain of her manpower and leaving her open to conquest (ch. 13–14). His record in the ninth-century *Historia Brittonum*, where he appears as a doublet under the names Maximianus and Maximus, is more neutral (chs. 26–27).
53. Jankulak (2010: 1–4): "Geoffrey introduced 'Britain' itself, a concept already familiar to the Welsh, to English historiography, and in doing so permanently affected the way English writers thought about Britain and its constituent regions."
54. *HRB* 1.3–18 tells the story of this Brutus' birth as the great-grandson of Aeneas, his exile, travels around the Mediterranean, and arrival in what will be Britain (cf. *Historia Brittonum* 10–11). No such individual is attested in Greco-Roman sources.
55. On the spurious connection, see Matthews (1975: 175 n.3).
56. Jones (1996: 132).
57. Although the *Mabinogion* collection is considered a later text than Geoffrey's *Historia*, it is thought to draw on common sources rather than simply adapt it (Jankulak 2010: 53–4). See Mac Cana (1992) for the *Mabinogion* in the context of Welsh literature (1–20) and for "The Dream of Macsen Wledig" specifically (78–84), including as a by-product of the "pseudo-historical movement dominated by Geoffrey."
58. "Maxim" appears twice in the so-called Harleian genealogies, written in old Welsh and dated to the twelfth century. On the significance of "Wledig," see Stevens (1938: 89–91).
59. Jankulak (2010: 59–63); Mac Cana (1992: 78). Although the texts seem to treat two distinct Elens, they both appear as "Elen Luyddawg."
60. In Welsh translations of Geoffrey's *Historia*, Maximian's father-in-law, Octavius, is rendered as "Eudaf," implying a semi-coherent tradition (Jankulak 2010: 63).
61. The inscription, now faded into obscurity, was transcribed by Edward Llwyd in 1696. For the text and discussion, see Rhys (1908: 39–57), who posits that the pillar is a column spoliated from a Roman temple (50).
62. Macsen's talking head bookends the album's narrative, appearing in the lyrics to both "Inner Sanctum" and "Damnatio Memoriae," as well as on a t-shirt produced in conjunction with the album. It is unclear whence SuidAkrA formed the conviction that this is part of Macsen's story, but Antonik has maintained it in both a YouTube video discussing the album (SuidAkrAofficial 2013) and an interview (Rose 2013). Pacatus does include the image of Maximus' severed head carried from the battlefield "half-alive with eyes not yet closed in total death" (41.2), but this is presented as a counterfactual to his capture at Save. A comic included with the CD release of the album situates "Inner Sanctum" during the capture of Krak des Chevaliers, a crusader castle, by the Egyptian Sultan Baibars in 1271, but I have found no connection between Macsen and that place. A reference to "Baphomet" in the lyrics to "Inner Sanctum" suggests a link to stories of John the Baptist, whose head was supposedly worshipped by the Templar Knights. The heads of John and Brân have been connected as representing common folklore themes (Fee 2001: 183–84, 196–99; Knight 2012: 35).
63. Mac Cana (1992: 80). Compare another scholar's "regret" that they "cannot place much credence in the British connections of Maximus... alleged in the *Mabinogion*" (Matthews 1975: 175 n. 3).

64. The lyrics also show the depths of SuidAkrA's Classical erudition, since they refer to Maximus' campaigns with Theodosius in Africa, attested only in Ammianus Marcellinus (29.5.6, 29.5.21).
65. SuidAkrAofficial (2013); transcribed from subtitles.
66. They therefore elide the role of Andragathius—Maximus' general—in vanquishing Gratian (Zosimus 4.35; Lunn-Rockliffe 2010: 319).
67. Curley (1994: 33). In *BMW*, Cynan has all the local women's tongues cut out.
68. Riggsby (2006: 5) could be said to endorse this as "interdiscursive" practice.
69. Wilson (2008) explores the similar ambivalence in using capitalist forms of music to rail against capitalism.

CHAPTER 3
SCREAMING ANCIENT GREEK HYMNS: THE CASE OF KAWIR AND THE GREEK BLACK METAL SCENE
Christodoulos Apergis

Black metal ("BM" hereafter) represents one of the most extreme, manifold, and well-studied forms of heavy metal music and subculture. Originally a term used to describe pioneering thrash/speed metal bands of the 1980s who made extensive use of Satanic and anti-Christian themes, BM emerged as a distinct and self-conscious movement in the first years of the 1990s in Norway, where the infamous deeds of a now mythologized circle of musicians made it known to a wide audience as the epitome of blasphemy; murders, grave desecrations, and, above all, a terrorizing series of church burnings by members of the scene brought considerable attention to that nascent extreme metal subgenre, which since then has proliferated throughout the globe building a concrete, yet extremely diverse, ideological universe, whose only cohesive sentiment seems to be a strong anti-Christian hatred.[1]

In this chapter I focus on Kawir, a modern Athenian BM band named after the cult of the Kabeiroi that has devoted its entire discography to the worship of the Greek Pantheon.[2] Active since 1993, Kawir was probably the first BM band to pave the way for a practice that would later develop into a minor trend within (and to some extent beyond) the Greek BM scene: setting ancient Greek hymns to music. Kawir's approach to ancient Greek hymnography, however, indicates something more than a literary interest in hieratic poetry: the band is actively connected to the contemporary pagan movement in Greece that attempts to reconstruct ancient Greek religious practices,[3] having close ties to the ΥΣΕΕ—Ύπατο Συμβούλιο των Ελλήνων Εθνικών (The Supreme Council of Ethnikoi Hellenes, "YSEE," hereafter)—one of the largest pagan organizations promoting the revival of ancient Greek religion in Greece and beyond.[4] After laying out some preliminaries, I present and discuss the use of ancient Greek hymns in the discography of Kawir. Afterwards, through the analysis of two of their songs that consist of (mostly) original lyrics, I shall attempt to demonstrate how this band has utilized the formal conventions of the Greek hymnic tradition to compose some hymns on their own and then how a BM song has eventually become a liturgical hymn in contemporary pagan worship. Finally, I investigate the influence of Kawir on the Greek BM scene, and the far-right ideology espoused by some bands that have followed Kawir's characteristic practice of setting Greek hymns to music.

A brief introduction to ancient Greek hymnography

Jan Maarten Bremer's (1981: 193) influential definition of the hymn as a "sung prayer" reflects plainly the importance of music—in some form of singing, rhythmical recitation, or instrumental accompaniment—for ancient Greek hymnography and worship. That said, apart from a few exceptional cases, the original music(al notation) of Greek hymns is completely unknown.[5] The surviving hymnic texts represent a plethora of different periods of antiquity and circumstances of performance: there are hymns from as early as the Archaic Period and as late as the fifth century CE; some are cultic—written to be sung and/or danced in a specific religious context—while others can be found within literary works of different genres, such as lyric, dramatic, or epic poetry, in prose, and even in sub-literary sources.[6]

Thus, the term "hymn" does not correspond to a specific genre, but designates a broad category, a genus, diversely sub-classified by ancient and modern scholars.[7] One should bear in mind that, in addition to the original function of the hymns—about which there seems to be no definite consensus among Classicists—the way these texts have been read and re-imagined more than two thousand years after their composition might be substantially different and equally or even more important regarding their reception in contemporary art. However, virtually all types of Greek hymns follow more or less consistently the same tripartite scheme: *epiklesis* (invocation)/*eulogia* (praise)/*euche* (prayer).[8] Addressing the god in the second or third person singular (techniques known as *Du-Stil* and *Er-Stil*, respectively), Greek hymns typically open with an invocatory part (*epiklesis*) that contains the name, epithets, and title of the divine addressee, and end with a prayer (*euche*), which requests some kind of aid. Frequently the longest part of a hymn, the middle (*eulogia*), constitutes the proper praising of the divinity, and may include listing the god's powers, mythical narratives, and attempts to persuade him or her to be propitious and fulfill the final request.[9] As we shall see in the second section of this chapter, Kawir have attempted to follow this conventional hymnic structure in their original lyrics, placing themselves within a poetic tradition that, as with almost every form of religious expression, is inherently characterized by a degree of conservatism.

Black metal for beginners

Black metal is an extreme subgenre and subculture of heavy metal mainly known for its anti-Christian, Satanic, and misanthropic rhetoric against the modern world. Having its musical roots in the thrash scene of the early 1980s, this idiom is generally characterized by high-pitched/shrieked vocals, heavily distorted guitars, frenetic ("blast-beat") drumming, and music productions that are usually raw and primitive.[10] Lyrical themes frequently include devil worship, anti-Christian propaganda, war, death, mysticism, and pagan traditions; National Socialism and racism are also apparent in some cases, forming a small, but recognizable movement within BM.[11] BM artists typically adopt a fierce image on stage; most of them appear in corpse-paint make-up,[12] wear spikes, and use occult symbols such as the inverted cross or the pentagram in their live performances.[13]

BM turned to pre-Christian religions from a very early point, considering Christianity as an alien influence imposed upon a pure, idealized pagan past.[14] The infamous church arsons in Norway, although portrayed as acts of a circle of "Satanic Terrorists" by the mass media were, in fact, mainly justified as retaliation against the imposition of Christianity on the Nordic culture and religion. Varg Vikernes, one of the most emblematic figures of these events, has stated that "there was not a single Satanist in the whole Black Metal scene in Norway in 1991–92."[15] To the extent that it attacks and/or has been "demonized" by Christianity, BM may become a vehicle to promote various religious or anti-religious beliefs, including theistic or atheistic Satanism,[16] pre-Christian religions,[17] as well as occult and esoteric philosophies.[18] All of these have been adopted in varying degrees of sincerity, devotion, and eclecticism by BM artists.

Black metal worship: Ancient Greek hymns in the discography of Kawir

From their first demo in 1993 and throughout their over-20-year discography, the Greek BM band Kawir have set to music numerous ancient Greek texts. The lyrics of their 2005 album *Arai*, for example, are curses and prayers from the so-called Greek Magical Papyri;[19] the songs "Titanomachy" (Τιτανομαχία/Grunwald, 2011) and "Nyx" (*To Cavirs*, 1997) consist of excerpts from Hesiod's *Theogony*; and "The Adored Cry of Olympus" from the 1994 EP *Eumenides* sets to music a poem by the sixth-century BCE lyric poet Alcaeus (fr. 338). The great majority of Kawir's songs, however, are musical adaptations of ancient Greek hymns, a fact that clearly reflects the band's religious orientation. According to Therthonax—the founder, composer, lyricist, and sole permanent member of the band throughout its numerous lineup changes—Kawir "consists of persons who are worshipping of the gods."[20] In this section I shall examine the use of ancient Greek hymns in Kawir's discography, discussing what it can tell us about the band's reading of these texts as well as their appropriation of, and engagement with, ancient Greek religion and worship.

Table 3.1 below lists the songs of Kawir that contain excerpts from ancient Greek hymns, and the corresponding hymnic texts. As one can easily see, the *Orphic Hymns* (a set of eighty-seven anonymous, short religious poems dating between 200 and 400 CE) are by far the most represented hymnic group in the discography of Kawir:[21] thirty-four out of the forty-three identified hymnic texts belong to this collection, while there are only five *Homeric Hymns* (a set of thirty-three anonymous poems from the Archaic Period attributed to Homer), two hymns of Proclus (a neo-Platonist philosopher of the fifth century CE), one hymn of Callimachus (a major Hellenistic poet), and one hymn of the second-century CE lyric poet Mesomedes.

Significantly, with the exception of the lyrical hymns of Mesomedes,[22] all these texts have been preserved together in the manuscript transmission as a compiled collection of

Table 3.1

	Song, album	Ancient Greek hymns used
1	"Sinn (The Blazing Queen)," *Promo '93*	Homeric Hymn ("*HH*" hereafter) *to Selene* (in English)
2	"Hecate's and Ianos," *To Cavirs*	Proclus' *Hymn to Hecate and Janus*
3	"Hymn to Zeus," ———	Orphic Hymn ("*OH*" hereafter) *to Zeus*; *OH to the Sun*
4	"Hermes the Psychopomp," ———	*OH to Hermes*
5	"Daughters of Night," ———	*OH to the Erinyes*
6	"Hymn to Seline," ———	*OH to Selene*
7	"Persefone," ———	*OH to Persephone*
8	"Artemis," ———	Callimachus' *Hymn to Artemis*; *OH to Artemis*
9	"Δαίμων (Εμπουσα)," *Δαίμων*	*OH to Hecate*
10	"Moirae," *Ophiolatreia*	*OH to the Fates*; *OH to Dike*
11	"Rhea (Meter Theon)," ———	*OH to Physis*; *OH to Rhea*; *OH to the Mother of the Gods*
12	"Poseidon," ———	*OH to Poseidon*
13	"Nemesis," ———	*OH to Nemesis*; *OH to Dike*
14	"Ares (The God of War)," ———	*OH to Ares*; *HH to Ares*
15	"To Pallas," ———	Proclus' *Hymn to Athena*; *OH to Athena*
16	"Hephaistos," ———	*OH to Hephaestus*
17	"Ophiolatreia," ———	*OH to Protogonos*
18	"To Uranus," ———	*OH to Uranus*
19	"Kouretes," ———	*OH to the Kouretes* (37); *OH to the Kouretes* (38); *OH to Korybas*
20	"Daemon," *Isotheos*	*OH to Daimon*
21	"Hymn to Winds," ———	*OH to Boreas*; *OH to Zephyros*; *OH to Notos*
22	"To Demeter," ———	*OH to Eleusinian Demeter*
23	"Hail Bacchus," ———	*OH to Dionysus*
24	"Hades," ———	*OH to Pluto*
25	"Thanatos," *Νυχτός τελετήσιν: 20 Years of Recordings*	*OH to Death*

26	"Io Pan,"———	*OH to Pan*
27	"Εἰς βασιλέα Ἥλιον," *Πάτερ Ἥλιε, Μῆτερ Σελάνα*	Mesomedes' *Hymn to the Sun* (in modern Greek)
28	"Διόνυσος,"———	*OH to Dionysus Trieretikos*; *HH* (26) *to Dionysus*
29	"Ἡρακλῆς μαινόμενος,"———	*OH to Heracles*
30	"Εἰς Διόσκουρους,"———	*HH* (33) *to the Dioscuri*
31	"Η ταύριαν Ἄρτεμις,"———	*OH to Artemis* (in modern Greek); *HH* (27) *to Artemis* (in modern Greek)

hexametric hymns.[23] However, they differ greatly from each other in terms of date, style, and context of performance. The *Orphic Hymns*, carrying in their headings instructions on the proper incense to be burned when performed, are generally considered texts of a liturgical nature, and were probably used in the mystic rites of a small Orphic community in Asia Minor during the first centuries of this era.[24] On the contrary, the much earlier *Homeric Hymns*, as well as those by Callimachus, were not cult songs in any real sense; the former, distinguished as "rhapsodic," served probably as preludes to the recitation of epic poetry in rhapsodic competitions;[25] the latter, which exhibit a strong poetic influence by the hymns of the Homeric collection, are considered purely literary creations.[26] The late hymns of Proclus constitute a different case; although they, along with the literary hymns of Aristotle or the Stoic Cleanthes, have been classified as "philosophical," they were probably performed in a context that involved ritual acts. Proclus has been depicted as a deeply religious person, a theurgist and theologian who "preferred hieratic over philosophy," having been initiated into various mystery cults.[27]

Kawir's apparent emphasis on the hymns of the Orphic collection can thus be accounted for by the religious character of these texts in general, and their use in mystic rites in particular.[28] This hypothesis gains strength from the various references by the band to ancient Greek mystery cults. Apart, of course, from the cult of the Kabeiroi, after which the band is named, Kawir's second album, *Epoptia*, bears the name of the final initiation stage of the Eleusinian Mysteries (ἐποπτεία); the lyrics of "Isotheos" from the homonymous 2012 album translate a passage from the Magical Papyri connected to the Mithraic mysteries;[29] the title of their 2014 compilation album *Νυχτός Τελετῆσιν: 20 Years of Recordings* uses a word (τελετή) that exclusively refers to Greek mystery cults;[30] and their 2016 boxed set *ΑΜΥΗΤΟΝ ΜΗ ΕΙΣΙΕΝΑΙ* ("Let the uninitiated not enter") is named after an inscription (*Samothrace* II 1, 62) which prohibited the uninitiated from entering the sanctuary of the Great Gods in Samothrace (see Figure 3.1).[31] These references clearly demonstrate the band's fascination with the Greek Mysteries.

Kawir also take great pains to present their live performances as religious rituals. The live shows named "A Rite to the Hellenic Pantheon," "Nocturnal Ritual in Larisa," and

Figure 3.1 Kawir, *ΑΜΥΗΤΟΝ ΜΗ ΕΙΣΙΕΝΑΙ* (2016; Album cover).

"Kawir's ceremony in the Cerumnos Pagan Fest" are clearly indicative of this tendency. During its live performances, the band typically appears in cloaks reminiscent of the ancient Greek *himation*, and in some cases, the traditional BM corpse-paint make-up is replaced by masks, pointing to a cult atmosphere.[32] Furthermore, the singer of Kawir frequently raises his right hand while performing the hymns, a typical stance for praying in ancient Greece that has also been adopted by the contemporary devotees of Greek religion. BM performance in general seems to share some features of a mystery cult: its extreme and transcendental aesthetics have the effect of excluding the "uninitiated" and enhancing a sense of distinct identity, unity, and mystical experience among the "true" followers.[33]

Kawir's performance of Greek hymns, however, is not limited to BM live shows. Through its sister acoustic project ΚΑΒΕΙΡΟΣ, co-founded in 2007 by Therthonax, the band is actively engaged in worship. ΚΑΒΕΙΡΟΣ regularly perform ancient Greek hymns using guitars, bagpipes, and replicas of ancient Greek instruments (psaltery, lyre) in the revival of ancient Greek religious festivals. These have taken place in the last decade or so under the auspices of official religious organizations such as the YSEE and the Religious Community Labrys.[34] Therthonax seems to underline the importance of ΚΑΒΕΙΡΟΣ's religious role when he states in an interview that "all the members of the band are also members in YSEE . . . one of the few organizations that can perform, and the only one that has the authorization to practice ceremonies in open and in archaeological places."³⁵ Significantly, the *Orphic Hymns* are one of the main liturgical texts used in these religious festivals. Even if, as West (1983: 29) suggests, the hymns of the Orphic collection attest to "a cheerful inexpensive dabbling in religion by a literary minded burgher and his friends," they hold a prominent place in the religious practice of Greek neo-paganism.

A second aspect of Kawir's use of Greek hymns which deserves our attention is that, in some cases, Therthonax attempts a kind of syncretism, combining excerpts from hymns dedicated to different deities to praise a specific god. "Hymn to Zeus," for instance, contains excerpts from the *OH to the Sun* (row 3 of the table), and Rhea is praised in the homonymous song with excerpts from the *OH to Physis* and the *OH to the Mother of Gods* (row 11). Similarly, Dike, the goddess of Justice, is associated with Nemesis and the Fates in "Nemesis" and "Moirae" respectively (rows 13 and 10), while in "Kouretes" the Cretan "demons" are apparently identified with their Phrygian counterparts Korybantes (row 19). These identifications and associations between gods, however, are not arbitrary; all follow well-known syncretistic tendencies of Greek religion, common in late antiquity, and particularly prevalent in Orphic theological thought.³⁶ Such appropriation of Greek hymnic elements helps to inform the extent to which Kawir both engage with and perform the ancient material.

Hymnic conventions in the black metal mold: Kawir's contemporary hymns

The extensive use of ancient Greek hymns in the discography of Kawir would alone suffice to make it a fascinating case study of Classical reception. However, the band's engagement with the Greek hymnic tradition goes a step further; Kawir have also tried to incorporate some formal characteristics of ancient Greek hymnography in their original lyrics, composing songs that follow the traditional tripartite scheme of Greek hymns (*epiklesis/eulogia/euche*). Through the analysis of Kawir's songs "Zeus" and "Hymn to Apollo" from the albums *Epoptia* (1999) and *Isotheos* (2012) respectively, I examine how the conventions of ancient Greek hymnography are re-contextualized within the strongly anti-Christian framework of BM, as well as how a BM song has made its way into the religious practice of Greek neo-paganism.

First, I consider the song "Zeus" (track length, 8:55). The lyrics are as follows (I have added line numbers for convenience):

> We call upon Zeus,   1
> King of the Gods,
> Great Father guide us.
> Ἀρχὴ πάντων
> Πάντων τε τελευτή.   5
>
> Zeus is the Sun and the Moon
> Zeus is the winds and the storms

Zeus is the earth and the stars
Zeus is the unbending flame
Zeus is the Night and the Day   10
Zeus was born male and a nymph.

We remember the time,
when your Mother hides you
from the wrath of your Father Kronos
in a cave somewhere in Crete,   15
and Amalthia feeds you
with the horns of wisdom,
and Koryvantes dancing around you
the dance of men,
the dance of war.   20
Oh! You are the Archon of Lightning.

The years has [sic] passed away and then
the Christians have arrived,
they killed your Priests,
destroyed the Temples.   25
Oh! Zeus now guides us in a justified war,
this filthy sickness, must eclipse.
They tried many times to kill your children.
This divine Hellenic race.

And now the only vision that we have is ... (×2)   30
Revenge, Revenge, Revenge (×3)
STRIKE WITH LIGHTNING. (×3)

"Zeus" begins with a majestic melody performed by a solo flute (0:00–0:23), arguably to stand in for the ancient Greek aulos, the main instrument that accompanied the singing of hymns in antiquity.[37] When the rest of the instruments join, the flute melody continues, harmonized by the bass guitar, with distorted guitar chords in accompaniment; the theme remains the same throughout the first verse.

The first verse of "Zeus" (lns. 1–5 / 0:35–0:52) corresponds to the *epiklesis*, the invocation that opens Greek hymns, establishing contact between the speaking person(s) and the divine addressee. Typically, it contains the name of the god or the goddess addressed as well as attributes (epithets and titles) to win his or her attention and favor. This is exactly what we have in the first verse of "Zeus": the god is first invoked by name (1) and then is addressed as "King of the Gods" (2) and "Father" (3), two of the most common epithets of Zeus in Greek hymns and Greek literature in general.[38] In the following lines (3–5), the band use a formulaic Orphic phrase meaning "the beginning and the end of everything," which appears both in the *OH to Zeus*, 7 and *OH to Uranus*, 2.

The second verse (lns. 6–11 / 1:32–2:06) introduces the *eulogia*, which is usually the longest section of a hymn. Its main function is to praise the powers of the divine addressee in an appropriate and recognizable manner as well as to persuade him to be propitious and fulfill the final request(s). Although the form it takes differs considerably from case to case, common traits include anaphoric (repeated) address, *hypomnesis* (reminder of earlier benefits conferred by the deity or earlier worship offered by petitioners), *ekphrasis* (description of the god, his haunts, his actions) and, of course, narratives.[39]

The transition to this section in "Zeus" is signified by a change both in the lyrical content and music. The opening theme now gives way to another melody, and Kawir, obviously influenced by the Orphic fr. 243,[40] praise the oneness of Zeus as the personification of nature's antithetical elements in an anaphoric manner, with the word "Zeus" repeated at the beginning of each line. The *eulogia* continues in the next verse (lns. 10–16 / 2:18–3:27) with another typical feature of this section, a mythical narrative. Addressing Zeus in the second person singular (*Du-Stil*), Kawir recount the myth about his nursing in Crete by Amalthea and the shield-clashing Kouretes, who are apparently identified with their Phrygian counterparts Korybantes. Significantly, the upbringing of Zeus in Crete can also be found in the *eulogia* of Callimachus' *Hymn to Zeus* (10–14, 45–54),[41] and in the inscribed cult hymn to *Dictaean Zeus* from the site of Palaikastro on Crete (9–10).[42] This third verse ends with a direct invocation to Zeus (ln. 21),[43] which leads to a guitar solo by Therthonax (3:26–4:00).

When the solo ends, the music changes considerably. The distorted guitars, bass, and drums fade out, and for one-and-a-half minutes (4:01–5:37), synthesized strings and non-distorted guitars complement each other in an atmospheric instrumental duet. This creates an ethereal state preparing for the hearing of the tragedy: after this part, the drums rapidly build up tension, and when the rest of the instruments join in, the feeling of the song shifts into a mix of melancholy and hatred. Now Kawir, addressing Zeus again in the second person, recount the crimes of the Christians against the Greek religion ("They killed your priests, destroyed your Temples"). Christianity is described as a "filthy sickness," which "must eclipse" (ln. 27), and the band ask the god to guide his "children" in a "justified war" (ln. 26). Although the musical theme is now different, more aggressive and less grandiose, this non-mythical narrative (lns. 22–30) belongs in the *eulogia*, too, since it serves as an argument, a justification for Kawir's final request to the divine addressee. It is a strange type of *hypomnesis*: instead of using well-known motifs, such as *da quia dedi* ("give because I have given") or *da quia dedisti* ("give because you have given"), the band remind Zeus of what has been taken from his "children," and call on him to remedy this injustice.

A distorted and slow repetition of the phrase "and now the only vision that we have is," accompanied only by fast-paced guitars and drum-breaks, emphasizes the transition to the final part of the song, which corresponds to the prayer section (*euche*). "Zeus" now bursts into a frenetic tempo, with all the instruments played aggressively. The request is unambiguous: the word "revenge" is screamed nine times for one minute (7:20–8:20) within the musical maelstrom, then followed by an equally violent, triple repetition of the phrase "strike with lightning," which brings the song to an end.

In worshipping Zeus, Kawir adhere to the formal conventions of ancient Greek hymnography. "Zeus" begins with a typical *epiklesis* (lns. 1–5), continues with a long *eulogia* which includes the praise of Zeus (lns. 6–11), a *Du-Stil* mythical narrative about his upbringing in Crete (lns. 12–21), and a *hypomnesis* to persuade him to grant the final request (lns. 22–30), and concludes with an explicit *euche* (lns. 30–31). However, while Greek hymns usually end with a wish about the health, well-being, or prosperity of the worshipping community,[44] the conclusion of "Zeus" asks the divine addressee to cause harm, in a matter that recalls the requests of Greek revenge curses. This provides us with a great insight into how BM conceptualizes hymnody and religion. The "justified war" and the "revenge" that Kawir request from Zeus epitomize BM's retaliatory polemic against the imposition of Christianity upon "pagan" culture and religion. The black metalers who terrorized Norway with their pyromaniac interests justified the church arsons as a reprisal: the twelfth-century Fantoft stave church in Bergen, the first to be set on fire, symbolized one of the first emblems of Norway's violent Christianization, having been built on sacred pagan grounds.[45] Greece, too, like Norway, was Christianized and constitutionally recognizes Christianity as a "prevailing religion." Although Greek churches have not been burned, BM's fiery rhetoric is virtually the same. "Zeus" embodies the genre-defining anti-Christian sentiment of BM and exemplifies how it has shaped Kawir's reception of the ancient Greek hymnic tradition.

Before turning to the next song, it is worth noting that "Zeus" is not the only song of Kawir to follow the tripartite scheme of Greek hymns. "Gaia," for example, from the same album, similarly begins with an *epiklesis* ("Oh Gaia/Great Goddess,/who gives life to everything that grows and lives on the infinite body") and ends with a distinct request corresponding to the *euche* ("Show me the ancient secrets/Give me the universe's being/Give me eternal life/Give me the knowledge of the black arts for the final purpose"), while its middle part praises the goddess with a mythical *Du-Stil* narrative about her contribution to the creation of gods (e.g. "Thou mingled with the universe and gave birth to fearful gods"). Therefore, it is a plausible assumption that Kawir consciously try to employ the tripartite structure of Greek hymns in their songs, continuing a long tradition of hieratic poetry.

The next song in this discussion, the "Hymn to Apollo" (track length, 9:43), seems to have a special significance for Kawir, since its lyrics are written by Vlassis Rassias, the Secretary General of the YSEE, and constitute an original attempt in ancient Greek (blended, however, with elements from the Modern Greek language).[46] This is perhaps the reason why "Hymn to Apollo" is the only song of Kawir that does not contain typical BM screams, but is sung throughout with clean vocal lines.

The lyrics are as follows, accompanied by my translation into English (and with line numbers added):

Φοῖβε Θεὲ	1	Phoebus God
ἄναξ πυρφόρε		lord fire-bringer
τριποδιλάλε, ξανθὲ τοξευτά,		speaking from the tripod, blond archer
Ἄπολλον Θεὲ		Apollo God

μάντι, δαφνηφόρε,	5	prophet, laurel-bearer,
δαῖμον καθάρσιε καὶ αὐξητά,		purifying and increaser daemon
Ἐσένα καλοῦμε		we invoke Thee
Ἐσένα ὑμνοῦμε		we praise Thee
Πύθιε, Λατῷε, παιάν, κοσμητά. (×2)		Pythian, son of Leto, healer, orderer.

Following the pattern of "Zeus," "Hymn to Apollo" opens with a solo flute playing a grandiose melody, which is soon reinforced by distorted guitars playing the same phrase but in a fifth lower (00:17–1:18). Unlike in "Zeus," however, this musical theme is heard throughout the better part of the song in a repetitive flow. The nine lines of "Hymn to Apollo" are repeated in two verses (1:19–2:03 and 2:35–3:19), and from this point onwards there is a long instrumental part that consists of a guitar solo in the same melody (3:20–4:25), an acoustic bridge with flutes and whispers (4:26–6:18), and a concluding passage (outro) in which the guitars play a lead part along with the flute (6:19–end).

Thus, from a musical standpoint, the lyrics of "Hymn to Apollo" cannot be divided into sections. This continuous form is also reflected in this song's hymnic structure, which is modeled on shorter *Orphic Hymns*. As is the case with the poems of the latter collection, "Hymn to Apollo" does not have a clear transition between the *epiklesis* and the *eulogia*, consisting mainly of clustering cultic epithets.[47] Only two verb phrases (lns. 7–8) break the rule, thus signifying the division of this "hymn" into two main parts: an extended *epiklesis*—which also serves as *eulogia* (1–6)—and a closing section corresponding to the *euche* (7–9).

The first part of "Hymn to Apollo" consists of a list of cultic epithets taken from various ancient texts. They have a substantial role here, invoking Apollo by name ("Ἄπολλον Θεέ"), and praising his main attributes as god of light ("Φοῖβε"), archer ("ξανθὲ τοξευτά"), oracle ("μάντι," "τριποδιλάλε"), and god who cleanses from guilt or defilement ("καθάρσιε"). Two of the epithets used in this part, however, do not traditionally belong to the worship of this god: αὐξητής ("increaser," 6) is typically applied to Pan and to Zeus,[48] and πυρφόρος ("fire-bringer," 2) is used for various other deities, including Helios (the personification of the Sun),[49] Zeus, and Asclepius.[50] But this is another attempt at religious syncretism that evinces Kawir's tendency to echo Orphic theology, as for example in Orphic fragment 413.11–13: "Helios, also called Apollo, renowned archer,/Phoibos far-shooting, accurate seer of all,/and Asklepios, healer of diseases, all that is one."[51]

The *euche* of the "Hymn to Apollo" is introduced with a direct invocation to the divine addressee (ln. 7), and this is the first time a verb appears in this song. The verb used here, "καλοῦμε" ("we invoke"), is a typical formula for the transition to the final hymnic section, especially in the Orphic corpus.[52] Like the majority of the *Orphic Hymns*, however, "Hymn to Apollo" does not seem to ask for a specific divine favor in its prayer. As Graf (2009: 174) argues, "Everything these hymns demand from their gods is rather general—that the gods be present at the ritual;" thus, we can consider the verb "καλοῦμε" as a similar petition for Apollo to come in person, though milder than those typically found in the cletic hymns, which usually express the request for the god's epiphany with an imperative expression (ἐλθέ, "come"; φάνηθι, "appear," etc).[53]

The next verb phrase, "Ἐσένα ὑμνοῦμε" ("we praise Thee") is rather unconventional for the closing and usually appears at the beginning of hymns.[54] "Hymn to Apollo" ends with four consecutive epithets (9) praising specific attributes of Apollo: "Πύθιε" refers to his attribute as the protector of the Delphic oracle, "Λατῷε" to his genealogy ("son of Leto"), and "παιάν" to his power as god of healing. The last epithet, however, "κοσμητά" ("orderer"), is found nowhere else in praise of this god, being a cult title of his father, Zeus.[55] The fact that it is attributed to Apollo here further demonstrates the religious syncretism mentioned above. The epithets that Rassias uses in praise of Apollo seem to stress the importance of this god for Greek religion. They hail Apollo as κοσμητὴς, αὐξητὴς, and πυρφόρος to equate him with Zeus and Helios, two of the most powerful gods of the Greek Pantheon.

However, the main reason I examine "Hymn to Apollo" is not so much its hymnic form, poetics, or the religious syncretism it implies, but because it is a striking example of the extent to which BM may engage with religion and worship. More than just a song performed live at performances staged as religious rituals, Kawir's "Hymn to Apollo" has been established as a cultic hymn in the contemporary practice of the ancient Greek religion in Greece. With its music composed by Therthonax and its lyrics written by Rassias, this song is regularly chanted in the ancient Greek religious festivals that the YSEE revives, being accompanied by ritual acts such as the libation of red wine (σπονδή) or the burning of incense (θυμίαμα). Some examples of the song's performance in religious ceremonies include the 2012 and 2013 celebration of Aphrodisia,[56] a festival in praise of Aphrodite, and the 2012 celebration of Thargelia, a major Athenian festival in honor of Apollo and Artemis.[57] In every instance, the last three lines of the song, which I marked above as its prayer section, are repeated three times in a gradually increasing volume, thus reinforcing the assumption that this song should be considered a celtic hymn. What interests us here, however, is that a song composed by a BM band (although non-BM in its musical form) has apparently taken a prominent place in the contemporary worship of the Greek pantheon, standing alongside ancient hymns, and bearing a great religious significance for the devotees of ancient Greek religion, who chant it to express their faith.

The influence of Kawir and the extreme politics within the Greek black metal scene

Kawir's engagement with the Greek hymnic tradition appears to have influenced a good number of BM bands in Greece and, to a lesser extent, beyond. In 1998—the year following the release of Kawir's first full album—four Greek BM bands (Bacchia Neraida, Βάκχειος, Dithyramvos, and Uranus) went on to set Greek hymns to music.[58] As one can see in the appendix to this chapter, at least twenty-one BM bands have at some point used ancient Greek hymns in their songs, either in the original language or in an English or Modern Greek translation. With the exception of Behemoth (Poland), Hades Adorned (the Netherlands), Verberis (New Zealand), and Jose Beausejour (France), all of them hail from Greece, and at least four (Silent Dominion, Morbid Fog, Dizziness, and Archaeos) refer to Kawir as one of their main influences.[59] In this last section I offer a brief look at the reception of ancient Greek hymns by these bands as well as at the far-right ideology espoused by some of them.

These other BM adaptations of Greek hymns are largely similar to the ones by Kawir. The Orphic collection is again prevalent with thirty-five hymns, followed by fourteen *Homeric Hymns*, and one hymn of Proclus. Unlike Kawir, however, and their exclusive focus on the gods of the Greek Pantheon, the majority of the bands in question tend to follow a more eclectic approach, hybridizing Greek religious elements with references to Satanism and various occult symbolisms. The wide range of deities praised in the *Orphic Hymns* enables this collection to be embraced by diverse audiences: the *OH to Death*, for example, seems perfectly suitable to the Satanic milieu of the band Diabolical Principles, which has set it to music ("Orphic, to Death"); similarly, the *OH to Pluto* (the ruler of the Underworld), which appears in songs by at least five BM bands, is certainly at home within the morbid aesthetics of BM. Furthermore, the *Orphic Hymns* have been often viewed as texts of an occult nature, and this is another good reason why they are seemingly preferred by BM artists.

The nature of the BM bands that have used Greek hymns in their songs reflects an important (and generally well-discussed) aspect of BM's ideology. Although politics is not the main thrust of this chapter, one cannot overlook the fact that one of these bands (arguably the most popular alongside Kawir) is led by a member of the Greek Parliament for the ultra-nationalist (formerly openly neo-Nazi) party of Golden Dawn (Χρυσή Αυγή). Giorgos Germenis, the front man and leader (under the stage pseudonym Kaiadas) of the legendary Greek BM band Naer Mataron is, in fact, one of several MPs of Golden Dawn to have been arrested and held in pre-trial detention for the maximum limit of eighteen months while the party faced charges of forming a criminal organization.[60] Although Naer Mataron is not typically considered a National Socialist BM (NSBM) band, the political agenda of its leader is clearly related to the alt-right movement within BM.[61] Kaiadas was also a member of the homonymous NSBM band Kaiadas, as well as of three other NSBM bands (Bannerwar, Nekysia, and Stosstrupp).

Similarly, although none of the other BM bands that have used Greek hymnic texts in their songs self-identify as NSBM or is openly racist, the leading members of three of them have at some point formed NSBM bands, two of which are directly connected to Golden Dawn. MP, the founder and sole member of Bacchia Neraida, which in 1998 set twelve *Homeric Hymns* to music, has also formed Wolfnacht, a NSBM band bearing the banner of Golden Dawn in its logo. Voreas, the sole member of the short-lived band Βάκχειος, which in the same year set to music the *OH to Perikionios*, was also a founding member of F.R.O.S.T, whose logo is the emblem of Nazi Germany, while one of its few songs is entitled "Golden Dawn." Finally, the previous band of Acherontas V. Priest, the founder and frontman of Acherontas, which between 2015 and 2016 set seven *Orphic Hymns* to music, was Stutthof, a NSBM band named after one of the Nazi death camps in Poland.

As a result of the over-generalizing tendency to consider all pagan BM bands fascists or adherents to far-right ideologies, Kawir have also been accused of being NSBM or somehow associated with Golden Dawn. However, there is nothing in the lyrics, interviews, or long career of the band that indicates or implies such a fact, and Therthonax categorically denies these accusations, insisting that "Kawir promotes Greek Polytheism" and "has nothing to do with politics or political parties."[62] Christos "Pandion" Panopoulos, a member of ΚΑΒΕΙΡΟΣ, live member of Kawir (flutes, bagpipes), and one of the founders of the Religious Community Labrys has stated in a relevant interview that:

> Having as a defining characteristic a) religion and b) the Hellenic culture, we find almost all modern political ideologies more or less incompatible with our culture ... and even more so parties with fascist ideologies that are not only pro-Christian but totalitarian in the deepest and worst monotheistic example, which of course is the exact opposite of our ancestral culture. As such we see the Golden Dawn as a threat and even if we try to publicly abstain from political debates (in order to keep the religious character as our primary guide without further and for the most part objective distinctions) individually we usually raise our voices against such phenomena.[63]

While Therthonax's claim that "Kawir has nothing to do with politics" may sound slightly odd, given the band's active engagement in a movement that in a sense seeks to re-capture a pre-Christian Greek past, it is evident that the founder of Kawir wishes to emphasize the band's religious (as opposed to political) character as well as its detachment from the contemporary political scene. At any rate, Kawir's profile stands in stark contrast to the far-right ideology embraced by some bands who have followed its characteristic practice of screaming ancient Greek hymns.

Conclusion

Kawir's rich reception of the ancient Greek hymnic tradition constitutes a remarkable example of heavy metal's engagement with the Classical world. This pioneering BM band has not only set to music a considerable number of ancient Greek hymns, but has also attempted to incorporate various poetic conventions of ancient Greek hymnography into its original lyrics, composing songs that follow the traditional tripartite structure of Greek hymns. "Zeus" exemplifies this approach, and provides us with a great insight into the way BM conceptualizes hymnody and religion through its pervasive anti-Christian stance. Kawir's appropriation of ancient Greek hymnography represents something much more than a literary exercise; it is motivated by sincere religious conviction. The band openly promote the revival of ancient Greek religion and, through its sister project ΚΑΒΕΙΡΟΣ, is actively engaged in worship, performing praise songs to honor the gods of the Greek Pantheon in the religious festivals that the YSEE revives. Kawir's interaction with the Greek neo-pagan movement is so vital that one of its songs, "Hymn to Apollo," the lyrics of which were written by the Secretary General of the YSEE, has been established as a contemporary liturgical hymn among the Greek pagan community.

In addition to Kawir (and, to some extent, due to its influence), at least twenty-one more BM bands have at some point set ancient Greek hymns to music, making up an impressive total of ninety-three Greek hymnic texts being sung, recited, or screamed in BM songs. The vast majority of them are from the *Orphic Hymns*, and the popularity of this collection can be accounted for by the liturgical character of these texts (at least for the religiously oriented Kawir), as well as by their syncretistic nature and consequent appeal to occultists, which have made these hymns attractive to diverse audiences. Another important result of the study is Kawir's stark contrast to the extreme-right political ideology espoused by some bands of the Greek BM scene, among which the most notable example is Naer Mataron, whose front man is also an MP for the Greek ultra-nationalist party Golden Dawn.

Black metal—whether violent, politically charged, or captivated by ancient cultures, paganism, and the occult—is fairly consistent with its fundamental and relentless aversion to Christianity. From the infamous church burnings in Norway to Kawir's BM hymnody and religious devotion, this extreme metal subgenre has thematized religion, walking a tightrope between blasphemy and faith.[64]

Appendix

Table 3.2 BM bands who have used ancient Greek hymns in their songs

Βάκχειος, *Μάκαρ Κερασφόρε*, 1998	"Μάκαρ Κερασφόρε"	OH *to Perikionius*
Dithyramvos, *Pagan Perpetuation*, 1998	"Keravniou Dios"	OH *to Zeus Keraunios*
Bacchia Neraida, *Εις τους δώδεκα θεούς του Ολύμπου*, 1998	"To Zeus"	HH *to Zeus*
	"To Hera"	HH *to Hera*
	"To Athena"	HH (11) *to Athena*
	"To Poseidon"	HH *to Poseidon*
	"To Apollo"	HH (21) *to Apollo*
	"To Artemis"	HH (9) *to Artemis*
	"To Dimitra"	HH (2) *to Demeter*
	"To Hermes"	HH (4) *to Hermes*
	"To Aphrodite"	HH (6) *to Aphrodite*
	"To Mars"	HH *to Ares*
	"To Hephaestus"	HH *to Hephaestus*
	"To Hestia"	HH (24) *to Hestia*

Uranus, *The Clang of Lances*, 1998	"Χθόνιε –Σκηπτούχε"	OH to Pluto
	"Angaeus"	OH to Uranus
Naer Mataron, *Skotos Aenaon*, 2000	"Iketis"	OH to the Sun
Unholy Archangel, *Blessed by Aris*, 2000	"Blessed by Aris"	HH to Ares (in English)
Hades Adorned, *Crata Repoa*, 2002	"Orphic hymn to Hekate"	OH to Hecate (in English)
Athos, *Return to the Hellenic Lands*, 2004	"Nykta"	OH to Night
Athos, *The Awakening of Athos*, 2007	"Oneirou"	OH to the Oneiroi
Athos, *Crossing the River of Charon*, 2008	"Melinoe"	OH to Melinoe
	"Persephone"	OH to Persephone
	"Plutonas"	OH to Pluto
Ancestral Rhymes, *The Cosmic Law*, 2008	"Hymn to the Sun"	Proclus' *Hymn to the Sun* (in Modern Greek)
Behemoth, *Evangelion*, 2009	"Daimonos"	OH to Dionysus Bassareus
Lord Impaler, *Admire the Cosmos Black*, 2011	"Hymn to the Nymphe"	OH to the Nymphs
Morbid Fog, *Αρχέγονο Σκότος*, 2012	"An Ancient Chant to Worship Hades"	OH to Pluto
Silent Dominion, *Defending the Ancient Spirit*, 2013	"To Charites"	OH to the Charites
	"Amiable Goddess Hecate"	OH to Hecate
	"Modest Daughter"	OH to Athena
Silent Dominion, *Spiritual Flesh Around the Cycles of Inexistence*, 2013	"Themis"	OH to Themis
Dizziness, *Offermort Heritage*, 2013	"Triumph of a Superior Idea"	OH to Nemesis
Morbid Fog, *Daemones*, 2014	"Zephyros, the Son of Astraeos"	OH to Zephyrus
Diabolical Principles, *Manifesto of Death*, 2014	"Orphic, to Death"	OH to Death
Jose Beausejour, *Monetized Pagan Gods IV*, 2014	"To Aphrodite 1–6"	HH (5) to Aphrodite (in English)

Acherontas, *Ma-IoN (Formulas of Reptilian Unification,* 2015	"The Awakening of Astral Orphic Mysteries—Behind the Eyes of Irida"	*OH to the Sun; OH to the Stars* (in Modern Greek)
Nåstrond/Acherontas, *Chthonic Libations,* 2016	"Beneath the Infernal Seats (Hymn to the Titans)"	*OH to the Titans*
	"Secret Gates of Earth Unlocking (Hymn to Pluto)"	*OH to Pluto*
	"Human Life to Age Abundant Spare (Hymn to Thanatos)"	*OH to Death*
	"Mysteries of the Best Chthonic (Hymn to Persephone)"	*OH to Persephone*
	"The Oracle who Admonished the Unworthy (Hymn to Oneiroi)"	*OH to the Oneiroi*
Archaeos, *Archegono Miasma,* 2016	"Hymn to Zeus"	*OH to Zeus Keraunios*
Archaeos, *Forgotten Art of Sacrifice,* 2016	"Fiery Winds Over Acherontas"	*OH to Pluto* (in Modern Greek)
	"Hail Pan, The Horned One"	*OH to Pan* (in Modern Greek)
	"Hymn to Nymphs"	*OH to the Nymphs* (in Modern Greek)
Verberis, *Vexamen,* 2016	"Protogonos"	*OH to Protogonos* (in English)
Celtefog, *Sounds of the Olden Days,* 2016	"Nykta"	*OH to the Stars*
Aherusia, *Prometheus: Seven Principles on How to Be Invincible,* 2017	"Ὠκεανός (Ocean)"	*OH to Oceanus*

Notes

1. There are, however, some Christian BM bands, but they are a distinct minority and a clear response to the prevailing trend in the genre.
2. The cult of the Kabeiroi (also known as the Mysteries of the Kabeiroi) was an ancient Greek mystery cult in praise of the enigmatic gods Kabeiroi mainly attested on Lemnos and at Thebes. See Bremmer (2014: 37–48). The connection of Kawir's name to the Kabeiroi derives from Modern Greek usage; the Kabeiroi are pronounced as /kaviri/ in Modern Greek and Kawir as /kavir/.
3. The revival of pre-Christian religious traditions is a growing global tendency, diversely manifested in Europe and overseas. The Greek neo-pagan movement belongs to so-called

reconstructionist (as opposed to eclectic) paganism and comprises various groups in Greece and worldwide. For a recent discussion, see Voulgarakis (2014: 88–98).

4. For a study focusing on the YSEE, see Fotiou (2014).
5. To this it should be added that not all of the texts classified as hymns were originally meant to be sung. Aelius Aristeides' hymns, for instance, are in prose form.
6. For a brief survey of the extant remains, see Furley and Bremer (2001a).
7. Ancient theory subdivides hymns into many different forms (prosodion, paean, etc.), for which the surviving texts do not provide enough evidence. Modern scholarship classifies hymns depending on the context of their performance (cultic, rhapsodic, literary, etc.).
8. Several alternative appellations have been proposed; I follow the terminology suggested in Furley and Bremer (2001a: 51).
9. The formal elements of hymns are discussed in more detail in the second section of this chapter. For a comprehensive description of the hymnic form, see Furley and Bremer (2001a: 50–64).
10. For a detailed description of the BM sound, see Hagen (2011: 183–88).
11. On the rise of nationalism, racism, and the National Socialist BM (NSBM) scene, see Olson (2011).
12. Corpse paint is a type of white and black, demonic-like make-up mainly in the areas of face and neck, while sometimes it is mixed with real or fake blood.
13. Kahn-Harris (2007: 38).
14. The Swedish band Bathory is a prominent example; its fourth album, *Blood Fire Death* (1988), thematically based on the Norse gods, was among the first BM releases that deviated from the purely Satanic symbolism of the so-called First Wave of BM. For more on the importance of this album in the rise of Viking metal and thus of Mediterranean metal, see Fletcher (this volume).
15. See Midtskogen (2009).
16. For a discussion on the various types of Satanism in BM, see Mørk (2009).
17. For an overview of pagan BM and pagan metal generally, see Weinstein (2014b).
18. On Occult BM, see Granholm (2013). For more on the influence of esotericism and the occult on metal, see the chapters by Secord and Olabarria (this volume).
19. The Greek Magical Papyri is a collection of papyri from Greco-Roman Egypt that contains magic spells, rituals, curses, prayers, and hymns dating from the second century BCE to the fifth century CE.
20. See Therthonax's interview (in Greek) in Παπαγεωργίου (2018). It is common for artists in BM to use stage names.
21. These hymns constitute a part of the vast corpus of texts marked by modern scholars as "Orphic," a term used to designate anything somehow connected to the mythical poet, musician, and prophet, Orpheus. The most recent monographs on the *Orphic Hymns* are Ricciardelli (2000), Morand (2001), and Fayant (2014). See also Morand (2015).
22. It is worth noting that Mesomedes' *Hymn to the Sun* (row 27 of the table) is among the few Greek hymns that survive with musical notation; however, there is nothing to suggest that Kawir have taken into account the hymn's original music.
23. For a discussion on the transmission of these texts with previous bibliography, see Stephens (2015: 38–46).

24. Graf (2009).
25. See Furley (2011: 207).
26. As Haslam (1993: 125) suggests: "The Hymns, it goes without saying, are literary texts. To call them religious is simply to say that they inscribe themselves within the genre."
27. See Tanaseanu-Döbler (2013: 186–257) and van den Berg (2001: 86–111).
28. Moreover, the *Orphic Hymns* are short compositions, something that facilitates their adaptation into music, and constitute a large hymnic corpus, which is, of course, a good reason why these texts, as Johnston (2010: 125) notes, appear to be among the favorite texts of neo-pagans.
29. For a discussion on this text, see Betz (2003).
30. See Schuddeboom (2009).
31. See Dimitrova (2008: 239–40).
32. There is at least one piece of ancient evidence for the use of mask(s) in Greek mystery cults: Pausanias' description of the "major" initiation in the cult of Demeter Kidaria at Arcadia (8.15.1–3). For discussion, see Jost (2003).
33. See the insightful discussion of Satanic BM performances by Olson (2008: 40–68).
34. Labrys, founded by members of YSEE and originally one of its sub-organizations, is now independent. Some of the religious festivals at which ΚΑΒΕΙΡΟΣ has performed are the Olympeia (2008), the Prometheia (2008–9), and the Attika Dionysia (2009–11).
35. See Prassa (2008).
36. For a relevant discussion, see Bernabé (2010).
37. See Lozynsky (2014: 20).
38. See e.g., *βασιλεῦ* in the *OH to Zeus*, 3; *πάτερ* in Cleanthes' *Hymn to Zeus*, 34.
39. Furley and Bremer (2001a: 59).
40. See Bernabé (2004: 205–14).
41. Stephens (2015: 52–4).
42. Furley and Bremer (2001b: 1–20).
43. As Lozynsky (2014: 56) notes, invocations may be found anywhere in Greek hymns apart from the proper *epiklesis*.
44. Furley and Bremer (2001a: 60).
45. For more on the church arsons committed by members of the Norwegian black metal scene in Norway, see Moynihan and Søderlind (2003).
46. I refer to lines 7–8, where the verbs and the personal pronoun follow Modern Greek grammar, which is nonetheless similar to the original Greek in this case. As for the pronunciation, Kawir follow the universal way in which modern Greeks pronounce ancient Greek, by using the contemporaneous Greek phonetic system, a practice often called the "Reuchlinian pronunciation," as opposed to the reconstructed "Erasmian pronunciation" common among English-speaking countries.
47. See Lozynsky (2014: 75).
48. See *OH to Pan*, 11 and *OH to Zeus*, 8.
49. See e.g., *the Hymn to the Sun*, 23 from the Greek Magical Papyri (*PMG* IV 296–466).
50. *LSJ* (1996), s.v. "Πυρφόρος."

51. See Bernabé (2010: 431).
52. Lozynsky (2014: 75).
53. Furley and Bremer (2001a: 61).
54. See e.g., Callimachus' *Hymn to Artemis*, 2.
55. *LSJ* (1996), s.v. "Κοσμητής."
56. The performances of "Hymn to Apollo" at Aphrodisia may be viewed at ysee.gr (2012b) and (2013).
57. The performance of "Hymn to Apollo" at Thargelia may be viewed at ysee.gr (2012a).
58. For an up-to-date online resource on Hellenic/Greek BM bands, see the blog "Hellenic Black Metal Front."
59. See "Dizziness interview" (2013), Silent Dominion (2013), Morbid Fog (2015), and Γιώργος (2016).
60. The marathon trial of Golden Dawn began in April 2015 and is currently (June 2019) ongoing. On far-right politics in Greek music and the involvement of Golden Dawn, see Koronaiou, Lagos, and Sakellariou (2015). For the rise of Golden Dawn and the ways in which it has changed over the years in response to political developments in Greece, see Karpozilos (2018).
61. For more on NSBM and its relation to the practice of paganism, occultism, and National Socialism, see Gardell (2003: 284–323) and Moynihan and Søderlind (2003).
62. See Therthonax's interview (in Greek) in Γιαννακόπουλος (2017). See also Fotiou's discussion (2014: 221), who argues that YSEE's political discourse is "more internationalist rather than nationalist."
63. See Jason Pitzl-Waters (2013).
64. Special thanks for their insightful comments and suggestions go to the editors of this volume, Kris Fletcher and Osman Umurhan, the anonymous readers of Bloomsbury Press, Professor Andreas Michalopoulos (University of Athens), and to my friends and colleagues Katerina Kallivoka, Ioannis Kalofotis, and Ioannis Kaneris.

CHAPTER 4
CASSANDRA'S PLIGHT: GENDER, GENRE, AND HISTORICAL CONCEPTS OF FEMININITY IN GOTHIC AND POWER METAL

Linnea Åshede and Anna Foka

Introduction: Genres, gender, and the Classics

Heavy metal is associated with a variety of discourses, social practices, and cultural meanings, where the majority revolves around concepts, images, and experiences of power.[1] Metal as live performance is synonymous with intensity and loudness, with its fans often embodying and enacting power through strong physicality at concerts: headbanging, stage diving, crowd surfing, and shouting among other expressions. The physical character of the musical genre also manifests in the metal-specific rhythmic "dancing" style, moshing, an aggressive and dynamic swinging of arms in a windmill motion with occasional high kicks.

Heavy metal is, further, a musical genre that is stereotypically inspired by phenomenologies and narratives of powerful masculinity.[2] Indeed, in European metal cultures, and more precisely within the subgenres of power and epic metal, bands often appear aesthetically inspired by historical models of aggressive and powerful masculinity that range from fantasy heroes to medieval tales to figureheads of Classical antiquity. Often, this heavy investment in history belies mainstream media representations of heavy metal as a blue-collar, outspokenly non-erudite cultural expression. For example, the American band Manowar's twenty-eight minute song "Achilles, Agony and Ecstasy in Eight Parts" (from the album *Triumph of Steel*) draws heavily upon Homer's *Iliad*.[3] Similarly, Iron Maiden's take on Alexander the Great has already received some scholarly attention in the field of Classical Reception Studies.[4] The conceptual framework of songs such as these is laced with historical notions of powerful masculinities.

In this chapter, we wish to go beyond discussions of heavy metal as inextricably intertwined with historical masculinities by arguing that the genre has become more complex in its representation of gendered identities of the past. Our analysis is theoretically informed by the concept of "historical culture" (*Geschichtskultur*), a manner of understanding the relationship between a group and its past (i.e. how specific historical concepts may inspire and affect the present).[5] Furthermore, historical culture's scope is the examination of all the layers and processes of social historical consciousness, paying attention to the agents who compose notions of "history," the media by means of which it is disseminated, the representations that it popularizes, and the creative and artistic receptions found in popular culture. Like all cultures, heavy metal constitutes a site of continual negotiation over definitions, behaviors, aesthetics, and identity. While certainly inspired by and themed according to heroic masculinities of the past, we argue that metal also accommodates ancient paradigms of powerful femininities to a hitherto unrecognized degree.[6] Ultimately, we argue that in its representation of societal structures, especially in relation to gender, metal has evolved over time, specifically during the 1990s and 2000s.

We concentrate on how historical concepts of gender are communicated in two subgenres of European heavy metal: gothic metal and power metal, as represented by the bands Theatre of Tragedy and Blind Guardian from Norway and Germany, respectively. While a genre cannot be solely represented by a single band, our chosen examples are rather typical of their respective subgenres in terms of lyrics, musical style, and theatrical self-presentation, as they have been canonized in the early 1990s within a central European and a Scandinavian context. Since both of these bands originate in the geographical area of Central/Northern Europe at the turn of the twenty-first century—a time and place where both genres stood at the height of their popularity—we argue that these songs reflect a conscious transformation of popular culture in the 1990s, which urged the promotion of women's voices in traditionally male-dominated artistic fields.[7]

Gothic and power metal constitute fertile comparative ground for two main reasons. On the one hand, as we explain below, these two subgenres constitute each other's virtual antitheses in terms of mood and gender dynamics. On the other hand, both subdivisions are known for experimenting with instrumentation beyond the conventional rock/metal lineup of electric guitars, bass, drums and vocals; in particular, they incorporate symphonic elements, inspired by Classically composed pieces for orchestras that employ elaborate percussion set-ups and string and brass instruments. Both gothic and power metal also originate and retain strong followings in Europe, in part through heavy borrowing of form and content from European cultural traditions, from folk music to folk tales, and from historical events to historical texts—sometimes in a highly eclectic manner (see below on the influences of Blind Guardian), sometimes in the form of niche concept albums (for instance, Swedish Sabaton's *Carolus Rex*).[8] That said, there are obvious differences between our two case studies, as the musical structure of Theatre of Tragedy's songs falls within the tradition of popular music (e.g. verse, chorus, and bridge) while Blind Guardian incorporate more Classical symphonic elements in their structure.

We begin our investigation by observing how the gothic metal band Theatre of Tragedy and their 1997 album *Aégis* relate to topics from Classical antiquity. This album is notable for its many tracks that explore female figures of antiquity, such as "Venus," a track written partly in Latin, and "Poppæa." Moving from general models to specific examples we focus on the first single of the album, "Cassandra." In order to highlight how Theatre of Tragedy renegotiate the historical position of this character, we provide a comparative analysis of Cassandra's reception by German power metal band Blind Guardian in the songs "Under the Ice" and "And Then There Was Silence," both released in 2002 and so relatively close in time to *Aégis*.

This chapter aims to point out differences across metal subgenres in representations of gender that go beyond the supposed focus on hegemonic warrior-masculinity.

Importantly, metal lyricists' eclectic approach to historical sources of inspiration in no way makes the choice of Classical imagery random or insignificant. Iain Campbell, for example, argues that Classical allusions have the effect of appropriating "the traditional *gravitas* associated with the Classical world," creating a historical connection which may imbue a band and its music with authority, mystique, and intellectual capital.[9] This chapter, then, discusses how two metal bands at the turn of the twenty-first century make use of Classical figures to address themes and issues relevant to their own—and their audiences'—historical contexts, including contemporary receptions of historically situated gender roles. Metal as a musical genre and an artistic production may carry strong (albeit shifting) ideological investments, and to fans, the self-presentation of bands is often seen to endorse a particular set of values.[10] The choice of lyrical and material imagery can thus have strategic impact on how audiences view their heroes, themselves, and the world.

The nexus of genre and gender thus emerges as a crucial analytical instrument for the study of the relationship between heavy metal and the Classical world. Even more than most types of music, metal has become increasingly diffracted into a plethora of ever-evolving subgenres, distinguished by often-polemical ideals, ideologies, and socio-cultural codes (see the introduction to this volume). In his seminal work on metal culture, Robert Walser characterizes the function of genres as simultaneously providing "models of composition" for musicians and "horizons of expectation" for audiences.[11] This shared, dialectic discourse helps shape a common—but never absolute— understanding of musical style, lyrical content, and visual presentation. Harris M. Berger pursues a similar line of thought when he argues that "much of music's affective power comes when a composer creates musical forms that lend themselves to be grasped in a particular way by those with similar social-musical histories."[12] Therefore, each subgenre of heavy metal engages with a given phenomenon according to its own set of temporal, geographical, and socio-cultural specificities.[13]

By concentrating on two contemporary conceptions of Cassandra's myth, we show how its reception exemplifies "the two-way relationship between the source text or culture and the new work and receiving culture."[14] As an artistic product, metal music may be inspired by a historical culture, but it is also affected by the contemporary culture that receives this historical content, calling for a more precise focus on how female historical icons are portrayed in contemporary metal settings. We show that, with *Aégis*, Theatre of Tragedy utilize deep-rooted paradigms of ancient concepts of femininity in metal contrary to the popular belief that considers the genre to be primarily masculinist.

To this end, we have—perhaps controversially—chosen to analyze the bands' lyrics. Despite Dietmar Elflein's dismissive claim that metal lyrics are generally "less important than the music and the visuals or the image," the relative importance of lyrical content still remains a contested question among metal scholars.[15] We strongly believe that in our chosen subgenres—gothic and power metal—a fan's reading, discussing, and learning lyrical content by heart constitutes an optional, yet important practice by which she shows a commitment to her favorite band(s) and the musical community.[16] This is particularly relevant for the period under discussion, when music was disseminated as physical records/discs along with often-elaborate booklets, complete with the printed lyrics.[17]

Theatre of Tragedy: Under the *Aegis* of Classical antiquity

The term "gothic," an epithet that is mainly associated with architecture and literature, has been used to refer to aesthetic elements seen as dark and sinister, and is often invoked—especially in youth culture—to imply content that is supernatural and grim.[18] The term entered heavy metal music with the release of Paradise Lost's *Gothic* album in 1991, although fans have often been at odds over "which bands are, or most definitely are *not*, authentically Gothic."[19] Musically, gothic metal is generally characterized by its choice of timbres, commonly described as "dark," but also as romantic and passionate, and it has often been regarded as a combination of the melancholy theatricality of goth rock with heavy metal's volume and energy.[20] Over time, "gothic" has come to stand for an affinity with darkness that goes beyond music to encompass clothing, as well as narratives and emotional content, where the typical gothic version of the somber and sinister is often both glamorous and self-consciously feminine.[21]

Within this framework, gothic metal has developed aesthetics that vary between subgenres. One of the most important aspects of contemporary gothic metal is the use of melodic keyboards, synthesizers, and female vocals sung in an operatic style, with frequent use of minor chords and tri-tones. The term "beauty and the beast" refers to a style of vocals that combines a female and male vocalist, where soft and dulcet female vocals are deliberately contrasted with male growls or aggressive singing.[22] Tiamat (*Wildhoney,* 1994) and The Gathering (*Mandylion,* 1995) make use of this aesthetic on their earlier albums, but the band that made it an indispensable element of the gothic canon is Theatre of Tragedy in its self-titled debut in 1995. After a second album, *Velvet Darkness They Fear* (1996), the band's first critical success arrived after the release of *Aégis* in 1998.[23] On *Aégis,* the piano featured in earlier albums is replaced by synthesizers, while vocalist Raymond Rohonyi discards his black metal growls in favor of a softer, spoken, even whispering voice. The music is also less aggressive and less heavy than on previous albums.

As exemplified in part by their name, Theatre of Tragedy play on connotations of dark theatricality, a morose ambience, and themes beyond the hegemonic aggressive masculinities that used to be so integral to most metal subgenres before the 1990s.[24] The lyrical content of *Aégis* is centered on female stories, with every song named after a woman (more below). The title of the album itself also embodies strong connotations of femininity and power, since *aegis* is the Greek name of Athena's shielding armor (made in part out of a goatskin, from whence it derives its name), adorned with the head of the gorgon Medusa.[25] Athena's *aegis* is described in the *Iliad* as "fraught with terror; all around it fearful Flight is set as a crown, and on it is Strife, on it Valor, and on it Assault, that makes the blood run cold, and on it is the head of the Gorgon monster, terrible and awful" (*Iliad* 5.738–42).[26] The goddess herself is similarly portrayed as an awe-inspiring figure: "among them went bright-eyed Athena, holding the precious, ageless and immortal *aegis*: a hundred tassels of pure gold hang fluttering from it, all of them tightly woven, each worth a hundred oxen (*Iliad* 2.446–49)."[27] The battle-cries and immortal might surrounding Athena are images of Classical heroism that within Greek culture are normally attributed to male gods and heroes, and thus set her apart as exceptional in every aspect.

By choosing *Aégis* as a name and model, Theatre of Tragedy appropriate the iconic shield that embodies precisely that aesthetic of power traditionally valued in metal culture yet grounded in a warrior goddess. The name can thus be understood as a statement opposing the subordination of everything typically considered feminine or "unmanly" in cultural traditions that valorize masculinity,[28] foreshadowing the album's purpose to present portraits of strong female characters. Furthermore, the modern concept of doing something "under someone's *aegis*" refers to acting under the protection of a benevolent force—which in the context of Theatre of Tragedy's album becomes aligned with femininity. Moreover, every track is named after a female character adopted from European history and mythology: "Venus" and "Poppæa" are a Roman goddess and empress, respectively; "Aœde," "Cassandra," "Bacchante," and "Siren" are all drawn from Greek mythology, while "Lorelei" refers to a water sprite from German folklore.[29] As with Theatre of Tragedy's previous releases, the lyrics are written in an archaizing English with Latin passages on "Venus" add to the album's antiquarian feel.[30]

Watch your step, Cassandra: A Classical model of tragic femininity

To deepen our understanding behind Theatre of Tragedy's reception of female icons from antiquity, we will concentrate on the first track—and only single—from *Aégis*, "Cassandra." The ancient sources present Cassandra as a daughter of king Priam of Troy (a.k.a. Ilium). Her father and most of her brothers were killed during the siege of the city as recounted in the *Iliad*, while Cassandra herself was dragged from Athena's temple and raped by the warrior Ajax.[31] After the fall of Troy, Cassandra was allotted as a war prize to the conquering king Agamemnon, and upon their return to Mycenae, was murdered along with him by his vengeful wife, Clytemnestra. However, Cassandra is best known for her ill-fated prophetic gift. A virgin priestess of Apollo, she purportedly caught the god's eye and he bestowed the gift of prophecy upon her, but when she spurned him, he added the curse that no one would believe her. Everyone, including her family, thus came to regard Cassandra as mad. Though she tried to warn of catastrophes such as the Trojan horse and Agamemnon's murder as well as her own, her words were misunderstood or disregarded, and she could only watch in vain as her visions came true.[32]

Cassandra emerges in the Classical sources as the embodiment of tragedy, the powerless victim of gods, fate, and men.[33] The treacherous nature of her prophetic gift estranges her from her own family, and her absolute knowledge of past, present, and future only underscores the horror of her inability to influence her circumstances. Playwrights such as Aeschylus and Euripides utilize Cassandra as a figure whose impassioned monologues communicate vital information about past and future events to the audience. But as a woman who speaks in public she differs from the feminine norm; in ancient Greek contexts, a woman speaking publicly is always a woman speaking out of place.[34] Because her utterances are always ignored or misconstrued by her companions, Cassandra is effectively silenced even when she speaks.

Troubled heterosexuality: Beauty and the beast

None of the female icons from the album *Aégis* corresponds to the traditional mythological trope of the exceptional warrior woman who, as Frances Early points out, can be lauded for temporarily transcending the "weakness of her sex," but who ultimately disrupts patriarchal order and so must be suppressed.[35] Theatre of Tragedy's female icons are heroines in a different sense: they play leading roles, but are not warriors, not even necessarily protagonists. Cassandra's status as paradigmatic outsider, in particular, makes her an attractive figure to both the gothic and larger heavy metal communities who, as observed by Deena Weinstein, tend to self-identify with all types of outcasts.[36] As the band's name indicates (above), Theatre of Tragedy share gothic metal's special affinity for the dark and sinister, what Garry Sharpe-Young refers to as the subgenre's "somberness and depressive bent."[37] Alongside this special affinity, we argue that Theatre of Tragedy's positioning of their heroines in active communication with their male counterparts exemplifies an understanding of gender relations beyond the standard model of powerful men and oppressed women: women and men as equals, with equal accountability for their actions.

"Cassandra" exemplifies how Theatre of Tragedy integrate musical composition, lyrical style and content (discussed in greater detail below), and live performance in the construction of an affective ambience. The song (track duration 6:49) is dominated by a slow, pace-like andante tempo, and the band's trademark carefully arranged vocal contrasts. The minor-key instrumental intro contains few distorted guitars, but "heaviness" is provided by the slow, steady, software-augmented drumbeat punctuating the melody, with a plucking guitar and much reverberation. The morose mood intensifies as vocalist and lyricist Rohonyi murmurs the first lines in a slow, breathy legato, the pace smooth and flowing without any real breaks between the notes. His whispers with sustained vowels lend the song an intimate, confessional tone:[38]

> He gave to her, yet tenfold claim'd in return
> She hath no life, but the one he for her wrought
> Proffer'd to her his wauking heart, she turn'd it down (down, down)
> Riposted with a tell-tale lore of lies and scorn.
>
> Theatre of Tragedy, "Cassandra," Aégis, 1998

Theatre of Tragedy initiate the re-telling of Cassandra's fate by focusing on the source of both her gift and her affliction, the one in complete control of her life: the god Apollo. As the song moves into the chorus, Rohonyi—voice still gruff and undeniably masculine—also starts delivering lines in Cassandra's "voice," stating for her: "I ken to-morrow, refell me if ye can!" The chorus ends by a bitten off "'Sicker!' quoth Cassandra."

The female vocals of Liv Kristine do not enter the soundscape until the song's final half (at 3:35). Whether consciously or unconsciously, the theatrical composition of the song thus mirrors the structure of Aeschylus' tragedy *Agamemnon,* where the audience must wait for Cassandra's anticipated speech until line 1072, despite her entering the stage much earlier. While she is not referred to explicitly until line 950, where Agamemnon instructs Clytemnestra to "welcome kindly this foreign woman," it can be inferred that she arrives along with him in his carriage before line 781.[39] In the ancient play, despite being greeted and entreated by Clytemnestra and the chorus, Cassandra seemingly stubbornly remains mute for a long time, until her sudden cry for Apollo at line 1080.[40] So, too, Liv Kristine keeps the audience waiting. The effect is especially poignant in live performances of the song—as at the Metalmania Fest in Katowice, Poland (April 29, 2009)—where Liv Kristine is a visible presence on the stage from the first moment, contrastingly fair-haired, white lace-clad, and feminine beside the dark-clad, all-male band.[41] She remains mute for the first two minutes of the performance, which builds anticipation and makes the contrast that much sharper when her eerily distant mezzo-soprano enters to describe Cassandra's and Apollo's conflicting emotions without backing from Rohonyi.

Liv Kristine's visual as well as aural contrast from the rest of the band presents her as a stranger in their midst, and the two vocalists' self-presentation during live performances further augment the vocal construction of binary gender as opposing contrasts. During the first half of the song, Rohonyi delivers the lyrics with his microphone cradled between both hands, with Liv Kristine swaying silently and sensually in the background. The band and male vocalist always face the audience, but the female vocalist frequently turns her back or closes her eyes, presenting herself as apart and unattainable.

In "Cassandra," the lyrics focus not on her prophecies, but on the tragic consequences of Apollo's feelings toward the title character. Cassandra is named "Apollo's bane" in the chorus, but it is above all he who is presented as her destroyer—a powerful god driven to cruelty by wounded male pride.[42] This problematizing of the power dynamics of heterosexual desire is the core theme of *Aégis*. By locating part of the guilt in the male party and portraying the source of the tragedy as the relationship itself, rather than either one of its participants, Theatre of Tragedy make a subversive statement in relation to traditional heavy metal culture. Although metal is no longer as universally white, male, and heterosexual as often claimed,[43] the genre remains associated with a basic attitude of testosterone-fueled machismo.[44] Its prevalent representation of women as sexual objects and evil seductresses typically positions them as mysterious, potentially dangerous Others, whose inherent desirability can be blamed for causing both male desire and suffering. Male mistreatment of women is thus legitimized as just revenge or an act of self-defense.[45]

In addressing Apollo's self-justified revenge upon a woman who spurned him, Theatre of Tragedy call attention to the hidden logic behind the metal stereotype of the *femme*

Figure 4.1 Liv Kristine, vocalist. Theatre of Tragedy.

fatale. According to sociologist Sara Ahmed, feelings are often attributed to certain bodies. For instance, male hurt at being rejected is readily converted into a reading of the object of denied desire as inherently hurtful, a conceptual leap whereby "I feel bad" becomes "you *are* bad," locating the blame in the female body.[46] Hence, women who change their mind are routinely reviled as evil deceivers. Drawing on feminist theory and critical studies, Classical scholars have formulated several interpretations regarding female status based on nearly exclusively male-generated primary sources. From Hélène Cixous' *The Laugh of the Medusa* (1976) to Mary Beard's *Women and Power: A Manifesto* (2017), women from antiquity to the present appear discredited as a consequence of patriarchal social structures. Similarly, in Theatre of Tragedy's "Cassandra," Apollo attempts to discredit the prophetess by taking away her credibility in the eyes of others, effectively silencing her. Although Liv Kristine's part of the lyrics concedes that Cassandra "belied her own words" (5:46) and that "her naysay raught his heart" (5:32), Apollo's suffering is not represented as justifying revenge. On the contrary, Theatre of Tragedy emphasize his culpability by having asked outright at 2:30 why the god of prophecy himself could not foresee that Cassandra would accept his gift but reject his love.

While Theatre of Tragedy's use of an archaizing English of their own invention and the occasional Latin makes their lyrics incomprehensible to many listeners, Campbell observes that the incorporation of "ancient" languages fills a function in itself, appropriating the aforementioned privileged connotations of mysterious, nearly mythical cultures.[47] Theatre of Tragedy's strategic use of languages is exemplified by several tracks on *Aégis*. The chorus of "Siren," for example, constructs its image of the irresistible yet fatal effect of the siren upon her male victim through a gendered division of lyrics. As Liv Kristine sings "I speer thine pine," at the beginning of the chorus, Rohonyi declares "Thine voice is oh so sweet," the two utterances inextricably entangled. Similarly, her later call "list and heed" is immediately followed by his low "thou say'st," an interjection which turns him into the mediator narrating her siren song to the listener.

As an even more poignant example of musical gendering, the soft piano figures on the intro of "Venus" are joined by Liv Kristine's equally light mezzo-soprano as she slowly sings the first verse in Latin. The mezzo-soprano's high-pitched Latin is not necessarily understood by the uninitiated, yet it is likely identified as Latin by the listener. In sharp contrast, Rohonyi's subsequent growled vocals are accompanied by the introduction of grinding, distorted guitars. His lyrics are in archaizing English, and as he spits out bitter accusations against the flighty goddess—"Venus! I trow'd thou wast my friend" (1:21)—the female voice repeats the end of his phrases in English and in the same mezzo-soprano as her delivery of the Latin verses. Her repetition of his growled verses, but in mezzo-soprano, serves as a failed attempt to reconcile his displeasure, since for the remainder of the song Liv Kristine continues to communicate with Rohonyi in Latin after responding to his words in English. This alternation of Rohonyi's lines in English and Liv Kristine's in Latin creates a seemingly dysfunctional one-way communication. Perhaps as a comment on the popular conception of the inherent differences and subsequent communication-issues of men and women, the two voices in this song literally speak different languages even when they share some verses in English. Furthermore, the translation of the Latin further emphasizes their deep disconnect, as Venus herself laments the pain of beauty and desire, echoing the experience of the male voice, but without a direct answer to his appeals.

Their inability to communicate is just one of many representations of troubled heterosexual relations presented by *Aégis*. These tense relationships challenge not only the stereotypes of traditional metal, but also Theatre of Tragedy's own subgenre. Gothic metal is often characterized as more feminine in its aesthetics than most metal subgenres, and accommodates a higher percentage of female performers and fans.[48] The Goth scene has a strong investment in sexually active, independent femininity.[49] As Amy Wilkins demonstrates, however, this "empowered" feminine ideal can be as constrictive as it is liberating, because female beauty and heterosexual availability remain mandatory. Wilkins thus argues that the ideal of males and females as equally sexually liberated retains and "repackages" male sexual entitlement, because female participants are still denied the option not to be sexually invested in males.[50]

Aégis, then, breaks ground by bringing gender conflict to the forefront with its use of dueling and layered male-female vocals. Since, in Berger's words, "singers employ a wide range of vocal articulations and timbres, all of which are foundational aspects of their musical ideas,"[51] then Theatre of Tragedy's ideology on *Aégis* can be summed up in their distinct vocal style: "beauty and the beast." The lyrics of "Poppæa," for example, may initially appear misogynistic, painting a picture of the title character as cruel and willful, with a chorus of "And the wench doth bawdness to blow." However, most of the lines are sung together by Rohonyi and Liv Kristine. Their contrasting voices draw attention to the existence of a relationship between two distinctly individual subjects, and therefore the potential for conflict, between the title character and an unnamed male party who is watching, desiring, and judging her. According to Roman historians, Poppaea Sabina was the second wife of the emperor Nero, whose death he allegedly caused (then grieved excessively) by kicking her stomach while she was pregnant.[52] The initial line of the song —"Dream of a funeral, blest temptress—behest me!"—thus sets the stage for another tragedy, fueled by desire.

It is poignant that while a recurring line in the chorus of "Poppæa," "Stay my adamant/ Suffer me to transfix thee" (first at 1:48), can be seen as referring to Nero's inability to deal with Poppaea as an independent agent—firstly demanding that she accept his abuse, and secondly "fixating" her in time and space by taking away her life—it can also be understood as referring to the claim by some Roman historians that Nero in the course of his mourning had all female theatrical masks be made in her likeness, thus preserving her, albeit unmoving, for eternity.[53] However, Theatre of Tragedy ultimately refuse to participate in this removal of agency, for when Poppaea finally is addressed directly at 3:14, the duet of contrasting voices leads to Liv Kristine's more prominent voice that entreats "do what thou wilt" above the muted whisper of Rohonyi's simultaneous delivery of the same verse.

By employing a high-contrast combination of female high-pitched vocals and male death-metal growls to portray iconic females renowned for their troubled relationships with men, Theatre of Tragedy present an impression of heterosexuality based on contrast and opposition. Calling attention to gender as something relational rather than essential enables the band to locate liability, guilt, and agency in both parts of a relationship.[54] They thus challenge metal stereotypes of men as acting and women as acted upon,[55] while simultaneously criticizing the uneven power-relations of traditionally male-dominated arenas such as heavy metal and heterosexual relationships.[56] Songs like "Poppæa" and "Cassandra" call attention to the fact that when a woman is accused, there is usually a male accuser in the background, whose motives may be anything but just or justified. Theatre of Tragedy's re-presentations of historical femininity problematize gendered power-relations by presenting male and female as equal accomplices. The destructive potential of heterosexual desire is located not in sexual difference itself, but in its historical role as preventer of mutual communication.

Homosocial bonding: Blind Guardian and power metal

As an all-male group (fronted by a tenor) whose musical output takes the shape of "massively complex, intricate metal epics,"[57] the German Blind Guardian are a quintessential power metal band. As a subgenre known for its fascination with all things epic—including elaborate concept albums with fifteen-minute songs and ten-minute guitar solos—power metal has an established tradition of incorporating Classical imagery, particularly in the hyperbolically heroic self-presentation. However, the Classical allusions are only part of an eclectic mixture of influences, as illustrated by Blind Guardian's album *A Night at the Opera* (2002), for which lyrical inspiration is drawn from the Bible, *The Song of Hildebrandt*, *Tristan and Isolde*, Tolkien, Nietzsche, and Galileo Galilei, as well as the Dungeons & Dragons fantasy series *DragonLance* (the album's title is a nod to Queen's 1975 album of the same name).

Blind Guardian also treat Cassandra in two songs from the album *A Night at the Opera* (2002): "Under the Ice" and "And Then There Was Silence." The former recounts her fate after the Trojan War, closely based on Aeschylus' *Agamemnon*. When introducing the song during a live performance in Moscow (May 25, 2002), the male vocalist/lyricist Hansi Kürsch calls it a story about Cassandra's suffering.[58] Being feminine and tragic rather than masculine and heroic, Cassandra provides an unusual topic for a power metal band.[59] Blind Guardian's version of her fate is presented in a markedly different fashion than that of Theatre of Tragedy. "Under the Ice" has a melodic intro in Phrygian mode, the fifth and dominant mode of the harmonic minor scale, also known as the Mixolydian ♭9 ♭13 chord scale. The flatted second and the augmented step between the second and third degrees of the scale establish a distinctive sound, common, for example, in *Misirlou*, a popular modern Greek and Armenian song of the 1920s. The Phrygian mode is also frequently used in heavy metal due to the tense qualities and oriental/South-East Mediterranean character traditionally associated with its sequence of half- and whole-tone transitions in Western culture.[60] In Blind Guardian's "And Then There Was Silence," the Phrygian intro takes the form of a quiet combination of hi-hat and guitar to introduce the main theme of the piece. The song then launches into a sonic assault: the first heavy riff continues the Phrygian scale, in an eruption of a typically dense power metal soundscape with rapid-fire double kick-drums and multi-tracked distorted guitars. Kürsch delivers the first lines in an energetic wail ("Run 'til you find the answer/Time out for poor Cassandra/She's fairly safe within the fire") that quickly swells into a chorus of multiple backing vocals.

Blind Guardian's musical trademark consists of the liberal use of multi-tracking and overdubbing, where musical mass-effects are created by recording and adding multiple versions of guitar parts and vocals, and Kürsch sings his own backup vocals on the studio versions of songs (a fairly common practice within power metal).[61] The result is that a quartet backed by additional keyboards comes out sounding much like a musical army. Whereas on other albums, such as *Nightfall in Middle Earth* (1998), the vocal repetitions could be described as aiming toward a military march/choir effect, the collective harmonized presentation of Cassandra's tragedy in "Under the Ice" emphasizes panicked madness. Although phrases such as "cruelly admired" (0:45) allude to Cassandra's mistreatment at the hands of men like Ajax, Apollo, and Agamemnon, the chorus locates the crux of her tragedy elsewhere (1:20):

Enjoy your stay here
Welcome to the slaughterhouse
Release from rotten thoughts
No more pain, and no more gods.

Blind Guardian, "Under the Ice," A Night at the Opera, 2002

Blind Guardian's Cassandra can be said to embody the tragedy of the human condition in general, that of being a mere mortal at the mercy of circumstances beyond one's control, a definition of tragedy closely aligned with the Classical one.[62] The second line of the chorus echoes Aeschylus' Cassandra referring to Agamemnon's palace and his family tree (the house of Atreus) as a slaughterhouse, reflecting both its tragic history and the imminent murders.[63] For Blind Guardian's Cassandra, death marks the end of suffering, the final release from accusations of madness and fraud, and the whims of the gods.

Rather than fatalism, however, the song's distinct power metal delivery emphasizes resistance, positioning Cassandra within a context of intense homosocial bonding. By "homosocial" we mean a same-sex group or context defined by often emotionally intimate but self-professedly non-sexual bonding (i.e. a social rather than erotic preference for members of one's own sex).[64] Walser argues that women are typically represented as dangerous in heavy metal because "their attractiveness threatens to disrupt both male self-control and the collective strength of male bonding."[65] This does not apply to Blind Guardian's Cassandra, who is consistently represented as an object of (universal) compassion rather than (individual) desire. She provides a motivation for heroic resistance, a symbol around which to rally.

Blind Guardian deal with Cassandra in a sympathetic manner a second time in the lead single from *A Night at the Opera*, "And Then There Was Silence." This fourteen-minute *tour de force* of frequently changing vocal styles freely re-tells the fall of Troy in over 150 lines of lyrics. Because one characteristic of Blind Guardian is the complexity of Kürsch's lyrics, the song's viewpoint shifts multiple times. Sometimes the tone and pitch of the vocals signal a shift in narrative perspective, but often the listener/reader is left to decipher the lyrics based on whatever *a priori* knowledge they have about the events surrounding the Trojan War and its aftermath. In one of the bridges, Kürsch adopts the voice of a fallen Trojan soldier, presumably Hector, cautioning "Watch your step, Cassandra, you might fall/As I've stumbled on the field" (3:08) before addressing her as "sister mine." In contrast, later lines warn of Helen, the more typical *femme fatale* whose beauty "will bring in a murderous price" (6:20) (i.e. spark the Trojan War). War is the great horror of mankind, the end of everything that leaves only silence in its wake.

Once again, however, the context of the power metal subgenre shifts the focus from mourning to collective celebration of the heroic aspects of death on the battlefield, where the end of a war and the end of Troy prefigures the subsequent rise of Rome. This picture of war resonates with a line from Euripides' *Trojan Women*, where Cassandra claims that "The man of sense should avoid war, but, if it comes to it, a glorious death is not an accolade the city should despise."[66] Within the context of power metal as an arena of homosocial bonding, the tragedy of war as the breakdown of social bonds simultaneously becomes cause for celebration of mighty deeds, forging new bonds between heroic brothers in arms.

Blind Guardian enact homosocial bonding on multiple levels, starting with the liberal use of choruses that, in Walser's words, "serve to enlarge the statements of the solo vocalist, enacting the approval or participation of the larger social world."[67] Unlike the conflicting heterosexual harmonics of "beauty and the beast" style vocals, the all-male chorus chanting "Nothing to lose, like one we'll stand/We'll face the storm" ("And Then There Was Silence," 7:00) emphasizes oneness, a unified supporting community. Rapid-fire drums and multiple electric guitars produce the mass sonic effect. Because of the sonic power inherent in their volume and capacity to sustain tones almost indefinitely, heavy metal's characteristic distorted guitars are typically gendered as ultra-masculine, as borderline phallic extensions of the male body.[68] Weinstein argues that within metal, male vocalists and guitarists simultaneously contend for dominance, but also enact male bonding, particularly by interacting with each other during live performances, thus functioning as a symbol of the unity of the band.[69] In the case of Blind Guardian, the bonding effect of the chorus is even more marked in live contexts, where fans participate by singing along and clapping with the rhythm to an extraordinary degree. Conversely, it can be observed of Theatre of Tragedy's musical style that the distorted guitars typically follow the male vocals, whereas the female vocals tend to be accompanied by more femininely gendered instruments such as strings and piano.

It would be easy to reduce Cassandra within Blind Guardian's heroic ethos to a sort of homosocial "fetish" in the anthropological sense of an often inanimate mediator between the community and a higher/mystical force, in this case the force that inspires mere mortals to immortal deeds of heroism, like a fairytale princess to be rescued.[70] Indeed, "And Then There Was Silence" positions her within a framework of war, its losses and its further horrors, where she emerges as a passive image to inspire pity, rather than as an agent in her own right. However, "Under the Ice" tells a different story. Here, Cassandra is represented in ways that—even in the midst of her tragedy—both acknowledge her especially vulnerable position as a woman, yet claim for her a status as an exceptional, triumphal "warrior" rather than victim (0:44):

> Inside the fire
> Awakes desire
> Cruelly admired
> They'll torture her soul
> And they'll torment her heart
> But won't change her mind.
>
> Blind Guardian, "Under the Ice," *A Night at the Opera, 2002*

Blind Guardian's Cassandra stands fast, even as Clytemnestra is coming to decapitate her. By stoically facing her death, she will escape fate, gods, and painful thoughts—all those things by which even the band and audience who are currently engaged in celebrating together the strength of her character are still bound. We suggest that in this instance, the choice of a feminine, tragic subject matter rather than the more typical masculine, heroic one enables Blind Guardian to transcend their ethos of homosocial bonding to address the truly universal, human condition, drawing on the Phrygian minor that recalls Greek cultural stereotypes, and by association, Greek tragedy. In this song, the cementing and celebration of bonds between men is supplanted by comparatively humble recognition of a different type of strength—a mistrusted, doomed woman standing tall in the face of her lonely death—and a certain frustration with mankind's limited perspective (4:14):

> We're not allowed to see
> Beyond; that's your skill
> Will we ever learn the lesson?
> We can't fly with broken wings
> Break the chains
> Time to change.
>
> *Blind Guardian, "Under the Ice," A Night at the Opera, 2002*

Conclusion

Sharpe-Young describes Theatre of Tragedy's *Aégis* as "a conceptual work dedicated to mythological female beauty."[71] With our analysis, we hope to have shown this statement to be overly reductive of both the album's content and the wider gender-political discourse with which Theatre of Tragedy choose to engage. The album can rather be regarded as a problematization of heterosexual power dynamics, making use of the accumulated cultural capital of Classical imagery to highlight issues relevant to contemporary audiences. Like the Cassandra of Aeschylus and Euripides, Theatre of Tragedy's Cassandra may offer an alternative definition of gendered relationships that emphasizes mutuality and joint liability. This reception resonates with Pascale-Anne Brault's analysis of the Classical myth, where "through Cassandra, we come to see that tragedy is essentially related to the feminine, to a certain feminine element that tragedy must suppress or deny but can never totally ignore."[72] Because she is dominated and silenced by men, Cassandra is paradoxically capable of vocalizing the injustices of female—and human—conditions.

Steve Waksman has pointed out that "power is an issue that comes up repeatedly in academic treatments of heavy metal," and that is often identified as the genre's central preoccupation.[73] He goes on to claim that the presumption in metal scholarship is "that metal's projection of power proves empowering for its dedicated listeners, and that metal often fosters a distinct sense of empowerment among those whose social position teeters between privilege and marginality."[74] Indeed, we agree that "power" is integral to metal culture, but the concept must be understood as multi-faceted, just as Berger demonstrates how the "heavy" in heavy metal can refer to "a variety of textural, structural, and affective aspects of musical sound," capable of encompassing elements from gothic metal's dark aesthetics to power metal's sonic assaults.[75]

Both Theatre of Tragedy and Blind Guardian choose to raise the question of power in Cassandra's narrative by focusing on its perceived antithesis: powerlessness. Theatre of Tragedy call attention to the uneasy division of power in heterosexual relations, highlighting male accountability and ultimately problematizing power itself. Blind Guardian focus on the vulnerability of the human condition (to gods, fate, and war), but ultimately rejoice in the construction of a shared bonding-power to combat this powerlessness. In the hands of both bands, Cassandra becomes an embodied locus for discussing powerlessness in the terms and issues most relevant to their respective subgenres, within sexual/intimate relations and social/collective relations, respectively.

Even beyond the turn of the twenty-first century, heavy metal continues to render historical representations of gender germane to the present. Beginning in the 1990s, metal's borrowing and reinterpretation of historical female figures could be interpreted as being driven by shifts within a social group's hegemony. Heavy metal from this period onward represents a paradigmatic example of a male-dominated genre that with increasing frequency is interrupted by a strong feminine presence.[76] Some acts in heavy metal may provide a site for the positive incorporation of two groups traditionally constructed as oppositional: masculine and feminine. This social phenomenon, or what Antonio Gramsci calls an "equilibrium of hegemony," requires an historical process and a synchronic viewpoint that shifts between resistance and incorporation.[77] The understanding of heavy metal as popular culture and a different way to iterate hegemony theory may account for the sudden burst of powerful historical femininities in gothic and power metal.[78]

Notes

1. Walser (1993a: 2).
2. Walser (1993b: 343). See also the Introduction (this volume).
3. See Cavallini (2007).
4. See Umurhan (2012). Apart from Iron Maiden's "Alexander the Great," he further discusses notions of aggression and historical masculinity in heavy metal from the legionary soldiers of Ex Deo's track "The Final War." See also Djurslev (2014) and Fletcher (2015).
5. For a useful discussion of the concept, see Erdmann (2007).
6. For heavy metal as a genre of polymorphous masculinities, see Haenfler (2013: 64).
7. See Foka (2015a) and (2015b). For one study conducted by the European Parliament on the promotion of gender equality in popular culture, see Giomi, Sansonetti, and Tota (2013).
8. See Sharpe-Young (2007) and Freeborn (2010). Mattar (2004: 536) offers an example of how "power metal" was often used interchangeably with "European metal" at the beginning of the twenty-first century.
9. Campbell (2009: 113).
10. Wallach, Berger, and Greene (2011b: 8).
11. Walser (1993a: 28–9).

12. Berger (1999: 231).
13. Borthwick and Moy (2004: 139).
14. Hardwick (2003: 4).
15. Elflein (2013: 76).
16. On lyric memorization as display of commitment, see Weinstein (2000: 123).
17. Sharpe-Young (2007: 335).
18. Bardine (2009: 125–27).
19. Baddeley (2002: 271). Note the distinction between the terms "goth music" and "gothic metal," where the latter is considered by some a derivative of the former (as well as being influenced by traditional metal bands such as Black Sabbath, and doom metal).
20. Gunn (2007: 44).
21. Gunn (2007: 48) and Haenfler (2013: 92).
22. This term is generally used by fans describing this vocal combination in magazines and fanzines, both in print and online. See e.g., Reesman (2007) and Erik M. (2013).
23. Sharpe-Young (2007: 291).
24. Connell (1990: 83, 94).
25. *OCD* (2003), s.v. "aegis."
26. ἀμφὶ δ' ἄρ' ὤμοισιν βάλετ' αἰγίδα θυσσανόεσσαν / δεινήν, ἣν περὶ μὲν πάντη Φόβος ἐστεφάνωται, / ἐν δ' Ἔρις, ἐν δ' Ἀλκή, ἐν δὲ κρυόεσσα Ἰωκή, / ἐν δέ τε Γοργείη κεφαλὴ δεινοῖο πελώρου, / δεινή τε σμερδνή τε (trans. Murray and Wyatt, adap. Linnea Åshede). Cf. also Homer, *Iliad* 21.400–402.
27. μετὰ δὲ γλαυκῶπις Ἀθήνη, / αἰγίδ' ἔχουσ' ἐρίτιμον ἀγήραον ἀθανάτην τε, / τῆς ἑκατὸν θύσανοι παγχρύσεοι ἠερέθονται, / πάντες ἐυπλεκέες, ἑκατόμβοιος δὲ ἕκαστος (trans. Martin Hammond, adap. Anna Foka).
28. Krenske and McKay (2000: 288).
29. "Aœde" is a transliterated female form of the Greek ἀοιδὸς (epic poet), as well as the name of one of the earlier set of three muses (see e.g., Pausanias 9.29.2).
30. See Secord (this volume) for Bal-Sagoth's use of archaizing English.
31. The lesser or Locrian Ajax, to be distinguished from the greater Ajax, son of Telamon. For the story, see e.g., Vergil, *Aeneid* 2.403–6.
32. For various accounts of this episode, see e.g., Homer, *Iliad* 24.697–706, *Odyssey* 11.421–24; Aeschylus, *Agamemnon* 1064, 1289–94; Euripides, *Trojan Women* 355–60; Vergil, *Aeneid* 2.245–50.
33. Brault (2009: 199–202).
34. See Foley (2001) and Foka (2011, 2014).
35. Early (2003: 56–7).
36. Weinstein (2000: 219).
37. Sharpe-Young (2003: i).
38. As observed by Berger (1999: 230), the objective/sensory and subjective/affective elements of a song can only ever be described as an after-construction—during the experience of listening, they are inseparably entangled as sound begets emotion, which in turn affects the perception of sound.
39. Aeschylus, *Agamemnon* 950–1: τὴν ξένην δὲ πρευμενῶς / τήνδ' ἐσκόμιζε· (trans. Linnea Åshede).

40. See a detailed analysis of language and performance relating to Aeschylus' Cassandra and her belated speech in Mitchell-Boyask (2006: 273-74).
41. All references to the live performance of this song refer to the particular, but representative, performance in thegothictale (2011).
42. Compare Aeschylus' *Agamemnon* 1081, where Cassandra's cry of ἀπόλλων ἐμός· could mean both "my Apollo" and "my destroyer." Cf. Brault (2009: 207) and Mitchell-Boyask (2006: 271-76).
43. See e.g., Elflein (2013: 72).
44. Krenske and McKay (2000: 287), Weinstein (2000: 29), Borthwick and Moy (2004: 140-41, 144, 147), Campbell (2009: 117), and Umurhan (2012: 138).
45. Walser (1993a: 11), Hill (2011: 298), and Sloat (1998).
46. Ahmed (2004: 28).
47. Campbell (2009: 113).
48. Haenfler (2013: 98).
49. Gunn (2007: 46).
50. Wilkins (2004: 329-30, 333-34, 342, 346-47); also Gunn (2007: 53) and Haenfler (2013: 99).
51. Berger (1999: 46).
52. Suetonius, *Nero* 35.3; Tacitus, *Annals* 16.6; Cassius Dio 63.9.5, 63.27.
53. See Pliny, *Naturalis historia* 37.50 and Cassius Dio 63.9.5.
54. On gender as relational, see Haraway (1997: 28).
55. Weinstein (2000: 67).
56. Krenske and McKay (2000: 287) and Wilkins (2004).
57. Sharpe-Young (2007: 335).
58. See Kosiński (2007).
59. Campbell (2009: 117).
60. See Lilja (2009: 167-75) for the use of the Phrygian mode in heavy metal compositions.
61. Borthwick and Moy (2004: 141).
62. In her analysis of female characters in Greek tragedy, Foley (2001: 121) states: "The greater embeddedness of the female agent in social expectations, constraints, and realities and her (sometimes) more limited vision and knowledge of public affairs can be used to reflect the human condition in tragedy, where characters often face circumstances beyond human control."
63. Aeschylus, *Agamemnon* 1091-92. Cf. 1309 where Cassandra hesitates upon the threshold, claiming that φόνον δόμοι πνέουσιν αἱματοσταγῆ, "the house breathes blood-dripping slaughter" (trans. Linnea Åshede).
64. The term "homosocial" is coined and explored by Sedgwick (1985) in greater depth.
65. Walser (1993a: 118).
66. φεύγειν μὲν οὖν χρὴ πόλεμον ὅστις εὖ φρονεῖ· / εἰ δ' ἐς τόδ' ἔλθοι, στέφανος οὐκ αἰσχρὸς πόλει / καλῶς ὀλέσθαι, Euripides, *Trojan Women* 400-402 (trans. Shirley A. Barlow).
67. Walser (1993a: 45).
68. Waksman (1999). Cf. Walser (1993a: 41-2), Bayton (1997: 43-4), Berger (1999: 58), and Umurhan (2012: 138).

69. Weinstein (2000: 25, 221).
70. In this sense, "fetishes" do not necessarily stand for displaced sexual yearning but rather, in Emily Apter's words, for more ideological instances of "displaced lack, [that is] dream surrogates for better values" (1993: 2).
71. Sharpe-Young (2007: 291).
72. Brault (2009: 199).
73. Waksman (2011: 190).
74. Waksman (2011: 190).
75. Berger (1999: 58).
76. Foka (2015b).
77. See Jones (2006).
78. The authors express heartfelt gratitude to: Mattias Eklund, Stefan Bränberg, and Robin Rönnlund for sharing musical expertise; Liv Kristine Espenæs for her time and generosity with communication and band photos; our volume editors, Kris Fletcher and Osman Umurhan, for encouragement and for conceiving of this volume, which allowed us to combine many passions; and not least the bands, for inspiration in this and many other endeavors.

CHAPTER 5
HEAVY METAL DIDO: HEIMDALL'S "BALLAD OF THE QUEEN"

Lissa Crofton-Sleigh

Dido, the queen of Carthage in Vergil's *Aeneid*, has captivated audiences, artists, and academics since the epic poem was first published in Rome in the first century BCE. She is often considered Vergil's most beloved, compelling, and memorable character in both the ancient and modern worlds, while *Aeneid* 4, where her story is prominently featured, has been deemed the most famous book of the epic, because it depicts a sad, yet fascinating story of forbidden love between Dido and the main character, Aeneas. In antiquity public recitations of stories from the *Aeneid*, particularly the story of Dido, were common.[1] Ovid, a Roman poet and younger contemporary of Vergil, comments that the most read part of the *Aeneid* was the story of Dido and Aeneas and their unlawful love (*Tristia* 2.533–6), and St. Augustine famously wept upon reading the death of Dido (though later rebukes himself for doing so; *Confessions* 1.20–21).

In music, Dido has also proven to be a popular character, particularly in the realm of opera, where most treatments of the *Aeneid* focus upon the story of Dido and her tragic downfall (Cavalli's *Didone*, Purcell's *Dido and Aeneas*, Metastasio's *Didone abbandonata*, and Berlioz's *Les Troyens*, to name a few).[2] The overwhelming popularity of Dido and the *Aeneid* in opera leads Fitzgerald to remark in his contribution to a book on the reception of Vergil:

> the best rationale for a chapter on Vergil in music is the fact that, for the late twentieth century and early twenty-first century, Vergil's *Aeneid* has become opera ... it is arguable that the most exciting development in the reception of the *Aeneid* over the last half century has been the gradual entry of Berlioz's *Les Troyens* into the operatic repertoire.[3]

Fitzgerald's decisions to ground the discussions in his chapter solely in opera, a genre now often considered elitist, and to ignore modern popular music are troublesome. This is not to say that Classical reception in opera is unimportant or uninspiring; quite the contrary, it is an exciting development that operas about Vergil's *Aeneid* have become part of the standard repertoire. But this chapter and this volume aim to shift the focus toward a less-studied (and often less-appreciated), but more contemporary and important genre, heavy metal, examining both the music and its audience.[4]

Heavy metal has often incorporated the themes and characters of Classical and other ancient mythologies into its musical, visual, and verbal dimensions, and displays a particular appreciation for the value of power, especially masculine power, viewed as a core element of heavy metal.[5] The literature of the Greeks and Romans similarly contains many examples of powerful men and masculinity, frequently in opposition to female inadequacies,[6] while the underrepresentation and marginalization of women in metal, both as artists and as fans, has often been highlighted by scholars, as has the tendency of heavy metal to be "read as a bastion of sexism and patriarchal oppression in terms of lyrical content, album imagery, and video performance."[7] With these issues in mind, here I will examine the implications surrounding one representation of a powerful female in metal music, not necessarily to explore the complicated perceptions of gender in metal, but to understand how metal music can inform and change our own perspectives and reception of Classical characters and texts, even one as famous and well-studied as Vergil's *Aeneid*.[8]

The song "Ballad of the Queen," written and sung from the perspective of Dido, comprises part of the 2013 concept album *Aeneid* by the Italian power metal band Heimdall.[9] Though it is rare for metal music to "articulate 'feminized' emotions,"[10] the genre is known to present a range of emotions such as rage, sadness, and fear.[11] All of these emotions are experienced by Dido, not only in "Ballad of the Queen" but also in the fourth book of Vergil's *Aeneid*. Taking into consideration the similar themes and emotions in the lyrics, music, and liner notes of the metal song as well as its inspiration, I argue that Dido's struggle in Book 4 between being a rational figure in a position of power (traditionally a male position) and a scorned woman (based in part on other mythical female figures such as Medea and Ariadne) is echoed in the song, which attempts to reconcile traditionally masculine elements of metal music (loud male vocals, themes of hatred and rage) with a feminine point of view. Dido's transition from a more masculine, powerful queen in *Aeneid* 1 to a more feminine, powerless lover in *Aeneid* 4 is in part an issue of gender and identity, fraught with emotional tension, and is problematic both for her and Carthage, leading to her own downfall and the eventual downfall of her city.[12] The divide between femininity and masculinity is similarly tense in the metal community, where female masculinity may be viewed as a "failure" and as a "defective copy of the male body."[13] Nonetheless, while in Vergil's *Aeneid* Dido's emotions can be seen as causing her weakness and eventual downfall, her range of emotions in "Ballad of the Queen" serves to empower her character and endow her with a heroic status similar, if not equal to, that of Aeneas.[14] As Fitzgerald (2014: 341) remarks, "music can supply what Vergil's text occasionally calls for but cannot contain." The emotive power of Dido in "Ballad of the Queen" shows how music, and metal music in particular, can interpret themes and emotions found in *Aeneid* 4 and deepen or add new levels of meaning and understanding to Vergil's characters. While many ancient and modern readers may be fascinated by and feel sympathy toward Dido, the heavy metal audience presents a group who potentially understands and even identifies with Dido's position of isolation, rather than pitying her for it.

Heimdall was formed in 1994 in Salerno, Italy by brothers Fabio Calluori (guitars) and Nicolas Calluori (drums).[15] Released in 1998, their acclaimed first album, *Lord of the Sky*, explores the mythology of the eponymous Norse god Heimdall. Subsequent albums (*The Temple of Theil* (1999), *The Almighty* (2002), and *Hard as Iron* (2004)) also deal with themes of mythology, gods, and war. After a six-year hiatus, due in part to several lineup changes and a new label (Scarlet Records), the band reformed in 2011 with both Calluori brothers, past member Carmelo Claps (guitars) and new member Gandolfo Ferro (lead vocals), as well as the addition of bass player Daniele Pastore in 2013. For their next project the band chose to create a new album around one of the most famous Italian myths, the story of Aeneas.[16] Each song on *Aeneid* is inspired by a book of Vergil's epic, which traces the destiny and journey of the Trojan hero Aeneas to Italy to found the Roman race.[17] The album presents important characters found in the *Aeneid*, such as Aeneas' father Anchises (in the song "Underworld"), his lover Dido ("Ballad of the Queen"), and his enemy Turnus ("The Last Act"), who all motivate Aeneas' actions in various ways in Vergil's poem. The album also draws upon significant themes from the epic, including references to the fate that drives Aeneas throughout the poem ("Forced by Fate," "Save You," "Waiting for the Dawn," "Night on the World"). Associations, both explicit and implicit, between Aeneas and the Roman emperor Augustus in the poem are highlighted in the song "Hero," focused around *Aeneid* 8, a book that most directly connects Aeneas to Rome and Augustus. Evander, king of the Arcadians, guides Aeneas on a tour of Pallanteum, the future site of Rome, while Aeneas' goddess mother Venus presents new armor to her son, including a shield which depicts the glorious future of Aeneas' descendants, particularly Augustus in his victory over Antony and the Egyptian queen Cleopatra in the Battle of Actium in 31 BCE, represented in the center of the shield.[18]

The epic themes contained musically and lyrically on the *Aeneid* album replicate themes not only of Vergil's poem, but also of Heimdall's earlier work, such as mythological struggles between men and gods, war and the fight for glory and honor, the sadness or difficulties of love, and journeys of exploration. In the album *The Almighty*, for instance, the tracks are linked by common themes of searching and journeying to find someone or something that is missed or longed for, even and especially when that someone or something is increasingly distant, unattainable, or inexplicable. This journey can take many different forms, including movement through death, dreams, love, art, glory, or immortality. The band's exploration of these themes throughout their work can help to explain their choice to refer to their own members as "Heroes" and their biography as their "Saga" on the website. Yet, Heimdall can be seen as heroes not only in their musical talent and history, but also in creating a new epic metal album they consider worthy of representing a Classical epic.

Most of the songs on Heimdall's album feature a first-person male perspective, whether as the protagonist Aeneas, his father Anchises, or other Trojans, as the "singer(s)" of the song.[19] These songs reflect their masculinity in the musical arrangements: they have similar chord structures, quick tempos, epic choirs, and symphonic arrangements, all characteristic of power metal, known for its soaring vocals and clean production values. In particular, these songs incorporate heavy usage of distorted guitars, seen as the most crucial and most masculine element of heavy metal.[20] For example, the song "Underworld," based on the sixth book of Vergil's epic, in which Aeneas travels down to the Underworld to consult with Anchises, contains a lightning-fast tempo and a barrage of distorted electric guitar riffs and power chords. The drums rage at a furious rate behind the wall of sound and Gandolfo Ferro's belting vocals.

"Ballad of the Queen," however, strikes a different sound and tone.[21] Based on Book 4, the song concerns Queen Dido, who is first introduced when she welcomes Aeneas to Carthage after his shipwreck in Book 1. The first book of the *Aeneid* establishes many similarities between Dido and Aeneas; they are both leaders of their respective peoples, as well as exiles (as Heimdall's explanatory liner notes point out). Dido flees Tyre because her brother kills her husband Sychaeus, whose shade approaches her in a dream and suggests that she lead an expedition to find a new home (*dux femina facti*, "a woman was the leader of the exploit," *Aen.* 1.364).[22] Having founded the new city of Carthage, she is then presented as a woman delighting in her official duties: *se laeta ferebat/per medios, instans operi regnique futuris* ("happily she was carrying herself/through the midst of her people, pressing on in the work for her future kingdom," 1.503–4). Yet Dido's position as a single woman with political power in northern Africa presents a danger to Aeneas and his mission, and a transgression of the patriarchal order in Vergil's time, when the Romans were painfully aware of the dangers presented to Rome by Cleopatra, the exotic foreign ruler of Egypt.[23] As Nugent (1999: 260, 269) remarks, "the great female characters of the *Aeneid* ... refuse, in various ways, their traditional roles of passivity, domesticity, and insubordination," yet the "oppositional and alternative views they present seem largely discredited by their own failure."[24] Dido's eventual failure as a queen, as a woman in a masculine position of power, stems from her falling in love with Aeneas (sparked by the intervention of Venus, fearing for the safety of her son Aeneas, at *Aen.* 1.667–722). Construction projects symbolizing the rise of Carthage at *Aeneid* 1.421–29 are left abandoned in Book 4.86–9. The queen, encouraged by her sister Anna at *Aeneid* 4.39–49 to view a marriage with Aeneas as a prudent political alliance against the threat of hostile neighboring peoples, loses both her alliance and Aeneas, who is reminded of his true destiny, Italy.

Heimdall's liner notes to the *Aeneid* album offer a brief summary of the important events in each book to provide background for the listener who may not be familiar with the story. The synopsis for Book 4 reads:

> Though bound by a vow to her husband Sychaeus, Dido fell in love with Aeneas. Juno got Venus to agree to their union and arranged a hunt and a storm to take them together into a cave ... but Aeneas' destiny was different. The father of the gods, Jupiter, through the words of Mercury, reminded the Trojan of his noble and sacred duty. The cold farewell words of Aeneas, prompted by Jupiter, caused the anger of Dido who swore vengeance. Warned by Mercury, Aeneas and his people hastily departed in their ships. Abandoned and wrapped by pain and desperation, the Carthaginian queen ascended to the pyre and took her sword, cursing him and prophesying eternal hatred and war between Carthage and the descendants of the Trojans.

Such a brief introduction to the complex nature of Book 4 necessitates omissions. The liner notes exclude the fact that Aeneas does love, or at least cares about, Dido and bitterly wrangles with how he should inform her of his need to leave (*Aen.* 4.279-95). However, this omission enables the song to focus upon Dido's bitterness over his rejection. The notes also do not make clear that Dido kills herself with Aeneas' sword (*ensem ... Dardanium*, 4.646-47), only referring vaguely to "her sword"—though one can argue that Aeneas has left her this sword, thereby making it her own instrument by which she can choose to die (see Figure 5.1).

Finally, the liner notes do not highlight how the majority of *Aeneid* 4 is told from Dido's perspective, through her actions in sacrificing to the gods (4.56-85) and in deciding to commit suicide, as well as the act itself (4.450-76, 504-21, 642-47, 688-92). Dido's point of view is also featured in the poem's conversations between Dido and her sister Anna (4.1-55: Anna persuades her to pursue Aeneas; 416-36: Dido asks Anna to persuade Aeneas to stay; 477-503: Dido asks Anna to have a pyre built for the purpose of burning Aeneas' personal effects in a magic spell),[25] and Dido and Aeneas (4.296-392: Dido tries to convince Aeneas to stay, but is rebuffed by Aeneas, whom she then reproaches), as well as Dido's own internal and external monologues about Aeneas and her impending death (4.534-53, 590-629, 651-62).[26] Although the liner notes do not mention the emphasis on Dido's perspective in *Aeneid* 4, Dido's position as the focalizer in "Ballad of the Queen" is clearly derived from the structure of the fourth book, as will be discussed below. Heimdall's

Figure 5.1 Alexander Runciman, *Dido on the Seashore with a Sword in her Hand* [Verso: *Woman and Child*]. National Galleries of Scotland. David Laing Bequest to the Royal Scottish Academy transferred 1910.

introduction may not include every detail of *Aeneid* 4 (and it cannot be expected to do so), but it does give the listener a basic understanding of the important themes of the poem and the song (and heavy metal): love, hatred, and vengeance.

As the liner notes inform us, "Ballad of the Queen" presents the love-stricken queen, having seen that Aeneas has left her, on the funeral pyre, about to tragically end her life. These details would seem to require a song with a different sonic quality from the rest of the album (except perhaps "Away," which focuses on the funerals of the Trojan and Latin warriors described in *Aeneid* 11). Aeneas' glorious mission to battle for and found Rome is highlighted in most of the other songs, but "Ballad of the Queen" offers the opportunity to see his mission from another perspective, that of those he has left behind. The introduction begins with ominous-sounding synth, which slowly fades into the crescendo of an acoustic guitar riff (track time 0:00–0:40). The mood is somber (E♭ minor, 3/4 meter), and the music builds upon a Classical music-inspired framework of "theme and variation," where a musical theme is first revealed in its basic form, then reappears in slightly altered forms throughout the song.[27] No heavily distorted guitars and no blasting drums appear on this track. Although the song employs the word "ballad" in its title, it is not a power ballad in the style of glam metal, but uses a slow tempo to investigate the cold and tragic nature of love and its consequences.[28] The listener expects a more subdued sound, and the song seemingly strives for themes of sadness and death, particularly in the featuring of the melodic piano interlude after the first chorus (1:29–1:47).[29] Heimdall's extensive emphasis of the piano occurs on only one other track on the album, "Away," the lyrics of which describe the dead warriors' glorious ascent to the sky. The piano in "Ballad of the Queen," as well as Dido's position on the funeral pyre during the song, associate her both musically and thematically to the strong male heroes who have sadly lost their lives in battle. Dido, too, will lose her life.

Lyrically, the first-person narrative indicates that the person singing is Dido herself (through the voice of Ferro), which establishes a female perspective for the song. Dido employs second-person pronouns to question Aeneas' intentions and her own willpower, yet whether she is addressing Aeneas directly or indirectly is unclear, as Aeneas is given no opportunity in the song to respond. The structure of the lyrics exhibits a familiarity with the structure of Book 4. The first verse (0:40–1:14) begins as follows: "Why did you find rest here on my shores? Why did your words light the flame in my heart?" The series of direct and/or rhetorical questions stylistically echoes Dido's first speech to Aeneas at *Aeneid* 4.305–30, where she lambastes him for trying to deceive her in his departure. These lines also illuminate Dido's internal conflict between her roles as powerful ruler of the Carthaginians and lover of Aeneas.[30] Dido's first question refers in part to the tradition of *hospitium* that she upheld in her position as queen of Carthage, offering food and shelter to the shipwrecked Trojans, hospitality which she now wishes she had never bestowed.[31] Her second question alludes to the extensive fire imagery that Vergil employs throughout Book 4.[32] At *Aeneid* 4.23, Dido comments to her sister Anna that she "recognizes the traces of an old flame" (*agnosco veteris vestigia flammae*), referring to a love which had once been solely for her dead husband Sychaeus. She realizes that same flicker of love is now burning for Aeneas, creating shame for the noble widow.[33] In the song, Dido, unaware of the gods' role in her consuming love for Aeneas, seemingly questions and chides both Aeneas and herself about the efficacious and poignant nature of his words, which would have sent her into a devastating passion. She simultaneously explores both her internal and external conflicts. Fire imagery then reappears during the bridge, with the line "The flames burn on into my heart." Dido realizes her loss of power and control, and searches to find a way to regain them, turning to cold steel to cease the fiery pain in her heart.

Gandolfo Ferro's singing style similarly mirrors Dido's conflict between her more masculine and feminine sides. His vocals through the first verse are softer, more controlled, and less projected and aggressive, which can be interpreted as echoing Dido's polite, diplomatic nature in *Aeneid* 1. For most of the verse Ferro sings in the same low chest register, lower than heard in most of the other songs on the album. Ferro ascends to a higher register to highlight one word in the verse: "love" (in the third line, matched also by the final word of the verse, "suns"). This vocal style seemingly encapsulates Dido's struggle to remain calm and rational regarding her troublesome love for Aeneas, concealing an inundation of fiery emotions just beneath the surface. A struggle between masculine and feminine can also be seen in both choruses (1:14–1:29, 2:20–2:52): "Hear the ballad of the queen / a melody of pain / hear my memories and dreams / hate for the years to come." The chorus lyrics juxtapose Dido's pain, memories, her hatred for Aeneas, and the future enmity between Rome and Carthage. Ferro's chorus vocals are doubled and in perfect fourths, emphasizing the articulation of her heightened, conflicting emotions by means of harmonized voices.

In the second verse (1:47–2:19), Dido's lyrics show her switching from being a victim of love toward rage and hatred. We see her concern for integrity and reputation, and her hurt pride, as she berates herself for being so foolish as to listen to Aeneas' words, which "now are as cold as blades." These lines serve to equate words with war; because Dido trusted Aeneas, she was unprepared for the battle ahead and has left herself (and her city) vulnerable. Comparing Aeneas' words to "blades" that have stabbed her also foreshadows her eventual death by Aeneas' sword.[34] This sentiment underscores an issue prominent in Vergil's *Aeneid*, where the personified *Fama*, "Rumor," casts Dido and Aeneas as "captured by a shameless love" (*turpi. . .cupidine captos*, 4.194) and Dido as neglectful of her city (*Aen.* 4.173-95), an identity with which she bitterly wrangles for the rest of Book 4.[35]

As mentioned earlier, Dido's role as a female ruler is already problematic in the ancient world, particularly in the wake of Cleopatra, whom Octavian portrayed as a threat to Rome. Dido similarly considers destroying "Rome" (though never directly completes the action) when she imagines setting fire to the Trojan ships, forcing them to abandon their journey to Italy (4.604-6). Dido tries to reverse the damage *Fama* has done in her eulogy to herself (4.651-58), reclaiming her more masculine, political side and recalling with pride her achievements as a sound leader who founded a great new city. Her castigation of herself in the song represents a similar attempt to remove herself from the spell Aeneas' words cast upon her and reclaim her strong, stately identity. Both works emphasize Dido's persistent desire for a good reputation, both as wife to Sychaeus and as political leader.[36]

Dido's masculine side continues to dominate in the rest of the second verse, as she sings more about hatred and war. Dido finishes the verse by singing, "Your friends will be your enemies / And the sun will start to cry / Hate will domain between our mates [*sic*] / I swear it to the stars." Aeneas' quick transition from friend to foe here is reflected in Vergil's text, as Dido shifts from calling Aeneas "spouse" (*coniuge*, 4.324) to "enemy" (*hostis*, 4.424, 549). Dido politicizes her words by drawing her nation into the conversation with the plurals "friends ... enemies ... mates." As Dido hates Aeneas, so too must the Carthaginians sustain an everlasting hatred for the Trojans (mirrored in the line in the chorus, "Hate for years to come"). The domain of hatred echoes Dido's curse at *Aeneid* 4.607-29, where Dido beseeches her people to always persecute Aeneas and his descendants and never succumb to an alliance (*nullus amor populis nec foedera sunto*, "let there be no love or treaties between our peoples," 4.624). Dido's words have immense power, as Vergil implies that her everlasting enmity explains the origins of the Punic Wars between the Romans and Carthaginians, a series of wars between 264 and 146 BCE, which ended with the devastating sack of Carthage in 146.[37] Likewise, Dido's words in "Ballad of the Queen" decree future hostilities between the Trojans and Carthaginians.

In the second verse, a change in singing style reflects Dido's growing power. Ferro sings in head voice: the timbre is rougher, and the pitch rises an octave higher than the first verse. It could be argued that Ferro's higher register here comes off as more emotional, i.e., more feminine; that, in turn, could allude to Dido's gradual deterioration in *Aeneid* 4 as charted by Vergilian scholars, who have often linked Dido's emotionality to her downfall. Her amorous passion leads to madness and places her in a position of fatal weakness, which in part enables Vergil to elicit sympathy for Dido from the reader.[38] But "Ballad of the Queen" does not seek sympathy alone for Dido. Though still singing from the perspective of Dido, Ferro's higher, more aggressive metal vocals indicate strength and virtuosity, which propel Dido into a position of higher power and prestige. While discussing the influences of opera on rock music, Ken McLeod argues that, among fans of both opera and rock, there is a distinct aesthetic preference for artists who exhibit ability in upper registers. The same could be said to apply to metal if we consider, for example, the immense popularity of Judas Priest, whose singer Rob Halford can be said to exhibit operatic qualities in the use of falsetto and the *messa di voce* style.[39] McLeod (2001: 190) continues:

> Such similarities of expression rest largely on a sense of transgression either of the bondage of social norms and conventions in the case of rock singers, or of the bondage of unrequited love or other dramatic tragedy in the case of the opera singer. In both cases it is the transgressive voice which is able to transcend bodily or emotional constraints.

In Vergil's *Aeneid*, Dido's raging emotion weakens her, but in metal, her emotions of hate and anger enhance her position of power.[40] Her "transgressive voice" (via Ferro's vocal range and more aggressive tone) allows her to transcend her own constraints as a lovelorn female victimized by Aeneas. She uses her voice to battle Aeneas, who not only has no response, but is also, perhaps, unworthy of responding to Dido here. Susan McClary ([1991] 2002: 80–111), in her examination of the nature of madness in relationship to femininity in Classical music, points to hyper-masculinized madness in heavy metal as a sign of a shift in the discourse of gender in music.[41] Madness may lead to feminized weakness and destruction in Classical music (and in Vergil's epic), but it fosters masculine power and heroism in heavy metal. Dido's rage and vocal supremacy against Aeneas in the second verse thus elevates her to an extent not seen in Vergil's poem.

The tone of the music and lyrics evolves again at the bridge (2:52–3:24). The music continues in a minor key, but the bridge is dominated by one lead vocal and accompanying piano.[42] Gloomy minor chords, as Walser suggests, are similar to manifestations of women, filled with mystery and dread that threaten male self-control and power.[43] Walser's characterization of women in metal is strikingly similar to the representation of heroines of Greek tragedy. Their very presence on the stage signals danger for the male protagonists, just as Dido symbolizes danger for Aeneas here.[44] The bridge's lyrics and minor chords evoke the tragedy of Book 4, as Dido resorts to suicide, seemingly her only remaining option for closure.[45] Once Dido decides upon suicide by sword, she calms herself and eventually finds peace. While her suicide links her to tragic heroines such as Phaedra, Dido's choice of the sword as her death weapon is inherently more masculine; men die by swords in battle.[46] Her choice aligns her with Ajax, the famous Greek hero who likewise dies by his own sword because of shame and an affront to his reputation.[47] Dido's decision to die has often been seen as the means by which she resumes at least some of her dignity and heroic stature in Vergil's epic.[48]

In "Ballad of the Queen," Dido demands that her "cold friend," the sword, free her and finally bring her peace from the destructive flames of love. Ferro's vocals emote still more passion and intensity than in the second verse and hit a virtuosic crescendo in the very last line, where Ferro sings "give me peace, give me peace, give me peace," weaving an operatic melisma into the last word of the line (and song). Dido desires peace for herself even as she rejects peace for Aeneas (and their respective peoples). Yet each repetition of "give me peace" crescendoes in urgency, which makes the listener question whether she actually achieves her peace. Dido is never mentioned again in Heimdall's album (except for a possible reference in "Underworld," where Aeneas is walking in "a dark world full of tears"), but in Vergil's epic Dido sees Aeneas once again in the Underworld and rebuffs his pleas to her with stony silence (*Aen.* 6.450–76). We might read Dido's pleas for peace as the reason for her not to reappear in later songs on the album; Dido wants no further association with Aeneas, not even in his meeting with or remembrances of her later in Vergil's epic.

The song's near ninety-second conclusion (3:25–4:50) combines a choral arrangement consisting of several voices singing in short, distinct, yet repeated wordless harmonies in a minor key along with string, piano, and guitar accompaniment (the last twenty seconds are sung *a cappella*). The triple repetition of the last line as well as the repetition of vocal riffs in the finale could be seen as the musical equivalent of a prayer or even a magic spell, representing the magical elements of Vergil's *Aeneid*, where Dido feigns knowledge of an incantation meant to rid her of desire for Aeneas as a pretext to hide her actual plan (4.474–503). Additionally, the musical conclusion captivates with its overwhelmingly tragic sound, leading the listener to expect that the song will end sadly. In fact, the song unexpectedly closes on a major chord, as do many of those on the album that deal with masculine glory and honor. Dido has died with and for her honor and found peace as a hero.

Furthermore, retaining Ferro as the vocalist (as opposed to having a guest female singer on the track) is indicative of the same issue with which Vergil dealt, as a male writing and narrating the strong female character of Dido.[49] The intricacies and variations of the music, lyrics, and vocals throughout the song reflect Dido's complexity as a character, as well as her tragic struggle to reconcile the different sides of her identity; this song, along with the rest of the album, serves as an example of how metal music functions as a particularly apt setting for exploring some of the complex issues of Vergil's poem. Heimdall's sophisticated treatment of the background material might surpass the typical listener's knowledge of Vergil's ancient epic, but the band has aimed for accessibility with synopses of each book of the *Aeneid* along with the lyrics in the liner notes (see Fletcher, this volume). By the end of the album, between the songs and the synopses, the listener ought to have a reasonably strong sense of the plot, themes, and characters present in Vergil's epic and might even be inspired to go read the work, in translation or possibly in the original Latin. As Juhana Rossi and Ellen Emmerentze Jervell noted in *The Wall Street Journal* on June 4, 2013, heavy metal music frequently inspires fans to learn foreign, even obscure languages, to better comprehend the themes and content of the music and/ or its background sources. Given the strong likelihood that even fans from Italy have not studied Latin,[50] learning this ancient language might present the kind of challenge metal fans around the globe would embrace to better understand Vergil's as well as Heimdall's *Aeneid*.

The reception of Dido by metal audiences may also differ dramatically from how the Romans would have perceived her in the *Aeneid*. Servius' late antique commentary on the *Aeneid* remarks that the phrase *dux femina facti* (*ad Aen.* 1.364), which indicates the nature of Dido as a leader, "should be proclaimed as if astonishing" (*pronuntiandum quasi mirum*). The mid-fourth-century grammarian Donatus is even less charitable, declaring that this line must have been included to mock Pygmalion, Dido's brother (*Interpretationes Vergilianae* 1.80.2–3). On Donatus' commentary Keith observes, "To Donatus' androcentric gaze, the effectiveness of a female leader necessarily implies the concomitant inadequacy of the male who should master her."[51] Dido's status as a foreign female in power is not normative in the Roman world; she is to be viewed as a dangerous outsider or other. According to Syed, "As a woman and a Carthaginian, Dido embodies otherness in a double sense against which Aeneas' identity can be defined."[52] Dido's otherness allows not only Aeneas' identity to be defined, but also that of the Romans. As Reed suggests, "the Roman self is clearly opposed to an Oriental 'other'—suggesting a Carthaginian identity narrowly avoided, an Egyptian identity rejected ... or a Trojan identity left behind."[53] Not only should Romans not identify with Dido, but even pitying her places a Roman reader or audience in a precarious position, as they are temporarily siding with the "enemy."[54]

Metal fans, however, can identify with Dido, particularly her status as an outsider. Dido's disempowerment in Vergil's *Aeneid* can be seen as establishing a rapport with metal bands and fans throughout the globe, who may feel the same emotions of frustration, rage, hatred, and sadness, and use those emotions to fuel powerful songs that transcend everyday experience.[55] Heavy metal fans, and queer heavy metal fans in particular, according to Clifford-Napoleone, constantly have to negotiate their identity in hostile situations, as Dido must do in the *Aeneid*. But, as Clifford-Napoleone notes, "music goads individuals into questioning their own identities and allows them to use the sonic gestures of music to negotiate their identities," and heavy metal, in particular, is identified by fans as a vehicle for opposing marginalization.[56] Dido's appearance in Heimdall's *Aeneid* is brief, but strong. Heimdall's music progresses beyond Vergil's sympathetic reading (*Aen*. 4.408–15, lamenting Dido's sight of Aeneas leaving and the nature of love) to offer what can be seen as a sympathetic reading of Dido and *Aeneid* 4 which suggests to an audience new ways of contemplating and interpreting Vergil's epic. "Ballad of the Queen" functions to empower Dido's character and allows her to express emotions which may have caused Romans to pity (or condemn) her but instead encourages metal fans instead to understand and respect her. Clifford-Napoleone refers to an "ethos of acceptance" in heavy metal, providing queers and other outsiders an association and a sense of belonging, also known as "outsider togetherness."[57] Dido finds in the heavy metal audience what she rarely or never would have found in ancient, and perhaps some modern, audiences: acceptance.[58]

Notes

1. On the famous and beloved nature of Dido and Book 4, see, e.g., Spence (1999: 80, 95) and Syed (2005: 143). On the public recitations of Vergil's work, see Syed (2005: 14). Vergil himself was reputedly a delightful reader, who performed portions of *Aeneid* Books 2, 4, and 6 (if not more) to the public (*Vita Vergilii* 95–98) in an effort to judge reader response and improve his epic.
2. For more about Dido in music, see Kailuweit (2005: 351–423).
3. Fitzgerald (2014: 341).
4. The limited appreciation of the metal genre encompasses not only many Classics scholars, but also much of academia in general. For more on the history and development of metal studies, including discussion of its rising (and very recent) legitimation, see Hickam (2014: esp. 15–17) and Brown (2016a).
5. On masculine power in heavy metal, see Walser (1993a: 76, 108–10), Weinstein (2000: 104), Wong (2011: 83), and Gascot-Hernández (2015). The nature of rock music in general as a male domain is discussed by Whiteley (1997: xix, xxv); in the same volume, Cohen (1997: 28–9) suggests that metal presents "a spectacle of male power and offers a means through which men can demonstrate their manhood."
6. See, for example, the famous funeral oration of the Athenian general Pericles during the Peloponnesian War between Athens and Sparta, where he suggests that women will have the best reputation if they do nothing that might cause them to be the subject of men's conversation (Thuc. 2.45.2). On the appropriation of myth and history regarding strong male figures such as Alexander the Great and Octavian, and the lessons that they impart upon a traditionally male heavy metal audience with typically masculinist predispositions, see

Umurhan (2012). Similarly, see Djurslev (2014). On military and wartime masculinity in heavy metal, see Kartheus (2015: 324–27).

7. On the underrepresentation and/or marginalization of women in metal, see, among others, Walser (1993a: 108–11), Weinstein (2000: 36, 67), Hill (2018). Quotation is from Barron (2013: 68). See also St. Lawrence and Joyner (1991). Cope (2010: 142–45) opposes the view that women are not welcome in the metal world, arguing instead that space in metal is developing for women, especially as musicians; cf. Riches (2015). In his work Cope separates hard rock and heavy metal into genres with distinct musical codes, disputing Led Zeppelin's position as an originator of metal, and also disagrees with Walser's arguments about gender anxieties in heavy metal, claiming that misogyny and other marginalization of women occur only in blues-influenced hard rock. Lilja (2009: 24–5), however, argues that no distinction can be made in musical terms between hard rock and heavy metal, as both are influenced by the blues. I tend to agree with Lilja that it is difficult to make a clear distinction, as literary and musical genres quite often and quite naturally overlap.

8. Cf. Åshede and Foka on Cassandra (this volume).

9. For more on Heimdall, this album, and the question of nationalism, see Fletcher (this volume).

10. Overell (2013: 201).

11. Wallach, Berger, and Greene (2011b: 14).

12. Fletcher (2014: 31, 144–45, 154–55) argues that Dido stands for her city, and her struggle to prioritize her love for her new country over her love for Aeneas leads to her demise. Aeneas, however, recognizes the need to regard his love for his new *patria,* or "fatherland"—Rome—as more important than his personal love (*amor*) for the Carthaginian queen. Cf. Syed (2005: 145, 172) and Reed (2010: 73).

13. Clifford-Napoleone (2015: 93, 98). She argues, however, that the understanding of the performance of male masculinity in metal as an illusion covering the queerscape (that is, the strong presence of the LGBTQ community within metal, both as fans and as performers) causes the hypermasculinized presuppositions to break down, and points to Joan Jett as a great example of a female rocker breaking down the barriers of masculinity.

14. Dido can be seen as a hero in Vergil's *Aeneid,* but typically she is viewed as a tragic hero, whereas Aeneas is the stronger epic hero. For a recent discussion, see Panoussi (2009).

15. Biographical information is derived from the band's official website (www.heimdallband.com), as well as from *Encyclopaedia Metallum.*

16. Heimdall may have been inspired to create an album around the mythology of their own culture from remarks such as those made by Mortiis, keyboardist for the Norwegian black metal band Emperor: "Bands from fucking Greece and Italy going pagan Viking metal—how stupid can people be? . . . A guy from Greece holding on to Thor's hammer, what's the point of that? He should have a Zeus symbol or a Cronus symbol. At least respect that, his own mythological gods!" (quoted in Christe 2003: 284). Additionally, the *Aeneid* album cover art is an image of a cross, a "symbol of solidarity" to Scandinavian and Norwegian metal, according to Christe (2003: 284).

17. For more on the structure of this album, see Fletcher (this volume).

18. The Battle of Actium was the culmination of the series of civil wars in Rome, beginning in 49 BCE, when Caesar marched on Rome. After his defeat of Pompey and his allies in 46 BCE, Caesar was assassinated in 44 BCE. Caesar's supporter Antony and his adopted heir Octavian (later Augustus) ruled over the eastern and western halves of the Roman Empire, respectively, and solidified their alliance with the marriage of Antony to Octavian's sister Octavia in

40 BCE. They fought as allies against Sextus Pompey in the second round of civil wars, but tensions had already begun to mount between the two leaders and came to a head when Antony divorced Octavia to be with Cleopatra (his lover since 41 BCE). Out of spite, Octavian declared war against Cleopatra in 32 BCE, and finally defeated the lovers in 31 BCE, forcing their swift retreat back to Egypt and a mutual suicide in 30 BCE.

19. *Aeneid* 2 and 3 are also first-person male perspectives: in these books Aeneas narrates his own story to Dido of his futile fight to save Troy and his travels from Troy to Carthage.
20. On guitars and gender see, e.g., Walser (1993b), Bayton (1997), and Waksman (1999).
21. Similarly, the fourth book of Vergil's *Aeneid* has often been seen as the outlier, unnecessary to the linear plot and in conflict with some of the other books, but beloved and essential to the emotional appeal of the epic; see, e.g., Austin (1966: ix) or Spence (1990: 80, 95).
22. All translations of the Latin are my own.
23. On Dido as a threat to the mission of Aeneas, see, e.g., Keith (2000: 115–16) and Fletcher (2014: 142, 151, 162). On Dido's dangerous and transgressive position as a female in power, see Monti (1981: 32, 59, 77) and Panoussi (2009: 135, 187–88).
24. Nugent (1999: 260) also argues that Dido's "unusual choices in how she lives her life are seen by those around her as specific *rejections* of more normal roles."
25. Though Anna can be seen as an important player in persuading Dido to seek a marriage with Aeneas, her role is relatively minor in *Aeneid* 4.
26. Syed (2005: 96) suggests that there are, in fact, more monologues than dialogue in Book 4. For more on the dialogue of Book 4, see Highet (1972).
27. On this Classical theme in metal, see Umurhan (2012: 137). On the influence of Classical music on heavy metal, see Walser (1993a: 57–107) and Lilja (2009).
28. Christe (2003: 155) describes glam power ballads as "the ultimate sellout ... pseudo-acoustic love [songs] complete with weepy guitar solo and lovelorn sing-along chorus." As Christe notes on the same page, British heavy metal dealt mostly with tragic romance when talking about love at all; we might think of "Ballad of the Queen" as following along the same thematic lines.
29. According to Walser (1993a: 130) male fans of the harder genres of metal tend to perceive keyboards and/or the piano as "feminine." Perhaps the piano's prominence here suggests that the band may be actively pursuing a feminine sound, in addition to a sad sound. On the problematic nature of "feminine" or "feminized" instruments in metal, see DiGioia and Helfrich (2018: 368).
30. For more on Dido's internal conflict of masculinity and femininity in Vergil's *Aeneid*, see especially West (1980) and Panoussi (2009: 135, 187). Nappa (2007) argues that Dido's conflict stems from the realization that she never wished to be married at all, thus potentially pointing to Dido's desire to retain her masculine status and power.
31. At *Aeneid* 4.657–58, Dido's last words are a lament about how happy she would have continued to be as queen and leader of the Carthaginians, had Aeneas never landed on her shore. On the nature of Dido's and Aeneas' relationship in terms of *hospitium,* the conventions governing Roman hosts and guests, see Gibson (1999).
32. On Vergil's fire imagery, see, e.g., Knox (1950), Rudd (1990: 152, 164–65), and Gutting (2006: 269).
33. Roman women who were faithful to their husbands throughout their lives were held in the highest esteem. Though a widow, Dido's alleged infidelity offers one reason why, as some have suggested, she and Aeneas could not have remained together and left for Italy. On Dido's

struggle and shame about being an *univira* ("one-man woman"), see Rudd (1990) and Panoussi (2009: 185–86).

34. Wound imagery appears in Vergil's *Aeneid* as well. The *pectore vultus/verbaque* "(face and words [of Aeneas] in her heart," *Aen.* 4.4–5) help to kindle in Dido the flames of love which she describes to Anna at the beginning of Book 4. After Anna convinces Dido to let down her guard and open herself up to loving Aeneas, the flames kindled by Aeneas' appearance and words eventually create "a wound in her heart" (*pectore vulnus*, *Aen.* 4.67).

35. For more on Dido and her reputation, see Moles (1987: 153–61), Tatum (1996: 448–51), and especially Syson (2013).

36. Dido's desire for a good reputation aligns her with many of the famous Greek heroes, both male and female. Achilles stopped fighting in the Trojan War when he felt that his reputation was being shamed by Agamemnon's usurpation of his war trophy Briseis (Homer, *Iliad* 1, esp. 161–71). Medea's refusal to be ashamed (Euripides, *Medea* 381–406) also provides a clear model for Dido.

37. On the political and military ramifications of Dido's curse, see Monti (1980: 60–1), Hardie (1986: 283–84), and Panoussi (2009: 196).

38. For example, Hardie (2014: 63, 69) writes, "Dido is brought low when she succumbs to love by an all too 'feminine' weakness … majestic Dido descends from the epic throne into erotic obsession reminiscent of self-absorption typical of Latin love elegy." For additional discussions of Dido's emotionality and madness, see, e.g., Otis (1963: 87–91) and McLeish (1972). On reader sympathy for Dido, see, e.g., Farron (1980). In contrast, Schiesaro (2008) suggests that Dido is not a hapless victim, but instead poses a considerable threat to Aeneas through a desire for revenge akin to Euripides' characterization of Medea, who killed her own children to enact vengeance upon her ex-husband, Jason.

39. McLeod (2001: 189–90).

40. For more on power for women and other marginalized groups, both semantically and in heavy metal music, see Gascot-Hernández (2015: 98–102). On the heavy metal scene as a transgressive space where women can perform resistance, see Riches (2015: esp. 266–68), and Savigny and Sleight (2015).

41. For recent responses to McClary ([1991] 2002) and the gendered nature of metal music, see Hill (2015) and (2016).

42. Overell (2013: 216) argues that minor keys are found in more typically feminized genres of music such as emo and are usually avoided in male rock genres.

43. Walser (1993a: 119).

44. Dido's representation as an abandoned woman, as well as a woman who commits suicide, is often linked with tragic Greek heroines such as Medea, Ariadne, and Phaedra. On the connections among these characters, see, e.g., Oksala (1962: 167–97), Segal (1990: 11), and Schiesaro (2008).

45. The tragedy of *Aeneid* 4 has been well examined in scholarship as early as Pease (1935: 8–11). For a recent discussion with relevant bibliography, see Panoussi (2009). Some scholars have argued that Dido's death is sacrificial, to allow Aeneas' journey to continue; see, e.g., McLeish (1972) and Horsfall (1990: 131).

46. For more on female death by sword as masculine mode in Greek tragedy, see Loraux (1987).

47. Ajax views himself as the best warrior after Achilles, so when Odysseus instead receives Achilles' armor, Ajax and his reputation are fatally insulted. On Dido's relationship to Ajax, see Tatum (1996: 445–51) and especially Panoussi (2009: 182–97).

48. E.g., in Lyne (1987: 46), Rudd (1990: 162), and Heinze (1993: 105).
49. Lovatt (2013: 11) speaks of the masculine nature of epic but also claims that Vergil, by "writing Dido . . . makes his own voice (at least partly) feminine."
50. Due, perhaps, in part to the typically working- and lower-middle class background of metal fans, as noted by Krenske and McKay (2000: 293) and Weinstein (2000: 286). For a recent, in-depth study of the class backgrounds of heavy metal fans since the 1970s, see Brown (2016b). See also Fiori (1984). Those of the working class in Italy often begin vocational school as adolescents, suggesting a high improbability of enrollment in academic courses such as foreign language; see also Pozzoli (2007).
51. Keith (2000: 24).
52. Syed (2005: 144).
53. Reed (2010: 67). Cf. Syed (2005: 191–92). For more on Roman and/or Italian identity within *Aeneid*-based albums in heavy metal, see (Fletcher) this volume.
54. As suggested by Spence (1999: 90–5). Cf. Syed (2005: 136–93).
55. On the transcendent and communal power of metal music, particularly for female fans, see Hill (2015: 243–45) and Riches (2015: 266–68).
56. Clifford-Napoleone (2015: 18, 67 (quoted), 70). On the empowerment and identity negotiation of female metal fans, see also Patterson (2016) and Savigny and Sleight (2015: 348–51). On the empowerment of female fans through the creation of metal fan fiction, see Hoad (2017).
57. Clifford-Napoleone (2015: 58). The title of her third chapter is "Outsider Togetherness." Yet there may be some contradiction in metal identity: see Hill, Lucas, and Riches (2015), which discusses how "internal practices of marginalization within metal act to preserve and (re) produce hegemonic power structures" (295).
58. Many people have helped to guide the development of this chapter; I'd like to thank Kris Fletcher, Osman Umurhan, and Cody H. Smith for their illuminating comments and recommendations on earlier drafts. The "Dido In and After Vergil" panel at the 2018 SCS annual meeting in Boston, sponsored by the Vergilian Society, as well as audiences at Santa Clara University and the University of San Francisco, also posed insightful questions and offered useful suggestions for me to explore as I was in the process of researching and writing. Any remaining errors are my own.

CHAPTER 6
A METAL *MONSTRUM*: EX DEO'S CALIGULA
Iker Magro-Martínez

This chapter analyzes the treatment of the emperor Caligula in two songs and their accompanying music videos by the Italian-Canadian death metal band Ex Deo that portray the emperor as brutal and violent. First, I briefly study metal's interest in themes related to evil, bloody, dark tales. Second, I sketch the reception of Caligula to show how, since the very first accounts of his reign, the emperor has always had a terrible reputation, which continues to affect his depiction in modern literature and cinema. The music of Ex Deo is no exception. Specifically, I examine the portrayal of the emperor in the lyrics and videos of two songs from Ex Deo's second album *Caligvla* (2012): "I, Caligvla" and "The Tiberius Cliff (Exile to Capri)." Their depiction of the Roman emperor is emblematic of the fascination with evil and brutality that permeates many metal subgenres and shows how the reception of Caligula makes him an obvious choice for metal songs.

Metal and evil

Since its origins, heavy metal music has shown a deep interest in relating grim, scary, and evil tales. Black Sabbath, one of the most influential bands in the early days of the genre, reveal a clear interest in the occult on their first album, *Black Sabbath*, released in 1970.[1] The parallel development of the shock rock of Alice Cooper and Kiss, pioneers in the use of sophisticated theatrical scenography in their shows, contributed a horror film visual aesthetic to heavy metal's bag of tricks (Weinstein 2000: 21) and had a profound influence upon later hard rock and heavy metal bands such as Mercyful Fate/King Diamond, Lizzy Borden, W. A. S. P, Rob Zombie, and Lordi, among many others. The themes of evil and darkness flourished with the emergence and expansion of the extreme metal scene in the mid-1980s and 1990s.[2] Death metal, regarded as one of the most aggressive and visceral forms of music (Dunn 2004: 107), deals in its vivid and unambiguous lyrical style with death, suicide, misanthropy, madness, and diabolical, anti-religious, and gory themes (what Weinstein (2000: 38–42) calls "themes of chaos"), which transgress and cross boundaries, question and break taboos and established values (Hjelm, Kahn-Harris, and LeVine 2013b: 10). Metal's depiction and narration of the darkest side of humanity's degradation has from time to time placed this genre at the center of a noticeable moral panic (Klypchak 2013: 37).[3]

While there are numerous explanations offered for the rise of extreme metal, most scholars agree on the sense of empowerment afforded by death metal music.[4] Metal music and its preoccupation with violence, horror, the occult, and evil themes are the reflection of the contemporary tensions of its time. The exploration of the "other," that is, of what hegemonic society does not want to acknowledge, has allowed metal music to find forms of transgression and appropriate sources of empowerment whereby controversy becomes a tool of identity (Hjelm, Kahn-Harris, and LeVine 2013b: 5), and the control of unsettling fantasies, of the fascinating abject, empowers both the music and its audience to control the threats of the modern world (Berger: 1999 and Kahn-Harris 2007: 43). Furthermore, metal music brings images of chaos and death to the forefront because it empowers them with its vitalizing sound (Weinstein 2000: 38). Reciprocally, aggression, anger, violence, and brutality become the source of metal's vitality, a vitality that produces an energy that excites and "charges up" the body and leads to a catharsis (Kahn-Harris 2007: 52).

At the same time, metal music has always shown a special interest in historical themes and events. History offers a wide array of bloody and sinister episodes and figures that fit in with the style played by metal bands, especially—but not exclusively—those belonging to the extreme metal scene. The connection between metal music and evil characters from the past is reflected in different ways. For example, bands' names allude to these historical figures. Bathory is a Swedish band that became fundamental in the development of extreme metal styles, like black and Viking metal. Their name derives from Erzsebeth Bathory (1560–1614), also known as the Bloody Countess, a Hungarian noblewoman accused of murdering over 700 women.[5] The examples of this phenomenon are countless, including bands named after infamous Classical characters: Neron Kaisar (Russia), Tiberius Project (Brazil), and Elagabalus (US).[6]

Furthermore, historical characters with a terrible reputation have become the subject matter of concept albums. For example, in 2008 the English symphonic black/gothic metal band Cradle of Filth released *Godspeed of the Devil's Thunder*, based on the story of Guilles de Rais (1405–1440), a French serial killer of children.[7] On their album *Nightwing* (1999), Swedish black metal band Marduk based many songs on the figure of Vlad Tepes III Draculea (1431–1476), also known as Vlad the Impaler, the Wallachian prince who inspired Bram Stoker's Dracula.

Some metal musicians also use the names of such characters for their stage personas. It is very common for musicians of black and death metal to adopt artistic *noms de guerre* based on demonology or pagan mythology that sound blasphemous and sinister. This trend goes back to Venom, the pioneer extreme metal band, whose bassist and singer adopted the name Cronos, the titan and father of Zeus in Greek mythology. Meanwhile, Magnus Broberg, the black metal singer and ex-member of the Swedish black metal band Dark Funeral, is known in the extreme metal scene as Emperor Magus Caligula. Because evil and the recreation of historical events are a defining aspect of some metal music, Caligula, traditionally portrayed as a bloody, insane, and lustful tyrant, is an obvious choice for a genre fascinated by evil figures.

The transmission and reception of Caligula

Gaius Julius Caesar Augustus Germanicus, better known as Caligula (12–41 CE), was the third emperor of the Roman Empire (37–41 CE).[8] He is also arguably the most infamous of the emperors, depicted since antiquity as cruel, incestuous, delusional, and egomaniacal. Although recent scholarly works have argued that this portrait of him is overblown or even completely fictional, it is so pervasive and well-established that it still dominates outside of academia, and influences Ex Deo.[9] As so much work has been done on the reception of Caligula, only a brief overview is needed here to sketch out his main characteristics in the tradition. I will return to individual negative details as they appear in Ex Deo's songs and videos.

The three most influential early authors for subsequent views of Caligula are Philo, Seneca, and Suetonius. Philo (*ca.* 20 BCE–50 CE), an Alexandrian Jew who personally met Caligula when he led a Judean embassy to Rome, describes the emperor as a wild, delirious person possessed by a great frenzy and insanity (*Legat.* 93). Seneca the Younger (*ca.* 4–65 CE), a senator and philosopher, was another contemporary of Caligula. He alludes to the emperor in many of his treatises, and describes him as an unstable and furious ruler greedy for human blood (*Ben.* 4.31.2). Although Suetonius (*ca.* 70–*ca.* 138 CE) was not a contemporary, his biography has exerted the most influence on the modern reception of Caligula. Because he worked as a manager of public libraries and the imperial archives during the reign of Hadrian, his account was long supposed to be based on reliable sources. While recent work has criticized the likely senatorial bias of such sources, Suetonius' biography of the emperor is the most scandalous of the twelve in his *De vita caesarum* (*On the Life of the Caesars*), and is the source of most of the (in)famous details about Caligula's life and character.

After a dramatic childhood and youth in which his siblings either died or were executed, Caligula became the successor to Tiberius (14–37 CE). The ancient authors record that after a hopeful beginning and an enigmatic illness, his reign deteriorated into a string of countless scandals, arbitrary abuses of the senatorial class, and megalomaniac whims that would eventually lead to his assassination.[10] As Suetonius so memorably puts it (*Calig.* 22): *Hactenus quasi de principe, reliqua ut de monstro narranda sunt* ("So much for Caligula as emperor; we must now tell of his career as a monster").[11]

Seneca's and Suetonius' presentation of Caligula are complementary. The emperor appears in eight of Seneca's twelve *Dialogi* as an example of vice, and the antithesis of every Stoic virtue: excess of emotion, waste of money, verbal abuse, cruelty, anger, cowardice, and hubris.[12] Suetonius may have been influenced by the depiction of Caligula in Seneca (Lindsay 1993: 9), and the part of his biography that depicts the emperor as a monster (*Calig.* 22–60) presents the quintessential bad ruler, focusing on the sensational and the shocking (Southon 2017: 188). Suetonius goes so far as to describe Caligula using the Latin word *monstrum* (*Calig.* 22), which suggests something unnatural and, when applied to a human being, has a pejorative sense: atrocious, evil, offensive, and brutal.[13] Caligula thus becomes the incarnation of all the vices of the bad emperor; he is the totalization of evil.

Many modern scholars now consider that this view of Caligula as a monster is the result of a hostile senate; regardless, it has persisted throughout antiquity, through the Middle Ages and Renaissance, and into modern times. It has been so enduring that whenever people schematize the rulers of Rome into "good" and "bad" emperors,

Caligula is almost universally one of the first to be put in the latter category. The only emperor who rivals Caligula for the position of "worst emperor" is Nero, due to his reputation for persecuting the Christians.[14]

In the twentieth century, this image of Caligula persisted, in part through the depiction of the emperor in popular culture.[15] Twentieth-century literature and cinema reproduced the image of Caligula as a depraved and disturbed ruler and he—along with Nero—has become the archetypal bad emperor or evil ruler (Lindner 2013: 211). Like their predecessors since antiquity, these authors tend to focus on the same anecdotes and a simplistic portrayal of Caligula (Southon 2017: 187). Among the numerous books and films about him, it is worth mentioning two in particular, because of their popularity and their influence on Ex Deo's presentation of the emperor.

In 1934, Robert Graves published his wildly successful novel, *I, Claudius*, following it with a sequel, *Claudius the God and His Wife Messalina*, a year later. Graves, who would later publish a translation of Suetonius (1957), was greatly inspired by this ancient author's portrait of Caligula. In Graves' books, Caligula is inhuman from his infancy: he kills his own father Germanicus. He becomes an aberrant and monstrous emperor, a madman who believes he is a god and who is an unpredictable murderer, responsible even for the death of his sister Drusilla (Southon 2017: 190).

Jack Pulman adapted Graves' two novels for the BBC series *I, Claudius* (1976), which achieved enormous popularity with audiences. John Hurt's brilliant and histrionic performance as Caligula shows a deranged, cruel, and capricious ruler obsessed with his divinity. However, unlike Graves' Caligula, Hurt's is not unambiguously evil; he suffers an evident mental illness and shows a great dependence upon Drusilla, the only one who is able to soothe him until the emperor murders her at the height of his insanity (Southon 2017: 196).

One of the depictions of Caligula that most influenced Ex Deo is the infamous 1979 film *Caligula*, an erotic film produced by the adult magazine Penthouse.[16] Gore Vidal, who wrote the script in 1976, was also inspired by Suetonius' writings (he was then kicked off of the project by producer Bob Guccione, who went on to record pornographic scenes and add them to the film).[17] In *Caligula*, Malcolm McDowell plays the role of an arbitrary and eccentric emperor obsessed with his own divinity, ruling in an age of decadence and corruption. Caligula is not mentally ill, but he is a traumatized young man who constantly fears for his life and whose only solace from corruption is his true love Drusilla, who is the moral heart of the film and who mothers him until her death (Southon 2017: 199–201).

This film gained such notoriety that after its release many B-movies used the figure of Caligula to symbolize an imperial court of lust and corruption.[18] Because of his depiction in *Caligula*, the emperor's hubris, despotism, and obsession with divinity were neglected in favor of the picture of a depraved emperor full of sexual fantasies and excesses, and he continues to appear in pornographic and erotic movies.[19] As we will see, this depiction is especially important for Ex Deo's music video about Caligula. In short, the modern portrayal of Gaius can be described as an even more radicalized vision of the old one. Despite the most recent scholarly trends, his name is automatically associated with the corruption of power and uncontrolled sex.[20] He is a depraved, mentally ill figure who—whatever promise he may have shown as a young man—turns into a monster.

Caligula in metal

According to the online database of metal bands *Encyclopaedia Metallum*, there are eleven bands who either use or have used the emperor's nickname in some form.[21] The vast majority of them play or played extreme metal music such as thrash, death, black, etc., including the disbanded Belgian group Caligula, who played thrash/avant-garde metal (although they humorously describe their style as "True Belgian Tralala Metal").[22] The cover of their album *Greatest Hits* (2013) features the emperor's bust dressed up in party style, thus diminishing his bloody and cruel reputation.[23] Caligula's Horse is an Australian progressive metal band, and despite the fact that their songs are not about the emperor, the band's name clearly alludes to one of the most popular anecdotes about Caligula: supposedly, he appointed his beloved race horse Incitatus as a consul (Suet., *Calig.* 55). Yet another band is Dominion Caligula, led by Masse Blomberg, the aforementioned Emperor Magus Caligula, who released a single album, *A New Era Rises* (2000), with such explicit song titles as "In Love with the Gods," "Let Them Hate Me," and "Drink the Royal Seed (Fellatio Me Scrotum)."[24]

In addition to bands named after Caligula, the same database lists over forty songs about the emperor. One of the more recent is "Caligula," released by the veteran German thrash metal band Sodom on their album *Decision Day* (2016). The song does not attempt to provide a narration of any type, focusing instead on Caligula's mental illness and paranoia, listing ominous phrases such as "scream of doom," "king of the dead," "sperm profusion," "inner rotting," "aristocrated prostitution," "demonic creature," and "crowned with kinky insanity." The multitude of descriptions offers a sense of the associations a metal band is likely to have with the name "Caligula," and shows the persistence of the emperor's reputation within this medium.

Caligula in Ex Deo

I turn now to Ex Deo's characterization of Caligula. I have chosen Ex Deo both because they are an active band and offer music videos for the two songs I analyze below and because they exemplify the recent turn to the ancient world by bands with a connection to Italy or Greece. (In fact, all the guest musicians on the album I will be discussing are of Italian or Greek descent.) In keeping with the canons of extreme metal music, Ex Deo portray a ferocious, bloody Caligula, and focus on his association with evil. Moreover, Caligula embodies the ancient Rome Ex Deo wish to present to its audience: a domineering civilization whose history is packed with bloody events. I focus on the aspects of Gaius' life that the band emphasizes alongside the sources (ancient and modern) used to highlight his depraved qualities and to create a captivating figure for metal fans. As Ex Deo's songs will show, the modern reception of Caligula and the concerns of extreme metal are a perfect match.

Ex Deo is a melodic/symphonic death metal project conceived and founded by Maurizio Iacono in 2008. The singer and lyricist of Ex Deo is also the leader of the acclaimed melodic death metal band Kataklysm, whose members also take part in this project. In spite of his Canadian nationality, Iacono has declared that he comes from Rome[25] and his two parents were born in Italy.[26] He speaks Italian and uses the language in a few lines of Ex Deo's songs (e.g., "The Roman," *Immortal Wars*, 2017), as well as Latin.[27] The name of the band is also Latin, and its meaning ("Out of god") and origin are explained in a Facebook post by the band.[28]

Iacono has been able to combine the ancient history of the Roman Empire with a melodic death metal enriched with symphonic and cinematic elements to make Ex Deo's music complex, epic, and grand.[29] When asked why he started a band based on Roman history, Iacono answered that "the Roman historical subject fits perfectly into Metal, there is something brutal, hard, obscure in both" (Donatoni 2018). In Iacono's opinion, Roman history is "a great factual storytelling concept for a metal band because it is real, it happened and it has got lots of everything blood, sex, fire, etc." (Rebecca 2017).

Romulus (2009), the band's first album, begins with the title track, which introduces the album and the band's general focus on topics related to Roman antiquity, beginning with the story of Rome's foundation:

Romulus, with my brother's blood I opened the gates of time (…)
Within my beating heart, the sword and spear shall govern (…)
Remus defied me, and I shall strike upon those who disobey me with death …

Ex Deo, "Romulus," Romulus*, 2009*

This vision of a dominating and merciless Rome continues throughout the rest of the album, which focuses mainly on the events and characters of the military conflicts of the final years of the Republic: the Gallic wars ("Storm the Gates of Alesia"), Julius Caesar ("Invictus") and his 13th Legion ("XIII Legio") and the civil war between Octavian (later Augustus Caesar) and Marc Antony ("Cry Havoc," "The Final War (Battle of Actium)").[30]

The second album, *Caligvla*, was released on August 31, 2012, exactly 2,000 years after Caligula's birth.[31] Iacono said in an interview: "I really love the emperors, their characters were atypical and sometimes they were incredibly intelligent and real intellectuals, while on the other side there were incredibly perverse and crazy people. I like the extreme of both parts that are also present in Metal in general" (Donatoni 2018). Despite its title, only the first two songs deal with the emperor: "I, Caligvla" and "The Tiberius Cliff (Exile to Capri)." Then there are tracks about wars like Teutoburg ("Ambush of Varus"), the rebellion of Spartacus ("Along the Appian Way"), the persecution of Christians under Nero ("Burned to Serve as Nocturnal Light"), and the Roman games ("Pollice verso (Damnatio ad Bestia)").

If most of these topics seem relatively well known, that is by design. In an interview, Iacono explains his reasoning for choosing the material he has:

If I go too far into history and start referencing the war against Hannibal, the story of Scipio and the start of the Roman civilisation, people will never really manage to get into Ex Deo. I will have to slowly bring these subjects in. "Romulus" was the foundation story, Julius Caesar is and always will be the most popular theme and "Caligvla" is also a popular figure and I also wrote a song about Nero in the new record. I have to move in such a careful way that people will become truly attached to the concept and once they are attached I can begin explaining things more.

Yiannis 2013

Iacono's desire to focus initially on more familiar aspects of Roman history (e.g., Romulus, Remus, and the foundation of Rome) likely accounts for fans having to wait an additional five years until the 2017 release of the third album, *Immortal Wars*. This album is a chronological narration of the 2nd Punic War between Romans and Carthaginians, including Hannibal, and—in light of his comments above—may suggest that Iacono considered his fans had been duly prepared to get further into the history of Rome.

As the song titles and topics make clear, Ex Deo's music and lyrics present us with a cruel Roman history full of violent and bloody episodes. Iacono, by using the emperor's nickname as the album's title, not only transports us back to Imperial Rome, but also

Figure 6.1 Ex Deo, *Caligvla* (2012; Album cover).

evokes all the negative connotations of Caligula. As the analysis of the two songs will show, Iacono views Caligula as both a product and an agent of this violence and cruelty.

Although I am aware that an understanding of heavy metal also requires comprehension of its sound, an element that defines its power and meaning (Weinstein 2000: 123), as a Classicist by training I will approach these songs primarily through their lyrics. But other aspects—such as the cover, the visual idiom, and clothing—also define the musical genre (Fletcher 2015: 1, 3, and 8). In the case of *Caligvla*, the album cover introduces us to Ex Deo's dark Classical world (See Figure 6.1).

Designed by Seth Siro Anton, the leader of the Greek symphonic death metal band Septicflesh, the cover shows an equestrian statue, a crowned Caligula atop a horse (possibly Incitatus?) standing on its hindquarters, surrounded by the steam of Roman baths with a coffered ceiling crammed with busts and friezes in the background. The faces of the horse and the rider are extremely aggressive and unsettling. They seem to be commanding an attack. While one of the rider's arms is missing, the other holds a shield with the face of Jupiter, which is also carved on the emperor's chest. Human skulls hang from one side of the horse. The letters of the album title evoke traditional Roman inscriptions, in part because the *U* of "Caligula" has been presented as the Latin *V* (the Romans did not distinguish between vocalic and consonantal "u," and represented both with capital "v").[32] Among the letters of the title appear the numbers 12–12–41 in Roman numerals. It is unclear what these mean but they likely have some connection with the dates of Caligula's birth and death, as he was born August 31, 12 CE and died January 22 (or 24), 41 CE. Altogether, these elements and the mainly gray coloring of the artwork introduce us to the dark and violent world of Caligula's Rome, which fits with the genre's code.

"I, Caligvla"

"I, Caligvla," the first track on *Caligvla*, can be viewed as a parallel to the opening song of Ex Deo's first album, *Romulus*. These characters, Romulus and Caligula, represent the bloody and pitiless ancient Rome Iacono shows us, and Caligula can be thought of as a second Romulus; he is going to refound Rome with great violence, as did the founder and first king of Rome. The track's title clearly plays on that of Graves' novel, *I, Claudius*, connecting the audience with Graves' and Pulman's literary and cinematographic legacy, as well as with imperial Rome.[33] The listener discovers that, as in these recreations of the Julio-Claudian dynasty, Ex Deo's Caligula is the antithesis of the cautious and fearful Claudius.

"I, Caligvla" starts with a brief choral section that evokes the epic feeling of the type of symphonic death metal the band plays while also recalling the soundtracks of so-called "sword and sandal" films.[34] Again, this is by design, as Iacono frequently refers to the influence of films about Rome on the band, as in an interview about this album: "The first one (*Romulus*) had a very organic sound, we wanted to do something a little bit more underground sounding. This one though, we went with a much bigger production, we wanted to have more of a soundtrack environment, to give it justice and to have a big sound." He also said that "every time we do a new record we watch Roman-themed movies, we remove the sound and we play our music to them. If the music can relate to the action taking place then we are doing the right thing—if it won't then we have to redo the whole thing. This is what we do every time" (Yiannis 2013).[35]

As the song continues, the guitar riff increases in volume just before Iacono's clear voice announces Caligula's installation as emperor, and this is the first and the only time we hear the real name of the *princeps:* "On this glorious day, I declare Gaius Augustus Germanicus emperor of Rome."[36] Because the rest of the song is in the first person, perhaps we can read this as Caligula himself speaking, declaring himself emperor of Rome. We thus might assume a firsthand perspective of the emperor and in this way the song becomes more dramatic. Immediately after this declaration, Iacono begins to sing in his death-metal growl:

> I, Caligvla, am God made flesh, the rope around your neck,
>   this is the will of the gods!
> I, Caligvla, am master of all your fears, thy might colossal,
>   these hands are drenched in blood!
>
> *Ex Deo,* "I, Caligvla," Caligvla, *2012*

The first lines of the song present the audience with the two basic ideas upon which the lyrics are focused. On the one hand, Caligula is a ruler convinced of his own divinity; he is a god made flesh, and he embodies and represents the will of the gods. On the other hand, the will of the gods as executed by Caligula is cruel and merciless. He is the rope around the neck and the master of fears, showing that his reign is a bloodthirsty one. The description of Caligula's hands as drenched in the blood of his subjects recalls the ancient sources' depiction of him as a merciless and ruthless ruler (especially Suet., *Calig.* 26–32).

The lyrics continue:

> Bow to me, you worthless swine . . . the sky will fall from grace
> All these voices left unheard, dead and buried in my dominion
> Whisper . . . Whisper . . . whisper words of domination . . .
>
> *Ex Deo,* "I, Caligvla," Caligvla, *2012*

Caligula's dominion acquires even a cosmological dimension;[37] not only is he a tyrannous ruler of people, defined as "worthless swine," but his power is so absolute that he threatens even the gods of the sky—as he is said to have done in some of the ancient sources.[38] The cruelty of, and fear inspired by, his rule are made clear once again; the voices of the subjects executed under his reign have been muted to mere whispers. He is a ruler that shows no mercy to the worthless swine.

Ex Deo press Caligula's megalomania further, as the next lines of the song insist on the absolutism of his power:

I am life, I am death, your souls laid to rest
I am everything you need and all the things you fear
Whisper ... Whisper ... Whisper words of insanity ...

Ex Deo, "I, Caligvla," *Caligvla*, 2012

His authority is all-encompassing, and, as in a modern totalitarian state, he provides everything needed, and he is everything to be feared. Absolute terms such as "life," "death," "everything," and "all things" emphasize that nothing escapes Gaius' control. Furthermore, there is an allusion—the only one in the two songs—to the emperor's disturbed mind ("whisper words of insanity") echoing the early sources' allusions to Caligula's mental illness in relating anecdotes highlighting his abuse, capriciousness, and irascibility.[39]

The next lines of the track take us into the details of Caligula's biography, including his tragic infancy and youth, and show how Iacono attempts to explore the character's motivations and thoughts: "They killed my mother (they killed my mother ...), they killed my father (they killed my father ...) who am I but the true face of Rome!" When Caligula was seven, his father Germanicus died under suspicious circumstances during his stay in Syria, and Tiberius was suspected of planning his murder (Suet., *Tib.* 52; *Calig.* 2). His mother and brothers were also accused of conspiracy and they all died in exile or were executed (*Tib.* 53) when he was around twenty. According to the song, what Caligula has been experiencing since his tragic childhood is the true face of Rome. But the inclusion of his parents' death in the song does not function as a justification for his actions or as a token of empathy with Gaius; it is a signal that the way he rules is a perpetuation of the inherent cruelty and violence of ancient Rome, as is also apparent in "The Tiberius Cliff (Exile to Capri)."

This emphasis on the death surrounding Caligula suggests the influence of the 1979 film's depiction of him, because the movie presents a young Caligula in constant fear for his life and frightened of the wrath of Tiberius who put Caligula's siblings to death.[40] In fact, the very next, symphonic section of the song contains part of a dialogue from this film:

Tiberius: Serve the state, Caligula, although the people in it are wicked beasts.
Caligula: But they love you, lord.
Tiberius: ... they fear me ...[41]

The inclusion of this dialogue demonstrates the profound influence of the modern perception of Caligula upon Iacono's characterization of the emperor, especially the recreations based on Suetonius and influenced by the perceived abuse of power by Augustus' two successors. This passage shows how Caligula promises to continue Tiberius' oppressive policy, and it is a clear reminder of what became a kind of political slogan for Caligula, captured by Suetonius (*Calig.* 30): "*Oderint dum metuant*," that is, "let them hate me as long as they fear me."[42]

The next lines of the song further develop the sinister portrait of Caligula: "Traitors shall be crucified, the women and children thrown from the Tarpeian rock/ I thirst your blood, I want it all!" These lines explicitly portray the emperor as a bloody, evil, and merciless tyrant, and the two types of punishment chosen emphasize Caligula's cruelty. Crucifixion is a well-known method of torture because of its prolonged torment and its visibility, which gives it an exemplary function.[43] Similarly, the claim that women and children, vulnerable and fragile, are going to be thrown from the Tarpeian Rock connects them with the most ignominious offenders since Republican times, who were smashed to death against the ground after a quick fall.[44] At this point of the song, the first lines of the track—from "I, Caligvla, am God made flesh" to "these hands are drenched in blood"—are repeated again, and the ring composition emphasizes Caligula's cruelty and divinity.

The track ends with a clean guitar backed by a dark chorus that expresses Caligula's self-proclaimed divinity: "Kneel, kneel, kneel … before for me/Kneel, kneel, kneel … for I am God!" Caligula's declaration that he is a god reflects the ancient tradition—first attested by Philo (*Legat.* 11)—that he believed himself to be a living god and wished to be worshipped as one.[45] While it is possible that this tradition is overblown, and that Caligula was doing nothing that his predecessors had not, to some extent, already done, the perception of him has made his self-proclaimed divinity indicative of his evil megalomania.[46] By having the phrase "I am God" be the last line of the song, Ex Deo treat this aspect of Caligula's reception the same way.

The music video for "I, Caligvla" visually reinforces Ex Deo's portrait of the wicked Caligula.[47] The members of the band perform the song dressed up as Roman soldiers of the 13th legion while we see Caligula surrounded by his court:[48] women in lascivious poses, soldiers, and silent men whose identity will not be revealed until the lengthy credits, which name the main characters. At the beginning, the emperor beats an almost naked female slave with a stick, then a gladiatorial contest takes place in front of the throne. During the brutal combat between the gladiators, Caligula's face is splashed with drops of blood, which he wipes away then licks from his fingers as he stares at the fight, laughing with the women whenever a gladiator is injured. The scene perhaps reflects the reports that Caligula adored combat in the arena (Suet., *Calig.* 26 and 54), but it also shows an aspect of ancient Rome immediately recognizable to the general viewer.

The music video ends when one of the gladiators is defeated and Caligula orders the other fighter to execute the one who has fallen. The music stops and the emperor allows the winner to keep his life. The credits then inform us about the identity of the characters in the music video. Besides Caesonia, Caligula's fourth and last wife, the women around the emperor in immodest postures, touching and kissing his face quite lasciviously, are his sisters Agrippina, Drusilla, and Livilla.[49] Thus, the video suggests that the emperor maintained sexual relationships with all of them, drawing on one of the best-known anecdotes about Caligula (e.g., Suetonius *Calig.* 24, 36). Although scholars have questioned the veracity of these details and offered suggestions for the motivation behind such accounts, Caligula's incest fits and reinforces the image of a perverted imperial court.[50]

Among the men in the video are such important personalities as Claudius, Caligula's uncle and his successor; Lepidus, Drusilla's husband, who led a conspiracy against him and appears indifferent to his wife's coquetry with her brother; and Seneca, the aforementioned philosopher who later became the emperor Nero's mentor and one of the main shapers of the emperor's reputation. In addition, one of the guards accompanying the victorious gladiator is Cassius Chaerea, the praetorian tribune who played an important part in the emperor's assassination. Although the video does not explain why these people are important, their inclusion reinforces the idea that it purports to show something historical and even educational.

After the credits, there is a short sequence where Caligula pours his wine on the female slave's buttocks, providing one more sexual element at the end of the video. The scene then goes black, and the words "la fine" appear, giving one final Italian touch to the video, as well as a further nod to the cinematic.

The video exudes a testosterone-fueled masculinity based on mastery and domination, on despotism and sexual control. We are presented with a cruel emperor surrounded by a silent and complicit court. Caligula appears as a symbol of power, surrounded by women—his own sisters!—in sexually suggestive gestures, enjoying the blood shed by the gladiators and deciding the fate of a human being. As a whole, the video reflects many of metal's traditional concerns, demonstrating the ways in which Caligula is an obvious figure for a band such as Ex Deo.

Although things have been changing, metal has historically been a masculinist, heterosexual, and male-dominated music scene,[51] and among the many metal styles, extreme metal magnifies masculinity (as a code of power and domination), with its sonic power, gruesome subject matter, and visual imagery (Weinstein 2016a: 16–19).[52] In addition, the control and conquest of the female, as the video explicitly shows, is one of the most recognizable elements of death metal imagery (Kahn-Harris 2007: 36). Iacono and the members of Ex Deo emphasize the masculine potency of the music and the content of the video by their movements and facial expressions, as well as their martial dress. Ex Deo is thus another example among many in the extreme scene (black or Viking metal especially) that constructs a highly masculinized past drawing on the notion of a place (Dunn 2004: 117; Heesch 2010: 74–5), in this case the imperial Rome of Caligula. Gaius' masculinity is thus not based on his military skills as a warrior, as is the case of, say, Alexander the Great in Iron Maiden's song, but on pure sexual domination and violent aggression.[53]

"The Tiberius Cliff (Exile to Capri)"

The next song on the album, "The Tiberius Cliff (Exile to Capri)," takes us back to the government of Caligula's predecessor, Tiberius. Like Caligula, Tiberius has generally had a negative reputation since antiquity—and, like Caligula's reputation, Tiberius' may also be overblown.[54] The last years of Tiberius' reign are often described as bloody by the ancient authors (among others, Suet., *Tib.* 61–67), particularly after the death of his mother Livia and the treachery of Sejanus, the praetorian tribune and right-hand man to whom he delegated the administration of the Empire. In the most influential sources, Tiberius spends these final years unpopular and paranoid, fearful of plots on all sides.[55]

The first lines of the track, growled by Iacono, situate us in a specific time and place, during this final phase of Tiberius' life:

> 26 A.D. exile to Capri, paranoia infects the mighty Tiberius
> Assassins lurk throughout the glorious land, like Germanicus,
>   dead by a poisoned tongue!
>
> Ex Deo, "The Tiberius Cliff (Exile to Capri)," Caligvla, 2012

Tiberius spent the last eleven years of his life on this small island in the bay of Naples; he never returned to Rome. These lines also introduce the audience to the stifling atmosphere of the political scene during Tiberius' reign: a dense network of spies and agents spread around the vast lands of the Empire are following the orders of the old Tiberius. As mentioned above, some believe that Caligula's father, Germanicus, was one of the victims of this sort of intrigue (as were some of Caligula's siblings), and the death of Caligula's father comes up again near the end of the song.[56] The reference to Caligula's father here foreshadows the way in which Ex Deo view Tiberius and Caligula as being inseparable.

The lyrics reflect this atmosphere of tyranny and absolutist power:

> What is a king without a leash on his kingdom?
> What is all power . . . without fear to feed it?
> On to Capri to rule, bring forth desire of a god
> . . .
> My reign as a Julio-Claudian, will be remembered as the greatest of them all
> Statues will be erected in all corners of Rome!
>
> Ex Deo, "The Tiberius Cliff (Exile to Capri)," Caligvla, 2012

Here we are once again witness to a brutal and limitless power based on fear, horror, and oppression. Ex Deo modifies the character of Tiberius to make it even more negative than in hostile writers such as Suetonius or Tacitus. In this song, the old emperor is convinced of his divinity and believes that his reign will be the most glorious in the Julio-Claudian dynasty.[57] However, according to the ancient sources, Tiberius accepted no honors, which makes it difficult to believe that he saw himself as a god and ordered his subjects to worship him as such (e.g., Suet., *Tib.* 26–27; Tac., *Ann.* 2.88, 6.37–38).[58] Although the portrait of Tiberius by the ancient authors is extremely negative, even this is altered to present the "divine" tyrant to whom Caligula is the heir and successor.

This second song also contains more familiar biographical details about Tiberius, including the emperor's well-known sexual debauchery:

Servants to please, my wildest dreams . . .
I am Tiberius and you shall bring me your children,
You shall bring me your wives; you shall bring me everything . . .

Ex Deo, "The Tiberius Cliff (Exile to Capri)," Caligvla, 2012

The line, "You shall bring me your children," alludes to Suetonius' shocking description of the pools of the caves of Capri where little children, Tiberius' "little fishes," were trained to satisfy the emperor's wildest sexual dreams (*Tib.* 43–44). The emperor has been transformed in Suetonius' account from a paranoid tyrant into a depraved and sexually deranged, vicious ruler. As in Ex Deo's depiction of Caligula, megalomania and debauchery go hand in hand.

Ex Deo makes this connection between Tiberius and Caligula explicit, as the song includes the "teachings" with which the old emperor aims to educate his successor to the Roman throne:

Watch closely Little Boots,
As I bathe in their blood and crush their dignity to nothing,
One day you will be the same, boy . . . oh what a sight it will be . . .

Ex Deo, "The Tiberius Cliff (Exile to Capri)," Caligvla, 2012

The influence of the film sequence from *Caligula* (1979) where Caligula visits Tiberius in Capri is evident in the lyrics. In this part of the film, Tiberius calls Gaius "Little Boots" many times after swimming with his little fishes (film minute 00:15).[59] After that, they talk about the political situation of Rome (the dialogue quoted in part in "I, Caligvla"). The lyrics also show that Tiberius recognizes Caligula as his successor, even though he is aware of the terror Gaius is going to spread. In fact, the bloodshed Caligula will unleash and the humiliation of his subjects constitutes a pleasing spectacle. Tiberius is eager to observe the terrible consequences of his decision, tragic for the Roman people, and Iacono punctuates the line with diabolical laughter. Both the movie and the lyrics depict Tiberius as the prime corrupter of a young Caligula. The lines from the song remind us strongly of Suetonius' claim about Caligula's "savage nature," which

> was so clearly evident to the shrewd old man that [Tiberius] used to say now and then that to allow Gaius to live would prove the ruin of himself and of all men, and that he was rearing a viper for the Roman people and a Phaethon for the world.

Suetonius, Calig. 11[60]

Phaethon was the son of the sun god Helios. When he borrowed his father's chariot, which takes the sun across the sky, he lost control of the horses and almost destroyed the world. Along with the flood, this is one of the great catastrophes of the mythical period and shows just how dangerous some considered Caligula to have been.

In the next verse, Tiberius explains to young Gaius why he had to murder his father Germanicus, recalling what Caligula had said about his parents' fate in the previous song. Iacono introduces us to the complex political game at the imperial court. The continuous rise in Germanicus' prestige and fame was a situation that Tiberius felt was a threat to his own political power:[61]

> (Dear Caligvla) Your father was a hero of Rome; I could not let him rise
> One day you will understand and worship me as a god
> My enemies will tremble, my wrath unmerciful
> *Avt vincere avt mori.*
>
> Ex Deo, "The Tiberius Cliff (Exile to Capri)," Caligvla, 2012

The end of the dialogue—"*Avt vincere avt mori*" ("Victory or death")—while also being a very metal sentiment, sums up the traditionally negative view of the macabre and paranoid policy adopted by Tiberius in his last years.[62] The old Tiberius regards the imperial court and policy as a battlefield, and he has to strike first and directly at the heart of the enemy, the senators, before he is killed. This line, like so much else in these two songs, insists on the suffocating atmosphere of the reign of Gaius' predecessor and his paranoid abuse of power.

Finally, Tiberius invites the future emperor to throw their enemies off a cliff on the precipitous island of Capri: "Caligvla! ... Rise with me ... Rise, and all shall fall from the Tiberius cliff." This alludes to a passage in Suetonius, who claims that Tiberius liked to throw his victims off the cliff, a 300-meter fall near Villa Jovis, the luxurious palace built by him on Capri (*Tib.* 62). This cliff functions as the perfect metaphor for the situation of those close to the old emperor: they were continuously walking on a razor's edge and dependent on Tiberius' capricious nature.

Like "I, Caligvla," "The Tiberius Cliff (Exile to Capri)" has its own music video, though it is very different in scope (and presumably cost). It was released in February 2013, with clips from a live performance, the band dressed in their legionary uniform and accompanied by a female belly dancer. Her inclusion reinforces the theatricality of Ex Deo's music and live shows and adds an exotic touch to the video, underlining the otherworldliness and mystique evoked by the band's music. The belly dancer may even be an allusion to the *spintriae,* the sexual dancers of the court of Tiberius in Capri (Suet., *Tib.* 43). Iacono has said in an interview that in the show in Canada that was filmed for the video they had tried to make things more visually exciting, and "the end result was a hit. The belly dancer on stage worked" (Yiannis 2013).[63]

Despite the references to Caligula's infancy and youth, both songs of Ex Deo are far from being a historical biography of the emperor, in contrast with songs such as Iron Maiden's "Alexander the Great" (*Somewhere in Time*, 1986), which provides a chronological narration of the most glorious passages of the life of the Macedonian king and his extraordinary legacy. "I, Caligvla" is mostly a sketch of an absolute, limitless, and terrifying power, the depiction of an evil tyrannical monster who fits perfectly with the dark and epic music played by Ex Deo and the way Iacono brings Roman history to an extreme metal audience craving bloodshed and violence. In the same way, "The Tiberius Cliff (Exile to Capri)" presents Gaius' predecessor as the one who introduces him to the corrupted imperial policy and delights in the fact that this young man is going to continue with the violence and the aggressive treatment of his subjects. Therefore, Iacono depicts the second and third emperors of Rome in a way that generally corresponds to accounts offered by the ancient authors and his treatment has also been adjusted in keeping with the most infamous modern portrayal of them in the film *Caligula* (1979).

Conclusion

The basic topics of the two Ex Deo songs I have examined revolve around absolute power, strengthened by an image of self-divinization, and how this absolute power is translated into a despotic and merciless domination of Roman subjects. Ex Deo's lyrics and their representation of ancient Rome, exemplified by characters such as Caligula and Tiberius, connect directly with the dialectic of power and control articulated by metal music, especially its most extreme version. Iacono and his band construct an experience of power built up both lyrically and musically that draws on many topics typical of extreme metal: madness, violence, aggression, and the iconography of horror (Walser 1993a: 108–9). Supported by a radicalized modern portrait of this traditionally monstrous emperor, Ex Deo and their audience evoke a mythical past with a brutal historical murderer, a narrative that emphasizes power, conflict, violence, and death.

In the two songs analyzed here, Tiberius and especially Caligula become the incarnation of evil tyranny, despotism, cruelty, and abuse. Both tracks, "I, Caligvla" and "The Tiberius Cliff (Exile to Capri)," succeed in reproducing the oppressive and sinister image of the political scenario in which Tiberius and Caligula ruled and dominates the reception of these two emperors, especially the latter. The tracks are not an historical reconstruction of Caligula's life, but the depiction of a brutal and merciless monster. Even so, the inclusion in the lyrics of a few biographic and historic details (e.g., the meaning of the emperor's nickname, the name of the reigning dynasty, the murder of Caligula's siblings, the reason why Tiberius—supposedly—ordered the assassination of Germanicus, the specific place and time) reveal that Iacono has immersed himself in the Roman past. He has said that he saw his father reading constantly about this period and that he was "always surrounded by books about it and I decided to do a lot of research into the Roman Empire to try and find good things about it." He continued: "the more I researched it, the more I fell in love with the idea of evolution and how [the Romans] shaped the world" (James 2017). Though it is not clear which books Iacono read, the influence of Suetonius' biography of Caligula is obvious, and there is no sign of awareness that the negative stories about Caligula have been questioned by recent scholars—nor should we expect it. But Iacono's Caligula is also inspired by the image of the emperor in the 1979 film, which reinforces Suetonius' depiction. However, Iacono's preference for Suetonius' Caligula over the more nuanced image now advanced by some scholars is far from surprising, given the suitability of the emperor to the brutal and violent Rome Ex Deo presents.

There also remains the issue of any inherent political message behind Ex Deo's use of ancient Rome. I believe that, generally speaking, Ex Deo's music and lyrics must be disconnected from ethical and political dimensions (Phillipov 2006: 80).[64] The brutality, the violence, the despotism, and aggression Iacono transmits through his musical project is a product of his desire to pay tribute to ancient Rome, described in terms of dominance for an audience used to these conventions. It is undeniable that many Ex Deo songs promote a nationalistic agenda in their approach to Roman antiquity, an agenda that in songs such as "The Roman" (*Immortal Wars*, 2009) verge on an imperialist and militaristic discourse.[65] However, this, like the portrait of a brutal tyranny, must be understood in the context of what Kahn-Harris (2007: 144–56) calls the "reflexive anti-reflexivity" of metal, the capability of metal musicians to produce reflexive practice without being involved or attached to it. Reflexive anti-reflexivity allows Ex Deo to draw this image of a tyrannical, bloody, and insane ruler to maximize transgression and to protect the dynamics of power playing in extreme metal music. Ex Deo's music plays with the imagery of violence, domination, and absolute power, but the experience of listening to it hardly requires listeners to connect the music and lyrics with real actions or the musician's values (Phillipov 2013: 162).[66]

Iacono has said that while the music and lyrics of his main band Kataklysm deal with everyday life and and inner struggles, Ex Deo is the antithesis of that: "Kataklysm and Ex Deo are two different worlds. One is an anger filled social-based band that deals with modern emotions and the other is an epic journey into History and testosterone filled angst" (Sciarretto 2009). The Ex Deo singer states that he wants to "do his part by playing metal and putting some sort of idea out there. As far as Italy was concerned, initially I was concerned about people's reaction as Italy is very political and the message they see me trying to spread is completely different from the one that I am trying to push" (Yiannis 2013). I think his message and his goals are quite clear. On one hand, he wants listeners to have the feeling that they "can be back in those times [Roman times]" (Yiannis 2013). On the other hand, he has shown a firm desire to educate people through his music, "because the world that we live today is not all that different from the world that our ancestors lived in back then" (Yiannis 2013).

Iacono has claimed that at his first show with Ex Deo in Italy (specifically, in Milan on September 30, 2009), he rejected any connection between his musical project and fascist policies or ideologies. Part of the audience stood quietly during the first song because they had seen the eagles on the legionary standards that the band use as part of its stage set and thought it was a fascist symbol. Iacono delivered a short speech in Italian in response (which he paraphrased in a later interview):

> It's not what you think. It's about your history. Embrace it! If you don't want to embrace it, then YOU'RE the bad guys, man, because what happened is none of our faults. We're up here talking about history. You should be proud of what you've done because you brought the world into advancement.
>
> *OverkillExposure 2012*

In another interview, he spoke about the same show:

> We came on stage, we raised our eagle standards, our Roman banners and pictures of the Romulus record and the crowd was dead silent! They were all heads down, looking almost as if they were ashamed of us! We played our first song and there were only a couple of people screaming and I knew what type of people they were which was most likely fascists. I decided to do a short speech explaining that this show was not a political statement but I am presenting our history and that those who feel ashamed should leave the place as it meant that they are ashamed of who they were. I said to them: "There is nothing wrong with what you brought to the world" (...). Then the show was awesome!
>
> Yiannis 2013

Although there may be a certain cognitive dissonance in saying that modern Italians are not responsible for fascism and yet can somehow claim credit for the cultural achievements of the Romans, it is clear that Iacono does not see himself as presenting a whitewashed vision of antiquity to an explicitly political end. Indeed, he uses the themes of bloodshed, cruelty, violence, and evil when focusing on Caligula's most brutal features to excite his metal audience. Ancient Rome is a rich source from which to draw for writing and transmitting epic and exciting stories (such as that told in Vergil's *Aeneid*), but Iacono and his band have demonstrated how metal music can also present the Roman Empire's most horrible events and characters.[67] Iacono's band, with their traditional—yet also creative and suggestive—use of Caligula, play their part in the constant recreation of this emperor, as enigmatic and fascinating a character today as he ever was.[68]

Notes

1. The band was named after a horror film directed by Mario Bava, starring Boris Karloff and released in 1963. In fact, the development and popularity of metal music coincided with a period of great success for horror films (especially slashers) and books (Walser 1993a: 161). The blues, which exerted a key influence on the sound of early heavy metal, had been dealing with the occult for some years by the time heavy metal spread (Farley 2009: 87–91). For more on the influence of the occult on metal, see Secord (this volume).
2. I use the term "scene" to refer to both a flexible space and context for musical practice as well as to a decentralized, global, and diffuse network of producers and consumers of a specific kind of music (Harris 2000: 14).
3. Definition of "moral panic" in Cohen (2002: 1).
4. Walser (1993a: xvii, 163) connects extreme metal to dissatisfaction with the capitalist security state and dominant identities and institutions of a tumultuous era. The metal scene criticized the world as it saw it, and its themes of horror and violence were but a replication of the ruthless individualism that capitalism had naturalized. Similarly, Harrell (1994: 91) argues that death metal was the expression of industrialism's emotional isolation and violence, while Petrov (1995: 5) links this metal subgenre to the violence of the process of suburbia's urbanization. However, Arnett (1996) sees in metal a form of survival in an

insecure world and the failure of the state properly to socialize its adolescent members. Halnon (2006: 34) suggests that metal music was a "carnival" where the social rules (authority, morality, the sacred, etc.) were challenged. Other authors, however, have pointed to the commercial purposes of the evil aura that permeated this music. For instance, Scott (2007: 208) states that evil themes were a commercial gimmick to woo an interested audience into purchasing the product.

5. I cannot confirm whether the name of the band reflects Bathory's interest in the Hungarian aristocrat or is a tribute to the well-known Venom song "Countess Bathory" (*Black Metal*, 1982), which was destined to become a classic in the extreme metal scene. On the tendency within metal bands to pay tribute to "classic" bands, see Wallach, Berger, and Greene (2011b: 27) and Fletcher (2015: 1).
6. For more on bands named after figures from Classical antiquity, see Lindner and Wieland (2018).
7. Ten years earlier, in 1998, Cradle of Filth released *Cruelty and the Beast*, one of their most celebrated albums, based on the life of the countess Bathory.
8. Caligula is the diminutive of *caliga*, the military boots of the Roman soldiers. He received this affectionate nickname from the legionaries of the German camps, where he spent part of his childhood with his parents (Suet., *Calig.* 9).
9. For arguments that Caligula has been portrayed unfairly, see Nony (1986), Barrett (1989), Winterling (2011), and Wilkinson (2015).
10. On the benevolent start to Gaius' reign, then his radical change, see Philo, *Legat.*14 and 22; Flavius Josephus *AJ* 18.7.2; Cass. Dio 59.3.1 and 59.6.1.
11. Trans. J. C. Rolfe.
12. Notably, see e.g., *Cons. Polyb.* 17.3–6; *Helv.* 10.4; *Tranq.* 14.4–10 ; *Const.* 18.1–3; *De ira* 1.20.7–9 and 3.19.2. See also Wilcox (2008: 452).
13. See *OLD* (2012), s.v."monstrum;" see also Riddle and Arnold (1864) and Alfaro (2012: 18).
14. For a collection of primary accounts (in English) regarding Nero's persecution of the Christians, see Barrett, Fantham, and Yardley (2016: 166–70). For more on the reception of Nero, see the collection of chapters in "Part V: The Neros of Reception" in Bartsch, Freudenburg, and Littlewood (2017).
15. For a recent survey of Caligula in pop culture, including in cartoons, comics, graphic and historical novels, pulp fiction, film and TV, and board games, see Lindner (2013); see also "Some Other Caligulas, Part II: 1960–2012" on www.caligula.org.
16. There are 42 known versions of the film, many of which have been lost (Southon 2017: 188); see also www.caligula.org. The film has been strongly criticized by authors such as Solomon (2001) and Strong (2013). For more on the making of the film and its impact, see Hawes (2009) and Tuschinski (2013).
17. Gore Vidal then tried to separate his name from the film, claiming artistic differences (Raucci 2013: 149).
18. Lindner (2013: 215) counts a dozen films and TV series, mainstream and B-movies, where this emperor is a protagonist. He is often depicted as a mentally unstable tyrant, who symbolizes the corruption of power.
19. Some recent examples include *Caligula 2000*, *Caligula's Spawn* (2009), and Francesco Vezzoli's short art film, *Trailer for a Remake of Gore Vidal's "Caligula"* (2009).
20. The Italian Prime Minister Silvio Berlusconi was likened to Caligula when sex scandals involving the politician came to light. See Squires (2011): "The Caligulan court of Silvio Berlusconi laid bare."

21. *Encyclopaedia Metallum* is the largest online database of metal music. See www.metal-archives.com.
22. See their website: https://caligulabelgium.bandcamp.com.
23. Although the lyrics of this band's songs never relate to Roman history, one of their pictures shows its members dressed up as Roman soldiers, but in a humorous manner.
24. The album has eight tracks, all of which are based on Caligula's reign.
25. In the band's Facebook profile Rome is said to be the birthplace of Ex Deo.
26. His father was born in Catania and his mother in Bari. For additional discussion of Iacono's roots, tradition, and his family, see interviews with Iacono in Sciarretto (2009), James (2017), and Donatoni (2018).
27. For more on the use of ancient Greek and Latin, see Umurhan (this volume).
28. See "Ex Deo—Out of God" (2014).
29. I use the term "cinematic" to describe the bombastic, orchestral style influenced by film soundtracks and complemented with the inclusion of dialogues and narrations. Luca Turilli's Rhapsody (Italy) is a paradigm of cinematic metal. On the importance in metal of the epic and the grandiose, see Fletcher (2015: 1, 8). In Ex Deo's Facebook profile the band describe their style and music as "Epic Roman Metal" and say that their influences are "Jupiter, Mars and all gods of Rome."
30. See Umurhan's (2012) discussion of Ex Deo's music video for the track "The Final War (Battle of Actium)."
31. Iacono affirms this was a total coincidence, because he had not realized during the prolonged recording process that the anniversary was coming up (see OverkillExposure 2012). The music video for "The Final War (Battle of Actium)" was released on March 15 2010, commemorating the assassination of Julius Caesar (100-44 BCE) on the Ides of March. When the title of the second album was announced, Iacono posted on the band's Facebook profile Caligula's opening words from the film *Caligula* (1979): "I have existed from the morning of the world (…). Although I have taken the form of Gaius Caligula, I am all men as I am no man and so, I am a God" (10/14/2010).
32. Fletcher (2015: 8–9) and Campbell (2009: 121) argue that the use of ancient languages provides the music and a band's image with a certain otherworldliness, arcaneness, historical gravitas, and mystique. As mentioned above, Ex Deo uses Latin in many of its tracks, e.g., "Cruor nostri abbas," *Romulus* (2009).
33. Other historical productions have also appropriated the famous title of Graves' novel such as Hortense Dufour's *Moi, Neron* (1999).
34. Also known as *pepla,* films about ancient—primarily Roman—history (Cano Alonso 2011: 74).
35. In another interview, Iacono described the album as a "much bigger sounding, a very big album. It is like watching a movie" (OverkillExposure 2012).
36. The emperor's complete name is Gaius Julius Caesar Augustus Germanicus, but here "Julius Caesar" is omitted.
37. The words "dominion" and "domination" appear twice in two following lines and speak strongly to Iacono's fascination with Roman demonstrations of power. He remembers "watching these films [*swords and sandals* movies] and being really attracted by the Romans as they wielded so much power and control over so many people. It wasn't the armour or the weapons: I was attracted by the sheer power they possessed" (Yiannis 2013).
38. Seneca narrates how Caligula challenged Jupiter to combat when the sky was thundering and his actors were performing (*De ira* 1.20). Meanwhile, Suetonius affirms that, after ordering

the statues of the Olympic gods to be brought to Rome from Greece, he chopped Jupiter's head off and substituted it with his own (*Calig.* 22).

39. Philo was the first to mention Caligula's illness in *Legat.* 29. Suetonius in *Calig.* 50 also portrays Caligula as both physically and mentally ill, with symptoms including insomnia, epilepsy, fainting, and delusions.
40. Southon (2017: 203) believes that the 1979 film responds, in particular, to what Neiman (2015: 9) called the "problem of evil," or that after the Second World War, when the reality of the Nazi holocaust was brought to light, its evil needed to be explained and controlled. Therefore, Caligula is not pure evil, but largely a product of a time of decadence and corruption.
41. *Caligula* (1979, film minute 00:19). After uttering these words, Tiberius (played by Peter O'Toole) smiles in quite a sinister way. Iacono has seen the film, and describes it as "a little bit cheesy," asserting that, in contrast, "the album is an incarnation of Caligula. We are making it serious on this record" (OverkillExposure 2012). Audio samples are frequently used in Ex Deo's music. At the beginning of the track "Once were Romans" (*Caligvla*, 2012) we can hear a scene from the first episode of the TV series *Rome*, "The stolen eagle."
42. It was a quotation from a tragedy by Accius (*ca.* 170–*ca.* 85 BCE), also used by Tiberius with a modification: "*Oderint dum probent*," which means "let them hate me as long as they respect me" (Suet., *Tib.* 59).
43. Crucifixion was a humiliating form of execution practiced around the Mediterranean. The Romans used it for low-status criminals like slaves and provincial rebels (for more on crucifixion, see Cook (2015)). Iacono has joked about crucifixion in many interviews. He has said "it was the Romans who invented crucifixion! How metal is that?" (Sciarretto 2009), alluding to the traditional bond between metal music and anti-Christian and satanic themes. The Romans did not, however, invent crucifixion, but Iacono corrected himself in a later interview: "crucifixion is the most satanic thing you could ever see, and it was made popular by the Romans" (OverkillExposure 2012).
44. Death on the Tarpeian Rock brought great shame, and was a method of execution reserved for notorious traitors. See Gell., *NA* 20.1; Sen., *Controv.* 1.3; Tac., *Ann.* 6.19. See also Richardson (1992) and Höcker (2003).
45. Josephus also refers to that fact (*AJ* 19.1). However, one must bear in mind that Gaius had recently ordered the cult to the emperor, already present in the rest of the provinces, to be introduced in Judea and a statue of himself to be erected in the temple of Jerusalem. This was blasphemy and sacrilege in the eyes of both Jewish authors, but the cult to the emperor was not new at all and was the way the provincial elites demonstrated their loyalty to the Roman state.
46. Already in the Republic, Roman generals had dressed up as Jupiter in triumphal processions and enjoyed temporary godlike status (Beard 2007: 272–75), and Julius Caesar had been offered divine honors by the Senate, which he refused. Subsequently, Roman emperors and imperial family members were worshipped as gods in the Eastern cities, where the Hellenistic cults of the kings and dynasties had a long tradition (Gradel 2002).
47. See Napalm Records (2012) for the music video, which was released almost a month before the album by way of promotion.
48. The *Legio tertia decima Gemina*, commanded by Julius Caesar during his campaign in Gaul, has its own song on the album *Romulus* ("XIII Legio"). The band also wears legionary uniform during their concerts and in their other music videos.
49. The role of Agrippina is played by Iacono's wife, the Colombian model Surtsey Castaño.

50. Alfaro (2012: 19–24) and Winterling (2011: 3) argue that these kinds of statements were false and were meant to depict Caligula as evil and depraved.
51. Regarding the depiction of sex and gender roles in metal music, see Walser (1993a: 108–36), Weinstein (2000: 36–8; 2009, and 2016a), and Heesch and Scott (2016: 121–29).
52. For explorations of gender identity in metal, see the chapters by Åshede and Foka, Crofton-Sleigh, and Umurhan (this volume).
53. See Umurhan (2012) and Djurslev (2015).
54. For arguments against the veracity of the hostile tradition about Tiberius, see Nony (1986: 109–79) and Winterling (2011: 23–38). Winterling argues that Augustus' legacy required Tiberius to play a complex role into which he never grew.
55. See Tacitus, *Ann.* 1.60–64.
56. On the death of Germanicus and Caligula's siblings, see Nony (1986: 71–87, 145–53) and Winterling (2011: 33–8).
57. As Djurslev (2015: 134) says in discussing Kamelot's "Alexandria," the ideas of posterity and destiny are important in the world of metal music.
58. See the film *Caligula* (1979, 00:15), in which Tiberius denies being a god when Caligula tells him that he is.
59. Southon (2017: 197) argues that Tiberius uses the English translation of Gaius' nickname in this scene in an attempt to dissociate the young Caligula from the symbolic meaning that his name has acquired in modern times.
60. Trans. J. C. Rolfe. Suetonius also says that Tiberius was able to conceal Caligula's true brutal character, although he had already described the young Gaius' extraordinary capacity to hide his emotions and preserve appearances, an ability he needed to save his life (Suet., *Calig.* 10; Winterling 2011: 47).
61. Germanicus is a character greatly praised and idealized by ancient sources. Tacitus, for example, compares him to Alexander the Great (*Ann.* 2.73). On the relationship between Tiberius and Germanicus, see Nony (1986: 31–41, 51–61).
62. The Latin phrase has inspired some variation in metal songs: "Victory or die" (Motörhead, *Bad Magic*, 2015) and "For victory or death" (Amon Amarth, *Surtur Rising*, 2011).
63. Iacono attaches great importance to the theatricality and spectacle of his band's shows. He has said: "I wanted to get more into theatre, I wanted to bring the concert experience more to almost a theatre level and I couldn't do that with Kataklysm. I have a very big vision for [Ex Deo] and I want to bring it to a level where people will see a concert, and it's not just music and a band headbanging, it's like you go to see it and it's a whole theatre set-up. I want to bring something different to the music industry" (Falzon 2012).
64. For an opposing view, where metal may be read as political, see the chapters by Apergis, Olabarria, Fletcher, Taylor, and Umurhan (this volume).
65. Iacono has expressed a considerable fascination with ancient Rome and has developed an almost apologetic discourse with regard to its civilizing dynamics, but he also admits that Rome invented "a lot of bad things too." Iacono states it is "like a double-edged sword. [The Romans] created freedom and democracy (with the Greeks) but they also created dictatorship and tyranny. But that is how we started the concept of the current world, which can be at the same time big and chaotic. People try to put this black label on everyone, cataloguing something as 'evil' or 'bad.' But for me . . . you know, I explored the world of the Roman Empire more and fell in love with it. As bloody as it was, it was romantic at the same time" (OverkillExposure 2012 and Donatoni 2018).

66. However, in the extreme metal scene there are bands with an unequivocal political aura, both ultra-left (among many, Napalm Death) and ultra-right (the National Socialist Black Metal scene). See Walser (1993a), Purcell (2003), Kahn-Harris (2007: 141–56), Nilsson (2009), Wallach, Berger, and Greene (2011a), and Scott (2010) and (2011). However, in most cases, the conflict with politics is addressed privately and not publicly challenged by the members of the scene (Allet 2013: 168).
67. For the use of this Roman epic poem by metal bands, see Fletcher (this volume) and Crofton-Sleigh (this volume).
68. I would like to thank: Mark Hounsell, who helped adapt and improve an earlier draft of this chapter; my thesis director, Maite Muñoz (Classics Department of UPV/EHU - University of the Basque Country), for her advice, and Antonio Duplá (Classics Department of the UPV/EHU), who let me know about this interesting project. I would also like to thank Maurizio Iacono and Ex Deo for their powerful and inspiring music.

CHAPTER 7
OCCULT AND PULP VISIONS OF GREECE AND ROME IN HEAVY METAL
Jared Secord

Introduction

Just as its name suggests, the Flemish black metal band Ancient Rites displays a major interest in the premodern world, including Greco-Roman antiquity. Greece and Rome are represented especially on the band's 2006 album *Rubicon*, which features songs about Julius Caesar, the Battle of Thermopylae, and Arminius, who inflicted on Rome the great defeat at the Battle of the Teutoburg Forest in 9 CE. But the band's fascination with the premodern world extends beyond Greece and Rome, revealing an approach to antiquity that differs in many ways from the academic study of the Classics and Greek and Roman history. This approach is prominently on display in the band's 2001 album *Dim Carcosa*, and the substantial liner notes that accompany it. Written by Gunther Theys, the band's lyricist and vocalist, the notes explain the background for the album's songs, with emphasis on the books that inspired them. There are Greek and Roman books among this list: Homer's *Iliad* and Caesar's *Gallic War*.[1] Medieval books are likewise present, including the *Song of Roland*, and, more obscurely, a twelfth-century history that describes a Viking attack on the British monastery of Lindisfarne in 793 CE.[2]

Theys, however, also describes his interests in even more arcane subjects. These revolve around the ancient and mysterious city of Carcosa that appears in the album's title. This city is entirely fictional. It first appeared in a story by the American writer Ambrose Bierce (1842–1914), and then took on a long afterlife in horror and fantasy literature, even making a prominent recent appearance in the first season of HBO's *True Detective*.[3] As Theys reveals, he was first exposed to Carcosa by a reference to it in a popular occult book, Anton Szandor LaVey's *Satanic Bible*.[4] This reference inspired Theys to research whether Carcosa might be a real place, leading him to read deeply in what he describes as "mystical esoteric" subjects, including the Knights Templar, freemasonry, and something called "Tantric Alchemy." Theys' search led him to conclude that Carcosa was unlikely to be real, but he remained intrigued by the possibility that it may have been connected to the French town of Carcassone, whose name under the Roman Empire was Carcaso.[5] Clearly, Theys has a major interest in the ancient and medieval history of Europe. This has been fueled by reading books on eclectic topics, and a desire to explore esoteric questions about the world's premodern past.

The esoteric interests of Ancient Rites are not uncommon in heavy metal (henceforth simply "metal") and my focus here is on how esotericism informs the reception of Greek and Roman antiquity within the genre. The scope of my examination is limited to what I shall call "esoteric metal," a label that includes bands from a few different subgenres, especially black, death, and symphonic metal.[6] I use this label to describe not the sound or musical style of the bands, but rather the themes that they explore in their albums and lyrics. As with Gunther Theys and Ancient Rites, esoteric metal bands tend to be interested in the more arcane and mysterious aspects of the ancient world, which are not typically connected to Greco-Roman antiquity. The bands that interest me approach arcane material in a particularly bookish manner, a common phenomenon within the extreme metal scene.[7] Bookishness is a key part of the production and reception of esoteric metal, which allows both musicians and fans to discover and explore things that intrigue them about the world's ancient past. Esoteric metal is defined by the act of reading, and the process of trying to find new and unfamiliar arcane subject matter worthy of exploration for musicians and fans.[8] Like Gunther Theys, lyricists in esoteric bands read broadly and eclectically, exploring many topics revolving around the world's premodern past. This wide reading reflects the bands' deep fascination with the world's ancient past, and not just Greece and Rome. Esoteric bands often take an indiscriminate approach to the history of the ancient world, favoring books and ideas that are not taken seriously by professional Classicists and ancient historians, and exploring mysterious subjects like the entirely fictional ancient city of Carcosa. This approach to antiquity is a fundamental part of esoteric metal, and of its engagement with Greece and Rome alongside other aspects of the world's ancient past.

Two key sources inform the reception of Greece and Rome in esoteric metal. The first of these is the occult tradition, which is the subject of the chapter's first section. Occultism is heavily concerned with hidden or rejected knowledge from the ancient world, such as astrology and magic.[9] Its influence encourages esoteric bands to turn away from Greek and Latin works that have been accepted as Classics, a category that has often been linked with the ideas of harmony, balance, and rationality.[10] It has likewise prompted esoteric bands to link Greece and Rome with other ancient civilizations, and to seek out commonalities between their religious traditions, in keeping with occult views on this point. The chapter's second part then considers the influence of the other key source for esoteric metal: pulp fiction, especially as represented in the horror and fantasy stories published in the magazine *Weird Tales* in the first half of the twentieth century.[11] The influence of these stories helps to explain why esoteric bands tend to focus more of their attention on ancient civilizations besides Greece and Rome, deeming them too civilized to be appropriate sources for terror and alienation. Stories in *Weird Tales* are also responsible for a popular idea within esoteric metal: entirely fictional ancient books that contain terrifying information about the world's distant past. Both occultism and pulp fiction therefore help to fuel the interests of esoteric metal bands in the ancient world, while steering them mostly away from Greece and Rome.

The influence of *Weird Tales* stories and the occult tradition means that esoteric metal tends to present the world's premodern history in ways that now seem old-fashioned, and sometimes even problematic, from the perspective of professional Classicists and ancient historians. In one sense, this is a straightforward consequence of esoteric metal bands drawing from nineteenth- and early-twentieth-century views on history for their presentations of the ancient world. Greece and Rome consequently still appear largely as familiar, safe places, and insufficiently mysterious or exotic for sustained exploration.[12] There are definite traces here of Eurocentrism and Orientalism of the type that feature prominently in *Weird Tales* stories and the occult tradition.[13] Sometimes there are even definite signs of nationalism, such as in the case of Gunther Theys, who has become a controversial figure in Belgium because of his emphasis on Flemish history and identity.[14] But the esoteric bands that interest me in the remainder of this chapter are emphatically not fascist in their views, much less members of the marginal National Socialist Black Metal scene, which is widely condemned by other metal fans and musicians.[15] These bands have nothing explicit to say about contemporary politics or race in their music, a phenomenon that fits in with a generally apolitical tendency in many subgenres of metal around the turn of the twenty-first century.[16] Eurocentric and Orientalist ideas nonetheless do still abound in esoteric metal, fueled in large part by the older attitudes on history found in occultism and pulp fiction, which help to make ancient civilizations besides Greece and Rome seem more interesting.

What emerges in esoteric metal's view of premodern history is a complicated reception of Greece and Rome that depends much on their connotations of familiar antiquity. Both civilizations are valuable because they can easily evoke feelings of the ancient world, while sometimes providing glimpses of other, less familiar and civilized aspects of antiquity, as in their encounters with peoples to the north, east, and south of the Mediterranean world. Greece and Rome are defamiliarized somewhat by these associations, and by the interests that esoteric metal bands sometimes display in forms of rejected knowledge from the two civilizations, such as magic. These interests mostly parallel developments within the academic study of the Classics and Ancient History, which have increasingly treated Greece and Rome as less familiar places in the last four decades.[17] But a Eurocentric, Classical perspective still generally prevails within esoteric metal. This Eurocentrism is especially prominent in the common assumption that knowledge of the world's ancient past is filtered through Europe and its reception by Classically trained scholars. Esoteric metal consequently has a paradoxical attitude toward the world's ancient past. It regards Greece and Rome as basically uninteresting places for exploration, mostly avoiding songs and albums on topics that are popular within Mediterranean metal. At the same time, though, esoteric metal bands tend to present Greco-Roman antiquity in a larger context, associating it with other, more arcane and mysterious aspects of the ancient world.

The great beast and a perennial philosophy: The ancient world in esoteric metal via the occult

Metal's fascination with the occult is obvious, and it has been part of the genre from its earliest beginnings, as is clear from Black Sabbath's engagement with magical and arcane subject matter on their debut album from 1970.[18] Much of this interest in the occult, however, has taken generic forms, inspired and sanctioned by the presence of demons and sorcerers in the cover artwork and lyrics of bands like Black Sabbath, and by the popularity of Aleister Crowley (1875–1947), the massively influential occult figure who titled himself "The Great Beast."[19] Little real engagement with the ancient world has resulted from this generic type of occultism, apart from vague appeals to antiquity of the sort parodied in Spinal Tap's "Stonehenge" ("In ancient times . . . / Hundreds of years before the dawn of history / Lived a strange race of people . . . the Druids").[20] But some metals bands, beginning in the 1980s, have engaged more directly and creatively with the occult tradition, and with the ancient sources of wisdom that continue to inspire it.

This section focuses on two significant examples of esoteric metal's engagement with the occult tradition. The first is a Swiss band, Celtic Frost, which was influential in the early development of more extreme forms of metal in the 1980s, anticipating and inspiring the experimentation of many subsequent black and death metal bands.[21] Celtic Frost's use of Greek helps to reveal how this language is often valued in metal for its significance within occult traditions, and the evocative associations that it consequently has. Outside this occult context, Greco-Roman antiquity has little presence in Celtic Frost's work, despite the band's major interest in the ancient world. The second example treated is Therion, a Swedish band influential for its pioneering blend of metal with Classical instruments and choral vocals.[22] Therion stands out even within esoteric metal for the closeness of its connections to the occult tradition. Like Celtic Frost, Therion is interested in the ancient and occult associations of Greece and Rome, but the band has a much broader interest in the world's premodern past. Greco-Roman antiquity has a place in Therion's music, but always alongside the ancient civilizations of Egypt and the Near East, and even Atlantis and Lemuria, in keeping with the unorthodox views on the world's history championed in the occult tradition.[23] Therion presents all of these ancient civilizations as part of the *philosophia perennis* ("perennial philosophy") identified by occult scholars who wished to establish a basic unity between the world's different religious traditions.[24] Celtic Frost and Therion both defamiliarize Greece and Rome somewhat by approaching them via the occult tradition, while still regarding both civilizations as insufficiently exotic for much exploration.

To take Celtic Frost first: the band's approach to the world's premodern past reveals a deep fascination with arcane and occult subject matter at the expense of Greece and Rome. Such fascination derives in large part from the attitude that one of the band's founding members, Tom Gabriel Fischer, has concerning formal education. "I love learning things," writes Fischer, "but I hate being told what to learn."[25] Fischer found an outlet for his desire to learn outside of school, reading books about "ancient and modern history, occultism, religion, [and] the supernatural," all topics that also interested Celtic Frost's bass player, Martin Eric Ain.[26] Ain was raised in a strict Catholic family, but even in his teens he would make trips to a library in Zurich, which was the only place where he could access books by Crowley and other occult authors.[27] Greco-Roman antiquity evidently was insufficiently arcane to be worthy of exploration on Celtic Frost's albums, which instead are dotted with references to other ancient civilizations; Egypt, Carthage, and Babylon all make multiple appearances.[28] These civilizations are accompanied by the Celts represented in the band's own name, reflecting Fischer's interest in the ancient peoples of his native Switzerland.[29] Greece and Rome are conspicuously absent amidst such company.

The wide reading of Fischer and Ain nonetheless led them to explore some of the more obscure corners of Greco-Roman antiquity. The best sign of such exploration comes from the odd title of Celtic Frost's 1992 album, *Parched with Thirst Am I and Dying*. This title is a common phrase used in the Orphic gold tablets, which were interred in graves in many regions of the Greek world from as early as the fifth century BCE.[30] The tablets have received increasing attention from scholars, and have become much more accessible to non-specialists, in keeping with the ongoing movement within Classics to defamiliarize the ancient world.[31] But Celtic Frost's album was released before this recent boom of interest. The band evidently accessed the tablets through a brief discussion published in 1977 by Joseph Breslin, which offers a translation of three tablets, two of which include the phrase "Parched with thirst am I, and dying."[32] In his memoir, Fischer says that the quotation comes from "a fourth-century Greek-Roman poem found among the ashes of a dead man."[33] This identification is not entirely accurate: the tablet in question seems to be one found at Hipponion in southern Italy, hence Fischer's use of the odd "Greek-Roman" label. The tablet does date to *ca.* 400 BCE, but it was discovered on top of a woman's skeleton, not "among the ashes of a dead man," as Fischer claims.[34] Fischer's identification nonetheless makes clear the appeal he saw in the phrase, which fits in well with the band's morbid and dark interests. The obscurity of the tablet, combined with the circumstances of its discovery, made it more appealing to the band than less mysterious and sinister aspects of Greek and Roman antiquity.

Greco-Roman antiquity is present in Celtic Frost's albums via the use of Greek phrases, but this depends on the more occult and evocative associations of the language. These associations are especially clear from the title of the band's 1985 album, *To Mega Therion*, which is transliterated from the Greek for Crowley's preferred title of "The Great Beast" (he frequently claimed that he was the beast from Revelations 13). The Greek phrase here is familiar to those with occult interests, for whom the phrase evokes Crowley (and possibly the New Testament) rather than anything to do with Greco-Roman antiquity. Celtic Frost's fondness for using Greek album titles with occult associations continues in Fischer's new band Triptykon, whose name is transliterated directly from the Greek, in preference to the Latinized spelling of the English "Triptych." The band's 2010 album is called *Eparistera Daimones* (literally: "Left-side Demons"), a phrase that is taken from a ritual included in Crowley's 1913 *Book of Lies*.[35] This phrase clearly has intrigued fans of Triptykon, who have discussed its meaning and occult significance on the band's online discussion forum.[36] This forum also contains much speculation about the meaning of the Greek phrase used for the band's 2014 album title, *Melana Chasmata*. There is no occult significance to this title, which simply means "Black Chasms." Fischer writes on the forum that it was meant to reflect "the circumstances around the creation of the album as well as [its] atmosphere."[37] But fans of the band nonetheless have sought to discover deeper meanings in the title, based on the implicit assumption that Greek words and phrases used by the band cannot be translated so simply into English.[38] Fans of Celtic Frost and Triptykon evidently enjoy the process of trying to find significance in the Greek titles used by the bands. Greek is unfamiliar to most of their fans, but is simultaneously resonant, due to its continued use in a variety of different contexts, scientific, occult, and otherwise. As an ancient language, Greek clearly seems to possess power for some fans of esoteric metal, who treat each use of it almost as a magical incantation.[39] Though Celtic Frost engage sparingly with Greco-Roman antiquity, Greek is still valuable to the band because of its evocative unfamiliarity and esoteric associations.

Celtic Frost's influential example helped to inspire Therion, a band that has offered since its foundation in the late 1980s a brand of occult-tinged metal that continues to draw on the more esoteric associations of Greco-Roman antiquity. Therion's occult interests are clear first from the band's name, which was itself a shortened form of an earlier version: Megatherion.[40] The name looks back to Celtic Frost's *To Mega Therion*, and from it to Crowley, demonstrating again how metal uses Greek to evoke the occult tradition, rather than Greek antiquity.[41] But Therion's occult connections go far beyond those of Celtic Frost. Since 1991, the band's founder, Cristofer Johnsson, has been a member of Dragon Rouge ("Red Dragon"), a Swedish magical order that values individualism and antinomianism, and is similar in some respects to the Church of Satan.[42] The founder of Dragon Rouge, Thomas Karlsson (b. 1971) was, in turn, the main lyricist on Therion's studio albums released between 1996 and 2010.[43] As Kennet Granholm notes, Therion has not been a "mouthpiece" for Dragon Rouge, but the order still has a notable presence in the band's music.[44] Even before Karlsson began contributing lyrics, Therion's albums showed signs of the band's connections to Dragon Rouge, notably through the use of transliterated Greek. The band's 1993 album, *Symphony Masses: Ho Drakon Ho Megas* ("The Great Dragon"), includes as its subtitle a phrase often used in rituals performed by Dragon Rouge.[45] As was the case for Crowley nearly a century ago, Greek still has a place in the rituals of a modern occult order. This ritualistic, occult usage of Greek has been passed on to Therion.

Despite the band's use of Greek in some song and album titles, Greco-Roman antiquity has a small place in the albums of Therion, which offer wide-ranging engagement with the world's ancient wisdom in keeping with the perennial philosophy championed by Dragon Rouge and its founder. The order's perennialist outlook is supported by its academic and eclectic approach to the study of ancient religions. Its founder has a Ph.D. in the History of Religions from Stockholm University, and some of its members have learned Arabic, Sanskrit, and other languages to further their studies.[46] All of this training is put to use in the academic-style presentations that take place at retreats sponsored by the order, which cover a range of topics, including the depiction of dragons in Arabic literature and mythology.[47] The order's rituals likewise contain a heavy dose of eclecticism. To cite one significant example, its Dragon Ceremony includes a list of "dragon-like creatures drawn from various mythologies," climaxing with the repeated chanting of the Greek phrase "*Ho Drakon Ho Megas*."[48]

Therion's coverage of the premodern world is similarly eclectic. The band's double-album *Lemuria/Sirius B*, released in 2004, features songs that engage with Norse, Egyptian, Indian, and Greek mythology, not to mention the lost civilization of Lemuria named in the title.[49] The eclecticism of the order's rituals and presentations also appears in both the lyrics and the music of Therion's songs. Even in Therion's earliest days as a death metal band, its music included keyboards and choral vocals, both elements that were foreign to the genre at the time.[50] As Therion made the transition to a symphonic metal band in the mid-1990s, incorporating Classical instruments and yet more choral vocals into its sound, it continued to explore non-Western styles of music, particularly in songs with lyrics relating to Egyptian mythology.[51]

A telling example of the band's eclecticism comes in the song "Adulruna Rediviva," from the 2007 album *Gothic Kabbalah*. This is a concept album based on the subject of Karlsson's Ph.D. dissertation, the Swedish scholar Johannes Bureus (1568–1652), who found mystical significance in the runic alphabet of early Germanic languages.[52] Bureus presented his theories in a work called *Adulruna Rediviva* ("The Noble Rune Reborn"), hence the title of Therion's song.[53] This song explores multiple sources of ancient wisdom from different traditions, including in its lyrics a call to a group of prophetesses and goddesses: the Sibyls, the Gnostic figure Sophia (who is called the "female Christ"), Aphrodite, and Venus. There is also an appeal to a diverse group of real and imagined philosophers: "Hermes Trismegistos, Orpheus, Zarathustra, Pythagoras, and Plato."[54] The list of philosophers is organized according to early-modern views on their relative chronology, and implies a continuity to their teachings, thus combining Egyptian, Iranian, and Greek traditions into one.[55] The literature linked to Hermes Trismegistus has long since been identified as late pseudepigrapha, but his name still stands in Therion's song at the head of this succession of philosophers.[56] Fittingly, all of this takes place in a song that combines male and female vocalists, a full choir, and a mix of metal and symphonic instruments, all displaying the many different musical influences acting on the band.[57] The title of the song is in Latin, and it contains references to Greek and Roman philosophy and mythology, but it nonetheless owes most to the occult tradition, drawing on the works of Bureus and others who sought to unite the world's ancient religious traditions into one.

Occult perspectives on the world's premodern past have thus had a considerable impact on the reception of Greco-Roman antiquity within esoteric metal. Celtic Frost and Therion provide two particularly significant examples of occultism's influence, thanks to their popularity and influence within the genre. But there also are many bands with similar interests, including others with links to Dragon Rouge.[58] For all these bands, occultism offers a more compelling perspective on the premodern past than one that emphasizes the Classical associations of Greece and Rome. Like Therion and Celtic Frost, these bands might well have a major interest in these countries exclusively, but most of this interest is likely to be directed at arcane and mysterious material such as the Orphic gold tablets than what we might think of as the mainstream Classical world. Greco-Roman antiquity's connections to the occult tradition are what matter most to esoteric metal bands.

Exotic pasts and forgotten books: The ancient world in esoteric metal via Robert E. Howard and H. P. Lovecraft

Alongside metal's fascination with the occult, many bands also have a major interest in pulp literature from the first half of the twentieth century, particularly the stories of

H. P. Lovecraft (1890–1937) and Robert E. Howard (1906–1936), many of which were originally published in *Weird Tales*.[59] Lovecraft has enjoyed a significant following among metal bands since the 1980s, when his characters, especially the ancient octopus-headed entity called Cthulhu, began to appear with some frequency in metal songs, such as Metallica's "The Call of Ktulu."[60] Howard's stories, too, have had an increasing presence in metal since the early 1980s, when his most famous creation was played by Arnold Schwarzenegger in the film *Conan the Barbarian*.[61] Lovecraft's appeal to metal bands owes much to the genre's longstanding interest in horror and madness, just as Howard's popularity in metal depends heavily on the violence and darkness of his hyper-masculine stories.[62]

But the interest of esoteric metal bands in Lovecraft and Howard is often linked to a larger fascination with the world's premodern past. One band with such interests is Britain's Bal-Sagoth, who engage at length with the premodern world in six albums released between 1995 and 2006.[63] Bal-Sagoth may not enjoy the popularity and influence of other metal bands that have been inspired by the stories of Lovecraft and Howard, including the American band Nile, and the Danish band Mercyful Fate,[64] but their albums offer an unmatched level of engagement with the works of Lovecraft and Howard that can illustrate, in concentrated form, the larger influence that these authors have had on esoteric metal's reception of the ancient world.[65] This engagement with Lovecraft and Howard is owed largely to Bal-Sagoth's founder and lyricist, Bryon A. Roberts, who is also an aspiring author of dark fantasy and horror stories.[66] Roberts was responsible for the naming of the band, which comes from a story by Howard called "The Gods of Bal-Sagoth," originally published in *Weird Tales* in 1931.[67] Dark fantasy and horror stories are an entirely fitting source of inspiration for the unusual music of Bal-Sagoth, which Roberts describes as "symphonic baroque fantasy black metal."[68] In Bal-Sagoth's albums, the typical screamed vocals and high-treble guitars of black metal are joined with frequent use of spoken dialogue, and supplemented further with symphonic effects produced by synthesizers, giving the band a distinctive sound that takes much inspiration from film music.[69] The band is also notorious for having song titles of great length, written in the overwrought and archaizing style familiar from the works of Howard and Lovecraft.[70]

The eclecticism of Bal-Sagoth's music is matched by its wide-ranging engagement with the premodern world. The stories of Howard and Lovecraft serve as a major source of inspiration for the band's treatment of the world's distant and forgotten past, which mostly bypasses Greco-Roman antiquity. This treatment takes the form of an invented history filled with a diverse mix of peoples and places, complete with an imaginary work of ancient literature. Roberts has even put together a large online glossary of his invented world, identifying the hundreds of peoples and places that appear in it.[71] Bal-Sagoth does draw from Greco-Roman antiquity as a source of inspiration for its invented history, but the band has only limited interest in Greece and Rome.[72] As was the case for Lovecraft and Howard, Greco-Roman antiquity is simply too civilized to have a major place in Bal-Sagoth's exploration of premodernity. The band is instead more interested in civilizations that evoke a lost ancient world, following the lead of Howard and Lovecraft in exploring the imaginative and horrific potential of humanity's forgotten history.

Bal-Sagoth's exploration of the world's distant past via an invented history of humanity follows the lead of Howard, whose own invented "Hyborian World" was meant to convey to readers a feeling of familiar but mysterious antiquity.[73] The invented worlds of Bal-Sagoth and Howard do include many Greek and Latin words and names, but they draw on many other sources besides Greco-Roman antiquity, mixing together a wide range of traditions. The mix of names that form Bal-Sagoth's invented "antediluvian world" is clear even from a cursory examination of the band's album and song titles, which include references to Atlantis, Hyperborea, Lemuria, Mu, and Ultima Thule.[74] Atlantis derives ultimately from Plato, and Hyperborea and Ultima Thule were used by Greek and Roman authors to refer to far-off places in the mysterious north.[75] The lost continents of Lemuria and Mu, however, were inventions of the nineteenth century that have gained popular familiarity as signifiers of the world's distant past.[76] All of these places are also part of Howard's invented world, which used names that were meant to be familiar to readers.[77] Roberts follows Howard's example, and places the lost continents, along with Hyperborea and Ultima Thule, in their "correct" places on the map of his world, which fittingly includes a "Middle Sea" where one might expect to find the Mediterranean.[78] Howard and Bal-Sagoth both, therefore, offer a familiar map, filled with an eclectic range of names that have ancient associations. Within this mix, Greece and Rome are slightly defamiliarized by being linked with lost continents, but they still serve as the most familiar parts of the maps.

More signs of the eclectic nature of Bal-Sagoth's invented antediluvian world derive from the anachronistic use of Latin. In one of the band's several songs about Hyperborea, the warriors of this land inexplicably hail their king with a Latin phrase "Imperius Rex," which is evidently intended to mean "Imperial King."[79] Latin has a prominent place in another of the band's songs, where it is used alongside a bewildering range of other words and concepts that are meant to convey a feeling of antiquity. The song concerns a force of "Dragon Lords" in an allegorical version of ancient Britain, which is called by its alternative Latin name of "Albion."[80] Remarkably, the song includes a quotation from *Beowulf* in the original Old English, a reference to a system of writing called "Dragon Runes," and the implication that the Dragon Lords of Albion followed the convention of the Roman army in naming their units, one of which is called the "IX Legio Draconis" ("Ninth Legion of the Dragon").[81] Latin does have a prominent place in the song, but is linked with other languages, both real and invented, that also have ancient connotations. Bal-Sagoth's invented antediluvian world, much like Howard's Hyborian world, exploits Greek or Roman names in its attempt to create an atmosphere of familiar antiquity, joining these names with an eclectic mix of other ancient signifiers that have nothing to do with Greece or Rome.

Bal-Sagoth's invented world is accompanied by an imaginary, evil book of great antiquity that surely qualifies as an example of rejected knowledge but is nonetheless linked to Greco-Roman antiquity through its title and the history of its transmission. This book, *The Chthonic Chronicles*, is the subject of Bal-Sagoth's 2006 album, which was inspired by the example of Lovecraft and a group of other writers, including Howard, who all contributed to the creation of an entire body of imaginary ancient literature that they would cite in their stories.[82] By far the most famous of these books is Lovecraft's own *Necronomicon*, which shares with Bal-Sagoth's *Chthonic Chronicles* a complicated relationship with Greco-Roman antiquity, spelled out at length by both Lovecraft and Roberts in transmission histories of their fictitious books.[83] Tellingly, neither book was originally written in Greek, despite the Greek roots used in their titles. The *Necronomicon*, as Lovecraft explained in his essay "The History of the *Necronomicon*," was originally the work of a "mad Arab" of the eighth century named Abdul Alhazred, but it was translated into Greek in the tenth century.[84] Lovecraft evidently recognized that *Necronomicon*, with its clear connotations of death to English-speakers, would resonate much more strongly than the book's original Arabic title of *Al Azif* that he had assigned to it.[85] Bal-Sagoth's book, meanwhile, was written in "Old High Atlantean," and addressed to a divinity named Khthon, who was worshipped in several different forms by the peoples of Lemuria, Atlantis, Ultima Thule, and Hyperborea.[86] There is nothing Greek about the divinity Khthon, though his name is a transliteration of the Greek word for "earth," evidently spelled with an initial K to make the name seem more exotic.[87] "Chthonic" may not be used much in English, but Roberts evidently liked both its strong associations to the Underworld, and its similarity to Lovecraft's Cthulhu; Roberts even explains on his website that this similarity to "Cthulhu," a tri-syllabic word, is why he pronounces "chthonic" incorrectly ("katonic") on the album.[88] The album's title still has some remote associations with Greek antiquity, but the similarity of "Chthonic" to "Cthulhu" may ultimately resonate most for some listeners of the band.[89] Roberts follows Lovecraft in ensuring that there is separation between his invented book and Greece, despite the prominent use of a Greek root in its title.

Additional signs of this separation from the Classical world come from the handling of the purported Latin translations of the *Necronomicon* and the *Chthonic Chronicles*, which are identified as the only extant forms of the two fictitious books by both Lovecraft and Bal-Sagoth. The Latin translation of the *Necronomicon*, Lovecraft explained, was made directly from the Greek in the thirteenth century, and is the version most often mentioned in his stories.[90] Though the *Necronomicon* is not a Greek or Roman book, Lovecraft took for granted that its contents would be transmitted to the world thanks to the continuing knowledge of Greek and Latin among European and American scholars. The characters in his stories, even if they are professors of geology, are all able to read the Latin *Necronomicon*; one of them even displays his Classical biases by noting that the translation was in "awkward Low Latin."[91] Despite its seeming connections to Greco-Roman antiquity, the *Necronomicon* is fundamentally non-Western, and this is exactly why it was able to serve as an effective source of horror and alienation in Lovecraft's works.[92]

Bal-Sagoth handles its *Chthonic Chronicles* in much the same way, including excerpts from the work that derive from its "sixth Latin edition."[93] This Latin translation, though, was evidently still interspersed with "glyphs, sigils, [and] occult pictograms" that revealed the text's Atlantean origins, and established its non-Western credentials.[94] The Latin translation of the *Chthonic Chronicles* is accessible to the narrators of Bal-Sagoth's songs and associated stories, who tell the story of the band's larger fictional world in lyrics and accompanying liner notes. All these narrators are antiquarians active around the turn of the twentieth century, much like the characters in Lovecraft's stories.[95] But these antiquarian narrators direct almost all their scholarly attention away from Greco-Roman antiquity, despite their evident familiarity with Latin. Instead, all the songs featuring these antiquarians are about other premodern sites and civilizations: Angkor Wat, Atlantis, Babylon, and Egypt, along with the Olmec, Mayans, and Aztecs.

In contrast, Greco-Roman antiquity has a muted presence in the *Chthonic Chronicles*, appearing in only one song. This is a short, lyric-less piece (it includes wordless vocals) called "To Storm the Cyclopean Gates of Byzantium" and is accompanied in the album's liner notes by a short story written from the perspective of a centurion serving in the army of the emperor Septimius Severus during the Siege of Byzantium (193–195 CE).[96] Tellingly, this song has no connection to the antiquarian narrators who appear in all of the other songs and stories about the *Chthonic Chronicles*. It scarcely even qualifies as a conventional metal song; there are no guitars, drums, or bass, much less any screamed vocals, as there are in all the other songs on the album about the *Chthonic Chronicles*. These other songs and stories all emphasize the horrific and mysterious associations of non-Western civilizations, again following the example of Lovecraft.[97] Evidently, Roberts was unable to imagine a song that explored the lurking evil and danger that might be encountered by an archaeologist in a Greek or Roman ruin, as he was easily able to do for the ruins of non-Western civilizations in several different songs. These make extensive use of the tritone, an interval called by music theorists the *Diabolus in musica* ("the Devil in music") that has traditionally been used to evoke feelings of danger and fear.[98] Even when one of the antiquarian narrators displays his Classical training and swears an oath "by the erudite tongue of Herodotus," it immediately becomes clear that he is celebrating the discovery of "arcane secrets" about the non-Greek divinity Khthon in an "ancient Coptic papyrus."[99] Consciously or not, Bal-Sagoth follows the example of Lovecraft in turning away from Greco-Roman antiquity in its exploration of the premodern world. Just as Lovecraft found little potential for horror in Greco-Roman antiquity, likewise Bal-Sagoth has deemed Greece and Rome an inappropriate source for exploration in its unique brand of metal.

The influence of Lovecraft and Howard has led Bal-Sagoth to engage little with Greco-Roman antiquity in its reception of premodernity, following the same pattern that appears in the albums of Celtic Frost, Therion, and other esoteric bands. Bal-Sagoth's albums contain none of the explicit references to the occult that are so obvious in the albums of Celtic Frost and Therion, but the band still shares their fascination with the most arcane and mysterious elements of the premodern world, rather than Greece and Rome. Bal-Sagoth nonetheless follows the example of Lovecraft and Howard in drawing inspiration from Greco-Roman antiquity in its exploration of the world's distant and forgotten past, again much as Celtic Frost and Therion employ Greek and Latin words and phrases in their albums. The pulp and occult influences working on these three bands have helped them to present an alternative vision of the premodern world that mostly bypasses Greece and Rome, even as they take for granted nineteenth and early-twentieth century assumptions about these civilizations. Greco-Roman antiquity is still present in the albums of Bal-Sagoth, Celtic Frost, and Therion, but only alongside larger engagements with other periods and civilizations of the world's premodern past. In the end, the more familiar and famous aspects of Greece and Rome have little place in the music of the three bands, which instead look to authors like Howard, Lovecraft, and Crowley as sources of inspiration for their engagement with antiquity.

Conclusion

The three bands discussed in this chapter serve to establish that Classical reception in metal needs to be placed within the broader context of the genre's fascination with premodernity, and its interest in the occult tradition and pulp literature. Works of Greek and Latin literature have only a minor place in the receptions of Greco-Roman antiquity by Celtic Frost, Therion, Bal-Sagoth, and other esoteric bands. Esoteric bands are more likely, overall, to be captivated instead by a completely spurious piece of "ancient" literature. This is none other than Lovecraft's own *Necronomicon*, which a large number of people with interests in the occult believe is a real book, rather than an invented fiction.[100] Support for this belief comes from the many versions of the book that have been published and presented as authentic, above all the "Simon" *Necronomicon*, which has been a fixture in the occult sections of bookstores since its first publication in the late 1970s.[101] With prefatory material and an introduction authored by the mysterious Simon, this *Necronomicon* claims that there are major links between the fictional world depicted in Lovecraft's stories, the occult teachings of Crowley, and the magic and mythology of ancient Sumer.[102] Though the book is presented as the work of Abdul Alhazred, Lovecraft's own "Mad Arab," Simon's preface claims that the manuscript he accessed was in Greek, rather than Arabic, recalling Lovecraft's suggestion that the *Necronomicon* was translated from Arabic to Greek in the tenth century.[103] Simon's *Necronomicon* thus serves as a fitting symbol for the status that Greco-Roman antiquity has for many metal bands. Though the work has a Greek title and was ostensibly even translated from a Greek manuscript, Simon's *Necronomicon* brings together the major interests of esoteric metal bands in pulp literature, the occult tradition, and the most arcane aspects of the world's ancient history. Simon's *Necronomicon*, which has been quoted or alluded to in the lyrics of many death metal bands, is a strong contender for the title of the most popular and influential "ancient" book within metal.[104] The major influence of this book provides a final reminder that esoteric metal bands display limited interests in Greece and Rome when they approach the ancient world. Alternative traditions about antiquity and alternative canons of ancient literature, real or imaginary, have instead been of greater significance within esoteric metal.[105]

Notes

1. Both appear in the notes accompanying the song "(Ode to ancient) Europa."
2. *The Song of Roland* is the inspiration for the song "...And the Horns Called for War." The twelfth-century account of Lindisfarne is Symeon of Durham's *Book on the Origin and*

Progress of this the Church of Durham (see Rollason 2000 for Latin text and translation). Symeon's account serves as inspiration for the song "Lindisfarne (Anno 793)."

3. Bierce's story was called "An Inhabitant of Carcosa." It has been republished many times, including in a collection by Theys (2002: 55–60). For the later history of Carcosa, including its appearance in *True Detective*, see Tybjerg (2016: 110–12).
4. Theys' claim is confused. There is no reference to Carcosa in *The Satanic Bible* (LaVey 1969). There is, however, a reference to Carcosa in a companion volume to this work, *The Satanic Rituals* (LaVey 1972: 54).
5. These comments all come in Theys' liner notes accompanying the lyrics to the song "Dim Carcosa." For the history of Carcaso and its status in the Roman Empire, see Bekker-Nielsen (2008: 248–50).
6. For characteristics of these subgenres, see Introduction (this volume).
7. See Kahn-Harris (2007: 61).
8. For discussion, see Granholm (2011a: 518).
9. For the occult tradition, and its emphasis on rejected knowledge, see especially Hanegraaff (2012).
10. See Schein (2008: 79).
11. For the history of *Weird Tales*, see Haining (1990) and Hoppenstand (2013).
12. For discussion of the Classical tradition as it was conceived in the nineteenth and early twentieth centuries, see Budelmann and Haubold (2008: 13–14) and Schein (2008: 79).
13. For Orientalism in *Weird Tales* stories, see McGeough (2015: 373–86), and further discussion below. For the occult tradition, see Granholm (2011b: 22–4). For more on the influence of Orientalism on metal, see Olabarria (this volume).
14. For the controversies surrounding Theys and his interests in Flemish history, see his comments in Geegor (2015). On nationalism in black metal, see Spracklen, Lucas, and Deeks (2014: 56–60).
15. See Olson (2011: 147–48).
16. For the apolitical status of Norwegian black metal in this period, see Olson (2011: 138).
17. Note the growing interest in the study of magic, as observed by Collins (2008: xi). Consider also the increased attention on Greek and Roman astrology, including studies by Barton (1994) and Greenbaum (2016).
18. See Farley (2009: 78–80).
19. For the influence of Black Sabbath on later bands treating occult subjects, see Granholm (2011a: 517). For Crowley and his reception in popular music, see Lachman (2014: 322–46).
20. Spinal Tap, "Stonehenge," *Spinal Tap* (1984). The ellipses are in the original.
21. See Sharpe-Young (2007: 479–82) and Wagner (2010: 116–24). Note also that Celtic Frost's first three albums appear among the top 500 metal albums as voted by fans in a major worldwide poll (Popoff 2004: 90–3 and 102).
22. For overviews of the band's history and significance, see Ekeroth (2006: 411); Sharpe-Young (2007: 488–91) and Wagner (2010: 233–38). Note that Therion's album *Theli* (1996), the band's first to feature extensive use of Classical instrumentation and choral vocals, appears among the top 200 albums of metal history, as voted by fans (Popoff 2004: 165–66).
23. See Trompf (2013: 375–403). Therion's *Beloved Antichrist* (2018), a three-CD-length rock opera, contains one track entitled "Hail Caesar!"

24. See Hanegraaff (2012: 7–12).
25. Fischer (2000: 58).
26. Fischer (2000: 74), Fischer (2009: 133).
27. Fischer (2009: 138).
28. Note especially the songs "Babylon Fell (Jade Serpent)," from *Into the Pandemonium* (1987), and "A Descent to Babylon (Babylon Asleep)," from *Parched with Thirst Am I and Dying* (1992).
29. See Fischer (2009: 187).
30. For an overview of the tablets, including an edition with translation, see Graf and Johnston (2013).
31. See Edmonds (2011: 3–14) and Graf and Johnston (2013: 50–65) for a history of scholarship on the tablets.
32. Breslin (1977: 4, 6). Previous English translations of the tablets which might have been available to the band in 1992 rendered the key phrase differently. Note Guthrie (1952: 173) and Harrison (1908: 666), both of which translate the phrase as "I am parched with thirst and I perish."
33. Fischer (2000: 333 n. 90).
34. See Breslin (1977: 6) and Graf and Johnston (2013: 4–5).
35. Crowley (1913: 35).
36. See "Eparistera Daimones" ("n.d.").
37. Fischer (2013) in a reply posted to DrMorbid (2013).
38. One fan notes that the word "chasma" is used in the field of astrogeology, while another speculates wildly that *Melana* might refer to the river Nile. See the replies to DrMorbid in DrMorbid (2013).
39. For the magical power attributed to ancient languages in contemporary culture, see Pitcher (2009: 29).
40. For the name-change, see Ekeroth (2006: 121).
41. For the influence of Celtic Frost on Therion, see Wagner (2010: 234).
42. See Granholm (2014: 60–1). My discussion of the order depends heavily on the studies of Granholm (2005) and (2014); the latter is an updated, but shorter, version of the former, and I shall cite from both.
43. Granholm (2012: 563). For more on Karlsson, see Granholm (2014: 70–2). Karlsson was not the lyricist for Therion's two most recent studio albums, though both differ in character from the band's previous releases. *Les Fleurs Du Mal* (2012) contains fifteen covers of French pop songs from the 1960s and 1970s. *Beloved Antichrist* (2018), meanwhile, is a massive rock opera, and something of a passion project for the band's founder.
44. Granholm (2014: 195).
45. For the use of the phrase in Dragon Rouge rituals, see Granholm (2014: 107).
46. Granholm (2014: 198; 76, 107–8).
47. See Granholm (2014: 107–8), with additional details on the order's lectures in Granholm (2005: 201–3).
48. See Granholm (2005: 197–98; the quotation is from 198 n. 76).
49. See also the discussion of Granholm (2012: 568–69).

50. See Ekeroth (2006: 194–95), Wagner (2010: 233–35), and especially "Interview with Christofer Johnsson" (2004), which includes an album-by-album overview of the band's early experimentation.
51. Note especially "In the Desert of Set," *Theli* (1996). For Egypt in metal, see Olabarria (this volume).
52. See Granholm (2012: 563). For more on Bureus, see Håkansson (2012: 500–22).
53. See Håkansson (2012: 505–7).
54. Therion, "Adulruna Rediviva," *Gothic Kabbalah* (2007).
55. See Ebeling (2007: 62) for a similar succession in the works of the influential Renaissance scholar Marsilio Ficino, who translated both the works of Plato and the works attributed to Hermes Trismegistus into Latin.
56. See Ebeling (2007: 91–3).
57. On the music that has influenced Therion, see "Interview with Christofer Johnsson" (2004).
58. See Granholm (2013: 5–33).
59. For biographies of Lovecraft and Howard, see, respectively: Joshi (2013) and Finn (2013).
60. Metallica, "The Call of Ktulu," *Ride the Lightning* (1984). The band offered an alternative spelling of Cthulhu to make the word easier to pronounce, and to avoid the possibility of legal action for copyright infringement. See McIver (2009: 122). For a thorough review of Lovecraft-inspired songs in metal, see Hill (2006: 43–114) and Norman (2013: 193–208).
61. Hall (2007: 4–11) offers a discussion of Howard's sizable presence in metal. See also Sammon (2007) for the influence and reception of Conan in popular culture.
62. On the appeal of Lovecraft to metal, see Norman (2013: 203–4). On Howard's appeal, see Hall (2007: 7).
63. For an overview of the band's history and discography, see Sharpe-Young (2007: 478–79).
64. On Nile, see Hill (2006: 95) and Olabarria (this volume). On Mercyful Fate, see Hill (2006: 88–9).
65. For other bands with interests similar to Bal-Sagoth's, note, especially, the example of Ancient Rites (above), Manilla Road (see Sharpe-Young 2007: 310–11), and Absu (see Sharpe-Young 2007: 224–25).
66. See Roberts (2015) for his first published story in a collection written by metal musicians.
67. The story has not been included in the recent multi-volume edition of Howard's works published by Del Rey. It is, however, included in several older collections, such as Howard (1963: 91–128).
68. See the interview of Stefanis (2006) for the band's self-characterization.
69. See Messer (2006).
70. For the most extreme example in the band's discography, note "And Lo, When the Imperium Marches Against Gul-Kothoth, then Dark Sorceries Shall Enshroud the Citadel of the Obsidian Crown," *Starfire Burning Upon The Ice-Veiled Throne Of Ultima Thule* (1996). See Åshede and Foka (this volume) for Theatre of Tragedy's use of archaizing English.
71. See Roberts (1998). This is the only version of the glossary currently available to me online; it includes content only from the band's first four albums.
72. The band's most sustained engagement with Greco-Roman antiquity comes in a single song. This is "Blood Slakes the Sand at the Circus Maximus," *Battle Magic* (1998). It concerns the experience of an Iceni gladiator in the aftermath of Boudicca's rebellion against Rome. See below for discussion of another song that engages briefly with Greco-Roman antiquity.
73. See Shanks (2013: 13–34).

74. Note the titles of three albums for references to Atlantis, Lemuria, and Ultima Thule, respectively: *Atlantis Ascendant* (2001), *A Black Moon Broods Over Lemuria* (1995), and *Starfire Burning Upon the Ice-Veiled Throne of Ultima Thule* (1996). Hyperborea appears in three songs that all form part of the same sequence: "The Splendour of a Thousand Swords Gleaming beneath the Blazon of the Hyperborean Empire." Part I is on the band's 1996 album; Part 2 is on *Battle Magic* (1998); and Part III is on the band's 2001 album. Mu appears in "The Thirteen Cryptical Prophecies of Mu," from *The Power Cosmic* (1999).
75. For the influence of Plato's fictitious Atlantis, see Vidal-Naquet (2007). For Hyperborea, see Bridgman (2005) and, for Ultima Thule, see Mund-Dopchie (2009). See also Romm (1992) for discussion of the interests of Greek and Roman authors in places located at the edges of the world.
76. See de Camp (1970: 44–50) for Mu and (1970: 51–75) on Lemuria.
77. See Howard (2002: 381–98 and 423–25) for his famous essay "The Hyborian World," and for two of his own hand-drawn maps of this world, respectively. For the intended familiarity of his world, see Shanks (2013: 14).
78. For the band's map, see Roberts (2009a). One version of it is also included in the liner notes to *The Chthonic Chronicles* (2006).
79. Bal-Sagoth, "The Splendour of a Thousand Swords Gleaming beneath the Blazon of the Hyperborean Empire (Part III)," *Atlantis Ascendant* (2001). "Imperius" is not a word attested in Classical Latin, and it is used only as a noun in later Latin, where it means "emperor." See Souter (1949, s.v. "imperius").
80. "Draconis Albionensis," *Atlantis Ascendant* (2001). The song's title is evidently supposed to mean something like "English Dragon(s)." See *OLD* (1996), s.v. "albion."
81. The quotation is from *Beowulf* 3180: "Wyruld Cyninga" ("of the earthly kings"). I cite from the edition of Fulk, Bjork, and Niles (2008), which includes a glossary entry for the phrase at 460.
82. See "The Haunter of the Dark" in Lovecraft (1999: 344) for citations of many of the books invented by Lovecraft and his circle, with the accompanying explanatory note on the passage by Joshi (2013: 418 n. 15).
83. On Lovecraft's *Necronomicon*, see Harms and Gonce (2003: 3–28).
84. Lovecraft (1995: 52–3).
85. Lovecraft (1995: 52). As Lovecraft here notes, *Al Azif* refers to the "nocturnal sound" made by insects and is associated with the "howling of daemons."
86. All these peoples are mentioned in the album's liner notes for the song "The Sixth Adulation of his Chthonic Majesty," *The Chthonic Chronicles* (2006). There is a reference to "Old High Atlantean" in the notes for "Six Score and Ten Oblations to a Malefic Avatar," *The Chthonic Chronicles* (2006).
87. As a parallel, note the example, cited above, of Metallica spelling "Cthulhu" as "Ktulu." Compare also the common alternative spelling of "true cult" as "trve kvlt" within black metal, where the phrase is meant to signify authenticity. See Lucas, Deeks, and Spracklen (2011: 286 and 289).
88. See Roberts (2009b).
89. Note the remarkable suggestion of Hill (2006: 56): "I believe the term 'Chthonic' means 'related to Cthulhu.'"
90. See Lovecraft (1995: 53), who explains that the original Arabic version was lost in the eleventh century, and that the Greek translation may also be completely lost, despite some rumors of its continued survival.

91. See "The Festival," in Lovecraft (1999: 117). Note also "At the Mountains of Madness," in Lovecraft (2001: 250) for the familiarity of a geology professor with the Latin translation of the *Necronomicon*.
92. On Lovecraft's reception of the ancient Near East in his stories, see McGeough (2015: 373–86).
93. See the liner notes to "The Sixth Adulation of his Chthonic Majesty," *The Chthonic Chronicles* (2006).
94. "Six Score and Ten Oblations to a Malefic Avatar," *The Chthonic Chronicles* (2006).
95. See Müller (2013: 57–8) for discussion of Lovecraft's antiquarian characters.
96. From *The Chthonic Chronicles* (2006). The story explains that Septimius Severus was eager to find a copy of the *Chthonic Chronicles* in the library of Byzantium. It is interesting to note that Severus did actively seek out copies of ancient magical books when he visited Egypt (Cass. Dio 75.13.2), though it is by no means clear that Roberts' use of the emperor in the story is anything more than coincidental.
97. See McGeough (2015: 377) for discussion of how the ancient Near East served in Lovecraft's stories as a "meaningful referent for danger, anarchy and mysticism."
98. Note, especially, the use of the tritone interval in the first twenty seconds of "The Dreamer in the Catacombs of Ur," *Atlantis Ascendant* (2006). For more on the tritone, see Kahn-Harris (2007: 31).
99. "Unfettering the Hoary Sentinels of Karnak," *The Chthonic Chronicles* (2006).
100. See Harms and Gonce (2003: xvi). Note also Steadman (2015) who offers a discussion of Lovecraft's reception by contemporary occult groups.
101. Simon (1977). See also the discussions of Harms and Gonce (2003: 39–48) and Steadman (2015: 93–116).
102. Simon (1977: xi–xiii) and the "Chart of Comparisons" between Lovecraft, Crowley, and Sumer on (1977: xxxix–xl).
103. Simon (1977: xxxi).
104. See Hill (2006: 66, 73–4, 95) for discussion, respectively, of songs by Morbid Angel, Vader, and Nile that quote or allude to the Simon *Necronomicon*.
105. I am grateful to Ralph Patrello, Matt Unangst, Sean Wempe, and the volume editors, Kris Fletcher and Osman Umurhan, for their comments on drafts of the paper at various stages of the project, and to Jason Gersh for providing valuable advice on matters relating to musicology.

CHAPTER 8
"WHEN THE LAND WAS MILK AND HONEY AND THE MAGIC WAS STRONG AND TRUE": EDWARD SAID, ANCIENT EGYPT, AND HEAVY METAL
Leire Olabarria

Introduction: Egyptomania and heavy metal

The exhibition *Discovering Tutankhamun* held at the Ashmolean Museum in Oxford from July 24 to November 2, 2014 explored the reception of ancient Egypt after the discovery of the tomb of Tutankhamun in 1922, featuring ornaments, fashion outfits, and even popular dancing songs such as the hit "Old King Tut was a wise old nut" (Collins and McNamara 2014: 67–75). Focusing on early-twentieth-century Egyptomania, this exhibit illustrated how ancient Egypt has been an important part of Western collective imagery for centuries, with pyramids, mummies, and hieroglyphs attracting the attention of scholars and laymen alike. From film (Serafy 2003, Lupton 2003, Day 2006: 64–93) to painting (Blaschek 2010), from architecture (Humbert and Price 2003, Moser 2012) to literature (Parramore 2008, Fleischhack 2015), ancient Egypt continues to permeate popular culture, and its reception has become a burgeoning area of study, as the large number of publications, conferences, and events around Egyptomania indicates (e.g. Seipel 2000, MacDonald and Rice 2003, Colla 2007, Brier 2013).

This chapter aims to address the image of ancient Egypt in heavy metal music, which has not escaped the fascination with this ancient culture, as exemplified by the well-known songs "Powerslave" (Iron Maiden, *Powerslave*, 1984) or "Egypt (The Chains Are On)" (Dio, *The Last in Line*, 1984). Despite the abundance of allusions to Egypt in lyrics, album covers, and music videos, its impact on this musical genre has been entirely overlooked by Egyptologists, possibly due to the social stigma often connected with the metal scene. Associations with teenage suicide, Satanist rites, or violence in general have usually prevailed over its artistic quality and values and hence affected the perception of metal among the general public.[1] In this sense, ancient Egypt and heavy metal share some common ground, as they are both governed by popular (mis)conceptions that have deeply affected their reception. Particularly, the current understanding of Egypt is shaped by a tension between academic and so-called alternative visions of this culture, which are in effect competing views of ancient Egypt. Metal bands also make a choice of the vision of Egypt that they adhere to, generally leaning toward the latter.

Not all the bands present Egypt in exactly the same light, as the type of metal they perform may exert a direct influence on the choice of topics and their focus.[2] With this caveat in mind, I take the death metal band Nile as a case study because they are the most prolific band whose discography is entirely devoted to ancient Egyptian themes. This provides a rich repository of imagery of this culture—especially of pre-Hellenistic times—that can then be complemented by and contrasted with the lyrical concerns of other bands to achieve a fuller understanding of the reception of Egypt in heavy metal. Nile are also a prime example to illustrate the tension between academic and alternative Egyptology, as they explicitly reject an exclusively scholarly vision of ancient Egypt, while still providing extensive liner notes in their albums describing the historical background to some of their songs. Their portrayal of Egypt, reinterpreted through the lens of death metal, also has an impact on their fans, and I include some comments and quotes extracted from the Internet that attest to Nile's potential to construct and instill an image of the past.

An analysis of frequently recurring topics in heavy metal's representation of Egypt indicates that esoteric knowledge and violence are regarded as some of this civilization's most salient traits. This seems to be in line both with the themes most frequently employed in metal music and with the popular depiction of a mysterious Egypt that is also stressed by Egyptomania. As the concept of "mystery" embodies the unknown, and something that is not known is by definition different, Egypt is effectively being portrayed as an "Other" that contrasts with what is familiar.

The notion of Orientalism, as formulated by Edward Said (1935–2003), can be a thought-provoking tool for exploring these issues. Egypt is regarded as part of an "East" that was first delineated by scholars from a Eurocentric perspective and in opposition to a hypothetical Western identity. I argue that the Orientalist approach to ancient Egypt that has permeated popular culture is also prevalent in metal: Egypt is "otherized" and "exoticized" in keeping with the usual expectations of an allegedly mysterious ancient land where "magic was strong and true" (Dio, "Egypt (The Chains Are On)," *The Last in Line*, 1984). Heavy metal is therefore perpetuating a constructed idea of ancient Egypt that is present in society at large and whose roots can be traced back to Classical antiquity.

Conventionalism and transgression: Nile as a case study

Heavy metal is captivated by "the origins of things" (Umurhan 2012: 147), as evidenced by its numerous references to the history and mythology of ancient cultures, including Greece and Rome. In the introduction to this volume, Fletcher and Umurhan convincingly advocate the use of the label "Mediterranean metal" to refer to the increasing number of bands that share an interest in the history of Classical civilizations. The reception of Greece and Rome in heavy metal has received some attention over the last few years, and indeed topics such as "glory, war, trauma, and military prowess" (Umurhan 2012: 130) have been identified as some of the main motifs behind lyrics and music videos. Campbell (2009) argues that the selection of those themes is based on the appeal of the role of the warrior, with his code of honor, as an idealized masculine archetype of the Classical past that one may wish to emulate.[3]

The case of Egypt, which seems to have gone almost unnoticed by scholars of metal studies, offers an interesting counterpoint to the treatment of Classical civilizations. Images of aggression are also a major component of the portrayal of Egypt in heavy metal and the figure of an anonymous warrior thirsty for violence who appeases brutal gods abounds. However, the idea of an outstanding champion with heroic qualities seeking individual glory is largely absent. In addition, while connections of the Classical world with the occult are prominent in heavy metal (see Secord's contribution to this volume), magic and esoteric knowledge are perhaps more intimately imbricated in the construction of an image of Egypt as a mysterious land. These two major topics, namely violence and esotericism, are explored in detail below.

A variety of metal genres can be identified among the bands that have dealt with ancient Egypt in their compositions, for instance traditional metal,[4] power metal,[5] thrash metal,[6] progressive metal,[7] and death metal.[8] As pointed out in the introduction to this volume, these distinct musical styles have their own idiosyncrasies in terms of sound, lyrics, and even general aesthetics, which necessarily shape the image of ancient Egypt that they transmit. This ancient civilization, however, is featured only occasionally by the majority of metal bands, who do not seem to show a specific Egyptological interest and draw entirely on commonplace generalizations about ancient Egypt in their lyrics. In this chapter I analyze primarily the death metal band Nile due to their almost exclusive focus on ancient Egypt in all their albums. This emphasis, combined with an extensive discography and the occasional inclusion of album liner notes outlining their inspiration, provides a fascinating case study. Songs and albums from other bands are used as complementary evidence to achieve a more wide-ranging picture of the reception of Egypt in heavy metal.

Nile were founded in Greenville (South Carolina, USA) in 1993, and have remained active ever since despite considerable changes in the original lineup.[9] The band currently has eight full-length albums and two demos and is often classified as a technical or progressive death metal band, a subgenre defined by the sheer complexity of the music, which includes "dynamic song structures, uncommon time signatures, atypical rhythms and unusual harmonies and melodies" (Kegan 2015: 108–9).

The band's front man and founding member, Karl Sanders, has a long-term interest in the study of Egypt and ancient Near Eastern cultures that plays a pivotal role in the inspiration for their music.[10] References in Nile's songs show an impressive array of Egyptological knowledge, although this well-informed approach to Egypt is combined with other "alternative" sources of inspiration such as horror literature and esoteric writing. Nile's website used to have a forum on which band members interacted with fans, occasionally responding to questions about their lyrics, historical inspiration, and composition process.[11] This has provided an interesting outlet to explore to what extent the band has contributed to creating and solidifying an image of ancient Egypt among their fan base, and for this reason I occasionally refer to these discussions below.

Some peculiarities of death metal as a subgenre of heavy metal need to be discussed here to contextualize Nile's portrayal of Egypt within the expected themes of the subgenre. Indeed, the few other bands that also devote entire albums to ancient Egypt (e.g. Coffin Texts, Maat, Scarab) are classified under the same label as well, so the association of death metal with this ancient culture might be not entirely coincidental; it is possible that the speed and fierceness of this abrasive music allows for the exploration of a supposedly aggressive and violent ancient Egypt.

Growling vocals and distorted guitars characterize death metal as one of the so-called "extreme" subgenres of heavy metal (Purcell 2003: 9–24). In terms of composition, it attempts to defy the listeners' tonal and harmonic expectations by means of a variety of techniques including unexpected half-steps, sudden tempo changes, tritones, pitch axis melodies, and heavy palm-muting.[12]

In addition to these formal features, death metal bands share an interest in the darker aspects of life, "especially the triad of death, disease, and decay" (Weinstein 2000: 51).[13] The passion for destruction and violence is classified under labels such as "brutality" or "extremity" in the metal scene. These notions, which are an essential part of the dominant aesthetic of death metal, are regarded by metal fans as overwhelmingly positive and sought-after qualities. Although brutality is often only a pose that responds to expectations of disenfranchised crowds, it has had serious consequences in the public sphere, where heavy metal in general and extreme metal in particular have been vilified.[14] Thus, the supposed motivations behind these seemingly deviant inclinations have been scrutinized by many of the detractors of heavy metal with the intention of discrediting this musical genre, a practice denounced by Metal Studies scholars such as Weinstein (2000: 237–75).[15]

A more unprejudiced approach to brutality could frame it within the anthropological models of "transgression" (Kahn-Harris 2007: 29–46) or "controversies and countercultures" (Hjelm, Kahn-Harris, and LeVine 2013a). Transgression, as controversy, can be used as an analytical tool to articulate the study of excessive situations that test the boundaries established by communal norms (Jenks 2003: 3).[16] Both these approaches are very similar in that they address the idea that metal bands are presented—sometimes from within the metal scene itself—as challenging and eventually breaking socially imposed boundaries. This need for controversy or transgression is inherent in metal (Hjelm, Kahn-Harris, and LeVine 2013b: 3) and to a certain extent defines it as a musical genre.[17]

Kahn-Harris (2007: 30–46) identifies three types of transgressions occurring in extreme metal, namely discursive, sonic, and bodily. In this investigation I understand these transgressions as referring to themes, sound, and performance, respectively, although at times there may be a certain degree of overlap among them. In the following subsections I outline each of the three types separately, exploring to what extent the choice of ancient Egyptian themes may have had an influence on the character of some of these transgressions. In this sense, Kahn-Harris' analytical framework provides an opportunity to approach the treatment of Egypt in Nile—and other bands—systematically.

Discursive transgressions: Metal narratives of Egypt

First, I consider the usual themes that metal bands use to craft their discourse on ancient Egypt and to what extent that discourse can be characterized as transgressive. Although a given image of Egypt can be transmitted through a variety of means—including the music itself, as I argue below—in this section I focus primarily on the lyrics.[18] Lyrics have been widely neglected in metal studies, as they tend to be considered less relevant than sound (see Weinstein 2000: 26), but I believe they provide an insight into the eloquent narratives that bands like Nile try to construct. For example, they demonstrate how bands show a clear preference for what is widely perceived as the "Classical" period of Egyptian history, namely the pre-Hellenistic time. This could be due to a general interest in the "origins" of any culture, but it could perhaps be linked to the process of "otherization" initiated in Classical antiquity that I discuss further below.

Kahn-Harris (2007: 34–5) has argued that the typical themes favored in extreme metal, such as abjection, destruction, and decay, can be understood as transgressive because they seem to be testing social boundaries, for example, by elaborating upon explicit descriptions of violence. Nile's main lyrical concerns do not differ entirely from those of other death metal bands, but their focus on ancient Egypt allows them to mobilize some of those conventional themes in innovative ways. Death, battle carnage, and the ritual destruction of enemies are omnipresent throughout their albums, often interwoven with other topics like mysticism and forbidden arcane knowledge. In the following I demonstrate how Egypt is used to illustrate the subjects of violence and esotericism.

Nile define Egypt as an essentially violent civilization that takes pride in ruthless annihilation of its enemies. For instance, the ferocious way in which enemies were supposedly treated in the battlefield is described in quite graphic terms in the song "Black Seeds of Vengeance":

> You shall gore them with sticks, hack off their testicles
> And cut their phalluses to pieces, suffer none of them to live
> Dismemberment and slaughter shall you perform on them.
>
> Nile, "Black Seeds of Vengeance," Black Seeds of Vengeance, 2000

The cutting of the hands and phalluses of the enemies is a recorded practice in ancient Egypt, but it is not usually described in the passionately ferocious manner implied by Nile. Instead, mutilation was used as a practical way to count and keep records of enemy losses in battles. A representation of an almost bureaucratic recount of hands and genitals can be seen on the walls of Medinet Habu, which was the mortuary temple of Ramses III (late twelfth-century BCE), in the West bank of Luxor (Murnane 1980: 12–13).

In Nile's lyrics, battles are not usually depicted as glorious, but simply as brutal, as demonstrated by their account of the battle of Megiddo, which took place under Thutmose III in the first half of the fifteenth century BCE in northern Israel (Redford 2003: 1–56):

> Fearlessly I smote their center
> Savagely we broke the enemy's will
> Heavy slaughter and bitter suffering did we inflict upon them
> At the Word of the God Amun I waged war

> In the Name of the God Amun I sanctioned atrocities
> Wanton cruel remorseless in the Name of the God Amun.
>> Nile, *"In the Name of Amun,"* What Should Not Be Unearthed, *2015*

In this section of the song, military actions undertaken by the Egyptian army against their enemies are defined as wanton atrocities. The description of this battle in the original sources is much less explicit; instead of placing the emphasis on the destruction of the enemies, the ancient Egyptian account focuses on the figure of the pharaoh himself and the terror that his mere presence would instill in his enemies: "When they saw his majesty charging against them, they fled headlong to Megiddo with faces of fear, abandoning their horses and their chariots of gold and silver" (Sethe 1906: 657, 17–658, 3).[19]

While the battle of Megiddo is a known historical event, Nile do not always refer to specific battles. Sometimes they present an almost timeless image of a pharaoh smiting his enemies that does not necessarily correspond to a particular historical event. In songs such as "Ramses Bringer of War," carnage seems to be emphasized for its own sake.

> My chariot wheels trample the fallen
> Cut to pieces before my steeds
> And laying in their own blood
> I crush the skulls of the dying
> And sever the hands of the slain.
>> Nile, *"Ramses Bringer of War,"* Amongst the Catacombs of Nephren-Ka, *1998*

Their treatment of war mutilation and the battle of Megiddo shows that Nile take a general interest in Egyptian history, but they read it through a death metal lens which magnifies violent parts in accordance with the aesthetic that is expected of the genre. Specific pharaohs do not tend to be singled out in Nile's tracks, and if they are (e.g. "Ramses Bringer of War") it is on account of their aggressiveness in battle rather than their historical agency.

An interesting detail is that the Egyptian god Amun—both in the lyrics and the primary sources—is said to support Thutmose III in his military endeavors at Megiddo, so that war, and consequently violence, seem to be sanctioned by the gods. The notion that Egyptian gods are violent and cruel is widespread in Nile's universe and it ties in with the interest in paganism and the rejection of Christianity that often underlies extreme forms of metal.[20] Egypt, as well as other ancient cultures, offers a window into a time before Christendom, when the gods were old and thirsty for blood.[21] On some occasions, alleged sacrificial rites for those deities are described in extremely explicit terms, without sparing any gory details, as illustrated by the song "Masturbating the War God":

> We impale them on the massive stone member of the Ithyphallic War God
> Until the backs of their throats are torn out
> And their bowels are ripped apart.
> One by one we force the female captives to serve the Ahati

Until the God's legs are awash with blood
And his phallus drips with red and black gore

> Nile, "Masturbating the War God," Black Seeds of Vengeance, *2000*

The ancient Egyptian fertility god Min is represented as an ithyphallic figure in the Egyptian pantheon, so he might be the divinity that is alluded to in this scene. However, he is not connected to war (a role often reserved for the god Montu), and certainly no religious rituals involving the impalement of captives are attested in the primary sources.[22] The theme of a violent ithyphallic war god is revisited in the 2007 album *Ithyphallic*, the cover of which features the fictitious colossal statue of an ithyphallic god being transported with the pyramids of Giza in the background (see Figure 8.1). In the album's title track, an unnamed individual curses his enemies with the consent of that war god and finishes his speech by saying: "Anoint my phallus with the blood of the fallen".[23] This is a clear example of appropriation and reinterpretation of Egyptian imagery to suit the portrayal of ancient Egypt presented by Nile, namely a land of cruel gods who require bloody human sacrifices.

The overarching subject of violence can stretch beyond descriptions of battles and brutal sacrifices. Nile conform to the general preoccupation among death metal bands with decay and putrefaction of the flesh, which often serves to highlight the misery of humanity and the inexorable advent of death. The existence of mummification practices

Figure 8.1 Nile, *Ithyphallic* (2007; Album cover).

in ancient Egypt, however, seems to imply that a focus on decay may not be pertinent, as bodies would generally have been preserved.[24] This is no hindrance for Nile, and they choose to explore the Egyptian fear of putrefaction to give a twist to death metal's focus on decay. The artwork of the cover of some of the band's albums features mummies, showing that the corpse may look gruesome even when some skin is still visible. *Black Seeds of Vengeance* is a particularly good example, as it displays an anonymous warrior surrounded by bloody spears, whose facial skin is only partially preserved. In addition, songs like "The inevitable degradation of flesh" give Nile a chance to describe the things that could happen to a human body after death with singular bluntness:

> I have become corrupt decayed putrid
> Worms gorge upon me
> Maggots infest my organs
> Vermin gnaw my skull
> My eyes have been eaten, my ears are deaf
> Rotten flesh falls from my bones
> My head has removed itself from my neck
> My tongue taken away
> My hair has been cut off, my eyebrows stripped
> I have become what I abhor.
>
> Nile, "The Inevitable Degradation of Flesh," At the Gate of Sethu, 2012

This aversion toward the rotting of the flesh mentioned in the lyrics is documented in a variety of Egyptian sources, including some spells from the Coffin Texts, a collection of funerary literature inscribed primarily on coffins of the First Intermediate Period to the Middle Kingdom (*ca.* 2150–1650 BCE).[25] For example, Spell 755, entitled "For a man not to rot in the necropolis," is an obscure text which reproduces the prayer of a man that assimilates himself to Osiris to avoid the putrefaction of his body (CT VI [755]: de Buck 1935–1961: 384–5, Nyord 2009: 324–27). According to various mythological accounts,[26] Osiris, the god of the Egyptian netherworld, was murdered and dismembered by his brother, the god Seth, but he was eventually resurrected by the goddesses Isis and Nephthys. For this reason, the deceased is often identified with Osiris in mortuary rituals so that he would be able to resurrect as the god did.[27]

Funerary ideas of the resurrection of the dead through magic and mortuary rituals are connected to the second main theme for which Egypt appears to offer boundless inspiration, specifically the existence of arcane, esoteric knowledge. This concern is particularly important, as it is one of the most commonly used by other metal bands, but it also plays a major role in Nile's lyrics. For instance, in the song "Whisper in the Ear of the Dead," communication with the dead seems to enable direct access to "unwritten knowledge" that would render the speaker powerful and wise:

> I dream of the dead
> And their shades showeth me visions

> Which no living man can know
> I whisper in the ear of the dead
> And mine is the UnWritten Knowledge
> That lieth under the black earth
>
> *Nile, "Whisper in the Ear of the Dead," In Their Darkened Shrines, 2002*

References to necromantic rituals that allow the practitioner of magic to meddle with dark powers and resurrect the dead abound in heavy metal's portrayal of ancient Egypt. Those who perform magic often remain anonymous, but occasionally they are named after historical figures, as in the track "Im-Ho-Tep (Pharoah's Curse)" [*sic*] (*Horror Show*, 2001) by Iced Earth.[28]

In connection with necromancy, the topos of a deceased returned from the realm of the dead to slay those who disturb his eternal sleep has become recurrent in popular culture, and heavy metal is no exception. The so-called "curse of the mummy" has been one of the most self-perpetuating myths in Egyptology since the beginning of the twentieth century (e.g. Luckhurst 2012, Moser 2015: 248), and it is often associated with the figure of powerful pharaohs, as in the case of Mercyful Fate's "Curse of the Pharaohs," from their album *Melissa* (1983).[29] The curse of the pharaoh also appears in Iron Maiden's "Powerslave," arguably the most well-known metal song on ancient Egypt:

> Now I am cold but a ghost lives in my veins,
> Silent the terror that reigned
> Marbled in stone
> A shell of a man God preserved
> A thousand ages,
> But open the gates of my hell
> I will strike from the grave
>
> *Iron Maiden, "Powerslave," Powerslave, 1984*

Iron Maiden's "Powerslave" features a mummy who addresses the living from the afterlife, threatening to smite anyone who desecrates his tomb. Some lines of the song make it clear that this is the mummy of a pharaoh who was worshipped almost like a god in life until he encountered death.[30] The track uses this setting to explore ideas about the futility of existence and the inexorability of death, which strikes even those who are seen as immortal. As frontman Bruce Dickinson (2017: 151) states in his recent autobiography, it could be taken as a "partial allegory of life as a rock-star pharaoh."

In his study of the treatment of Alexander the Great in metal music, Djurslev (2014: 135–38) argues convincingly that Iron Maiden could almost be seen as trendsetters, since their perception of Alexander informed most subsequent attempts to approach this historical figure in heavy metal. While the theme of the curse of the mummy is also employed by other bands in reference to the pharaohs, their interpretation does not exclusively draw on Iron Maiden's, as they all make use of commonplace generalizations, portraying Egypt as a mysterious land where even the dead could rise again.[31]

The popular image of Egypt as a land shrouded in mystery fits with the interest that metal bands of all genres show in the occult (Walser 1993a: 151–60).[32] Nile's lyrics are saturated with references to esoteric knowledge, secret books, and divine revelation. Some examples include "The Essential Salts" (*Ithyphallic*, 2007), which deals with a cult of necromancers devoted to the resurrection of the dead, and "Liber Stellae Rubeae" (*What Should Not Be Unearthed*, 2015), which describes the contents of an old secret book.[33]

Many other bands share this interest in the occult in relation to ancient Egypt. Scarab is a particularly interesting case study because they are a death metal band from Egypt, but nevertheless seem, to some extent, to approach their country's past in ways that echo those of non-Egyptian bands. Their track "Serpents of the Nile," for example, advances notions of mysticism in which the entities that they refer to as the "serpents of the Nile"—which are not a known figure from ancient Egyptian mythology under that name—are asked to fulfill their roles and slay the enemies of the one who pronounces the prayer:

Signs I meet through my destiny
Showing me the way and the true path
Opening my vision to intuition,
I see the absolute.
Bring in me the wisdom from high above,
Bring in me the strength from down below,
Bring in me the gift of wise choice
For choosing is how we create.

Scarab, "Serpents of the Nile," Serpents of the Nile, 2015

Although a song such as "Serpents of the Nile" may not seem political at first glance, Scarab are using their own past to transmit a message, thus performing their understanding of national identity through their music.[34] In this case perhaps they are invoking the "serpents of the Nile" as representatives of the wisdom of their past to illuminate them in their current political circumstances. Furthermore, some of Scarab's other songs, such as "Blinding the Masses" (*Blinding the Masses*, 2010), are explicit condemnations of the pre-Arab spring political climate in Egypt, even if they do not feature any explicit references to ancient Egypt.[35] Although the use of the past to advance modern political agendas is not the main focus of this chapter, it is still worthwhile to see how their nationalistic vindications are framed within the traditional esoteric discourse on ancient Egypt favored by other metal bands.

In conclusion, while "no single lyrical theme dominates the genre" (Weinstein 2000: 34), history and the occult can be counted among the most recurrent matters in heavy metal, and I argue that focusing on ancient Egypt offers bands a singular opportunity to combine the two. Violence and access to arcane knowledge are some of the most pervasive themes in metal songs dealing with ancient Egypt. Most heavy metal bands exploit conventional assumptions about Egypt, namely the curse of the mummy and the ubiquity of magical practices, often accompanied by a clear sense of inglorious violence that reaches extreme brutality in the case of Nile's death metal. These themes are also approached through sound and performance in a way that does not essentially contradict the image presented in metal narratives of Egypt.

Sonic transgressions: Evoking the other

In this section I analyze how the music and overall aural impression that bands try to achieve may contribute to constructing a given notion of ancient Egypt. The sounds sought by extreme metal bands can also be productively analyzed as transgressions (Kahn-Harris 2007: 30–43), since they provide innovative alternatives to the typical elements of Western music. As a result, they may feel unpleasant to the untrained ear— or, to quote my long-suffering mother, sound like "an unbearable racket." Nile's music shows the same sonic transgressions as most other death metal bands, namely distorted and down-tuned guitars, constant change of tempo, complex drumming patterns, and growling vocals (Berger 1999: 59–63). Nevertheless, Nile make use of some exceptional sonic tools that are, in my view, reliant on the band's lyrical concerns.

First, several songs incorporate Middle Eastern microtonal intervals (Griffiths, Lindley, and Zannos 2001; see also Rushton 2001), mainly through the introduction of series of quarter tones, octatonic scales, and Phrygian mode into riffs and rhythms.[36] Examples of these are the bridge in "Eat of the Dead" (*Ithyphallic*, 2007; e.g., track time 3:29–3:39) or the main theme of "In Their Darkened Shrines: IV. Ruins" (*In Their Darkened Shrines*, 2002; e.g., 0:01–2:05). In an interview Karl Sanders, front man and main songwriter of Nile, explains how he employed similar methods to create an illusion of an ancient Egyptian sound through his music, an endeavor which he knew would result in a completely subjective rendering:

> I went to my jazz guitar teacher and said, "I need some guitar chords that sound like ancient Egypt." He looked at me blankly and said "What? There are none. What the fuck are you talking about?" So I thought to myself that if there are none then maybe I could invent some. That just told me that the field is wide open, so I found my own way.[37]

The use of quarter tones and Middle Eastern scales is not an exclusive feature of death metal, as bands of other subgenres also incorporate comparable sonic devices into their music with the aim of providing an appropriate setting for their Egyptian-themed songs, including, for example, the intros of "Powerslave" (*Powerslave*, 1984) by Iron Maiden (e.g., 0:04–0:14) and "Egypt (The Chains Are On)" (*The Last in Line*, 1984) by Dio (e.g., 0:15–0:29). The use of quarter tones is relatively unfamiliar to Western ears, creating a certain halo of mystery around the music.[38] The reason behind the association of the Middle Eastern quarter-tone scale and ancient Egypt is related to the Orientalization of some cultures, a mechanism that is further explored below.

Second, violent imagery is not only sung about in death metal, but it is also emulated by means of a variety of samples and frantic riffs. These offer the listener an aural experience of chaos that serves as a subtle embodiment of the violent and wicked world that is being recreated. Nile follow the trend of other bands of the genre, but they take care to incorporate elements that are reminiscent of their perception of ancient Egypt. Samples play a crucial role in this respect, as they are sometimes used to give a markedly Egyptian flavor to their compositions by including sounds of animals typical of the region such as crocodiles, or repetitive chants that may symbolize some kind of ritual incantation. Karl Sanders explains in his liner notes how they used the noises of crocodiles in the instrumental piece "Spawn of Uamenti" (*Annihilation of the Wicked*, 2005) to attain a disturbing atmosphere: "after experimenting with juxtaposing these various reptilian sounds—slithering, crawling, fighting, mating and what-not—against more orchestral-type sounds, the mix featured this evil quality that effectively built tension in such a creepy, eerie way." In the same notes, Sanders also refers to the riffs in "The Burning Pits of the Duat" (*Annihilation of the Wicked*, 2005) as being evocative of the Underworld: "Dallas [a vocalist and guitarist in Nile] really felt that the lyrics and title unquestionably called for utter underworld sorcery—riffs so fast, chopping and iniquitous as to musically capture the sensation of being consumed in pits of fire." Hence, their riffs and changes of tempo are painting an image of ancient Egypt that reinforces the themes explored in Nile's lyrics.

The last distinctive feature of Nile's extreme sound involves the use of lyrics in ancient Egyptian in some songs. The exact pronunciation of ancient Egyptian language is not known due to the lack of vocalization in the hieroglyphic script. Coptic, a later stage of Egyptian language written with a modified version of the Greek alphabet, is often used as a starting point for any attempt to discern the sounds of earlier Egyptian, on the understanding that an ultimate reconstruction remains impossible (Loprieno 1995: 28–50). Transliteration as employed by Egyptologists is not a guide to how ancient Egyptian would be pronounced, but a conventional way to represent the consonants to facilitate academic discussions about the language.[39]

In their songs, Nile sometimes include a few lines in ancient Egyptian relying on the currently superseded simplified transliteration system favored by E. A. Budge (1920: lix–lxii; Parkinson 1999: 68, n. 7), which features a suggested—and often arbitrary—vocalization. An example is "kheftiu Asar Butbiu," a phrase that occurs in "Kheftiu Asar Butchiu" (*In Their Darkened Shrines*, 2002). This sentence reflects Budge's incorrect transcription of a phrase extracted from funerary literature,[40] namely *ḫftiw wsir wbdiw*, "the enemies of Osiris, who are burned," which appears in the ninth hour of the *Book of Gates* (Hornung 1980: 219, lower register, scene 59).[41] The use of ancient Egyptian phrases such as this one can be considered a sonic transgression because the listener is being presented with unfamiliar sound combinations that are removed from the linguistic backgrounds they may have been exposed to.

In other occasions, their ancient Egyptian does not seem to be translatable, such as in the phrase "Mekhi Kherit Au Aqu, Mtum thai Peten Nekht An Aqu" in "Multitude of Foes" (*Black Seeds of Vengeance*, 2000). This string of words includes terms that may sound Egyptian (e.g., *nḫt* is "to be strong," *ḫriw* means "enemies"), but overall cannot be read as a meaningful text *per se*. However, this does not discredit Nile's work, since being grammatically accurate was never their intention. As Karl Sanders explained on the band's online forum:

> sadly folks that take a tunnel vision on which scales we use or do not use, or how much liberty is taken with grammar and syntax of a dead language are completely missing the point. Nile is NOT a Historical Society for the Preservation of Ethnomusicology. It's Entertainment, first and foremost, it's Death Metal secondmost.[42]

The words still sound Egyptian to modern ears, and that is what counts from the point of view of their performance; they are not reconstructing Egypt but recreating it, while also challenging the aural expectations of the listener.

Bodily transgressions: Performing ancient Egypt

Some forms of extreme metal may also be characterized by bodily practices that seek to transgress socially established boundaries (Kahn-Harris 2007: 43–6). These could potentially be interpreted from the point of view of the anti-social behaviors that are traditionally attributed to heavy metal, such as the use of drugs, alcoholism, self-destruction, and sexual indulgence that may verge on sexism by focusing on the subordinate position of women. However, extreme metal is often detached from these, showing an indifferent attitude to excesses or sometimes even a firm rejection of them through asceticism (Kahn-Harris 2007: 44). For this reason, I have chosen to reinterpret the approach to bodily transgression through the perspective of performance, including live shows and music videos. These performance elements often overlap with and serve to enhance the narratives of ancient Egypt that I analyze above as discursive transgressions, but here I focus on the impact of theatricality on the mobilization of an idea of ancient Egypt.

Some subgenres of metal give prominence to creative stage sets, decoration, and promotional photos as a way to transport the fans to a particular setting. A well-known use of Egyptian imagery to spice up a performance is that of Iron Maiden, who employed a full Egyptian-themed stage set during their World Slavery Tour (1984–85).[43] The stage props followed the artwork of their latest album *Powerslave*, whose cover showed a scene inspired by ancient Egypt, with a colossal version of the band's mascot, Eddie, carved into a stone pyramid in the guise of a pharaoh. During the tour, blocks with Egyptian hieroglyphs filled the stage, and a nine-meter model of a mummified Eddie was visible in the background on top of the drum set as he emerged from a golden sarcophagus, occasionally shooting sparks out of his eyes. During the songs "Iron Maiden" and "Powerslave" a walk-on Eddie also jumped on stage; this three-meter tall figure was dressed up as a mummy and would run around the stage mischievously stirring up the crowd. In addition, the album booklet for *Powerslave* included a photograph of the band members in a reproduction of an Egyptian tomb with a half-opened sarcophagus at the center.

Nile, however, do not seem to be so driven to provide a creatively curated stage set in live performances. It is worth noting that the aesthetics of death metal are often predicated on the key notion of "authenticity" (Harrell 1994: 92, 96). By virtue of that "authenticity" and in contrast with other metal genres, death metal musicians very rarely wear costumes or even make-up, and they are seldom featured on their album covers. The technical mastery of the band members and their engagement with the music is the only introduction they need in an environment that dismisses theatricality as "phony" (Berger 1999: 69–70).

In this context, it comes as no surprise that Nile do not make use of elaborate stage sets during their performances, often merely showing a banner with their emblem and/or an album cover in the background. While both band members and their fans engage with some bodily movements that characterize most metal subgenres, such as headbanging (Walser 1993a: 2, Weinstein 2000: 130–31) and mosh pits (Berger 1999: 70–3, Weinstein 2000: 228–29), the way these are performed is generic and non-specific to the band's interest in ancient Egyptian topics. In contrast, a theatrical approach to ancient Egypt is explored through the band's official music videos. While some of them only show a performance of the band in line with the philosophy of "authenticity" present in death metal (e.g., "Execration Text," *In Their Darkened Shrines*, 2002), others explore ideas of violence through pagan rites, effectively complementing the themes discussed in the lyrics (e.g., "Sarcophagus," *In Their Darkened Shrines*, 2002).

"Enduring the Eternal Molestation of Flame" (*At the Gate of Sethu*, 2012), for instance, is a fascinating case study because its music video features a dark reinterpretation of the ancient Egyptian judgment of the dead that took place in the Underworld after the passing of an individual. The heart of the deceased had to be weighed on a scale against a feather that symbolized *maat*—that is, cosmic order, justice, and truth. If the heart was found to weigh more than the feather, then the deceased had not led a virtuous life. They were deemed unworthy of entering the netherworld and faced ultimate destruction by Ammit, the devourer of the dead.[44] In Nile's version of this rite, the bloody heart of a sacrificial victim is set on the balance plate to the wild rhythm of a double bass drum beat accompanying frenzied dances and under the attentive gaze of a priest whose face and torso are smeared with body paint. The producer and director, Jon Simvonis, claims that the video mixes ancient Egyptian myth and voodoo rituals, possibly to incorporate a further element of harshness into the storyline.[45] One may wonder what kind of impact such a video may have among Nile's fans, and to what extent it may contribute to shaping their idea of Egypt. To judge from comments on online forums, it appears to consolidate the themes that are explored through discursive transgressions. For example, the aforementioned fear of putrefaction and enjoyment of violence proclaimed by Nile in their lyrics come across clearly in this music video, as demonstrated by the following emphatic comment of a fan: "The sidestory NEEDS more maggots and worms. As the main character obviously fears them feasting on his body, close-up HD views on those grisly little fuckers will only add to the brutality."[46] In this manner, music videos provide a visual counterpart to the violent and aggressive imagery that recurs in both lyrics and music.

As a summary, the image that Nile offer of ancient Egypt through discursive, sonic, and to some extent bodily metaphors is that of a brutal and mysterious civilization. These notions of Egypt also permeate other metal genres, but they are taken to an extreme in Nile, arguably because this fits in with the conceptual and aesthetic desiderata of death metal as a genre. Although the main focus may shift from violence to esotericism, the images of Egypt presented by bands of different genres do not contradict each other in essence, possibly because of the remarkable impact of Orientalism on all subgenres. The reasons why this ancient civilization may be so often linked to brutality and the unknown are explored in the next section.

Sources and inspiration: Egypt and the occult

Ancient Egypt tends to be perceived by modern Western society at large as an enigmatic, ruthless land. As Walser (1993a: 155) puts it: "Christianity, alchemy, myth, astrology, the mystique of vanished Egyptian dynasties: all are available in the modern world as sources of power and mystery." A vision of ancient Egypt as the cradle of esoteric knowledge, however, is not a mere by-product of contemporary society. Secrecy and initiation are significant components of Egyptian high culture itself, especially in terms of the display of power through knowledge and reaffirmation of hierarchies.[47] This arcane character was sensed by those who visited Egypt; various authors have commented on the influence that Greek and Roman accounts of Egyptian customs had on its perception as a land of secrets.[48]

Egypt has been surrounded since antiquity by an aura of mystery that has done nothing but grow over centuries until the present day, as evidenced by the ubiquity of the so-called curse of the mummy in popular culture (including, as seen above, the lyrics of several metal bands). I argue that this modern myth generated a keen interest of heavy metal in ancient Egypt, since it provides a clear link to horror stories, which have long been another source of inspiration for metal bands (Walser 1993a: 160–65, Weinstein 2000: 38–43).

Esoteric readings of ancient Egypt have rarely been assessed by academic Egyptologists (exceptions include Baines 1990: esp. 1–6, Hornung 2001), perhaps due to the polarization that exists between "professional" and "alternative" Egyptology. Some authors have challenged the appropriateness of such a clear-cut distinction (e.g., Picknett and Prince 2003: 191–92, Tully 2010: 23–6, Riggs 2015: 136–37), but the general consensus is that approaches focusing on the arcane are not to be taken seriously. In fact, the field often refers to authors with mystical inclinations scornfully as "pyramidiots."[49]

Most metal bands that refer or allude to ancient Egypt do not seek to pursue a historical reconstruction of ancient Egypt. They often prefer to draw on "alternative" Egyptology that leads them to present a colorful and appealing image of the ancient world, riddled with widespread clichés that have little grounding in historical evidence. For example, while I have not encountered allusions to aliens in the lyrics I have analyzed, old civilizations allegedly preceding Egypt are sporadically cited. The illustrator who designed the artwork of Nile's album *What Should Not Be Unearthed* (2015) stated: "with the art I excavated the theories of an elder ancient civilization which could give the origin to ancient Egypt."[50] On other occasions, Atlantis—or "the A-word," as Egyptologists sometimes refer to it informally—is mentioned openly, as in Symphony X's "Egypt" (*V: The New Mythology Suite*, 2000): "From the ruins of Atlantis / the Lord of Night rises from the sands).[51]

Nile show unparalleled awareness of Egyptological matters due to the interest of their front man Karl Sanders in the history and archaeology of Egypt.[52] An attention to detail often shines through their lyrics, with allusions in their liner notes to lesser known mortuary literature (e.g. the *Book of Gates*)[53] and archaeological sites (e.g. Mirgissa).[54] Despite this, they consciously favor "alternative" Egyptology as a source of inspiration because their aim is not to be historically accurate, but entertaining. In the words of Nile's front man Karl Sanders, "I guarantee you that if we remained strict absolute rule book (which in this case is an arbitrarily based system at best, anyway), the songs would suck about as much as when History authors write absolute pure text book regurgitation."[55] Here Sanders verbalizes the perceived clash between academic and alternative Egyptology, claiming that he makes his choice on the basis of which one of those interpretations will provide more entertainment to their fans.

Nile are open about their sources of inspiration and share their creative process and inspiration with their fans in the form of extensive liner notes in almost all their albums since *Black Seeds of Vengeance* (2000).[56] In these notes they acknowledge the influence of horror stories by H. P. Lovecraft and Robert E. Howard.[57] For example, the song "In Their Darkened Shrines" (*In Their Darkened Shrines*, 2002) unfolds in a landscape reminiscent of the forgotten ruins described in "The Nameless City" (Lovecraft [1921] 2011: 141–50). Meanwhile "Von Unaussprechlichen Kulten" (*Annihilation of the Wicked*, 2005) exploits the well-known topos of an ancient secret book that does not exist, in the line of Lovecraft's *Necronomicon*. Robert E. Howard introduced the fictional book *Nameless Cults* by the imaginary German author Friedrich von Junzt in his short story "The Children of the Night" (Howard [1931] 2008: 143–48). Lovecraft himself came up with the idea of giving this book a German title and, after several suggestions, the title that stuck was the grammatically incorrect *Unaussprechlichen Kulten* (literally *Unpronounceable Cults*), from which Nile seek inspiration for their song. Furthermore, the title of the album *Amongst the Catacombs of Nephren-Ka* (1998) carries a clear reference to Lovecraft: Nephren-Ka, or the Black Pharaoh, is a fictional character featured in several of the stories in the Cthulhu Mythos, such as "The Outsider" (Lovecraft [1926] 2011: 164–69). In the words of Sanders himself, this type of literature helps "bridge the gap" in tying together brutality and ancient Egypt.[58]

Although Nile claim not to be interested in reconstructing the history of Egypt with any precision, their liner notes often suggest otherwise: "we have faithfully and painstakingly adapted these words as closely as possible, in order to preserve the purity and integrity of the originals" (liner notes for "Masturbating the War God," *Black Seeds of Vengeance,* 2000). This assertion of authenticity, however, can also be framed within that

Lovecraftian tradition of creating an illusion of authenticity by constructing stories and sources to substantiate their arguments. Allusions to recognized academic Egyptologists, such as H. Brugsch (1827–1894), G. Maspero (1846–1916), or F. W. Petrie (1853–1942), often sprinkle their liner notes, together with references to nonexistent books.[59] The absence of contemporary scholars from these notes suggests that Nile may resort to relatively old resources, and rely on the works of E. A. Wallis Budge (1857–1934), to whom they refer in their liner notes for "The Burning Pits of the Duat" (*Annihilation of the Wicked*, 2005) as a "renowned Egyptologist."[60]

The case of Budge is quite controversial, as he is widely acknowledged by "alternative" Egyptology to be a reputable source (Hornung 2001: 2), while "academic" Egyptology avoids citing his work as much as possible. The reason for this ambivalence is perhaps based on Budge's attitude toward research and publications. On the one hand, he was one of the most prolific authors in the history of Egyptology, producing a number of popular works for the general public, which are widely reproduced and easily accessible still today. On the other hand, with over 140 books under his belt (Bierbrier 2012: 91), he could not hope to be as accurate as modern standards would require.[61] As Reade (2011: 451) puts it, "not all of Budge's ideas and cross-cultural references are necessarily mistaken, but he is inclined to adduce evidence that cannot be checked: modern students are severely warned against citing him as an authority."

I believe that one of the many reasons why Budge is not well regarded within the academic community is precisely the predilection that authors interested in esoteric Egyptology seem to show for him. Budge wrote extensively on magic (e.g., Budge 1899, 1934: 113–36), translated Egyptian texts dealing with the afterlife (e.g., Budge 1901), and compiled hymns to various gods (e.g., Budge 1934: 385–428), all of these being topics that could potentially spark the interest of the mystics. Budge's (1925) translation of the *Book of the Amduat*,[62] for instance, is cited as an essential resource by several websites dedicated to Hermeticism,[63] and a substantial quotation of this work is provided by Nile in the liner notes for "The Burning Pits of the Duat" (*Annihilation of the Wicked*, 2005).

Indeed, the predilection for this author may not have been based only upon the wide availability of his works. Budge's interest in the supernatural is beyond doubt, as he was an active member of the Ghost Club (Luckhurst 2012: 53–4), a society for the investigation of paranormal phenomena founded in London in the nineteenth century. Furthermore, his connection with societies like the Hermetic Order of the Golden Dawn, a secret organization for the practice of occultism, has been postulated although never verified (Tully 2010: 28). Hermetic societies such as the Golden Dawn often follow masonic rank structures and are based on the notion of knowledge through revelation for their initiates. The influence of ancient Egypt on this type of organization has received considerable attention over the years (e.g. Hornung (2001: 140–54, 181–84), Tully (2010), Vinson and Gunn (2015)).

A renowned example of these societies is the so-called religion of Thelema founded by Aleister Crowley at the beginning of the twentieth century as a spin-off of Golden Dawn.[64] Crowley has been a familiar figure in the metal scene, ever since Led Zeppelin's Jimmy Page, who was so obsessed with Crowley that he bought one of his houses, inscribed the Thelema-related phrase "Do what thou wilt" on the pressing of the vinyl of their 1970 album *Led Zeppelin III* (Farley 2009: 78–9).[65] One of the key pieces of the Thelemic belief was the "Stèle of revealing"—an otherwise ordinary late Twenty-fifth to early Twenty-sixth Dynasty (*ca.* seventh century CE) painted wooden stela[66]—which was said to contain the revelation of the *Book of Law* by Aiwass, the alleged messenger of the god Horus, to Crowley (Tully 2010: 39–43).[67] This is merely one example of a generalized appropriation and modern re-elaboration of Egyptian religion and funerary beliefs, but its contribution to the popularization of an arcane image of Egypt is undeniable.

Many heavy metal bands, inherently attracted to esotericism, have embraced these types of sources. The occultist Rollo Ahmed, for example, is openly mentioned by Nile in the liner notes to "The Black Flame" (*Black Seeds of Vengeance*, 2000) as an authority who supposedly worked on an ancient Egyptian funerary text. Although Crowley is not explicitly acknowledged by Nile, the spelling of the word "magick" on notes and song titles might betray his possible influence.[68] Metal, in this sense, adheres to the general conception of Egypt as a mysterious civilization, penetrating into the darker and more brutal sides of the occult which, in turn, feeds into the need for controversy and transgression often found in metal narratives. Egypt provides a repository of imagery that responds appropriately to the discursive concerns of heavy metal, but the question remains why this particular idea of Egypt has transcended into popular culture.

Orientalism and heavy metal: "Otherizing" Egypt

Reception Studies intend to explore the way(s) in which the past is represented, both inside and outside academic discourse. While scholars used to feel at ease with the notion that "the-past-as-it-really-was" could be reconstructed through the accumulation of factual, objective data obtained from modern readings of ancient texts (Martindale 2006: 2 and Kennedy 2006: 292), the rise in Reception Studies reflects the sentiment that every type of knowledge is mediated by the surviving sources and the way these are understood (see Umurhan, this volume). All the sources that are used to study the past are ultimately influenced by those who produced them in the same way modern scholars contribute to delineating what the past is and how it is perceived. Thus, the ancient Egypt that we know is undeniably a representation of ancient Egypt. To think that scholars can access a pure, real, and uncontaminated Egypt—that is, a Platonic idea of "the real Egypt"—is to ignore that any study of the past is indeed a study of its reception (Martindale 2006: esp. 12–13, Porter 2008: 474, Moser 2015: 244). In this sense, Egypt should not be regarded as a place, but as an idea (Said [1978] 2003: 177).

There does not exist, however, a single idea of Egypt, because different intellectual milieus may favor one aspect of its reception over others. Despite the role that the history of scholarship has played in the construction of knowledge about this ancient civilization, academics tend now to distance themselves from conceptions that regard ancient Egypt as the cradle of all esoteric lore. In opposition, the image of Egypt as an exotic, mysterious land remains the most prevalent in popular culture, as the case study of heavy metal demonstrates.

The predominance of an image of Egypt as a mysterious and, consequently, different land is exemplified particularly when the reception of Egypt in heavy metal is contrasted with that of Greece and Rome, which is extensively treated in this volume. A song like Manowar's "Achilles, Agony and Ecstasy in Eight Parts" (*Triumph of Steel*, 1992) presents a brave champion who seeks to avenge the death of his friend with the consent of the gods, knowing that he will be remembered as a hero.[69] This figure of the hero does not seem to be pursued in Egypt-related metal lyrics, where violence can be carried out to please the gods (Nile's "Masturbating the War God," *Black Seeds of Vengeance*, 2000), or to weaken one's enemies (Nile's "Execration Text," *In Their Darkened Shrines*, 2002), but apparently not to attain any kind of individual glory. I argue that various treatments of Greek or Roman civilizations and ancient Egypt in heavy metal illustrates this process of "otherization" to which Egypt has been subjected since Classical antiquity by authors such as Herodotus (Vasunia 2001: 11–13).

These related notions of Egypt as "an idea" and as "the Other" can be analyzed within the framework of Edward Said's ([1978] 2003) Classical paradigm of Orientalism. Despite the many criticisms the work has received (e.g., Bhabha 1994: esp. 94–120, Varisco 2007, Burke and Prochaska 2008), Said's ideas are essential when it comes to explaining the reception of Egypt in modern times.[70] Orientalism can be construed within three interrelated notions, namely an academic discipline for the study of the Orient, a mind-set based on a purported East-West dichotomy, and an idea of domination and subjugation (Said [1978] 2003: 2–3 and Mitchell [1989] 2009: 423). All these features of Orientalism still persist today in the conception of ancient Egypt upheld by popular culture, which has affected its reception in heavy metal.

According to Said, the "East" (or the "Orient") was artificially delineated by Western scholars as an undifferentiated unit that could be treated as an almost homogenous whole. Philology and textual studies were often privileged as the ultimate academic method to gain access to other civilizations (Said [1978] 2003: 121, 135–36), leading to the fallacy of "textual attitude." This approach presumed that the intricacies of human culture could be understood exclusively on the basis of what texts say (Said [1978] 2003: 92–4). Although comparable "Orientalizing" trends may seem outdated, there still exist a number of Oriental Institutes associated with several universities that frequently bring together the study of disparate societies under the same heading.[71] The object of Orientalism is consequently difficult to define outside the parameters of the methods of Orientalism itself.

This artificial homogenization of Oriental cultures is clearly present in heavy metal. For instance, despite the fact that Nile's main source of inspiration is ancient Egypt, they also have a few songs devoted to ancient Mesopotamia ("Die Rache Krieg Lied der Assyrische," [sic] *Amongst the Catacombs of Nephren-Ka*, 1998, a song that is sung in English despite its German title)[72] or Anatolian civilizations ("Hittite Dung Incantation," *Those Whom the Gods Detest*, 2009). Furthermore, the song "Black Hand of Set" (*In the Beginning*, 1999) combines ancient Egyptian, Indian, and Near Eastern deities in an extreme example of imposed homogeneity:[73] "Oh Kali/Oh Sekhmet/Oh Dagon."[74] The inclusion of Tibetan chants by a group of monks in the intro to "The Black Flame"

(*Black Seeds of Vengeance*, 2000) should be interpreted within the same homogenizing framework.

Whereas its object may be difficult to delineate, the approach and method favored by Orientalism seem to be relatively straightforward to identify. From the very beginnings of Orientalism, the purported exotic nature of distant lands was highly romanticized in travelers' accounts, artistic representations, and scholarly compilations. All these contributed—and to some extent still do—to inventing a monolithic identity that fitted Western expectations (e.g., Bohrer 2003: 11). An example of this, according to Moreno García (2015: 52), is the myth of an "eternal Egypt" that was regarded as a repository of tradition, esotericism, and spirituality.[75]

As explained above, this image may have originated in the early accounts of Classical authors, who were already presenting Egypt as the "Other." It is true that throughout history Egypt has been "reassigned" different identities to fit contingent purposes. An example of this is how ancient Egyptian monuments were employed as symbols of national pride in the context of the British occupation of Egypt at the turn of the twentieth century through the use of postal stamps featuring, for example, a pyramid and a sphinx.[76] Stamps would disseminate an image of Egypt linked to those architectural achievements that embodied the magnificence of their past. However, the exotic and essentially "Oriental" identity of Egypt persisted throughout history until modern days, when magic and mystery have become the widespread trademarks of an ancient Egypt that we Egyptologists have fashioned. The use of esoteric motifs in heavy metal should be framed within this trend of Orientalizing Egypt, of which conceptions of the afterlife—exemplified by the curse of the mummy—could be considered a prime example. In this context, it is worth recalling that even Scarab, a death metal band from Egypt, frame Egypt within the discourses of esotericism that could be attributed to Orientalizing trends.

It is a mistake to believe that there is a single Orientalist view, but all Orientalisms appear to share a confrontational outlook that emphasizes dichotomies and contrasts.[77] The East was thus automatically regarded as alien while being studied from a Eurocentric perspective. In other words, the East is described as the reverse of the West on the basis of some tropes of difference (e.g., Mitchell [1989] 2009: 409): the East is static where the West is dynamic, the East is religious where the West is secular, the East is passive where the West is active. This "otherization" of the East is ultimately used as justification for its politico-economic domination by the West.[78] When something is known it is more easily controlled, so the West had to construct an idea of the East as a mirrored image of itself to facilitate its subjugation.

An opposition I am particularly interested in here is that of a peaceful and democratic West to an allegedly violent and tyrannical East.[79] Said ([1978] 2003: 285–87) denounced the effect of the 1973 Arab-Israeli war on the popular presentation of the Arab, who went from being perceived as "the embodiment of incompetence and easy defeat" to someone "associated with either lechery or bloodthirsty dishonesty." In many cases, this brutality would be projected onto ancient "Oriental" civilizations, such as Egypt, to show that violence was an inherent characteristic of their peoples. Following this reasoning, by virtue of its static nature, the Orient of ancient times would not differ in theory from the Orient of today, as its essence remains untouched and unchanged (Mitchell [1989] 2009: 417). The shift in the perception of the Arab could be done effortlessly, because it fitted into the pre-existing conceptual dichotomy of East–West. The Arab was then presented as a menacing "Other" who had to be counteracted and neutralized, and this may readily become a justification for military interventions or policies of political control.

Although I do not claim that the reason why heavy metal bands portray Egypt as a violent culture is directly related to a discursive strategy of domination, it is obvious that the imagery these bands employ fits with Western expectations of the East as a savage, despotically ruled land in need of being either tamed or freed from the oppressor. I argue that this is a further example of how this Orientalist language of power and subjugation has become normalized in daily life and it is present even in a musical genre traditionally described as transgressive.

Conclusion: The reception of Egypt in heavy metal

This chapter has explored the perception of ancient Egypt in heavy metal music with a particular emphasis on the death metal band Nile. Although album covers, videos, and melodies have been taken into account, the lyrics remain the most informative way to explore metal's portrayal of Egypt. Some recurrent themes are violence, the putrefaction of the flesh, arcane knowledge and initiation, and the curse of the mummy. Esotericism and brutality are arguably the most notable among these themes, as they typically underlie other topics and fit into some of the most usual lyrical concerns of metal bands.

Some metal bands gravitate toward a darker and more brutal side of esotericism, because it provides an opportunity to describe gory scenes of violence. This image of a brutal and occult Egypt fits into the framework of dichotomies of Orientalism, since Egypt seems to be presented as a fierce "Other" that implicitly contrasts with peaceful and nonspiritual Western societies. Orientalist perspectives are essentially based on colonial ideologies of domination and distil the features of some ancient and modern civilizations into a few clichés based on tropes of difference. While an Orientalist interpretation of Egypt is part of its reception and should thus be taken into account, it is necessary to advocate for a more diverse insight into this culture.

Heavy metal is, perhaps unwillingly, fostering the oppositions that are the core of Orientalism, contributing to spreading a particular image of ancient Egypt among the general public. This conclusion may be shared by many other works on Reception Studies and may thus seem unremarkable. However, one may still wonder why heavy metal has hitherto not been treated in Reception Studies of ancient Egypt, especially since the message it transmits does not appear to diverge significantly from that obtained from other mainstream cultural products. Heavy metal is still a stigmatized musical genre to some extent, and this leads to an unjustified underestimation of its potential to inform scholarly work.

It is sometimes possible to identify the sources that heavy metal bands have employed to do research on ancient Egypt, either by indirect references (e.g., spellings such as "magick") or directly by means of interviews or in the case of the liner notes provided by Nile. These show that books dealing with occult aspects of ancient Egypt are, as a general rule, preferred to others that do not engage with alternative approaches. While the depiction of Egypt as an esoteric, mysterious land in Classical sources is respected in Egyptology and incorporated into its academic narratives, its continuation into modern esoteric movements is largely disregarded (Hornung 2001: 1; see also Secord, this volume). Picknett and Prince (2003: 192) suggest that alternative Egyptology is more popular among non-Egyptologists because "it stirs the imagination more immediately and profoundly than the dry and erudite books on the subject." Perhaps we, as Egyptologists, should take some responsibility in the matter and contribute to bridging the gap between academic and popular visions of Egypt by producing scholarly work that could reach a wide variety of audiences.[80]

Notes

1. Hjelm, Kahn-Harris, and LeVine (2013b: 2–9).
2. For a discussion on genre boundaries within heavy metal, see Walser (1993a: esp. 3–7) and Weinstein (2000: esp. 14–5), as well as the Introduction (this volume).
3. Examples of this fascination with individual heroes in their quest for glory include "Alexander the Great" by Iron Maiden (see analysis by Umurhan 2012: esp. 133–40 and Djurslev 2014), Virgin Steele's "Wings of Vengeance," or Manowar's "Achilles, Agony and Ecstasy in Eight Parts" (see Cavallini 2007, 2009, and Campbell 2009: 116–18).
4. Dio, "Egypt (The Chains Are On)," *The Last in Line* (1984); Iron Maiden, "Powerslave," *Powerslave* (1984).
5. Edguy, "The Pharaoh," *Mandrake* (2001); Freedom Call, "Pharao" [sic], *Crystal Empire* (2001).
6. Metallica, "Creeping Death," *Ride the Lightning* (1984); Iced Earth, "Im-Ho-Tep (Pharoah's Curse)" [sic], *Horror Show* (2001).
7. Symphony X, "Pharaoh" *The Divine Wings of Tragedy* (1997); Symphony X, "Egypt," *V: The New Mythology Suite* (2000).
8. Coffin Texts, *Gods of Creation, Death and Afterlife* (2000) and *The Tomb of the Infinite Ritual* (2012); Maat, *As We Create the Hope from Above* (2014); Nile, entire discography; Scarab, *Serpents of the Nile* (2015).
9. Further details on band members can be obtained on the website *Encyclopaedia Metallum*.
10. In an interview ("We brought Nile's Karl Sanders" 2018) Sanders stated: "I always had a casual interest in Ancient Egypt, but it wasn't until I found myself in a band called 'Nile' that the interest reached its zenith. I felt that in order to do a decent job writing songs for a band called Nile, I should really dig in and do a whole lot of reading and research to do the topic justice. That in turn deepened my interest, and I came to really enjoy all the time spent on the subject matter."
11. Unfortunately, Nile's official website (www.nile-catacombs.net/) was hacked in November 2017 and has not yet been restored, so the quotes extracted from the forums are no longer

available. The band, however, now communicate with their fan base on Facebook and Twitter.

12. Friesen and Epstein (1994: esp. 11), Harrell (1994: esp. 93–4), and Berger (1999: 62–3).

13. Harrell (1994: 93) provides a more comprehensive list of themes preferred by death metal (where he includes bands traditionally labeled as thrash and speed metal): "war, destruction, decay, disease, disillusion, death, pain, torture, vengeance, murder, blood, anarchy, corruption through power, confusion, chaos, darkness, isolation, insanity, monsters, weapons, and technology gone awry." Cf. Purcell (2003: 39–51).

14. While Kahn-Harris (2007: 45–6) states that violence within the metal scene is by no means more widespread than in any other subculture, Phillipov (2013) is more critical and argues that violence plays an important role in the definition and perception of some subgenres of extreme metal such as black metal.

15. In particular, Weinstein (2000: 270–75) rejects the use of what she calls "discursive terror," namely an intentional mischaracterization of one's opponents, to "otherize" and censor everything that is perceived as deviant from the normative public discourse.

16. Some of the authors that have discussed transgression include Emile Durkheim, Mary Douglas, and Victor Turner. See Jenks (2003: 15–48).

17. In the words of Karl Sanders ("Nile's Karl Sanders" 2018), "there is a happiness level, when you're playing your own music, and it's brutal, uncompromising music, no one can tell us what the fuck to do. We're doing what we want to do. There's a certain brutal joy in that."

18. The lyrics transcribed in this chapter are all extracted from the relevant CD booklets.

19. This emphasis on the fear-inspiring figure of the pharaoh is a recurrent topos in Egyptian royal inscriptions, such as on the Great Sphinx stela of Amenhotep II at Giza (late fifteenth century BCE): "He tramped the Bowmen under his feet, the Northerners bowing to his might and all the foreign lands being under his fear" (Sethe 1906: 1277, 3–6). All translations of Sethe (1906) are my own.

20. Among others, Moberg (2013: 91) has challenged the role of Satanism in black metal based on the existence of "unblack" or Christian black metal bands.

21. For example, Nile's song "The Eye of Ra," *Those Whom the Gods Detest* (2009) describes the wrath of the Egyptian war goddess Sekhmet: "Not one shall stand alive where I have been / As I rend the very flesh from their bones / I will wade in human blood and drink my fill / For the joy of killing gladdens my heart." This passage is probably based on an ancient Egyptian mythological narrative in which the god Ra sends his Eye, personified in the goddess Sekhmet, to punish mankind after they have plotted against him; see Guilhou (1989, 2010).

22. "Ahati," likely derived from an Egyptian term meaning warrior (ꜥḥꜣty), is not attested as an epithet of either Min or Montu. Assyrian reliefs illustrate the practice of impaling captives (Bleibtreu 1991), which may have inspired Nile's conflation of this custom with their description of female captives being impaled upon the Egyptian god's phallus.

23. Karl Sanders relates how they had started to refer to their own musical style as "brutal, ithyphallic metal" ever since they were a demo band ("Karl Sanders on Nile" 2008). The phrase "Anoint my phallus" was also printed on the back of the band's official t-shirt, cementing the connection between sex and violence in Nile's music. Aggressive sex and domination through violence are often interrelated aspects of a discourse of heavy metal that is essentially patriarchal and shaped by hegemonic masculinities; see Walser (1993a: 127–52).

24. Taylor (2001: 46–91) provides a well-researched and accessible introduction to mummification processes throughout Egyptian history.

25. For a catalogue of primary sources recording the fear of putrefaction, see Zandee (1960: 10–11, 56–60).

26. Snippets of this story are known from myriad sources throughout Egyptian history, but the most complete version of the myth was transmitted by the second-century CE Greek author Plutarch (Griffiths 1970).

27. For a comprehensive approach to the sources on the figure of Osiris and related funerary rituals throughout Egyptian history, see Smith (2017).

28. The success of the 1999 film *The Mummy* may have played a role in the perception of Imhotep as a dark magician, since one of the main characters was very loosely based on him. He held several offices, including those of high priest of Re, chief physician, and architect under king Djoser in the twenty-seventh century BCE. He was later deified in the seventh century BCE (Wildung 1977: 31–81) and eventually associated with Hermeticism (Hornung 2001: esp. 48–51).

29. "Way out in Egypt in the Valley of Kings / Where the mummified Pharaohs / Pretend dead in their sleep / Don't touch, never ever steal / Unless you're in for the kill / Or you'll be hit by the curse of the Pharaohs / Yes you'll be hit and the curse is on you."

30. "When I was living this lie fear was my game / People would worship and fall drop to their knees / So bring me the blood and red wine for the one to succeed me / For he is a man and a God and he will die too."

31. E.g. "Pharaoh's curse upon you / Who dares to invade his sacred ground / Gods of the Nile arise to strike you down," in "Pharaoh," *The Divine Wings of Tragedy* (1996) by Symphony X.

32. For metal's interest in the esoteric and the occult, see also Secord (this volume).

33. It is worth noting that the "essential salts" are a clear reference to H. P. Lovecraft's "The Case of Charles Dexter Ward" (Lovecraft [1942] 2011: 490–593), dealing with a young man who brings one of his ancestors back from the dead. "Liber Stellae Rubeae," composed in English by Aleister Crowley, represents a secret ritual of Apep, an Egyptian deity in serpent form who symbolizes the forces of chaos. Further connections of the image of Egypt propounded by metal bands with H. P. Lovecraft and Aleister Crowley are explored below.

34. For more on the influence of nationalism on bands' use of material from the ancient world, see Taylor (this volume) and Fletcher (this volume).

35. "Wake up now and face the massacre or run away and hide in a place where you can find your need / But if you want to stay then subversion is the only solution for your evolution / Open your eyes and see how they keep on manipulating."

36. On the use of the *hijaz* and the Phrygian scales to construct a "pseudo-oriental" modal system, see Lilja (2009: 172–75).

37. For the interview, see Pessaro (2018).

38. Karl Sanders stated in an interview that "if you put the quarter tone in the right place you can add a lot of dark mystery to a melody" (see "Biography: Karl Sanders" 2019).

39. For a brief outline of transliteration and transcription of ancient Egyptian, see Allen (2000: 13–19).

40. Budge (1911: vol. I, 206) provides an incorrect vocalization, as within his own system the phrase should read "kheftiu Asar ubudiu" instead. In addition, he erroneously ascribes this scene to the eighth division of the *Book of Gates* instead of to the ninth. For more on Budge and his influence outside of academia, see below.

41. The idea that the enemies of Osiris should be eradicated is well known in religious literature. See Zandee (1960: 217–24).
42. "Karl Sanders on Nilechat" (2015).
43. In an effort to target a younger audience that was not around for the original tour, Iron Maiden imitated the Egyptian-themed set in their 2008–09 Somewhere Back in Time tour.
44. For a brief overview of the judgment of the dead in ancient Egyptian eschatology, see Taylor (2010: 204–17).
45. See discussion in "Nile—'Enduring the Molestation'" (2012).
46. "Nile Fan Comment" (2015).
47. For an analysis of the importance of restricted knowledge in ancient Egyptian society, see Baines (1990: esp. 17–21).
48. See Hornung (2001: 19–25), Vasunia (2001: esp. 75–109), Harrison (2003: esp. 147–49), Stephens (2003: 20–73), Jordan (2006: 110–11), and Lloyd (2010). Egyptian magicians also play an important role in the Bible (see Exod. 7).
49. Cottrell ([1956] 1975: 164–74) devotes a section of his book on pyramids to the nineteenth-century astronomer Charles Piazzi Smyth, whom he identifies in the chapter's title as "the great pyramidiot."
50. See "Nile Catacombs" (2015). The illustrator's suggestion that his art might uncover some information behind the origin of Egypt contributes to a long tradition of belief that Egypt symbolizes a land of mystery and lost secrets where their answer lies interred. See Picknett and Prince (2003: 179).
51. This Classical myth of an allegedly ancient Egyptian origin is a further example of the extent to which the Greeks perceived Egypt as a land full of arcane secrets. See Vasunia (2001: 216–47).
52. In an interview, Sanders refers to the enjoyment that he experiences when doing research on ancient Egypt: "When I started researching the lyrics for Nile, I thought to do a really good job with it, it needed to be done right, so there was a lot of research involved. The more that I learned, the more I studied, the more I enjoyed it" ("Nile's Karl Sanders" 2018).
53. The *Book of Gates*, which shares many similarities with the *Book of the Amduat* mentioned below, is one of the compositions of royal funerary literature dealing with the sun's journey during the twelve hours of the night (see Hornung ([1997] 1999: 55–77)).
54. Mirgissa is a Nubian fortress located in the southern boundaries of Egypt by the Second Cataract. In the site an undisturbed deposit dating to the Twelfth Dynasty (early twentieth to late nineteenth centuries BCE) was found. It has been interpreted as an execration deposit for rituals of destruction of enemies because it included hundreds of broken vessels and mud figurines. The remains of a sacrificial victim were also unearthed 600 meters away from the fortress. See Ritner (1993: 153–80).
55. "Karl Sanders on Songwriting" ("n.d").
56. *Ithyphallic* (2007), the first one of the band with Nuclear Blast, is an exception because the liner notes were not included in the CD booklet. Instead, the limited edition of this album was presented in a pyramid-shaped box containing a small scroll with the lyrics and the liner notes.
57. On the influence of Howard and especially Lovecraft in metal lyrics, see also Norman (2013) and Secord (this volume).
58. Pessaro (2018).

59. The liner notes for the song "The Black Flame" (*Black Seeds of Vengeance*, 2000) mention an article supposedly published by G. Maspero in 1902 in the journal *The Cairo Archaeological Critiques*. This journal, however, never existed.
60. I also discuss above how Budge's transliteration system permeates the way Nile transcribe and pronounce ancient Egyptian language in their songs, thus proving the influence of this author on Nile's understanding of Egypt.
61. The 1994 science-fiction film *Stargate* echoes this stance when Daniel Jackson, a linguist who has been asked to translate some inscriptions, says: "The translation of the inner track is wrong. They must have used Budge. I don't know why they keep reprinting his books."
62. The *Book of the Amduat* is one of the so-called books of the netherworld, which are funerary compositions initially used for royal individuals. The *Book of the Amduat* outlines the nocturnal journey of the sun, describing the entities he would encounter every night (Hornung [1997] 1999: 27–53).
63. See, e.g., www.hermetics.org/.
64. Note that this is not the same as the right-wing political party Golden Dawn discussed by Apergis (this volume).
65. The figure of Aleister Crowley has also inspired some well-known metal songs, such as "Mr Crowley" (*Blizzard of Ozz*, 1980) by Ozzy Osbourne.
66. This stela is currently kept at the Egyptian Museum in Cairo with accession number A 9422 (previously Bulaq 666). For a published image of this stela, see Munro (1973: 187; pl. 2, fig. 5).
67. A translation of the text on this stela, which includes several fragments from the funerary composition known as the *Book of the Dead*, was provided to Crowley by the well-regarded scholars Battiscombe Gunn and Alan Gardiner. It is not certain, however, whether the latter knew whom he was ultimately working for (Vinson and Gunn 2015: 103).
68. Crowley used the spelling "magick" to differentiate his methods from "magic," which was practiced by stage illusionists (see e.g., Crowley [1954] 1988: chapter 1, "What is Magick?").
69. E.g., "For all shall come to know me / As they fall unto their knees / Zeus the Thunderer, control my destiny." See Cavallini (2009).
70. Egyptology has occasionally considered the implications of Orientalism, especially when assessing the accounts of early travelers (e.g., Thompson 2010) or the beginnings of the discipline (e.g., Harten 2000, Thomasson 2013: esp. 264–88), but this paradigm has not been systematically incorporated into Egyptological discourse (some exceptions include, e.g., Meskell 2000, Riggs 2014: 41–4, 2015, and Moser 2015). This shows a stark contrast with the study of Greco-Roman Egypt by scholars of Classics, in whose works Orientalism and the construction of the knowledge of the past seem to be prevalent approaches (e.g., Selden 1998, Vasunia 2001, Stephens 2003).
71. I have been based at one such institution myself, namely the Faculty of Oriental Studies at the University of Oxford (www.orinst.ox.ac.uk). Despite an ongoing effort to incorporate the archaeology and material culture of "Oriental" civilizations into the academic programs, language learning and text-based research continue to hold the faculty together.
72. The title of this song means "The vengeance war chant of the Assyrians," and Karl Sanders decided to give it a German title to honor the vast amount of archaeological work on ancient Assyria that is done by German scholars. For the full interview, see Deather (2000).
73. This song first appeared on the EP *Festival of Atonement* (1995).
74. The Mesopotamian fertility god Dagon may have been chosen because he was later appropriated by H. P. Lovecraft ([1919] 2011: 23–7); who is also a recognized source of

inspiration for Nile, in his short story entitled "Dagon." The other two goddesses mentioned are associated with destruction and violence.

75. Similar ideas are also explored by Vasunia (2001: 10–20) from the perspective of the Greek discourse.
76. See Reid (2002: esp. 205–12) and Moser (2015: 250).
77. Bohrer (2003: 17) prefers to use the term "exoticism" instead of Orientalism to avoid resorting to binaries such as West and East, but I believe that binary oppositions are at the heart of this phenomenon of "otherization" in which a "them" is always defined in contrast to an "us."
78. In this sense, the way an image of the East is constructed may simultaneously provide information about the self-fashioning of the West. This is especially revealing when examining the mechanisms of appropriation of certain notions or items originating in the East such as gunpowder (see Burke and Prochaska 2008: 49).
79. This dichotomy is also present in the treatment of the Persian Wars in heavy metal, which might also have been influenced by the release of the film *300* in 2006, based on Frank Miller's 1999 graphic novel of the same name. I am grateful to the volume editors for this insightful suggestion.
80. I am grateful to Kris Fletcher and Osman Umurhan for all the work and passion that they have put into this volume. I would like to dedicate my contribution to Iñaki Izarra, together with whom I have been doing "fieldwork" for this article since we first saw Nile live at Wacken 2003 together.

CHAPTER 9
CODA: SOME TRENDS IN METAL'S USE OF CLASSICAL ANTIQUITY
Osman Umurhan

The chapters collected in this volume demonstrate the enduring influence and deep impact of Classical antiquity upon the modern musical genre of heavy metal. Although this collection has merely scraped the surface of metal music's engagement with antiquity, its investigations demonstrate not only metal music's strong affinity for this period, but also how the medium of heavy metal—through its lyrics, music, videos, and album artwork—informs, recasts, and mediates between the seemingly distant and far-removed world of Greco-Roman antiquity and today. As a coda to this volume's collection of chapters, I recap some prominent trends explored by the contributors and offer additional observations about the importance of heavy metal for the future study of antiquity and the growing field of Classical Reception Studies. Metal, I argue, not only contributes to the increasing number of contemporary engagements with the Classical past, but—because of its growing international appeal—also promises to convey the legacy and discussion of Greece and Rome beyond academic discourses and in innumerable ways. Metal's international appeal illustrates the cultural and geographic extent to which Classical antiquity continues to reach new audiences across socio-economic boundaries.

The volume's introduction (Fletcher and Umurhan) argues that "reception" and its defining terms are frequently shifting and evolving as newer media engaging with the Classical world continue to emerge and challenge the predominating discourse about "what is" and "what is not" Classical Reception Studies.[1] The current discussion will show that metal both participates in and enriches current perspectives on approaches to the legacy of antiquity within and beyond academic discourses. In the following, I establish how the genre of metal fits appropriately alongside current forms of Classical reception, like film, TV, and other media, that seek to connect with and make sense of the distant past. From there I offer some additional thoughts on several metal artists' engagements with Greek and Roman antiquity—with a particular look at Ade, Imperium des Tenebras, and Ex Deo—that convey additional means by which some metal acts establish a substantive representation of and connection with antiquity. To conclude, I offer some preliminary opinions on the potential landscape of metal's engagements with Greece and Rome whereby these ancient cultures continue to acquire novel and added meanings in each musical interpretation. As metal spreads and reaches a larger, more international, and increasingly diverse audience, its practitioners' engagement with the Classical past promises to take on new shapes and forms increasingly informed by local, social, and politically motivated needs.

Metal's place in Classical reception

The study of Classical reception, both in material and theory, has continued to thrive since its inception as a sub-discipline of Classics. A greater number of forms of Classical reception is receiving deserved attention from Classical scholars. In addition to recent treatments of comics and science fiction, several scholars under the auspices of the Global Collaborative Network Fund (see www.postclassicisms.org) have embarked on a project that seeks to explore and expand the frameworks of studying antiquity.[2] Shane Butler's *Deep Classics* (2016), also, acknowledges a desire to re-evaluate and expand upon existing methodological means of historical inquiry to include disciplines ranging from philology to evolutionary biology. What proves salient about both of these approaches is their explicit desire to widen the scope of topics that constitute the study of the Classics:

> Deep Classics, in other words, is not opposed to some putatively "shallow" other; rather, it makes the claim that Classics is almost always "deep;" since, more or less constitutionally (we shall argue), it cannot easily be otherwise. Nor is our shift here from "Classical Reception Studies" to "Classics" tout court inadvertent, for like many others (including Goldhill and Martindale alike), we regard reception studies not as a detachable postscript to Classics but, rather, as a deep exploration—and, when needed, close interrogation—of our whole discipline's raison d'être.
>
> *Butler: 16*

> Our aim is to work collectively to extend the initial inquiries and methods of Reception Studies beyond reception narrowly understood to a broader inquiry into our own disciplinary practices and to situate those practices in more ambitious transnational and interdisciplinary configurations … we are as interested in examining the frameworks of studying antiquity that have prevailed as we are in giving new attention to the roads not taken, to the practices and approaches that we might from our disciplinary standpoint want to consider "mis-receptions."
>
> *postclassicisms.org*

Both acknowledge "Classical reception" as the foundation for inquiry about Greece and Rome beyond its immediate historical context. Furthermore, the aims of both represent a necessary advancement in their call to Classicists to reconsider the issue of the Classical tradition and its many permutations through the present beyond established theoretical and social paradigms of thought. But, where Butler imagines that the tradition of Classical reception requires more incisive thinking around the literary and artistic traditions, the scholars of postclassicisms.org wish to broaden the disciplinary standards for what constitutes Reception Studies beyond the potentially dismissive term "mis-reception." In fact, it is their stated aim to broaden the practices of disciplinary inquiry to include "transnational and interdisciplinary configurations" in much the same way the contributors of this volume have aimed to apply their vigorous scholarly training in linguistic, historical, critical, and philological approaches to metal's engagement with the ancient material. Moreover, metal's global appeal has only facilitated the awareness of Classical themes and figures on a transnational scale. James Porter, for example, has stated that one of the great ironies of Classical Studies is that they "have long been predicated on the reception of the Greek and Roman past outside of Classics for their own survival" (2010: 469). Metal, then, also serves as a testament to the value and interest of Classical antiquity to those approaching the material from an academic and non-academic perspective; that is, the former is determined primarily by the study of literary texts within the academic institution, while the latter engages with additional sources beyond the classroom such as in popular television, cinema, or comics. Both transnational and interdisciplinary views can only imbue Greece and Rome with new and added meaning(s).

Metal, then, offers a fertile bridge between Classical antiquity and a contemporary non-specialist audience of an international scale. It presents one key to broadcasting antiquity's value and worth to a growing contemporary audience in addition to other popular interactive modes, such as cinema, TV, or gaming.[3] Like movies, it has a wide range of circulation across many international markets and will continue to encourage an interest in antiquity that can also function as another component in the process of critical thought when considering the legacy of the Classical tradition. While metal originated in Britain of the late 1960s, it has since spread and gained traction across many of the world's continents, including South America, Africa, and Asia, and assumed new variations reflecting local musical forms and ideas.[4] Moreover, motivations for production have differed over time and across cultures. Though commercial success and subsequent profitability are desirable outcomes for many musicians as for the movie industry, for many metal artists these are not necessarily the sole and exclusive motives for composing and performing their music. In fact, many metal artists are not full-time musicians and never attain commercial success. Therefore, metal's artistic output tends to be uninhibited by commercial restrictions, such as suitability for popular radio play, and therefore free to engage with more esoteric material, such as that from Classical antiquity. Metal, therefore, represents another medium alongside cinema, TV, and gaming by which a contemporary audience may acquire greater familiarity, engagement with, and meaning about the Classical past.

Metal's mediation of Greece and Rome

The various chapters of this collection have explained in great depth the wide range of Mediterranean metal's use of antiquity. Now that this genre's fascination for and treatment of Greece and Rome has been established, it is worthwhile to ask what shape this medium's transmission of the past might take in the near future. The remainder of this analysis, then, seeks to disentangle and evaluate some of metal's encounters with antiquity to help illuminate how this subgenre and metal at large may transform in the near future given some current trends. Developments include the rise of metal's global spread as a by-product of globalization—along with its embrace and rejection—metal's increasing engagement with different media such as video and cinema, and its rising attraction among international artists and their audience across gender and socio-economic classes.

It is useful to reprise some discussion of the production and consumer expectation of Classical reception to better understand the future trajectory of metal's representation(s) of the Classical past. Though Martindale, for example, has asserted that a movie, like *Gladiator* (2000) "does not present a thoroughly imagined classical world," it seems that what constitutes this imagined world bears on personal preference, say, for the medium of literature over television or TV.[5] Regardless of difference in content or preference, each medium must be evaluated on its own terms. To expect Odyssean themes in Joyce's *Ulysses* to be articulated in like manner by metal act Symphony X's "The Odyssey" would be misguided for several reasons, primarily that one generally creates within the dictates of his chosen medium and its general rules of operation. In Martindale's words, to describe a literary text's engagement with the past, metal, too, participates in the dialogical process and, thereby, is a redescribable medium—that is, texts "are constantly being made rereadable in multifarious ways, and in that sense are always 'in production'" (13).[6] A medium's ability to be rereadable offers several opportunities for one to understand the past and the present. Metal, then, like other modes of reception, offers another contemporary medium by which one can engage in the reading of the past to help negotiate the present.

One metal case in point is Italian band Ade (Italian for "Hades") that connect with Classical antiquity on several levels—including the artistic, lyrical, and historical—to refashion the past in a novel way. Ade's logo and album cover art offer one artistic window into their portrayal of Rome (see Figure 9.1). The band logo "ADE," as on all its album covers, is emblazoned across the top in large calligraphic-like script. Upon closer inspection, the logo's initial and final letters—"A" and "E"—are embellished with flourishes in the form of an ancient Greek trireme. The descending strokes of both letters transform into a trireme's prow accompanied by protruding oars, whereas the ascending strokes shape into a trireme's overturned-stern also with projecting oars. This trireme motif pervades throughout the logo with hints of Celtic-like labyrinth patterns that move through and culminate above the letter "D" in crest-like fashion.[7] Below the band symbol is written the album title *Carthago Delenda Est* in regular, capital letters. The title itself represents a popular Latin phrase meaning "Carthage Must Be Destroyed," commonly attributed to the Roman senator and statesman, Cato the Elder, who strongly lobbied his fellow senators for the annihilation of Carthage, Rome's rival in a series of conflicts known as the Punic Wars (264 BCE–146 BCE).[8] The topic of the Punic Wars and the Latin phrase are further complemented below the logo with an illustration of a battle between Romans and Carthaginians. The scene portrays Roman soldiers, who brace themselves and duck behind their shields as Carthaginian war elephants approach caparisoned in full militaristic regalia. Archers mounted atop the beasts take aim at their Roman opponents below. Furthermore, the Roman soldiers' backs are to us, the viewers, who fall in line with their perspective, thereby making us Roman in a sense. Overall, the vignette, including the band logo, emphasizes war(fare) as its central

Coda: Some Trends in Metal's Use of Classical Antiquity

Figure 9.1 Ade, *Carthago Delenda Est* (2016; Album cover).

focus. The detailed logo and battle scene purposely serve as a fitting pair in light of other details discussed by band members in a recent biopic on Ade.

In a promotional video released by their record label, the members of Ade reveal great insight into the group's decisions behind the making of the album *Carthago Delenda Est* (2016).[9] It showcases how the band's embrace of a Roman historical topic such as the Punic Wars is motivated by a combination of interests in ancient history, literature, national identity, war, and violence. Ade's full-length album treatment of a specific topic from Classical antiquity is not unlike its many predecessors in its desire to tap into and glorify its national past.[10] For example, the band members go so far as to assume Roman names as their stage names, with the exception of the rhythm guitarist: Diocletianvs [*sic*] (vocals), Fabivs (guitars), Cornelivs (bass guitar), Decivs (drums), and Nerva (guitars).[11] Its rhythm guitarist and composer, Fabius, states that the band itself was first conceived in response to other Italian bands (for discussion of Heimdall and Stormlord, see Fletcher, this volume) who draw on historical and mythological topics of "Viking sagas, Pagan populations [and] Celtic culture" typical of Northern bands from Scandinavia. The band, Fabivs states, was ultimately inspired by the historical heritage of the Roman Empire. The topic, too, and musical style seemingly work hand in hand when Riccardo Studer, orchestral composer and audio engineer, determines that the band's instrumentation and orchestral accompaniment reflect the music's overall "aggressive and metal way." Then bass player and lyricist Caligvla explains how his research brought him to Livy's *The History of Rome* and former lead vocalist Traianvs to arsbellica.it to help infuse their music with a Latin language element and a greater appreciation for historical details concerning particular battles. The website offers an index of great battles in history from the period of ancient Egypt to the Second World War with detailed accounts and accompanying maps describing battle maneuvers, tactics, and military dispositions for specific battles based on various historians' accounts, including Livy, Polybius, and Caesar.[12] Consultation of these various sources enabled the band to better explore and articulate through their instrumentation and vocals "the dualism" between the two protagonists of the war, Hannibal and Scipio, and their "introspective psychological side."

Whether the band achieves this may be determined by the scholarly consumer; but what deserves more attention is the fact that the ancient topic has initiated both an artistic and intellectual impulse to revisit some feature or detail of the ancient past, and then reproduce it through music and cover art. If, as specialists of the field, we seek to impart the value of Classics to a broader audience, Ade's engagement surely illustrates the value of the ancient material for sparking independent research and critical thought. We bear witness to a band—through its lyrics, stage personae, and cover art—that has engaged in some earnest and critical thought about a topic of antiquity, informed in large part by their use of Livy and the website arsbellica.it to identify with and make sense of the past. For those engaged in the inquiry, like the musicians of Ade, this engagement with Rome seemingly comes hand in hand with the desire to add meaning to their musical persona and performance. Their dialogue with antiquity becomes an inextricable part of their metal identity.

An understanding and representation of the past for metal musicians, like those of Ade, are very much a product of the dialogical process that refashions the original narrative or text to deliver a new meaning within a new context. For example, whereas in the case of the Swiss band Eluveitie, which in a postcolonial move co-opts the Caesarian narrative in the service of reasserting contemporary Swiss identity over its historic subjugator (see Taylor, this volume), Ade avows its Italian identity (as do Heimdall and Stormlord; see Fletcher, this volume) by appropriating the perspective of Rome in its Punic War narrative in direct response to current Italian bands and their penchant for the Celtic and Nordic themes more typically embraced by the Norwegian metal scene. By its use of Rome, Ade reinforces its place among other Italian metal acts such as I Miti Eterni, Imperivm [sic], and Hesperia, who also stake a near autochthonous claim to material that is generally considered as tied to its national Italian heritage.[13] As the interview conveys Ade's members still engage—whether inadvertently or not—with those traditional means of meaning construction determined by some fundamental research tools of Classical scholarship such as with close readings of the primary text (e.g., Livy) or attention to language and vocabulary (e.g., Latin). However, this engagement is more likely geared toward the construction of the band's identity as Italian metal artists rather than to resolve debates that concern Classics scholars.

Metal, then, finds itself working within a tradition that not only mines the past, but also uses it as a vehicle for artistic and political expression (see more below). Greece and

Rome allow the scholar or musician an ideological platform upon which to negotiate the present. We have now observed this from looking at the construction of Kawir's black metal identity and anti-Christian stance derived from a rereading of ancient Greek hymnography (see Apergis, this volume) to metal's application of modern gendered perspectives on ancient narratives (see the chapters by Åshede and Foka and Crofton-Sleigh, this volume).

Metal and the future of Classical antiquity: More means of engagement

The reception of Classical antiquity promises to reach a larger and more varied audience thanks in part to metal's increasing global reach and appeal. Metal continues to garner worldwide attention and circulation around the globe and has been the subject of much discussion in the field of Metal Studies.[14] For example, Mark LeVine's *Heavy Metal Islam* details the appropriation of metal by North African and Middle Eastern countries. Today many metal musicians in Islamic countries have been targeted and ridiculed by their governments as purveyors of rebellion and threats to the religious status quo, and so have had to find alternate means of composing and performing. Consequently, metal in these countries, LeVine argues, has generated a virtual agora of sorts where collaborators by email may communicate, cooperate and contest social and religious values across different cultures. Metal in this regard becomes the platform by which a particular demographic may choose to negotiate its own social world. As metal's global reach expands, it continues to assume new forms to address local social and political needs. Its adaptability to indigenous modes, in turn, proves its potential value across different cultures.

My choice of the word "globe," too, is not coincidental, given the economic and political impact behind processes of globalization in the late twentieth and twenty-first centuries.[15] This volume alone has demonstrated the breadth of metal treatments of Classical antiquity, from Greece and Italy to Great Britain and the United States. In fact, the influence of Norwegian metal and "northern themes" on Italy illuminate a central facet of globalization, namely the ideas of diffusion and integration facilitated by the increasing flows of cultural and economic exchanges across localities and borders.[16] A key facet of (trans)cultural exchange involves the circulation of ideas, including any form of artistic output, such as music, art and/or performance. A major source of metal's diffusion in the last fifteen years has been due to advances in digital technologies,[17] thereby enabling a fairly smooth exchange of music between continental Europe and southeast Asia that in previous decades would not have been possible other than by means of traditional mail and illegal hardcopy bootleg media (vinyl, cassette, CD, DVD, etc.). Metal's global impact has been well documented and continues to circulate to more areas. It remains, however, to be seen to what extent a treatment of, say, Vergil's *Aeneid* or any other topic of antiquity may be redescribable, or in what ways it will continue to be rereadable or refashioned, by, for example, a metal act from Botswana or Southeast Asia. Perhaps this expectation, too, overlooks the possible permutations of antiquity beyond its geographic and cultural heritage of continental Europe and Great Britain. What new forms and voices the topics of Classical antiquity prevalent in Mediterranean metal will assume in burgeoning metal scenes in places such as South Africa or Malaysia remains to be seen.[18]

However, globalization has also had its polarizing effects. Whereas globalization has facilitated the exchange of ideas on a larger, international scale promising future novel forms, one cannot overlook other more contentious responses to it, such as its part in the rise of nationalism, right-wing ideologies, and even racism.[19] One does not need to look beyond the UK's Brexit of 2016 or Trump's presidency to notice increasing populist rhetoric in the face of controversial issues, like national security, borders, local economic interests, and immigration. Where in economic circles globalism is synonymous with free international trade—and has been a driving force behind the circulation of local metal forms abroad—the term "globalist" in some far-right and conspiracy theory circles constitutes a Jewish slur, one that President Trump, who declares himself a nationalist, has used to describe others in a negative light like, for example, his former economic advisor, Gary Cohn.[20] For some, such perspectives have been viewed as antithetical to the spirit of the unifying effects of globalization, while for others the very term "global" signals a threat to the principles embraced by more extreme ideologies.

It should be no surprise, then, that just as heavy metal has been the site for the celebration of nation or identity, so too can it be used as a musical vehicle for the expression of racist, fascist, or white supremacist ideologies. Some of our volume authors (e.g., Fletcher, Taylor, Olabarria, Apergis, and Magro-Martínez) have recognized some nationalistic, political, and racist elements in Mediterranean metal and National Socialist Black Metal (NSBM). In fact, their readings offer an illuminating cross-section of how Classical and Metal scholars vary in their impressions of metal's use of antiquity as either politically or apolitically charged. Fletcher and Taylor, for example, have argued for the politicization of the ancient material used by bands like Heimdall, Stormlord, Eluveitie, and SuidAkrA; some have argued that these bands draw on the glorious past of antiquity to formulate and communicate their national pride against the contemporary climate of dissolving borders and the reassertion of ethnic identity. Apergis, on the other hand, has argued that the Greek band Kawir deviates from the modern racist ideologies expressed elsewhere in European NSBM to promote, instead, a Hellenic national unity in the service of the YSEE (the Supreme Council of Ethnikoi Hellenes) and to divorce itself from any associations with contemporary Greek populist ideology of, for example, Golden Dawn.[21] Magro-Martínez considers Italian-Canadian Ex Deo's engagement with Roman antiquity apolitical, though the band's use of Roman military eagles on stage have conjured uncomfortable memories of a not-too-distant Fascist past among Italian concert goers.[22] Mediterranean metal, then, like other responses (e.g. right-wing or progressive) to globalization, may similarly appropriate a wide range of meanings imposed by the artist or its fan, alike. Whether that message is political, religious, or of theatrical import will continue to be determined by fan and artist negotiation of the Classical material, including instances when the artist and fan(s) may disagree about the message (see Magro-Martínez, this volume).

Another striking feature of Classical reception in metal beyond general treatments of ancient history and culture is the use of ancient Greek and Latin by Mediterranean metal bands.[23] Instead of looking for articulations of Classical antiquity as we might as

Coda: Some Trends in Metal's Use of Classical Antiquity

specialists of the field, it behooves us to consider how others might construe the ancient world more broadly. Many of the bands treated in this volume, for example, employ Latin rather freely, either as band name, track title, or as lyrics but, ultimately, with a view to exploring some additional aspect of antiquity and not necessarily as an end unto itself.[24] Some bands, like Ade, use Latin almost exclusively for album track titles or for lyrics in individual songs.[25] More often, a combination of Greek (see Apergis, this volume) and/ or Latin is interspersed within the lyrics of a particular track. Some have argued that the use of Latin or other ancient language by a metal band is generally done so to contribute an historical gravitas or authoritative weight to the musical mood.[26] Apergis, for example, argues that the Greek metal band Kawir's engagement with some ancient Greek hymns of the Orphic corpus reflect a Hellenic band's general anti-Christian sentiments. Through use of a language that predates Christianity, Kawir attempts to reassert the authority of an ancient Greek pagan religion and its language in place of the more contemporary and predominant religious system.

As the analyses in this volume have shown, the use of Classical material is pervasive in heavy metal—arguably more so than in any other contemporary musical genre. The use of Latin or any other ancient language (e.g., Gaulish by Eluveitie; see Taylor, this volume) is prevalent and goes hand in hand with metal's use of ancient history and fictional worlds. The search for a key Latin word such as *imperium* ("command," "power," or "empire") on the website *Encyclopaedia Metallum*, for example, generates fifty-one band entries, with *imperium* used either on its own as the act's name (sixteen) or in combination with another word (thirty-five). These bands hail anywhere from Chile and Mexico to Slovakia and the UK, demonstrating the range and diffusion of metal beyond its beginnings in North America and Europe. Some bands use the Latin *imperium* in combination either with an English word (i.e. Imperium Frost), or some other Latin word to produce a phrase (e.g. Imperium Sepulchri, Imperium Tenebrae, or alongside its misinflected counterpart Mundanus Imperium).[27] Of the remaining bands who employ the Latin *imperium* in whatever inflectional permutation, their national origins range anywhere from South Africa and Indonesia to Venezuela. The bands' use of the ancient languages, either in lyrical content and/or cover art, is not unlike many bands of Mediterranean metal, who mine antiquity for the exploration of themes from the occult, conflicts between gods or super humans to biblical narratives, to name just a few.

The Colombian metal band Imperium des Tenebras offers an interesting case study for the musical reception of Classical antiquity broadly construed. Although this band has not garnered the same international attention as, say, Ex Deo, Blind Guardian, or Eluveitie, the band deserves some attention here, to demonstrate how an act outside Europe or North America construes Greece and Rome. One track, "Nag Hammadi Gnosis Arcanus," from the band's split-EP *Absconditus Umbrae* engages with the subject of the sacred gnostic texts discovered in Nag Hammadi, Egypt, in 1945, texts which have had a significant bearing on studies of Christianity and Gnosticism.[28] The musical track begins with an English translation of one part of those texts, "The Gospel of the Egyptians," that proclaims the birth of Domedon Doxomedon, otherwise known as the great invisible spirit. In a similar vein to a Greek theogony, the narrative of the gospel goes on to outline the generation of gods and men, but the musical track offers an alternative narrative. The band's creative license includes somewhat garbled details about Egyptian pharaohs, Rome, and Seth—all topics that inform the cultural milieu of the gospels in general. Furthermore, those details are embellished with Latin lyrics and transliterated Greek. For example: "Nile tears of blood/ witness of our perdition/ ... sapientiam deperitum/ kyire ignis divine elsion/ ausum luctus/ kyire ignis divine elsion." To the Classical philologist the text above appears confused: the Latin is improperly rendered (*sapientiam deperitum*; incorrect gender agreement between noun and adjective), while the transliterated Greek for a common phrase found in the New Testament is misspelled and mispronounced in the audio recording (kyire . . . elsion for "Κύριε, ἐλέησον," or "Lord, have mercy"), then followed by additional Latin (*ignis*) and English (divine).

While it may be tempting for a Classicist to dismiss this as lazy and careless effort, viewing this is as a form of reception may be more constructive, specifically, as a "mash-up." "Mash-up" is a postmodern term used to describe the integration of complementary or disparate elements from two or multiple sources. In this regard, Imperium des Tenebras' formulation of the original languages may constitute a synthesis of disparate musical and lyrical elements. To view this expression as just a mistake, however, would distract from its contribution to the track's overall musical and lyrical mood. The misinflection would most likely go unnoticed, if not for the discerning listener looking for grammatical precision; it would not subtract from the artist's desire to evoke some general ambience and gravitas.

In addition to the feature of integration behind the concept of the "mash-up," it is useful to consider how hybridization, another facet of globalization, may shed light on how metal is currently—and may continue to be—received in popular culture. The sociological concept embraces the idea of mixture or developing new combinations from existing elements that I argue is similar to the term "mash-up." Hybridity reflects the outcome of "intensive intercultural communication, multiculturalism, growing migrations and diaspora lives, and the erosion of boundaries [and] has become a prominent theme in cultural studies."[29] As metal—and its novel articulations of antiquity—increasingly penetrates new regions and cultures it, too, has a tendency to encourage new debates local to its particular region.[30] Metal's international appeal is a testament to its adaptability and the medium's receptiveness to local forms.[31] In a contemporary era where the pace of exchange continues to accelerate, hybridity undoubtedly plays a significant role in an individual or band's formation of its musical identity. And, if metal continues to circulate as far and wide as it has, those bands that perform Classical antiquity promise to facilitate new dialogue between various communities and possible engagement with antiquity otherwise unexplored by other musicians and fans. In the case of Imperium des Tenebras we witness how some effects of globalization—the use of ancient Greek by a local Colombian band—might have played a significant factor in its articulation of Classical antiquity, through several traditions (e.g., the Gospels, ancient Egypt, and Rome).

Coda: Some Trends in Metal's Use of Classical Antiquity

Alongside the use of some ancient written and oral traditions, the music video and live performance offer additional forums by which metal artists may mediate between antiquity and other contemporary forms of artistic expression (see Magro-Martínez, this volume). Like the disparate elements of the "mash-up," Ex Deo's reception and representation of historical events do not derive from one particular source.[32] The band, moreover, continue to explore unique reconstructions of the past within the music video medium with the track, "The Roman," from their latest album *The Immortal Wars* (2016). As in their other videos the band appears in Roman period gear, specifically, military clothing representing Julius Caesar's Thirteenth legion, but here performing in a CGI Roman camp while enemy troops led by a one-eyed Hannibal enter the camp to engage in battle. Such attention to detail also informs the band's live performance in Roman battle accoutrements and other props such as Roman standards and armor.[33] They represent a growing trend among other Mediterranean metal bands such as Ade and Sacred Blood, who like to illustrate the historical or mythological period on their album cover art, in music videos, and/or dress the part on live sets.[34] Beyond the sartorial, some members of Mediterranean metal bands pay homage to Greece or Rome with body tattoos. For example, Iacono of Ex Deo has the "S. P. Q. R." and eagle brand on his shoulder, and the Latin phrase *invictus* ("unconquered") on his forearm, as well as a Roman centurion.[35] Metal's attention to Greece and Rome often reveals a more than superficial effort to treat and investigate its culture to include not only general events or historical figures (e.g. Julius Caesar or Hannibal), but also minutiae, down to the very look of period dress.

It is worth taking stock of another growing trend that some volume contributors have drawn attention to, namely the growing impact of female musicians on metal (see the chapters by Crofton-Sleigh and Åshede and Foka, this volume). Female metal artists continue to draw attention to Classical antiquity in their material, which further demonstrates the growing impact of metal across genders. In fact, the female presence in metal is growing steadily. The metal scene is no longer predominantly male and uniformly informed by masculinity as illustrated in part by the rise of female metal musicians, especially female lyricists, singers, and fans.[36] Acts include, for example, female-fronted bands, such as Nightwish (Finland), Epica (Netherlands), and Sirenia (Norway), some of which engage with mythology and fantasy themes such as Nightwish with J. R. R. Tolkien.[37] With particular regard for Classical antiquity, ShadowIcon, from Slovenia, feature a female lead singer-lyricist, Ana Prijatelj, and their album *Empire In Ruins* (2011) explores the period of the Roman Civil War through thirteen tracks, from the assassination of Julius Caesar to the murder of Caesarion, his illegitimate son by Cleopatra, in 30 BCE. Moreover, the album diverges from the usual focus on the celebration of war and masculinity, with a greater focus on the psychological trauma of war, with special attention paid to the voices of the "losers" such as Marc Antony, Cleopatra, and Caesarion. Female singer-lyricist Frederica "Sister" de Boni of Italy's White Skull also sings about topics relating to Rome such as the military ethos of Roman soldiers, the glory of Julius Caesar, and Cleopatra's political aspirations on the album *Public Glory, Secret Agony* (2000).[38] As Åshede and Foka and Crofton-Sleigh in this volume well explain, the increasing feminine presence in metal continues not only to challenge traditional views of sexuality and gender, but also amplifies the motif of the powerful woman occasionally discussed in ancient Greek and Roman discourses.

Classical antiquity has even helped encourage the formation of one all-female metal band, We Start Wars. In an interview with its lead member, Nita Strauss, she discusses how she took inspiration from antiquity for its band name.[39] She explains how many women since antiquity, with specific reference to Helen of Troy and Cleopatra, have been the source of great struggles and wars. Despite these women's seemingly poor historical reputation, Nita Strauss adapts the traditional narratives about them in the service of the band's and her own personal musical and gender empowerment when she states:

> I've always been fascinated by the idea of the female warrior, someone who fights her own battles and doesn't take shit from anyone, and equally fascinated with the concept that a woman's love or defending her honor would be worth so much that people would actually put their own lives and the lives of others at risk over it. The most famous story everyone thinks of first is, of course, "The face that launched a thousand ships," *Helen of Troy*. But there was also *Cleopatra and Marc Antony*, ... *Richard the Lionheart* rescuing his sister *Joan of England* during the crusades.[40]

Accordingly, Nita Strauss' inspiration draws upon the notion that women and war are not mutually exclusive; instead, a woman's act of defiance in the service of "defending her honor" fashions her a "female warrior" who, like other men in an ancient war narrative (e.g., Achilles, Hector, Aeneas, etc.), have risked their lives to protect the honor of family and state.[41] In like manner, the Classical examples of Helen of Troy, Cleopatra, et al., help facilitate for Nita Strauss a modern musical articulation of female empowerment within a generally male-dominated contemporary genre of music. The band name serves as a clear testament to this inspiration and the band's distinct female identity.

So, once considered the epitome of masculinity, metal now increasingly defies the popular stereotype of the genre as an arena for male performativity of aggression and masculinity. In fact, in the past twenty-five years, traditional gender discourses in metal have begun to be challenged beginning with the coming out of prominent front men such as Judas Priest's Rob Halford in the early 1990s and Norwegian black metal artist Kristiaan Eivindt Espedal (stage name "Gaahl") in 2008. Rob Halford, in particular, has been credited for pioneering heavy metal's distinct look in the late 1970s, with its male musicians clad in leather trousers and jackets, combat boots, spike gauntlets, and bullet studded belts.[42] However, once Halford came out, this sartorial image no longer represented metal's leading look.[43] Moreover, in coming out Halford has helped to challenge some stereotypes about metal and to encourage metal fans to "view the issue of masculinity and homosexuality in a different way."[44] Although male metal musicians still outnumber female metal performers, the recent rise of female-fronted and all-female groups suggest a narrowing of that gap. A marked rise in postfeminism (or postfeminist performance artists) in female metal bands, at least in the West, indicates that gender is no longer as prominent or contested as it once was thirty years ago.[45] Like the increasing and shifting theoretical approaches that have diversified approaches to the study of Classical antiquity from within so, too, metal is no longer defined exclusively as a musical medium that epitomizes masculinity, aggression, and teenage angst. Both disciplines address deeper cultural, sociological and political concerns and, therefore, account for their potential viability in contemporary society.

Conclusion

In short, this coda has addressed two larger issues surrounding the study of Classics and metal: one, the academic understanding and negotiation of metal's reception of Classical antiquity and, two, what new form(s) metal's engagement with this period has assumed. Although this coda has not addressed every facet of metal's reception as discussed by the volume's contributors, it has identified some prominent trends that inform the nature of many metal acts examined, especially Mediterranean metal. For one, metal's audience has become increasingly egalitarian. Due in large part to the processes of modern globalization, metal continues to circulate beyond national borders to pique the interest of musicians beyond, say, areas in Europe to Canada, North or South America, and Asia. Yet, as explored above, globalization has also had paradoxical effects in the drive of many to be more insular and protective of local culture and forms. This, of course, has led to the unfortunate implication of Greece and Rome in nationalist and racist ideologies among some Mediterranean metal bands. However, metal's increasing circulation has effected welcome change in expanding its traditional masculinist narratives beyond the concerns of one sex, especially with the rise of female acts and feminine perspectives. Mediterranean metal, too, has embraced some of these changes in its engagements with Classical antiquity and has presented new interest in and fresh perspectives for artists and fans that might not have otherwise found the material accessible outside the academic institution.

Metal's reception of antiquity, then, appears to be increasingly defined by a combination of factors related to processes of globalization, nationalism, politicization, and a growing egalitarian audience. Metal's appeal across socio-economic classes promises an array of voices about the Classical past in the near future. Several of this volume's contributors have identified some of these voices and the ever-broadening impact of Classics upon various media, and vice versa. Such a diverse and rich range of perspectives will undoubtedly continue to reshape—for better or worse—Classical antiquity. In the true dialogical sense, then, metal has afforded us a great opportunity to reflect upon the ways in which the exchange of ideas about and between antiquity and the present continue to make Greece and Rome and its legacy relevant, and how this legacy will continue to acquire new import from place to place and generation to generation.[46]

Notes

1. For more on Classical Reception Studies, its theories, methodologies, and definition(s), see Porter (2008), Kovacs and Marshall (2011), Martindale (2013), Jenkins (2015), Butler (2016), and Rogers and Stevens (2019: esp. 1–17). See also discussion in the Introduction (this volume).
2. For a brief discussion of other forms of Classical reception, see Introduction (this volume), with references.
3. Like Classical antiquity in heavy metal music, so, too have video games and gaming garnered recent interest from the field of Classics, see Ghita and Andrikopoulos (2009), Lowe (2009), Christensen and Machado (2010), and Reinhard (2018).
4. For a discussion of metal scenes across more than a dozen countries, see Wallach, Berger, and Greene (2011a) and Brown et al. (2016).
5. See Introduction (this volume) for another discussion of Martindale's sentiment.
6. Martindale describes the dialogical process as "a two-way process of understanding, backwards and forwards, which illuminates antiquity as much as modernity" (2013: 171). See Martindale (2013) for further discussion of the dialogical process and Martindale (1993: 13) for further discussion of the term "redescribable."
7. Celtic-like patterning in metal band logos is not an uncommon feature. See Taylor (this volume).
8. The Roman author Pliny the Elder (23/4–79 CE) offers the first explicit statement of the phrase in his *Naturalis historia* 15.74.4.
9. For the interview in two parts, see ADE Legions (2016a) and (2016b).
10. See *Encyclopaedia Metallum* for a full track listing of Ade's album *Carthago Delenda Est* (2016). See Introduction (this volume) and Fletcher (this volume) for a discussion of metal acts who use their nation's history.
11. See Magro-Martínez (this volume) for a detailed discussion of Caligula in contemporary film and Ex Deo.
12. The website's creators, Italian brothers Marco and Luca (2015), claim as their principal aim in their study, for example, of Julius Caesar's siege of Alesia (52 BCE) that "we discover the methods and principles of the "*ars bellica*" in which the Romans excelled ("*ars*" in this case should be understood with the meaning of "technique" and so "*ars bellica*" means technique of war) . . . we will try to make known the men, their history, their motivations and socio-political events which led them to have to compete on a battlefield."
13. See, e.g., I Miti Eterni's album *Historia Cumae* (2014), Imperivm's *Rome Burns* (2017), and Hesperia's *Caesar [Roma vol. I]* (2017). See also Fletcher (this volume) for a discussion of the various ways some Mediterranean metal acts forge connections between the Roman epic, the *Aeneid*, and the bands' national heritage.
14. For metal's impact felt around the world, see esp. Wallach, Berger, and Greene (2011a), Scott (2012), Lashua, Wagg, and Spracklen (2014), and Brown et al. (2016). See also discussion under "Metal Studies as Emerging Field" in the Introduction (this volume).
15. For some seminal studies on globalization and its various processes, see Giddens (1990), Harvey (1990), Appadurai (1996), and Tomlinson (1999).
16. Weinstein (2011), however, believes that metal's globalization is not brought on by "the cultural diffusion of diasporic communities, that took their culture with them when they migrated, but metal diffuses by one of the three social actors: musicians, fans, and mediators" (45) as though to suggest that these "actors" function apart from their own community.

Coda: Some Trends in Metal's Use of Classical Antiquity

17. Mayer and Timberlake (2014).
18. For the growth of heavy metal communities in Africa, see Banchs (2016).
19. For a discussion of globalization's stimulation of some forms of nationalism, racism, the Pagan Revival, and occult National Socialism, see Gardell (2003). See also Fletcher (this volume), with regard to globalization and nationalism.
20. Rosenberg (2018).
21. For racism in NSBM, see Gardell (2003: 284–323) and Olson (2008, 2013).
22. Scott (2010, 2011) represents one trend among metal scholars who suggest apolitical readings of metal.
23. See Fletcher (2015) and especially Fletcher (this volume) for a discussion of how some Italian metal bands understand, explain, and use Latin in their lyrics.
24. The use of Latin by metal bands is not limited to the treatments offered by contributors in this volume. Some other examples include but are not limited to: Epica's "Originem" (*Quantum Enigma*, 2014), Helloween's "Lavdate Dominvm," [sic] (*Better Than Raw*, 1998), and Iced Earth's "In Sacred Flames" (*The Crucible of Man (Something Wicked, Part 2)*, 2008). Latin is used exclusively throughout these tracks. Bands may also use Latin intermittently (see discussion of Imperium des Tenebras below).
25. The use of Greek and Latin by these Mediterranean metal bands varies by degree, from just track titles to entire songs in Greek and/or Latin. For some examples see Ade's *Prooemium Sanguine* (2009) and *Carthago Delenda Est* (2016), Ex Deo's *Caligvla* (2012) and *The Immortal Wars* (2017), Stormlord's *Hesperia* (2013), and Kawir's Πάτερ Ἥλιε Μῆτερ Σελάνα (2016).
26. Campbell (2009) and Fletcher (2015).
27. Grammatical rules for Latin require that both noun (*imperium*) and modifying adjective (*mundanus*) inflect appropriately to agree in gender, case, and number. The case endings in the phrase "Mundanus Imperium" do not agree; it should be expressed "Mundanum Imperium."
28. On the impact of the Nag Hammadi Library on early Christianity and Gnosticism, see Meyer (2007) and Bull, Lied, and Turner (2012).
29. Nederveen Pieterse (2012). Hybridity and hybridization are broad and contested terms even in globalization studies. The terms relate to the increasing diversity of local and global forms and the development of new combinations.
30. One interesting example is the metal scene in Botswana whose fans dress as cowboys, not because of any strong affinity to country music, but because many work on farms. Local fans often express their participation by sartorial competition, namely who can best dress as a cowboy in black leather. For more discussion, see Nilsson (2016).
31. Wallach, Berger, and Greene (2011b) refer to metal's global appeal as a form of "metallification," which suggests the "maturation of local scenes results from the flows of knowledge from more established scenes to newer ones, coupled with a desire among scene members to apply this knowledge constructively" (20).
32. For a consideration of the historical, cinematic, and pop influences on Ex Deo's tracks "I, Caligvla" and "The Tiberius Cliff (Exile to Capri)," see Magro-Martínez (this volume). See also Umurhan (2012: 140–47) for a discussion of cinematic and graphic novel influences on Ex Deo's video "The Final War (The Battle of Actium)."
33. See, for example, Ex Deo's live performance of the track "Storm the Gates of Alesia" (MrLechimp 2010) and Ade's "Carthago Delenda Est" (Chavez Roca 2016).

34. See, e.g. Pitch Black Records (2015) for the music video of Sacred Blood's "To Lands No Man Hath Seen" (*Argonautica*, 2008). The video description states the participation of re-enactors from the Hellenic re-enactment group "Koryvantes," who in this video perform the role of Greek hoplites, a siren/mermaid (pursued by those same hoplites), and a Greek maiden.
35. For a discussion with Iacono about his tattoos, see Matthijssens (2012).
36. Only recently has the discussion of gender and sexuality begun to receive full-length treatments by Metal Studies scholars. See, for example, the collection of essays in Heesch and Scott (2016). See also Clifford-Napoleone (2015).
37. See, in particular, Nightwish's track "Elvenpath" from the album *Angels Fall First* (1997).
38. Some tracks about Rome from this album include: "High Treason," "The Roman Empire," "In Caesar We Trust," and "Cleopathra" [*sic*]. Consult *Encyclopaedia Metallum* for additional tracks and accompanying lyrics.
39. See interview at "Nita Strauss" (2017).
40. See note above for link to interview (emphasis in original).
41. The idea of a "female warrior" from Classical antiquity also recalls Boudicca, the queen of the Iceni, who with native Britons in 60 CE led a rebellion against Roman rule in Britannia. Boudicca also appears on metal tracks, the following examples of which feature a female lead on vocals: Goat of Mendes, "Boudicca's Triumph" (*To Walk Upon the Wiccan Way*, 1997); White Skull, "Boudicca's Speech" (*Forever Fight*, 2009); and Serpentyne, "Boudicca" (*Myths and Muses*, 2014). For more on the reception of Boudicca, see Hingley and Unwin (2006) and Johnson (2012).
42. On metal fashion in general, see Weinstein (2000: 126–34) and Clifford-Napoleone (2015: 25–48).
43. Clifford-Napoleone (2015) argues that metal offers a queerscape, or a space for those who identify themselves as queer, for example, in the sartorial use of leather. Moreover, this queerspace, she argues, is not homophobic, but effeminophobic.
44. See interview with Rob Halford in Pittman (2010).
45. See Weinstein (2016b). For one account of a female musician's challenges in a male-dominated music industry dating back to the late 1970s and 1980s, see Lita Ford's account of her experiences with the band, The Runaways, and subsequent musical projects in her recent autobiography (2016).
46. I owe a massive debt of gratitude to Kris Fletcher for his suggestions on various stages of this chapter and to Filippo Carlà-Uhink for his insightful guidance and encouraging tenacity. All remaining errors are my own.

BIBLIOGRAPHY

Abate, A. (2013), "Intervista agli Heimdall", *www.rawandwild.com*, Available online at: www.rawandwild.com/interviews/2013/int_heimdall.php (accessed February 28, 2019).
ADE Legions (2016a), "ADE—Making of Carthago Delenda Est Part 1", *YouTube.com*, July 4. Available online at: www.youtube.com/watch?v=facVerXoVQc (accessed February 26, 2019).
ADE Legions (2016b), "ADE- Making of Carthago Delenda Est II", *YouTube.com*, July 15. Available online at: www.youtube.com/watch?v=K-SlPGgyRKc (accessed February 26, 2019).
Ahmed, S. (2004), *The Cultural Politics of Emotion*, Edinburgh: Edinburgh University Press.
Alfaro, J. P. (2012), "La imagen de Calígula en Suetonio: Realidad o Construcción", *Intus-Legere Historia* 6: 7–32.
Allen, J. P. (2000), *Middle Egyptian: An Introduction to the Language and Culture of Hieroglyphs*, Cambridge, New York: Cambridge University Press.
Allett, N. (2013), "The Extreme Metal 'Connoisseur'", in T. Hjelm, K. Kahn-Harris, and M. LeVine (eds), *Heavy Metal: Controversies and Countercultures*, 166–81, Sheffield and Bristol: Equinox.
Alston, R. (2015), *Rome's Revolution: Death of the Republic and Birth of the Empire*, Oxford: Oxford University Press.
Appadurai, A. (1996), *Modernity at Large: Cultural Dimensions of Globalization*, Minneapolis: University of Minnesota Press.
Appiah, K. A. (1991), "Is the Post- in Postmodernism the Post- in Postcolonial?", *Critical Inquiry* 17: 336–57.
Apter, E. (1993), "Introduction", in E. Apter and W. Pietz (eds), *Fetishism as Cultural Discourse*, 1–12, Ithaca and London: Cornell University Press.
Arnett, J. J. (1996), *Metalheads: Heavy Metal Music and Adolescent Alienation*, Boulder: Westview Press.
Ashby, S. P. and J. Schofield (2015), "'Hold the Heathen Hammer High': Representation, Re-enactment and the Construction of 'Pagan' Heritage", *International Journal of Heritage Studies* 21: 493–511.
Austin, R. G., ed. (1966), *P. Vergili Maronis Aeneidos, Liber Quartus*, Oxford: Clarendon Press.
Baddeley, G. (2002), *Goth Chic: A Connoisseur's Guide to Dark Culture*, London: Plexus.
Baines, J. (1990), "Restricted Knowledge, Hierarchy and Decorum: Modern Perceptions and Ancient Institutions", *Journal of the American Research Center in Egypt* 27: 1–23.
Bakhtin, M. M. (1981), "Forms of Time and of the Chronotope in the Novel", in M. Holquist and C. Emerson (trans.), *The Dialogic Imagination: Four Essays*, 84–258, Austin: University of Texas Press.
Banchs, E. (2016), *Heavy Metal Africa: Life, Passion and Heavy Metal in the Forgotten Continent*, Tarentum, PA: Word Association.
Bangs, L. (1980), "Heavy Metal", in J. Miller (ed.), *The Rolling Stone Illustrated History of Rock and Roll*, 332–35, New York: Random House.
Bardine, B. A. (2009), "Elements of the Gothic in Heavy Metal: A Match Made in Hell", in G. Bayer (ed.), *Heavy Metal Music in Britain*, 125–39, Burlington, VT: Ashgate.
Barlow, S. A. (1986), *Euripides Trojan Women: With Translation and Commentary*, Warminster: Aris & Phillips.

Bibliography

Barrett, A. A. (1989), *Caligula: The Corruption of Power*, New Haven and London: Yale University Press.
Barrett, A., E. Fantham, and J. Yardley, eds. (2016), *The Emperor Nero: A Guide to the Ancient Sources*, Princeton, Oxford: Princeton University Press.
Barron, L. (2013), "Dworkin's Nightmare: Porngrind as the Sound of Feminist Fears", in T. Hjelm, K. Kahn-Harris, and M. LeVine (eds), *Heavy Metal: Controversies and Countercultures*, 66–82, Bristol, CT: Equinox.
Bartolucci, F. (2019), "Enea non è un eroe 'pro migranti'. Insegniamo l'Eneide ai semicolti'", *Il Primato Nazionale*, January 29. Available online at: www.ilprimatonazionale.it/approfondimenti/enea-non-eroe-migranti-eneide-semicolti-102861/ (accessed February 27, 2019).
Barton, T. (1994), *Ancient Astrology*, Sciences of Antiquity, London and New York: Routledge.
Bartsch, S., K. Freudenburg, and C. A. J. Littlewood, eds. (2017), *The Cambridge Companion to the Age of Nero*, Cambridge Companions to the Ancient World, Cambridge: Cambridge University Press.
Bayton, M. (1997), "Women and the Electric Guitar", in S. Whiteley (ed.), *Sexing the Groove: Popular Music and Gender*, 37–49, New York: Routledge.
Beard, M. (2007), *The Roman Triumph*, Cambridge, MA: Belknap Press of Harvard University Press.
Beard, M. (2015), "Ancient Rome and Today's Migrant Crisis; The Romans would have been puzzled by today's hostility to migrants–and the EU's lack of political unity", *The Wall Street Journal*, October 16. Available online at: www.wsj.com/articles/ancient-rome-and-todays-migrant-crisis-1445005978 (accessed February 27, 2019).
Beard, M. (2017), *Women and Power: A Manifesto*, London and New York: Liveright Publishing Corporation.
Beard, M. and J. Henderson (1995), *Classics: A Very Short Introduction*, Oxford: Oxford University Press.
Bekker-Nielsen, T. (2008), "*Colonia Iulia Carcaso*? The Barbaira Milestone (CIL XVII 2, 299) and the Civic Status of Carcassone", *Zeitschrift für Papyrologie und Epigraphik* 164: 248–50.
Berg, R. M. van den (2001), *Proclus' Hymns: Essays, Translations, Commentary*, Leiden: Brill.
Berger, H. M. (1999), *Metal, Rock and Jazz: Perception and Phenomenology of Musical Experience*, Hanover: Wesleyan University Press.
Bernabé, A., ed. (2004), *Poetae Epici Graeci. Testimonia et Fragmenta. Pars II: Orphicorum et Orphicis Similium Testimonia et Fragmenta. Fasciculus 1*, München: K. G. Saur.
Bernabé, A. (2010), "The Gods in Later Orphism", in J. M. Bremer and A. Erskine (eds), *The Gods of Ancient Greece: Identities and Transformations*, Edinburgh Leventis Studies 5, 422–41, Edinburgh: Edinburgh University Press.
Betz, H. D. (2003), *The Mithras Liturgy: Text, Translation and Commentary*, Studien und Texte zu Antike und Christentum, 18. Tübingen: Mohr Siebeck.
Bhabha, H. K. (1994), *The Location of Culture*, London: Routledge.
Biddle, I. and V. Knights, eds. (2007), *Music, National Identity and the Politics of Location: Between the Global and the Local*, Abingdon: Routledge.
Bierbrier, M. L., ed. (2012), *Who Was Who in Egyptology*, 4th rev. edn, London: Egypt Exploration Society.
Billows, R. A. (2009), *Julius Caesar: The Colossus of Rome*, New York: Routledge.
"Biography: K. Sanders" (2019), www.spirit-of-metal.com, available online at: www.spirit-of-metal.com/en/biography/K._Sanders/9180 (accessed February 26, 2019).
Birley, A. J. (1981), *The Fasti of Roman Britain*, Oxford: Clarendon Press.
Blaschek, A. (2010), *Maler—Reisende—Aegypten: Die Wahrnehmung des Alten Ägypten im 19. Jahrhundert anhand von Malern als Reisebegleiter berühmter Persönlichkeiten*, Vienna: Phoibos.

Bibliography

Bleibtreu, E. (1991), "Grisly Assyrian Record of Torture and Death", *Biblical Archaeology Review* 17: 52–61, 75.

Bogue, R. (2004), "Violence in Three Shades of Metal: Death, Doom and Black", in I. Buchanan and M. Swiboda (eds), *Deleuze and Music*, 95–117, Edinburgh: Edinburgh University Press.

Bohrer, F. N. (2003), *Orientalism and Visual Culture: Imagining Mesopotamia in Nineteenth Century Europe*, Cambridge: Cambridge University Press.

Borthwick, S. and R. Moy (2004), *Popular Music Genres: An Introduction*, Edinburgh: Edinburgh University Press.

"Box Office Mojo: Gladiator" (2019), *www.boxofficemojo.com*, February 22. Available online at: www.boxofficemojo.com/movies/?id=gladiator.htm (accessed February 22, 2019).

Brault, P.-A. (2009), "Playing the Cassandra: Prophecies of the Feminine in the *Polis* and Beyond" in D. E. McCoskey and E. Zakin (eds), *Bound by the City: Greek Tragedy, Sexual Difference, and the Formation of the Polis*, 197–220, Albany: State University of New York Press.

Bremer, J. M. (1981), "Greek Hymns", in H. S. Versnel (ed.), *Faith, Hope and Worship: Aspects of Religious Mentality in the Ancient World*, 193–215, Leiden: Brill.

Bremmer, J. N. (2014), *Initiation into the Mysteries of the Ancient World*, Münchner Vorlesungen zu antiken Welten, Bd 1, Berlin: De Gruyter.

Breslin, J. (1977), *A Greek Prayer*, Malibu: J. P. Getty Museum.

Bridgman, T. P. (2005), *Hyperboreans: Myth and History in Celtic-Hellenic Contacts*, Studies in Classics, New York and London: Routledge.

Brier, B. (2013), *Egypt-omania: Our Three Thousand Year Obsession with the Land of the Pharaohs*, 1st edn, New York: Palgrave Macmillan.

Brown, A. R. (2011), "Heavy Genealogy: Mapping the Currents, Contraflows and Conflicts of the Emergent Field of Metal Studies 1978–2010", *Journal for Cultural Research* 15: 213–42.

Brown, A. R. (2015), "Explaining the Naming of Heavy Metal from Rock's 'Back Pages': A Dialogue with Deena Weinstein", *Metal Music Studies* 1: 233–61.

Brown, A. R. (2016a), "Introduction: Global Metal Music and Culture and Metal Studies", in A. R. Brown, K. Spracklen, K. Kahn-Harris, and N. W. R. Scott (eds), *Global Metal Music and Culture: Current Directions in Metal Studies*, 1–21, New York and Abingdon: Routledge.

Brown, A. R. (2016b), "Un(su)stained Class? Figuring Out the Identity Politics of Heavy Metal's Class Demographics", in A. R. Brown, K. Spracklen, K. Kahn-Harris, and N. W. R. Scott (eds), *Global Metal Music and Culture: Current Directions in Metal Studies*, 190–206, New York and Abingdon: Routledge.

Brown, A. R., K. Spracklen, K. Kahn-Harris, and N. W. R. Scott, eds. (2016), *Global Metal Music and Culture: Current Directions in Metal Studies*, New York: Routledge.

Budelmann, F. and J. Haubold (2008), "Reception and Tradition", in L. Hardwick and C. Stray (eds), *A Companion to Classical Receptions*, 13–25, Chichester: Blackwell.

Budge, E. A. W. (1899), *Egyptian Magic*, Books on Egypt and Chaldaea, 2, London: Kegan Paul, Trench, Trübner.

Budge, E. A. W. (1901), *The Book of the Dead: An English Translation of the Chapters, Hymns, etc. of the Theban Recension, with Introduction, Notes, etc. by E. A. W. Budge*, 3 vols, Books on Egypt and Chaldaea 6–8, London: Kegan Paul.

Budge, E. A. W. (1911), *Osiris and the Egyptian Resurrection*, 2 vols, London: Philip Lee Warner.

Budge, E. A. W. (1920), *An Egyptian Hieroglyphic Dictionary: With an Index of English Words, King List and Geographical List with Indexes, List of Hieroglyphic Characters, Coptic and Semitic Alphabets, etc*, London: J. Murray.

Budge, E. A. W. (1925), *The Egyptian Heaven and Hell, Being the Book of Amtuat, the Shorter Form of the Book of Am-tuat, the Book of the Gates and the Contents of the Books of the Other World*, London: M. Hopkinson and company.

Bibliography

Budge, E. A. W. (1934), *From Fetish to God in Ancient Egypt*, London: Humphrey Milford.
Bull, C. H., L. I. Lied and J. D. Turner, eds. (2012), *Mystery and Secrecy in the Nag Hammadi Collection and Other Ancient Literature: Ideas and Practices. Studies for Einar Thomassen at Sixty*, Leiden: Brill.
Burke E. and D. Prochaska (2008), "Introduction: Orientalism from Postcolonial Theory to World History", in E. Burke and D. Prochaska (eds), *Genealogies of Orientalism: History, Theory, Politics*, 1–71, Lincoln, NB; London: University of Nebraska Press.
Burrow, C. (1993), "Virgil in English Translation," in C. Martindale (ed.), *The Cambridge Companion to Virgil*, 21–37, Cambridge: Cambridge University Press.
Butler, S., ed. (2016), *Deep Classics: Rethinking Classical Reception*, London: Bloomsbury.
Cairns, F. (1989), *Virgil's Augustan Epic*, Cambridge: Cambridge University Press.
Campbell, D. B. (2010), "The Fate of the Ninth: The Curious Disappearance of Legio VIIII Hispana", *Ancient Warfare* 4: 48–53.
Campbell, I. (2009), "From Achilles to Alexander: The Classical World and the World of Metal", in G. Bayer (ed.), *Heavy Metal Music in Britain*, 111–24, Farnham: Ashgate.
Canfora, L. (1977), "Classicismo e fascismo", in Giuseppe Semerari (ed.), *Matrici culturali del fascismo: seminari promossi dal Consiglio regionale pugliese e dall'Ateneo barese nel trentennale della liberazione*, 85–111, Bari: Università di Bari, Facoltà di Lettere e Filosofia.
Cano Alonso, P. L. (2011), "Géneros Cinematográficos y Mundo Antiguo", in A. Duplá (ed.), *El "Cine de Romanos" en el siglo XXI*, 59–78, Vitoria: Universidad del País Vasco.
Carlà-Uhink, F. (2017a), *The "Birth" of Italy: The Institutionalization of Italy as a Region, 3rd–1st Century BCE*, De Gruyter: Berlin.
Carlà-Uhink, F. (2017b), "*Caput Mundi*: Rome as Center in Roman Representation and Construction of Space", *Ancient Society* 47: 119–57.
Cavallini, E. (2007), "Achilles in the Age of Metal", *Mythimedia.org*. Available at: www.mythimedia.org/Achilles_age_of_metal.html (accessed May 31, 2018).
Cavallini, E. (2009), "Achilles in the Age of Steel. Greek Myth in Modern Popular Music", *Conservation Science in Cultural Heritage* 9: 113–30.
Chavez Roca, O. t. (2016), "ADE—Carthago Delenda Est(live Madrid)", *YouTube.com*, September 14. Available online at: www.youtube.com/watch?v=u9sqGyrqXd8 (accessed August 30, 2018).
Checkel, J. T. and P. J. Katzenstein, eds. (2009), *European Identity*, Cambridge: Cambridge University Press.
Christe, I. (2003), *Sound of the Beast: The Complete Headbanging History of Heavy Metal*, New York: HarperCollins.
Christesen, P. and D. Machado (2010), "Video Games and Classical Antiquity", *The Classical World* 104: 107–10.
Ciampa, F. (2018), "Enea non era un migrante e, soprattutto, non era turco", *Giovani A Destra*, April 18. Available online at: http://giovaniadestra.it/2018/04/18/enea-non-era-un-migrante-e-soprattutto-non-era-turco/ (accessed February 27, 2019).
Cixous, H. (1990), "The Laugh of the Medusa", in D. Walder (ed.), *Literature in the Modern World*, 316–26, Oxford: Oxford University Press.
Clifford-Napoleone, A. R. (2015), *Queerness in Heavy Metal Music: Metal Bent*, New York and Abingdon: Routledge.
Cohen, S. (1997), "Men Making A Scene: Rock Music and the Production of Gender", in S. Whiteley (ed.), *Sexing the Groove: Popular Music and Gender*, 17–36, New York and London: Routledge.
Cohen, S. (2002), *Moral Panics and Folk Devils*, New York: Routledge.
Colla, E. (2007), *Conflicted Antiquities: Egyptology, Egyptomania, Egyptian Modernity*, Durham, NC: Duke University Press.

Collins, D. (2008), *Magic in the Ancient Greek World*, Blackwell Ancient Religions, Malden, MA: Blackwell Publishing.
Collins, P. and L. McNamara (2014), *Discovering Tutankhamun*, Oxford: Ashmolean Museum Press.
Comparetti, D. (1997), *Vergil in the Middle Ages*, Princeton Paperbacks, Princeton, NJ: Princeton University Press.
Connell, R. W. (1990), "An Iron Man: The Body and Some Contradictions of Hegemonic Masculinity", in M. A. Messner and D. F. Sabo (eds), *Sport, Men, and the Gender Order: Critical Feminist Perspectives*, 83–95, Champaign, IL: Human Kinetics Press.
Cook, J. G. (2015), *Crucifixion in the Mediterranean World*, Wissenschaftliche Untersuchungen zum Neuen Testament 327, Tübingen: Mohr Siebeck.
Cope, A. L. (2010), *Black Sabbath and the Rise of Heavy Metal Music*, Burlington: Ashgate.
Cottrell, L. ([1956] 1975), *The Mountains of Pharaoh: 2,000 Years of Pyramid Exploration*, London: Book Club Associates.
Crowley, A. (1913), *Liber CCCXXXIII: The Book of Lies, Which Is Also Falsely Called, Breaks: The Wanderings or Falsifications of The One Thought of Frater Perdurabo, Which Thought Is Itself Untrue*, London: Wieland.
Crowley, A. ([1954] 1988), *Magick Without Tears*, New York: Ordo Templi Orientis.
Cunliffe, B. (1997), *The Ancient Celts*, Oxford: Oxford University Press.
Curley, M. J. (1994), *Geoffrey of Monmouth*, New York: Twayne.
Dairianathan, E. I. (2009), "Vedic Metal and the South Indian Community in Singapore: Problems and Prospects of Identity", *Inter-Asia Cultural Studies* 10: 585–608.
Dairianathan, E. I. (2011), "Soundscapes in Vedic Metal: A Perspective from Singapore", *Perfect Beat* 12: 167–89.
Day, J. (2006), *The Mummy's Curse: Mummymania in the English-speaking World*, London: Routledge.
Deather (2000), "Nile—a very long story", *www.fobiazine.net*, February 28. Available online at: www.fobiazine.net/article/831/nile---a-very-long-story/ (accessed May 25, 2018).
de Buck, A. (1935–1961), *The Egyptian Coffin Texts*. 8 vols, Oriental Institute Publication, Chicago: University of Chicago Press.
de Camp, L. S. (1970), *Lost Continents: The Atlantis Theme in History, Science, and Literature*, New York: Dover.
De Francesco, A. (2013), *The Antiquity of the Italian Nation: The Cultural Origins of a Political Myth in Modern Italy, 1796–1943*, Oxford: Oxford University Press.
Dickinson, B. (2017), *What Does This Button Do?*, London: HarperCollins.
DiGioia, A. and L. Helfrich (2018), "'I'm Sorry, but It's True, You're Bringin' on the Heartache': The Antiquated Methodology of Deena Weinstein", *Metal Music Studies* 4: 365–74.
Dimitris (2015), "HESPERIA interview", *www.metalsoundscapes.com*, June 18. Available online at: www.metalsoundscapes.com/archives/20411/hesperia-interview (accessed February 26, 2019).
Dimitrova, N. M. (2008), *Theoroi and Initiates in Samothrace: The Epigraphical Evidence*, Hesperia Supplement 37, Princeton: The American School of Classical Studies at Athens.
"Dizziness interview" (2013), "House of the Whipcord Zine", *houseofthewhipcordzine.blogspot.com*, July 4. Available online at: http://houseofthewhipcordzine.blogspot.com/2013/07/dizziness-interview_4.html (accessed July 12, 2018).
Djurslev, C. T. (2014), "The Metal King: Alexander the Great in Heavy Metal Music", *Metal Music Studies* 1: 127–41.
Dobschenzki, J. V. (2015), "The Perception of the Middle Ages within German 'Mittelalter Metal': A Medievalist's View", in T.-M. Karjalainen and K. Kärki (eds), *Modern Heavy Metal: Markets, Practices and Cultures*, 113–21, Helsinki: Aalto University.

Bibliography

Donatoni, I. (2018), "Ex Deo—Il mio cuore all'Italia", *www.metalpit.ie*, May 26. Available online at: www.metalpit.it/interviste/ex-deo-il-mio-cuore-allitalia/ (accessed August 30, 2018).

Dr. Metal (2013), "Interview with Tomi Göttlich of REBELLION", *www.metalmeltdown.com*, February 20. Available online at: www.metalmeltdown.com/dr-metals-blog/interviews-rebellion2013 (accessed February 27, 2019).

Dr. Metal (2014), "Today's Show (March 28, 2014)", *www.metalmeltdown.com*, March 27. Available online at: www.metalmeltdown.com/dr-metals-blog/todays-show-march-28-2014 (accessed February 27, 2019).

Draheim, J. (1983), "Vergil in Music", trans. M. Armstrong, in C. Kallendorf (ed.), *Vergil: The Classical Heritage,* v.2, 317–44, New York: Garland Publishing.

Drinkwater, J. F. (1983), *Roman Gaul: The Three Provinces*, Ithaca: Cornell University Press.

DrMorbid (2013), "Triptykon Press Release", *www.triptykon.net*, October 22. Available online at: www.triptykon.net/forum/viewtopic.php?t=2409&sid=dc24cbcc8136934ea92d2cc41573242e (accessed April 1, 2018).

Dunn, S. (2004), "Lands of Fire and Ice: An Exploration of Death Metal Scenes", *Public: New Localities* 29: 107–25.

During, R., M. Muilwijk, S. de Klepper, and R. Saouma (2007), *Cultural Heritage and History in the European Metal Scene*, Utrecht, Netherlands: Belvedere Educational Network.

Early, F. (2003), "The Female Just Warrior Reimagined: From Boudica to Buffy", in F. Early and K. Kennedy (eds), *Athena's Daughters: Television's New Women Warriors*, 55–65, Syracuse, NY: Syracuse University Press.

Ebeling, F. (2007), *The Secret History of Hermes Trismegistus: Hermeticism from Ancient to Modern Times*, trans. D. Lorton, Ithaca and London: Cornell University Press.

Edmonds III, R. (2011), "Who Are You? A Brief History of the Scholarship", in R. Edmonds III (ed.), *The "Orphic" Gold Tablets and Greek Religion: Further Along the Path*, 3–14, Cambridge: Cambridge University Press.

Ekeroth, D. (2006), *Swedish Death Metal*, New York: Bazillion Points Books.

Elflein, D. (2013), "Overcome the Pain: Rhythmic Transgression in Heavy Metal Music", in J. H. Hoogstad and B. S. Pedersen (eds), *Off Beat: Pluralizing Rhythm*, 71–88, Amsterdam: Rodopi.

Eliot, T. S. (1945), "What Is a Classic?" in F. Kermode (ed.), *Selected Prose of T. S. Eliot*, (1975), 115–31, New York: Harvest Books.

Eluveitie.ch (2004), "Lupii Daciei", Available online at: http://eluveitie.ch/en/_index.php?view=press&id=34&lang=en (accessed July 27, 2018).

Encyclopaedia Metallum: The Metal Archives, www.metal-archives.com/ (accessed February 28, 2019).

"Eparistera Daimones" ("n.d."), *www.triptykon.net*, Available online at: www.triptykon.net/forum/viewtopic.php?t=1349 (accessed April 1, 2018).

Erdmann, E. (2007), "Geschichtsbewußtsein—Geschichtskultur. Ein ungeklärtes Verhältnis", *Geschichte, Politik und ihre Didaktik* 35: 186–95.

Erik M. (2013), "The Best '(Gothic) Beauty and the Beast' Albums", *metalstorm.net*, December 3. Available online at: www.metalstorm.net/users/list.php?list_id=2885&page=&message_id= (accessed May 31, 2018).

"Ex Deo—Out of God" (2014), *facebook.com*, December 17. Available online at: m.facebook.com/exdeo/photos/a.232835517041/10152916024362042/?type=3&theater (accessed February 28, 2019).

Falzon, D. (2012), "Ex Deo", *exclaim.ca*, September 25. Available online at: http://exclaim.ca/music/article/ex_deo (accessed August 30, 2018).

Farley, H. (2009), "Demons, Devils and Witches: The Occult in Heavy Metal Music", in G. Bayer (ed.), *Heavy Metal Music in Britain*, 73–88, Farnham and Burlington: Ashgate.

Farrell, J. and M. C. J. Putnam, eds. (2014), *A Companion to Vergil's* Aeneid *and Its Tradition*, Malden: Wiley-Blackwell.

Farron, S. (1980), "The Aeneas-Dido Episode as an Attack on Aeneas' Mission and Rome", *Greece & Rome* 27: 34–47.
Fayant, M.-C. (2014), *Hymnes Orphiques*, Collection des Universités de France. Série grecque, 509, Paris: Les Belles Lettres.
Fee, C. R. (2001), *Gods, Heroes, & Kings: The Battle for Mythic Britain*, Oxford: Oxford University Press.
Feldherr, A. (1995), "Ships of State: *Aeneid* 5 and Augustan Circus Spectacle", *Classical Antiquity* 14: 245–65.
Finn, M. (2013), *Blood & Thunder: The Life and Art of R. E. Howard*, Lexington, KY: R. E. Howard Foundation Press.
Fiori, U. (1984), "Rock Music and Politics in Italy", trans. M. Burgoyne, *Popular Music* 4: 261–77.
Fischer, T. G. (2000), *Are You Morbid? Into the Pandemonium of Celtic Frost*, London: Sanctuary Publishing.
Fischer, T. G. (2009), *Only Death Is Real: An Illustrated History of Hellhammer and Early Celtic Frost, 1981–1985*, with M. E. Ain. Brooklyn: Bazillion Point Books.
Fischer, T. G. (2013), "Reply to DrMorbid (2013)", *www.triptykon.net*, October 24. Available online at: www.triptykon.net/forum/viewtopic.php?t=2409&sid= dc24cbcc8136934ea92d2cc41573242e (accessed April 1, 2018).
Fitzgerald, W. (2014), "Vergil in Music", in J. Farrell and M. C. J. Putnam (eds), *A Companion to Vergil's* Aeneid *and its Tradition*, 341–52, Malden, MA: Wiley-Blackwell.
Fitzpatrick, A. P. (1996), "'Celtic' Iron Age Europe: The Theoretical Basis", in P. Graves-Brown, S. Jones, and C. Gamble (eds), *Cultural Identity and Archaeology: The Construction of European Communities*, 238–55, New York: Routledge.
Fleischhack, M. (2015), *Narrating Ancient Egypt: The Representation of Ancient Egypt in Nineteenth-century and Early-twentieth-century Fantastic Fiction*, Frankfurt am Mainz: Peter Lang Edition.
Fletcher, K. F. B. (2014), *Finding Italy: Travel, Nation, and Colonization in Vergil's* Aeneid, Ann Arbor: University of Michigan Press.
Fletcher, K. F. B. (2015), "The Metal Age: The Use of Classics in Heavy Metal Music", *Amphora* 12: 1, 8–9.
Fletcher, K. F. B. (2019), "Classical Antiquity, Heavy Metal Music, and European Identity," in M. Fernando Lozano Gómez (ed.), *The Present of Antiquity: Reception, Recovery, Reinvention of the Ancient World in Current Popular Culture*, Besançon.
Fleury-Ilet, B. (1996), "The Identity of France: Archetypes in Iron Age Studies", in P. Graves-Brown, S. Jones, and C. Gamble (eds), *Cultural Identity and Archaeology: The Construction of European Communities*, 196–208, New York: Routledge.
Foka, A. (2011), "Beauty and the Beast", *Classica et Mediaevalia* 62: 51–80.
Foka, A. (2014), "Material Girls: Humor and Female Professional Seduction in Greek Literature and Culture", *EuGeSta: Journal of Gender Studies in Antiquity* 4: 81–105.
Foka, A. (2015a), "Queer Heroes and Action Heroines", in M. G. Cornelius (ed.), *Blood, Sand, and Theory: Critical Considerations of Starz' Spartacus*, 186–206, Jefferson, NC: McFarland.
Foka, A. (2015b), "Redefining Gender in Sword and Sandal: The New Action Heroine in Spartacus (2010–13)", *Journal of Popular Film and Television* 43: 39–49.
Foley, H. P. (2001), *Female Acts in Greek Tragedy*, Martin Classical Lectures, Princeton, NJ: Princeton University Press.
Ford, L. (2016), *Living Like a Runaway*, New York: Dey St.
Fotiou, E. (2014), "'We Are the Indians of Greece': Indigeneity and Religious Revitalization in Modern Greece", *CrossCurrents* 64: 219–35.
Franklin, J. L. Jr. (1997), "Vergil at Pompeii: A Teacher's Aid," *Classical Journal* 92: 175–84.

Bibliography

Freeborn, R. (2010), "A Selective Discography of Heavy Metal Music", *Music Library Association Notes* 66: 840–50.
Friesen, B. K. and J. S. Epstein (1994), "Rock 'n' Roll Ain't Noise Pollution: Artistic Conventions and Tensions in the Major Subgenres of Heavy Metal Music", *Popular Music and Society* 18: 1–17.
Frith, S. (1996), *Performing Rites: On the Value of Popular Music*, Cambridge, MA: Harvard University Press.
Fulk, R. D., R. E. Bjork, and J. D. Niles (2008), *Klaeber's Beowulf and the Fight at Finnsburg*, Toronto: University of Toronto Press.
Furley, W. D. (2011), "Homeric and Un-Homeric Hexameter Hymns: A Question of Type", in A. Faulkner (ed.), *The Homeric Hymns: Interpretative Essays*, 206–31, New York: Oxford University Press.
Furley, W. D. and J. M. Bremer (2001a), *Greek Hymns: Volume 1. The Texts in Translation*, Tübingen: Mohr Siebeck.
Furley, W. D. and J. M. Bremer (2001b), *Greek Hymns. Vol II. Greek Texts and Commentary*, Tübingen: Mohr Siebeck.
Gardell, M. (2003), *Gods of the Blood: The Pagan Revival and White Separatism*, Durham: Duke University Press.
Gardenour W. B. S. (2015), "Through the Looking Glass Darkly: Medievalism, Satanism, and the Dark Illumination of the Self in the Aesthetics of Black Metal", *Helvete* 2: 13–27.
Gascot-Hernández, B J. (2015), "Power in Heavy Metal: A Positive Evaluation", in T.-M. Karjalainen and K. Kärki (eds), *Modern Heavy Metal: Markets, Practices, and Cultures*, 95–102, Helsinki: Aalto University & Turku: International Institute for Popular Culture.
Geegor (2015), "Interview with Gunther Theys (Ancient Rites)", *metalinvader.net*, April 19. Available online at: www.metalinvader.net/interview-with-gunther-theys-ancient-rites (accessed April 9, 2018).
Ghita, C. and G. Andrikopoulos (2009), "Total War and Total Realism: A Battle for Antiquity in Computer Game History", in D. Lowe and K. Shahabudin (eds), *Classics for All: Reworking Antiquity in Mass Culture*, 109–27, Newcastle-upon-Tyne: Cambridge Scholars Publishing.
Γιαννακόπουλος, Π. (2017), "Θερθώναξ (KAWIR) στο Rock Overdose", *rockoverdose.gr*, February 12. Available online at: www.rockoverdose.gr/θερθώναξ-kawir-στο-rock-overdose-το-νέο-μας-άλμπουμ-α/ (accessed July 19, 2018).
Gibson, R. K. (1999), "Aeneas as *hospes* in Vergil, *Aeneid* 1 and 4", *Classical Quarterly* 49: 184–202.
Giddens, A. (1990), *The Consequences of Modernity*, Stanford, CA: Stanford University Press.
Giomi, E., S. Sansonetti and A. L. Tota (2013), "Women and Girls as Subjects of Media's Attention and Advertisement Campaigns: The Situation in Europe, Best Practices and Legislations", *www.europarl.europa.ed/studies*. Available online at: www.europarl.europa.eu/RegData/etudes/etudes/join/2013/474442/IPOL-FEMM_ET(2013)474442_EN.pdf (accessed: January 25, 2019).
Γιώργος (2016), "Archaeos", *anthem.gr*, April 7. Available online at: www.anthem.gr/2470/sunenteuxh-archaeos/ (accessed July 15, 2018).
Giusti, E. (2018), "Romans Go . . . Where?; On Being an Italian Classicist", *Eidolon*, October 11. Available online at: www.eidolon.pub/romans-go-where-7641ef2a43b2 (accessed February 27, 2019).
Gradel, I. (2002), *Emperor Worship and Roman Religion*, Oxford: Oxford University Press.
Graf, F. (2009), "Serious Singing: The Orphic Hymns as Religious Texts", *Kernos* 22: 169–82.
Graf, F. and S. I. Johnston (2013), *Ritual Texts for the Afterlife: Orpheus and the Bacchic Gold Tablets*, Abingdon and New York: Routledge.
Granholm, K. (2005), *Embracing the Dark: The Magic Order of Dragon Rouge—Its Practice in Dark Magic and Meaning Making*, Åbo: Åbo Akademi University Press.

Bibliography

Granholm, K. (2011a), "'Sons of Northern Darkness': Heathen Influences in Black Metal and Neofolk Music", *Numen* 58: 514–44.

Granholm, K. (2011b), "Locating the West: Problematizing the *Western* in Western Esotericism and Occultism", in H. Bogdan and G. Djurdjevic (eds), *Occultism in Global Perspective*, 17–36, London: Equinox.

Granholm, K. (2012), "Metal and Magic: The Intricate Relation between the Metal Band Therion and the Magic Order *Dragon Rouge*", in C. M. Cusack and A. Norman (eds), *Handbook of New Religions and Cultural Production*, 553–81, Leiden and Boston: Brill.

Granholm, K. (2013), "Ritual Black Metal: Popular Music as Occult Mediation and Practice", *Correspondences* 1: 5–33.

Granholm, K. (2014), *Dark Enlightenment: The Historical, Sociological, and Discursive Contexts of Contemporary Esoteric Magic*, Leiden and Boston: Brill.

Gransden, K. W. (1996), *Virgil in English*, New York: Penguin Books.

Greenbaum, D. G. (2016), *The Daimon in Hellenistic Astrology: Origins and Influence*, Ancient Magic and Divination 11, Leiden: Brill.

Griffiths, J. G. (1970), *Plutarch's De Iside et Osiride*, Cardiff: University of Wales Press.

Griffiths, P., M. Lindley and I. Zannos (2001), "Microtone", in *Grove Music Online at: Oxford Music Online*. Available online at: www.oxfordmusiconline/subscriber/article/grove/music/18616 (accessed May 8, 2018).

Guilhou, N. (1989), *La Vieillesse des Dieux*, Publications de la recherche/ Université de Montpellier, Montpellier: Université de Montpellier.

Guilhou, N. (2010), "Myth of the Heavenly Cow", in J. Dielemann and W. Wendrich (eds), *UCLA Encyclopedia of Egyptology*, Los Angeles: http://escholarship.org/uc/item/2vh551hn (accessed May 8, 2018).

Gunn, J. (2007), "Dark Admissions: Gothic Subculture and the Ambivalence of Misogyny and Resistance", in L. M. E. Goodlad and M. Bibby (eds), *Goth: Undead Subculture*, 41–64, Durham, NC: Duke University Press.

Guthrie, W. K. C. (1952), *Orpheus and Greek Religion: A Study of the Orphic Movement*, London: Methuen & Co.

Gutting, E. (2006), "Marriage in the *Aeneid*: Venus, Vulcan, and Dido", *Classical Philology* 101: 263–79.

Haenfler, R. (2013), *Goths, Gamers, and Grrrls: Deviance and Youth Subcultures*, 2nd edn, New York: Oxford University Press.

Hagen, R. (2011), "Musical Style, Ideology, and Mythology in Norwegian Black Metal", in J. Wallach, H. M. Berger, and P. D. Greene (eds), *Metal Rules the Globe: Heavy Metal Music around the World*, 180–99, Durham, NC: Duke University Press.

Haining, P. (1990), *Weird Tales: A Selection, in Facsimile, of the Best from the World's Most Famous Fantasy Magazine*, New York: Caroll & Graf.

Håkansson, H. (2012), "Alchemy of the Ancient Goths: Johannes Bureus' Search for the Lost Wisdom of Scandinavia", *Early Science & Medicine* 17: 500–22.

Hall, S. (2007), "An Iron Harp Played through a Marshall Amp", *The Cimmerian* 4: 4–11.

Halnon, K. B. (2006), "Heavy Metal Carnival and Dis-Alienation: The Politics of Grotesque Realism", *Symbolic Interaction* 29: 33–48.

Hanegraaff, W. J. (2012), *Esotericism and the Academy: Rejected Knowledge in Western Culture*, Cambridge: Cambridge University Press.

Haraway, D. (1997), *Modest_Witness@Second_Millenium.FemaleMan©_Meets_OncoMouse: Feminism and Technoscience*, New York: Routledge.

Hardie, P. (1986), *Virgil's* Aeneid: *Cosmos and Imperium*, Oxford: Oxford University Press.

Hardie, P. (2014), *The Last Trojan Hero: A Cultural History of Virgil's* Aeneid, New York: IB Tauris.

Hardwick, L. (2003), *Reception Studies*, Oxford: Oxford University Press.

Hardwick, L. and C. Stray, eds. (2008), *A Companion to Classical Receptions*, Malden, MA: Wiley-Blackwell.

Bibliography

Harms, D. and J. W. Gonce III (2003), *The Necronomicon Files: The Truth Behind Lovecraft's Legend*, Revised and expanded edition, Boston: Weiser Books.
Harrell, J. (1994), "The Poetics of Destruction: Death Metal Rock", *Popular Music and Society* 18: 91–103.
Harris, K. (2000), "'Roots'? The Relationship between the Global and the Local within the Extreme Metal Scene", *Popular Music* 19: 13–30.
Harrison, J. (1908), *Prolegomena to the Study of Greek Religion*, Cambridge: Cambridge University Press.
Harrison, L. M. (2010), "Factory Music: How the Industrial Geography and Working-Class Environment of Post-War Birmingham Fostered the Birth of Heavy Metal", *Journal of Social History* 44: 145–58.
Harrison, S. J. (1990), "Some Views of the *Aeneid* in the Twentieth Century", in S. J. Harrison (ed.), *Oxford Readings in Vergil's* Aeneid, 1–20, Oxford: Oxford University Press.
Harrison, T. (2003), "Upside Down and Back to Front: Herodotus and the Greek Encounter with Egypt", in R. Matthews and C. Roemer (eds), *Ancient Perspectives on Egypt*, 145–55, London: UCL Press.
Harten, S. (2000), "Archaeology and the Unconscious: Hegel, Egyptomania, and the Legitimation of Orientalism", in W. Seipel (ed.), *Ägyptomanie. Europäische Ägyptenimagination von der Antike bis heute*, 323–28, Vienna; Milano: Kunsthistorisches Museum Wien.
Hartman, S. (2008), "Venus in Two Acts", *Small Axe* 12: 1–14.
Harvey, D. (1990), *The Condition of Post-Modernity: An Enquiry into the Origins of Cultural Change*, Oxford: Blackwell.
Haslam, M. W. (1993), "Callimachus' Hymns", in A. M. Harder, R. F. Regtuit, and G. C. Wakker (eds), *Callimachus*, Hellenistica Groningana, 111–25, Groningen: Egbert Forsten.
Hawes, W. (2009), *Caligula and the Fight for Artistic Freedom: Making, Marketing and Impact of the Bob Guccione´s Film*, Jefferson, NC: McFarland & Company.
Hedrick, C. (2000), *History and Silence: The Purge and Rehabilitation of Memory in Late Antiquity*, Austin: University of Texas Press.
Heesch, F. (2010), "Metal for Nordic Men? Amon Amarth´s Representation of Vikings", in N. Scott and I. von Helden (eds), *The Metal Void: First Gatherings*, 71–80, Oxford: Inter-Disciplinary Press.
Heesch, F. and N. N. Scott, eds. (2016), *Heavy Metal, Gender and Sexuality: Interdisciplinary Approaches*, New York: Routledge.
Heinze, R. (1993), *Virgil's Epic Technique*, trans. H. and D. Harvey and F. Richardson, Berkeley: University of California Press.
Hellenic Black Metal Front, http://hellenicblackmetalfront.blogspot.com/ (accessed February 28, 2019).
Heritage, G. (2016), "'It's Like a Mach Piece, Really': Critiquing the Neo-Classical Aesthetic of '80s Heavy Metal Music", in A. R. Brown, K. Spracklen, K. Kahn-Harris, and N. W. R. Scott (eds), *Global Metal Music and Culture: Current Directions in Metal Studies*, 50–67, New York: Routledge.
Hesperia Home Page (2015), "The 5th HESPERIA's album titled 'METALLVM ITALICVM' (Aeneidos … pars IV) is ready", *www.scena-italica.org*, January 25. Available online at: www.scena-italica.org/Hesperia/ENG/pages/novae.htm (accessed February 28, 2019).
HesperiaOfficial (2015), "METALLVM ITALICVM I (Album Version)", *YouTube.com*, July 18. Available online at: www.youtube.com/watch?v=egd2qZqSoIg (accessed February 28, 2019).
Hickam, B. (2014), "Amalgamated Anecdotes: Perspectives on the History of Metal Music and Culture Studies", *Metal Music Studies* 1: 5–23.
Highet, G. (1972), *The Speeches in Vergil's* Aeneid, Princeton: Princeton University Press.
Hill, G. (2006), *The Strange Sound of Cthulhu: Music Inspired by the Writings of H. P. Lovecraft*, Music Street Journal.

Hill, R. L. (2011), "Is Emo Metal? Gendered Boundaries and New Horizons in the Metal Community", *Journal for Cultural Research* 15: 297–313.

Hill, R. L. (2015), "Using Women's Listening Pleasure to Challenge the Notion of Hard Rock and Metal as 'Masculine' Music'", in T.-M. Karjalainen and K. Kärki (eds), *Modern Heavy Metal: Markets, Practices and Cultures*, 240–46, Helsinki: Aalto University & Turku: International Institute for Popular Culture.

Hill, R. L. (2016), "Masculine Pleasure? Women's Encounters with Hard Rock and Metal Music", in A. R. Brown, K. Spracklen, K. Kahn-Harris, and N. W. R. Scott (eds), *Global Metal Music and Culture: Current Directions in Metal Studies*, 277–94, New York and Abingdon: Routledge.

Hill, R. L. (2018), "Metal and Sexism", *Metal Music Studies* 4: 265–79.

Hill, R. L., C. Lucas, and G. Riches (2015), "Metal and Marginalization: Researching at the Edges of Exteriority", *Metal Music Studies* 1: 295–301.

Hingley, R., and C. Unwin (2006), *Boudica: Iron Age Warrior Queen*, London: Hambledon Continuum.

Hjelm, T., K. Kahn-Harris, and M. LeVine, eds. (2013a), *Heavy Metal: Controversies and Countercultures*, Bristol, CT: Equinox Publishing.

Hjelm, T., K. Kahn-Harris, and M. LeVine (2013b), "Introduction: Heavy Metal as Controversy and Counterculture", in T. Hjelm, K. Kahn-Harris, and M. LeVine (eds), *Heavy Metal: Controversies and Countercultures*, 1–14, Bristol, CT: Equinox.

Hoad, C. (2017), "Slashing Through the Boundaries: Heavy Metal Fandom, Fan Fiction and Girl Cultures", *Metal Music Studies* 3: 5–22.

Höcker, C. (2003), "Tarpeium Saxum", in H. Cancik and H. Schneider (eds), *Der Neue Pauly, Enzyklopädie der Antike*, 755, Stuttgart: J. B. Metzler.

Holopainen, T. (2013), "Interview—Cristiano Borchi & Francesco Bucci (Stormlord", *www.metal-temple.com*, October 23. Available online at: http://www.metal-temple.com/site/catalogues/entry/musicians/interview-cristiano.htm (accessed February 28, 2019).

Homer (1925), *Iliad, Volume II: Books 13–24*, trans. A. T. Murray, rev. by W. F. Wyatt, Loeb Classical Library 171, Cambridge, MA: Harvard University Press.

Homer (1987), *The Iliad: A New Prose Translation*, trans. M. Hammond, Penguin Classics, Harmondsworth, Middlesex: Penguin.

Hoppenstand, G. (2013), "On Pulp Fiction and *Weird Tales*", in G. Hoppestand (ed.), *Pulp Fiction of the '20s and '30s*, xiii–xxvii, Ipswich, MA: Salem Press.

Hornung, E. (1980), *Das Buch von den Pforten des Jenseits: nach den Versionen des Neuen Reiches. Teil II: Übersetzung und Kommentar*, Ægyptiaca Helvetica 8. Geneva: Editions de Belles-Lettres.

Hornung, E. ([1997] 1999), *The Ancient Egyptian Books of the Afterlife*, Ithaca, NY; London: Cornell University Press.

Hornung, E. (2001), *The Secret Lore of Egypt: Its Impact on the West*, Ithaca, NY: Cornell University Press.

Horsfall, N. (1990), "Dido in the Light of History", in S. J. Harrison (ed.), *Oxford Readings in Vergil's Aeneid*, 127–44, Oxford: Oxford University Press.

Howard, R. E. (1963), *The Dark Man and Others*, New York: Lancer Books.

Howard, R. E. (2002), *The Coming of Conan the Cimmerian*, New York: Del Rey.

Howard, R. E. (2008), *The Horror Stories of R. E. Howard*, New York: Ballantine Books.

Humbert, J.-M. and C. A. Price (2003), *Imhotep Today: Egyptianizing Architecture*, Encounters with Ancient Egypt, London: UCL Press.

"Ice Maiden (Interviewer) & Bucci, F. (Interviewee)" (2000), "Metal-Rules.com interview with Francesco Bucci, bass player for Stormlord", *www.metal-rules.com*. Available online at: http://www.metal-rules.com/interviews/Stormlord.htm (accessed: February 27, 2019).

"Interview with Christofer Johnsson from Therion" (2004), *alternative-zine.com*, May 3. Available online at: http://alternative-zine.com/interviews/en/6 (accessed April 1, 2018).

Bibliography

J. P. (2002), "Interview with Heimdall guitarist, Fabio Calluori", *www.metal-rules.com*. Available online at: www.metal-rules.com/interviews/heimdall.htm (accessed: August 30, 2018).

James (2017), "Maurizio Iacono of Ex Deo & Kataklysm", *moshville.co.uk*, February 19. Available online at: www.moshville.co.uk/interview/2017/02/interview-maurizio-iacono-of-ex-deo-kataklysm/ (accessed August 30, 2018).

Jankulak, K. (2010), *Geoffrey of Monmouth*, Cardiff: University of Wales Press.

Jenkins, T. E. (2015), *Antiquity Now: The Classical World in the Contemporary American Imagination*, Cambridge: Cambridge University Press.

Jenks, C. (2003), *Transgression*, London: Routledge.

Johnson, M. (2012), *Boudicca*, Ancients in Action, London: Bloomsbury.

Johnston, S. I. (2010), "Whose Gods are These? A Classicist Looks at Neopaganism", in F. Prescendi and Y. Volokhine (eds), *Dans le Laboratoire de l'Historien des Religions: Mélanges offerts à Philippe Borgeaud*, 123–33, Geneva: Labor et Fides.

Jones, M. E. (1996), *The End of Roman Britain*, Ithaca, NY: Cornell University Press.

Jones, S. (2006), *Antonio Gramsci*, London: Routledge.

Jones, T. (2018), "The fascist movement that has brought Mussolini back to the mainstream", *The Guardian*, February 22. Available online at: www.theguardian.com/news/2018/feb/22/casapound-italy-mussolini-fascism-mainstream (accessed February 27, 2019).

Jordan, P. (2006), "Esoteric Egypt", in G. G. Fagan (ed.), *Archaeological Fantasies: How Pseudoarchaeology Misrepresents the Past and Misleads the Public*, 109–28, London; New York: Routledge.

Joshi, S. T. (2013), *I Am Providence: The Life and Times of H. P. Lovecraft*, 2 vols. New York: Hippocampus Press.

Jost, M. (2003), "Mystery Cults in Arcadia", in M. B. Cosmopoulos (ed.), *Greek Mysteries: The Archaeology and Ritual of Ancient Greek Secret Cults*, 143–68, London: Routledge.

Kahn-Harris, K. (2007), *Extreme Metal: Music and Culture on the Edge*, Oxford and New York: Berg.

Kailuweit, T. (2005), *Dido—Didon—Didone: eine kommentierte Bibliographie zum Dido-Mythos in Literatur und Musik*, Frankfurt am Main: P. Lang.

Kallendorf, C. (1989), *In Praise of Aeneas: Virgil and Epideictic Rhetoric in the Early Italian Renaissance*, Hanover: University Press of New England.

Kallendorf, C. (2007), *The Other Virgil: "Pessimistic" Readings of the* Aeneid *in Early Modern Culture*, Oxford: Oxford University Press.

Karjalainen, T.-M. and K. Kärki, eds. (2015), *Modern Heavy Metal: Markets, Practices, and Cultures*, Helsinki: Aalto University.

"Karl Sanders on Nilechat" (2015), *www.nilechat.net*, "n.d." Available online at: www.nilechat.net/phpBB3/viewtopic.php?f=25&t=20835 (accessed June 6, 2015).

"Karl Sanders on Nile Tour Shirts: 'Consumers Deserve No Less'" (2008), *www.blabbermouth.net*, March 5. Available online at: www.blabbermouth.net/news/K.-sanders-on-nile-tour-shirts-consumers deserve-no-less/ (accessed May 8, 2018).

"Karl Sanders on Songwriting" ("n.d."), *www.nilechat.net*. Available online at: www.nilechat.net/phpBB3/viewtopic.php?f=25&t=20835 (accessed June 6, 2015).

Karpozilos, K. (2018), "Golden Dawn: From the Margins of Greece to the Forefront of Europe", in E. Doxiadis and A. Placas (eds), *Living Under Austerity: Greek Society in Crisis*, 67–89, New York: Berghahn Books.

Kartheus, W. (2015), "The 'Other' as Projection Screen: Authenticating Heroic Masculinity in War-themed Heavy Metal Music Videos", *Metal Music Studies* 1: 319–40.

Kegan, Y. (2015), *Subgenres of the Beast: A Heavy Metal Guide*, Lulu.com.

Kehoe, P. E. (1989), "Was Book 5 Once in a Different Place in the *Aeneid*?" *American Journal of Philology* 110: 246–63.

Keith, A. M. (2000), *Engendering Rome: Women in Latin Epic*, Roman Literature and Its Contexts, Cambridge: Cambridge University Press.

Kennedy, D. F. (1992), "'Augustan' and 'Anti-Augustan': Reflections of Terms of Reference", in A. Powell (ed.), *Roman Poetry and Propaganda in the Age of Augustus*, 26–58, London: Bristol Classical Press.

Kennedy, D. F. (2006), "Afterword: The Uses of Reception", in C. Martindale and R. F. Thomas (eds), *Classics and the Uses of Reception*, 288–93, Malden, MA; Oxford: Blackwell.

Keppie, L. J. F. (1984), *The Making of the Roman Army*, London: Batsford.

Klypchak, B. (2013), "'How You Gonna See Me Now': Recontextualizing Metal Artists and Moral Panics", in T. T. Hjelm, K. Kahn-Harris and M. LeVine (eds), *Heavy Metal: Controversies and Countercultures*, 36–49, Sheffield and Bristol: Equinox.

Knight, G. (2012), *The Secret Tradition in Arthurian Legend*, Cheltenham: Skylight Press.

Knox, B. M. W. (1950), "The Serpent and the Flame: The Imagery of the Second Book of the *Aeneid*", *The American Journal of Philology* 71: 379–400.

Knox, P. (2017), "In Today's Anti-immigrant Rhetoric, Echoes of Virgil's 'Aeneid'", *The Conversation*, March 20. Available online at: theconversation.com/in-todays-anti-immigrant-rhetoric-echoes-of-virgils-aeneid-74738 (accessed February 27, 2019).

Koronaiou, A., E. Lagos and A. Sakellariou (2015), "Singing for Race and Nation: Fascism and Racism in Greek Youth Music", in P. A. Simpson and H. Druxes (eds), *Digital Media Strategies of the Far-Right in Europe and the United States*, 193–214, London: Lexington Books.

Kosiński, M. (2007), "Blind Guardian—Under the Ice (live in Moscow 2002)", *YouTube.com*, April 8. Available online at: www.youtube.com/watch?v=VYFFivxw56A (accessed May 31, 2018).

Kovacs, G. and C. W. Marshall, eds. (2011), *Classics and Comics*, Oxford: Oxford University Press.

Kovacs, G. and C. W. Marshall, eds. (2016), *Son of Classics and Comics*, Oxford: Oxford University Press.

Krenske, L. and J. McKay (2000), "'Hard and Heavy': Gender and Power in a Heavy Metal Music Subculture", *Gender, Place, and Culture* 7: 287–304.

Lachman, G. (2014), *Aleister Crowley: Magick, Rock and Roll, and the Wickedest Man in the World*, New York: J. P. Tarcher/Penguin.

Lashua, B., K. Spracklen and S. Wagg, eds. (2014), *Sounds and the City: Popular Music, Place and Globalization*, New York: Palgrave Macmillan.

LaVey, A. S. (1969), *The Satanic Bible*, New York: Avon Books.

LaVey, A. S. (1972), *The Satanic Rituals*, New York: Avon Books.

Lilja, E. (2009), *Theory and Analysis of Classic Heavy Metal Harmony*, Publications of the Finnish Music Library Association 136, Helsinki: IAML Finland.

Lindner, M. (2013), "Power Beyond Measure—Caligula, Corruption and Pop Culture", in S. Knippschild and M. García Morcillo (eds), *Seduction & Power: Antiquity in the Visual and Performing Arts*, 211–24. London and New York: Bloomsbury.

Lindner, M. and R. Wieland (2018), "Horus and Zeus Are Playing Tonight—Classical Reception in Heavy Metal Band Names", *New Voices in Classical Reception Studies* 12: 32–46.

Lindsay, H. (1993), *Suetonius. Caligula*, London: Bristol Classical Press.

Liverani, E. (2009), *Da Eschilo ai Virgin Steele: Il mito degli Atridi nella musica contemporanea*, Bologna: Dupress.

Lloyd, A. B. (2010), "The Reception of Pharaonic Egypt in Classical Antiquity", in A. B. Lloyd (ed.), *A Companion to Ancient Egypt*, 1067–85, Malden, MA: Wiley-Blackwell.

Loprieno, A. (1995), *Ancient Egyptian: A Linguistic Introduction*, Cambridge: Cambridge University Press.

Loraux, N. (1987), *Tragic Ways of Killing a Woman*, Cambridge, MA: Harvard University Press.

Lovatt, H. (2013), "The Eloquence of Dido: Exploring Speech and Gender in Virgil's *Aeneid*", *Dictynna* 10: 2–11.

Bibliography

Lovecraft, H. P. (1995), "The History of the *Necronomicon*", in S. T. Joshi (ed.), *Miscellaneous Writings*, 52–3, Sauk City, WI: Arkham House.

Lovecraft, H. P. (1999), *The Call of Cthulhu and Other Weird Stories*, S. T. Joshi (ed.), London: Penguin.

Lovecraft, H. P. (2001), *The Thing on the Doorstep and Other Weird Stories*, S. T. Joshi (ed.), London: Penguin.

Lovecraft, H. P. (2011), *H. P. Lovecraft: The Complete Fiction, With an Introduction by S. T. Joshi*, New York: Barnes & Noble.

Lowe, D. (2009), "Playing With Antiquity: Videogame Receptions of the Classical World", in D. Lowe and K. Shahabudin (eds), *Classics for All: Reworking Antiquity in Mass Culture*, 64–90, Newcastle-upon-Tyne: Cambridge Scholars Publishing.

Lozynsky, Y. (2014), "Ancient Greek Cult Hymns: Poets, Performers and Rituals", Phd Diss., University of Toronto.

LSJ = Liddell, H. G., R. Scott, H. S. Jones, and R. McKenzie (1996), *A Greek-English Lexicon*, Oxford: Clarendon Press.

Lucas, C., M. Deeks, and K. Spracklen (2011), "Grim Up North: Northern England, Northern Europe and Black Metal", *Journal for Cultural Research* 15: 279–95.

Luckhurst, R. (2012), *The Mummy's Curse: The True History of a Dark Fantasy*, Oxford: Oxford University Press.

Lunn-Rockliffe, S. (2010), "Commemorating the Usurper Magnus Maximus: Ekphrasis, Poetry, and History in Pacatus' Panegyric of Theodosius", *Journal of Late Antiquity* 3: 316–36.

Lupton, C. (2003), "'Mummymania' for the Masses—Is Egyptology Cursed by the Mummy's Curse?", in S. MacDonald and M. Rice (eds), *Consuming Ancient Egypt*, 23–46, London: Routledge.

Lyne, R. O. A. M. (1987), *Further Voices in Vergil's Aeneid*, Oxford: Clarendon Press.

Mac Cana, P. (1992), *The Mabinogi*, Cardiff: University of Wales.

MacDonald, S., and M. Rice, eds. (2003), *Consuming Ancient Egypt* (Encounters with Ancient Egypt), London: Routledge.

Maggio, M. (2016), "Enea non era un 'profugo', il suo era un ritorno all'origine", *Il Primato Nazionale*, May 21. Available online at: www.ilprimatonazionale.it/cultura/enea-profugo-origine-45275/ (accessed February 27, 2019).

Maguire, D. (2015), "Determinants of the Production of Heavy Metal Music", *Metal Music Studies* 1: 155–69.

Marco and Luna (2015), "Ars Bellica: The Great Battles of History," arsbellica.it. Available online at: www.arsbellica.it/pagine/chisiamo_eng.htm (accessed February 28, 2019).

Marjenin, P. A. (2014), "The Metal Folk: The Impact of Music and Culture on Folk Metal and the Music of Korpiklaani", MA Thesis, Kent State University, OH.

Martindale, C. (1993), *Redeeming the Text*, Cambridge: Cambridge University Press.

Martindale, C. (2006), "Introduction: Thinking Through Reception", in C. Martindale and R. F. Thomas (eds), *Classics and the Uses of Reception,* 1–13, Malden, MA; Oxford: Blackwell.

Martindale, C. (2013), "Reception—A New Humanism? Receptivity, Pedagogy, the Transhistorical", *Classical Receptions Journal* 5: 169–183.

Martindale, C. and R. F. Thomas, eds. (2006), *Classics and the Uses of Reception*, Oxford: Oxford University Press.

Mattar, Y. (2004), "Evilized/Winterheart's Guild", *Popular Music and Society* 27: 536–38.

Matthews, J. F. (1975), *Western Aristocracies and Imperial Court: A.D. 364–425*, Oxford: University Press.

Matthijssens, V. (2012), "Ex Deo", lordsofmetal.nl, available online at: www.lordsofmetal.nl/en/interviews/view/id/4486 (accessed July 30, 2018).

Mayer, A. and J. M. Timberlake (2014), "'The Fist in the Face of God': Heavy Metal Music and Decentralized Cultural Diffusion", *Sociological Perspectives* 57: 27–51.

Bibliography

McClary, S. ([1991] 2002), *Feminine Endings: Music, Gender, Sexuality*, Minneapolis: University of Minnesota Press.

McCormick, M. (1986), *Eternal Victory: Triumphal Rulership in Late Antiquity, Byzantium, and the Early Medieval West*, Cambridge: Cambridge University Press.

McGeough, K. M. (2015), *The Ancient Near East in the Nineteenth Century: Appreciations and Appropriations*, 3 vols., Sheffield: Sheffield Phoenix Press.

McIver, J. (2009), *To Live Is To Die: The Life and Death of Metallica's Cliff Burton*, London: Jawbone Press.

McLeish, K. (1972), "Dido, Aeneas, and the Concept of 'Pietas'", *Greece & Rome* 19: 127–35.

McLeod, K. (2001), "Bohemian Rhapsodies: Operatic Influences on Rock Music", *Popular Music* 20: 189–203.

McParland, R. (2018), *Myth and Magic in Heavy Metal Music*, Jefferson: McFarland & Company, Inc.

Megaw, J. V. S. and M. R. Megaw (1996), "Ancient Celts and Modern Ethnicity", *Antiquity* 70: 175–81.

Mesiä, S. and P. Ribaldini (2015), "Heavy Metal Vocals: A Terminology Compendium", in T.-M. Karjalainen and K. Kärki (eds), *Modern Heavy Metal: Markets, Practices and Cultures*, 383–92, Helsinki: Aalto University.

Meskell, L. L. (2000), "The Practice and Politics of Archaeology in Egypt", *Annals of the New York Academy of Sciences* 925: 146–69.

Messer, O. (2006), "An Epic Adventure With Bal-Sagoth", *www.metalist.co.il*, May 26. Available online at: www.metalist.co.il/InterviewPrivate.asp?id=168&lang=eng (accessed April 1, 2018).

metalstorm.net (2018), Available online at: www.metalstorm.net/users/list.php?list_id=2885&page=&message_id= (accessed May 31, 2018).

Meyer, M. W., ed. (2007), *The Nag Hammadi Scriptures*, New York: HarperOne.

Midtskogen, R. (2009), "'Count' Regrets Nothing", *burzum.org*, July 4. Available online at: www.burzum.org/eng/library/2009_interview_dagbladet.shtml (accessed July 17, 2018).

Miller, F. and L. L. Varley (1999), *300*, Milwaukie, OR: Dark Horse Comics.

Miniconi, P. (1962), "La joie dans l'*Énéide*", *Latomus* 21: 563–71.

Mitchell-Boyask, R. (2006), "The Marriage of Cassandra and the *Oresteia*: Text, Image, Performance", *Transactions of the American Philological Association* 136(2): 269–97.

Mitchell, D. (2012), *Back Story: A Memoir*, London: HarperCollins.

Mitchell, T. ([1989] 2009), "Orientalism and the Exhibitionary Order", in D. Preziosi (ed.), *The Art of Art History: A Critical Anthology*, 409–23, Oxford; New York: Oxford University Press.

Moberg, M. (2013), "The 'Double Controversy' of Christian Metal", in T. Hjelm, K. Kahn-Harris, and M. LeVine (eds), *Heavy Metal: Controversies and Countercultures*, 83–97, Sheffield; Bristol CT: Equinox.

Moles, J. (1987), "The Tragedy and Guilt of Dido", in M. Whitby, P. Hardie, and M. Whitby (eds), *Homo Viator: Classical Essays for John Bramble*, 153–61, Oak Park, IL: Bolchazy-Carducci Publishers.

Monti, R. C. (1981), *The Dido Episode and the Aeneid: Roman Social and Political Values in the Epic*, Leiden: Brill.

Morand, A-F. (2001), *Études sur les Hymnes Orphiques*, Religions in the Graeco-Roman World, 145, Leiden: Brill.

Morand, A-F. (2015), "Narrative Techniques of the *Orphic Hymns*", in A. Faulkner and O. Hodkinson (eds), *Hymnic Narrative and the Narratology of Greek Hymns*, Mnemosyne Supplements, Monographs on Greek and Latin language and literature, 384, 209–23, Leiden: Brill.

Morbid Fog (2015), "Blackened Horde Zine", *blackenedhorde.com*, Available online at: http://blackenedhorde.com/morbid_fog/ (accessed July 8, 2018).

Bibliography

Moreno Garcia, J. C. (2015), "The Cursed Discipline? The Peculiarities of Egyptology at the Turn of the Twenty-First Century", in W. Carruthers (ed.), *Histories of Egyptology: Interdisciplinary Measures*, 50–63, New York; Abingdon: Routledge.

Mørk, G. (2009), "'With my Art I Am the Fist in the Face of God': On Old-School Black Metal", in J. A. Petersen (ed.), *Contemporary Religious Satanism: A Critical Anthology*, 171–98, Aldershot: Ashgate.

Morris, I. (2014), *"War! What Is It Good For? Conflict and the Progress of Civilization from Primates to Robots"*, New York: Farrar, Straus and Giroux.

Moser, S. (2012), *Designing Antiquity: Owen Jones, Ancient Egypt and the Crystal Palace*, New Haven, CT; London: Yale University Press.

Moser, S. (2015), "Legacies of Engagement: The Multiple Manifestations of Ancient Egypt in Public Discourse", in W. Carruthers (ed.), *Histories of Egyptology: Interdisciplinary Measures*, 242–52, New York; Abingdon: Routledge.

Moynihan, M. and D. Søderlind (2003), *Lords of Chaos: The Bloody Rise of the Satanic Metal Underground*, Revised and expanded edition, Los Angeles: Feral House.

MrLechimp (2010), "Ex Deo Storm the Gates of Alesia", *YouTube.com*, October 10. Available online at: www.youtube.com/watch?v=C_4ryClILJ4 (accessed August 30, 2018).

Müller, D. (2013), "Nostalgia in H. P. Lovecraft", in G. Hoppestand (ed.), *Pulp Fiction of the '20s and '30s*, 52–65, Ipswich, MA: Salem Press.

Mulvany, A. (2000), "'Reawakening Pride Once Lost': Indigeneity and European Folk Metal", MA Thesis, Wesleyan University, Middletown, CT.

Mund-Dopchie, M. (2009), *Ultima Thulé: histoire d'un lieu et genèse d'un mythe*, Histoire des idées et critique littéraire 449, Genève: Droz.

Munro, P. (1973), *Die spätägyptischen Totenstelen*. 2 vols, Ägyptologische Forschungen 25, Glückstadt: J. J. Augustin.

Murnane, W. J. (1980), *United with Eternity: A Concise Guide to the Monuments of Medinet Habu*, Chicago: Oriental Institute, University of Chicago.

Napalm Records (2012), "Ex Deo—I, Caligvla | Napalm Records", *YouTube.com*, July 27. Available online at: www.youtube.com/watch?v=SW01sWSPQYY (accessed February 28, 2019).

Nappa, C. (2007), "Unmarried Dido: *Aeneid* 4.550-552", *Hermes* 135: 301–13.

Nederveen Pieterse, J. (2009), *Globalization and Culture: Global Mélange*, 2nd edn, Plymouth, UK: Rowan Littlefield Publishers, Inc.

Neilstein, V. (2008), "Exclusive Interview with Eluveitie Mastermind Chrigel Glanzmann", *www.metalsucks.net*, July 16. Available online at: http://www.metalsucks.net/2008/07/16/exclusive-interview-with-eluveitie-mastermind-chrigel-glanzmann/ (accessed July 27, 2018).

Neiman, S. (2015), *Evil in Modern Thought*, Princeton: Princeton University Press.

"Nile Catacombs" (2015), *www.facebook.com*, May 26. Available online at: www.facebook.com/nilecatacombs/posts/10152823351341016 (accessed May 8, 2018).

"Nile—'Enduring the Eternal Molestation of Flame' video clip!" (2012), *www.nuclearblast.de*, November 30. Available online at: www.nuclearblast.de/en/label/music/band/news/details/2783527.71047.nile-enduring-the-eternal-molestation.html (accessed May 8, 2018).

"Nile Fan Comment" (2015), *www.nilechat.net*, "n.d." Available online at: www.nilechat.net/phpBB3/viewtopic.php?f=1&t=24023 (accessed June 6, 2015).

"Nile's K. Sanders Promises 'No Radical Departure' on Group's Forthcoming Album" (2018), *blabbermouth.net*, March 17. Available online at: www.blabbermouth.net/news/niles-K.-sanders-promises-no-radical-departure-on-groups-forthcoming-album/ (accessed May 11, 2018).

Nilsson, M. (2009), "No Class? Class and Class Politics in British Heavy Metal", in G. Bayer (ed.), *Heavy Metal Music in Britain*, 161–80, Farnham and Burlington: Ashgate.

Nilsson, M. (2016), "Race and Gender in Globalized and Postmodern Metal", in A. R. Brown, K. Spracklen, K. Kahn-Harris, and N. W. R. Scott (eds), *Global Metal Music and Culture: Current Directions in Metal Studies*, 258–71, New York and Abingdon: Routledge.
"Nita Strauss on WE START WARS: 'I've Been Trying To Put This Band Together Since I Started Playing Guitar'" (2017), *blabbermouth.net*, May 8. Available online at: www.blabbermouth.net/news/nita-strauss-on-we-start-wars-ive-been-trying-to-put-this-band-together-since-i-started-playing-guitar/ (accessed July 15, 2018).
Nixon, C. E. V. and B. S. Rodgers (1994), *In Praise of Later Roman Emperors: the Panegyrici Latini: Introduction, Translation, and Historical Commentary*, Berkeley: University of California Press.
Nony, D. (1986), *Caligula*, Paris: Fayard.
Norman, J. (2013), "'Sounds Which Filled Me With An Indefinable Dread': The Cthulhu Mythopoeia of H. P. Lovecraft in 'Extreme' Metal", in D. Simmons (ed.), *New Critical Essays on H. P. Lovecraft*, 193–208, New York: Palgrave Macmillan.
Nugent, S. G. (1999), "The Women of the *Aeneid*: Vanishing Bodies, Lingering Voices", in C. Perkell (ed.), *Reading Vergil's* Aeneid: *An Interpretive Guide*, 251–70, Norman, OK: University of Oklahoma Press.
Nyord, R. (2009), *Breathing Flesh: Conceptions of the Body in the Ancient Egyptian Coffin Texts*, CNI publications 37, Copenhagen: Museum Tusculanum Press.
O'Hara, J. J. (2006), "Review of Syed, *Vergil's* Aeneid *and the Roman Self*", *American Journal of Philology* 127: 317–20.
O'Neill, A. (2018), *A History of Heavy Metal*, London: Headline.
OCD = Hornblower, S. and A. Spawforth, eds. (2003), *The Oxford Classical Dictionary*, 3rd rev. edn, Oxford: Oxford University Press.
Oksala, P. (1962), "Das Aufblühen des römischen Epos: Berührungen zwischen der Ariadne-Episode Catulls und der Dido-Geschichte Vergils", *Arctos* 3: 167–97.
OLD = Glare, P. G. W., ed. (2012), *Oxford Latin Dictionary*, Oxford: Oxford University Press.
Olson, B. H. (2008), "I Am the Black Wizards: Multiplicity, Mysticism and Identity in Black Metal Music and Culture", MA Thesis, Bowling Green State University.
Olson, B. H. (2011), "Voice of our Blood: National Socialist Discourses in Black Metal", *Popular Music History* 6: 135–49.
Otis, B. (1963), *Virgil: A Study in Civilized Poetry*, Oxford: Oxford University Press.
Overell, R. (2013), "'[I] hate girls and emo[tion]s': Negotiating Masculinity in Grindcore Music", in T. Hjelm, K. Kahn-Harris, and M. LeVine (eds), *Heavy Metal: Controversies and Countercultures*, 201–27, Bristol, CT: Equinox.
OverkillExposure (2012), "Ex Deo, Kataklysm Frontman Maurizio Iacono: 'If The World Gives Me The Chance, I'll Give It Something It's Never Seen Before'", *www.metalunderground.com*, April 11. Available online at: www.metalunderground.com/news/details.cfm?newsid=79470 (accessed August 30, 2018).
Panoussi, V. (2009), *Greek Tragedy in Vergil's Aeneid: Ritual, Empire, and Intertext*, Cambridge: Cambridge University Press.
Παπαγεωργίου, Μ. (2018), "Κάβειροι-Kawir", *metafysiko.gr*, July. Available online at: www.metafysiko.gr/?p=3024 (accessed July 4, 2018).
Pardo, P. (2013), "After Nine Years, Power Metal Act Heimdall Return with Aeneid", *www.seaoftranquility.org*, March 3. Available online at: www.seaoftranquility.org/article.php?sid=2421 (accessed February 28, 2019).
Parkinson, R. B. (1999), *Cracking Codes: The Rosetta Stone and Decipherment*, London: British Museum.
Parramore, L. L. (2008), *Reading the Sphinx: Ancient Egypt in Nineteenth-Century Literary Culture*, New York: Palgrave Macmillan.
Patterson, D. (2013), *Black Metal: Evolution of the Cult*, Port Townsend, WA: Feral House.

Bibliography

Patterson, J. E. (2016), "Getting My Soul Back: Empowerment Narratives and Identities Among Women in Extreme Metal in North Carolina", in A. R. Brown, K. Spracklen, K. Kahn-Harris, and N. W. R. Scott (eds), *Global Metal Music and Culture: Current Directions in Metal Studies*, 245–60, New York and Abingdon: Routledge.
Pease, A. S. (1935), *Publii Vergili Maronis Liber Quartus*, Cambridge, MA: Harvard University Press.
Pendergast, J. S. (1988), "*Nachleben* is Where You Find It", *Classical Journal* 83: 323–5.
Perkell, C. (1999), "Editor's Introduction", in C. Perkell (ed.), *Reading Vergil's* Aeneid: *An Interpretative Guide*, 3–28, Norman: University of Oklahoma Press.
Pertile, L. (2014), "Italian Literature", in R. F. Thomas and J. M. Ziolkowski (eds), *The Virgil Encyclopedia*, v. 2, 674–80, Malden, MA: Wiley-Blackwell.
Pessaro, F. (2018), "How Nile Channeled Power of Egyptian Gods Game-Changing 'Catacombs' Album", *www.revolvermag.com*, April 26. Available online at: www.revolvermag.com/music/how-nile-channeled-power-egyptian-gods-game-changing-catacombs-album (accessed May 11, 2018).
Petrov, A. (1995), "The Sound of Suburbia (Death Metal)", *American Book Review* 16: 5.
Phillipov, M. (2006), "None So Vile? Towards an Ethics of Death Metal", *Southern Review* 38: 74–85.
Phillipov, M. (2013), "Extreme Music for Extreme People? Norwegian Black Metal and Transcendent Violence", in T. Hjelm, K. Kahn-Harris, and M. LeVine (eds), *Heavy Metal: Controversies and Countercultures*, 152–65, Sheffield; Bristol, CT: Equinox.
Phillipov, M. (2014), *Death Metal and Music Criticism: Analysis at the Limits*, Lanham: Lexington Books.
Picknett, L., and C. Prince (2003), "Alternative Egypts", in S. MacDonald and M. Rice (eds), *Consuming Ancient Egypt*, 175–93, London: Routledge.
Piotrowska, A. G. (2015), "Scandinavian Heavy Metal as an Intertextual Play with Norse Mythology", in S. A. Wilson (ed.), *Music at the Extremes: Essays on Sounds Outside the Mainstream*, 101–14, Raleigh, NC: McFarland.
Pitch Black Records (2015), "Sacred Blood—To Lands No Man Hath Seen (Official Video)", *YouTube.com*, October 10. Available online at: www.youtube.com/watch?v=6f1ju6el_r0 (accessed February 28, 2019).
Pitcher, L. V. (2009), "Saying 'Shazam': The Magic of Antiquity in Superhero Comics", *New Voices in Classical Reception Studies* 4: 27–43.
Pittman, S. M. (2010), "What Has Coming Out Meant to Rob Halford", *pollstar.com*, December 10. Available online at: www.pollstar.com/article/what-coming-out-has-meant-to-rob-halford-18367 (accessed August 30, 2018).
Pitzl-Waters, J. (2013), "Greece, The Golden Dawn, and Modern Paganism", *wildhunt.org*, October 3. Available online at: http://wildhunt.org/2013/10/greece-the-golden-dawn-and-modern-paganism.html (accessed July 25, 2018).
Plotkin, F. (1994), *Opera 101: A Complete Guide to Learning and Loving Opera*, New York: Hachette Books.
Pogorzelski, R. J. (2009), "The 'Reassurance of Fratricide' in the *Aeneid*," *American Journal of Philology* 130: 261–89.
Popoff, M. (2004), *The Top 500 Heavy Metal Albums of All Time*, Toronto: ECW Press.
Porliod, G. (2017), "Profughi come Enea: Scappava dalla guerra per cercare un destino migliore, lezione di storia sul mito fondante della nostra civiltà", *La Stampa*, November 11. Available online at: www.lastampa.it/2017/11/11/cronaca/profughi-come-enea- iQ91sxg2NdtAorBem9DBiL/pagina.html (accessed February 27, 2019).
Porter, J. I. (2008), "Reception Studies: Future Prospects", in L. Hardwick and C. Stray (eds), *A Companion to Classical Receptions*, 469–81, Malden, MA; Oxford: Blackwell.
Postclassicisms, *www.postclassicisms.org* (accessed February 28, 2019).

Pozzoli, D. (2007), "High School and Labor Market Outcomes: Italian Graduates", *Giornale degli Economisti e Annali di Economia* 66: 247–94.
Prassa, V. (2008), "KAWIR-THERTHONAX", *www.metalzone.gr*, February 22. Available online at: www.metalzone.gr/interviews/kawir-therthonax (accessed July 20, 2018).
Pratt, M. L. (2008), *Imperial Eyes: Travel Writing and Transculturation*, 2nd edn, New York: Routledge Press.
Puca, F. (1997), "L'*epic metal* e un' 'Achilleide' rock", *Kleos* 2: 107–33.
Purcell, N. J. (2003), *Death Metal Music: The Passion and Politics of a Subculture*, Jefferson, NC: McFarland.
Putnam, M. C. J. (2010), "Some Virgilian Unities", in P. Hardie and H. Moore (eds), *Classical Literary Careers and Their Reception*, 17–38, Cambridge: Cambridge University Press.
Putnam, M. C. J. (2013), *The Humanness of Heroes: Studies in the Conclusion of Virgil's* Aeneid, Amsterdam: Amsterdam University Press.
Raucci, S. (2013), "The Order of the Orgies. Sex and the Cinematic Roman", in M. S. Cyrino (ed.), *Screening Love and Sex in the Ancient World*, 143–55, New York: Palgrave MacMillan.
Reade, J. (2011), "Wallis Budge—For or Against?", in M. D. Ismail (ed.), *Wallis Budge: Magic and Mummies in London and Cairo*, 444–63, Kilkerran, Scotland: Hardinge Simpole.
Rebecca (2017), "Interview: Maurizio Iacono of EX DEO", *midlandsmetalheads.com*, February 28. Available online at: www.midlandsmetalheads.com/interview-maurizio-iacono-of-ex-deo/ (accessed August 30, 2018).
Redford, D. B. (2003), *The Wars in Syria and Palestine of Thutmose III*, Culture and History of the Ancient Near East, Leiden; Boston: Brill.
Reed, J. D. (2007), *Virgil's Gaze: Nation and Poetry in the* Aeneid, Princeton: Princeton University Press.
Reed, J. D. (2010), "Vergil's Roman", in J. Farrell and M. C. J. Putnam (eds), *A Companion to Vergil's Aeneid and its Tradition*, 66–79, Malden: Wiley-Blackwell.
Reesman, B. (2007), "They Will Rise: Metal's Female Ranks on the Move", *bravewords.com*, November 5. Available online at: http://bravewords.com/news/report-grammy-com-metals-female-ranks-on-the- move (accessed May 31, 2018).
Reid, D. M. (2002), *Whose Pharaohs?: Archeology, Museums, and Egyptian National Identity from Napoleon to World War I*, Berkeley; London: University of California Press.
Reinhard, A. (2018), *Archaeogaming: An Introduction to Archaeology in and of Video Games*, New York: Berghahn Books.
Rhys, J. (1908), "All Around the Wrekin", *Y Cymmrodor* 21: 1–62.
Ricciardelli, G. (2000), *Inni Orfici*, Milan: Mondadori.
Richardson, J. (2008), *The Language of Empire: Rome and the Idea of Empire from the Third Century BC to the Second Century AD*, Cambridge: Cambridge University Press.
Richardson, L. (1992), *A New Topographical Dictionary of Ancient Rome*, Baltimore and London: The John Hopkins University Press.
Riches, G. (2015), "Re-conceptualizing Women's Marginalization in Heavy Metal: A Feminist Post-structuralist Perspective", *Metal Music Studies* 1: 263–70.
Riddle, J. E. and T. K. Arnold (1864), *English-Latin Lexicon*. New York: Harper & Brothers.
Riggs, C. (2014), *Unwrapping Ancient Egypt*, London: Bloomsbury.
Riggs, C. (2015), "Discussing Knowledge in the Making", in W. Carruthers (ed.), *Histories of Egyptology: Interdisciplinary Measures*, 129–38, New York; Abingdon: Routledge.
Riggsby, A. M. (2006), *Caesar in Gaul and Rome: War in Words*, Austin: University of Texas Press.
Ritner, R. K. (1993), *The Mechanics of Ancient Egyptian Magical Practice*, Studies in Ancient Oriental Civilization 54, Chicago: Oriental Institute of the University of Chicago.
Rives, J. B. (1999), *Tacitus: Germania*, Oxford: University Press.
Roberts, Byron A. (1998), "Glossary", *www.balsagoth.com*, available online at: www.bal-sagoth.com/glossary.html (accessed April 1, 2018).

Bibliography

Roberts, B. A. (2009a), "Comics, Stories and the Lexicon", *byronbalsagoth.blogspot.com*, December 30. Available online at: http://byronbalsagoth.blogspot.com/2009/12/comics-stories-and-lexicon.html (accessed April 1, 2018).

Roberts, B. A. (2009b), "Thoughts from the Sanctum Sanctorum of Bal-Sagoth", *byronbalsagoth.blogspot.co.uk*, March 9. Available online at: http://byronbalsagoth.blogspot.co.uk/2009/03/popular-misconceptions-1.html (accessed April 1, 2018).

Roberts, B. A. (2015), "Into the Dawn of Storms", in D. M. Ritzlin (ed.), *Swords of Steel*, 12–33, Highland Park, IL: DMR Books.

Roche, H. and K. N. Demetriou, eds. (2017), *Brill's Companion to the Classics, Fascist Italy and Nazi Germany*, Leiden: Brill.

Rogers, B. M. and B. E. Stevens, eds. (2014), *Classical Traditions in Science Fiction*, Oxford: Oxford University Press.

Rogers, B. M. and B. E. Stevens, eds. (2019), *Once and Future Antiquities in Science Fiction and Fantasy*, Bloomsbury Studies in Classical Reception, London, UK: Bloomsbury Academic.

Rollason, D. (2000), *Symeon of Durham. Libellus de Exordio atque Procursu istius hoc est Dunhelmensis Ecclesie*, Oxford Medieval Texts, Oxford: Oxford University Press.

Romm, J. S. (1992), *The Edges of the Earth in Ancient Thought: Geography, Exploration, and Fiction*, Princeton, NJ: Princeton University Press.

Rose, R. (2013), "Interview with Arkadius of SuidAkrA, June 9, 2013 mp3", *YouTube.com*, June 11. Available online at: http://www.youtube.com/watch?v=Ywz76INsAs0 (accessed July 28, 2018).

Rosenberg, E. (2018), "Trump Called Gary Cohn a 'Globalist.' Here's Why Some People Find That Offensive", *Washington Post*, March 9. Available online at: www.washingtonpost.com/news/the-fix/wp/2018/03/09/trump-called-gary- cohn-a-globalist-heres-why-some-people-find-that-offensive/?__twitter_impression=true&__twitter_impression=true&utm_term=.2164e6f7e3ee (accessed February 28, 2019).

Rossi, J. and E. E. Jervell (2013), "To Really Understand Hevibändi, It Helps to Know the Language", *Wall Street Journal*, June: 4.

Rudd, N. (1990), "Dido's *Culpa*", in S. J. Harrison (ed.), *Oxford Readings in Vergil's Aeneid*, 145–66, Oxford: Oxford University Press.

Rushton, J. (2001), "Quarter-tone", in *Grove Music Online at: Oxford Music Online at:* Oxford University Press. Available online at: www.oxfordmusiconline at:.com/subscriber/article/grove/music/22645 (accessed May 8, 2018).

Said, E. W. ([1978] 2003), *Orientalism*, Modern Classics, London: Penguin Books.

Salway, P. (1997), *A History of Roman Britain*, Oxford: Oxford University Press.

Sammon, P. (2007), *Conan the Phenomenon: The Legacy of R. E. Howard's Fantasy Icon*, Milwaukie, OR: Dark Horse Books.

Savigny, H. and J. Schaap (2018), "Putting the 'Studies' Back into Metal Music Studies", *Metal Music Studies* 4: 549–58.

Savigny, H. and S. Sleight (2015), "Postfeminism and Heavy Metal in The United Kingdom: Sexy or Sexist?", *Metal Music Studies* 1: 341–57.

Scarsini, M. (2018), "Enea è un rifugiato? Il suo avo Dardano ci risponde con un categorico 'No'", *Il Primato Nazionale*, November 24. Available online at: www.ilprimatonazionale.it/cultura/enea-rifugiato-dardano-risponde-categorico-no-97219/ (accessed February 27, 2019).

Scego, I. (2018), *Anche Superman Era Un Rifugiato: Storie Vere Di Coraggio Per Un Mondo Migliore*, Milan: Piemme.

Schein, S. L. (2008), "'Our Debt to Greece and Rome': Canon, Class and Ideology", in L. Hardwick and C. Stray (eds.), *A Companion to Classical Receptions*, 75–85, Chichester: Blackwell.

Schiesaro, A. (2008), "Furthest Voices in Vergil's Dido", *Studi italiani di filologia classica* 100: 60–109, 194–245.

Schuddeboom, F. L. (2009), *Greek Religious Terminology—Telete & Orgia: A Revised and Supplemented English Edition of the Studies by Zijderveld and Van der Burg*, Leiden: Brill.

Sciarretto, A. (2009), "Kataklysm's Maurizio Iacono to Lay Down the Roman Law with Ex Deo", *noisecreep.com*, March 2. Available online at: http://noisecreep.com/kataklysm-s-maurizio-iacono-to-lay-down-the-roman-law-with-ex-de/ (accessed August 30, 2018).
Scott, N. (2007), "God Hates Us All: Radical Evil and the Diabolical Monstrous Human", in N. Scott (ed.), *Monsters and the Monstrous: Myths and Metaphors of Enduring Evil*, 201–13, New York–Amsterdam: Radopi.
Scott, N. (2010), "Politics? Nah Fuck Politics, Man: What can We Expect from Metal Gods?", in N. Scott and I. von Helden (eds), *The Metal Void: First Gatherings*, 211–18, Oxford: Inter-Disciplinary Press.
Scott, N. (2011), "Heavy Metal and the Deafening Threat of the Apolitical", *Popular Music History* 6: 224–39.
Scott, N., ed. (2012), *Reflections in the Metal Void*, Oxford: Inter-Disciplinary Press.
Scully, S. (2018), "Aesthetic and Political Concerns in Dryden's *Aeneis*", in S. Braund and Z. M. Torlone (eds), *Virgil and His Translators*, 275–87, Oxford: Oxford University Press.
Sedgwick, E. K. (1985), *Between Men: English Literature and Male Homosocial Desire*, Gender and Culture, New York: Columbia University Press.
Segal, C. (1990), "Dido's Hesitation in 'Aeneid' 4", *Classical World* 84: 1–12.
Seipel, W. (2000), *Ägyptomanie. Europäische Ägyptenimagination von der Antike bis heute*, Vienna; Milano: Kunsthistorisches Museum Wien.
Selden, D. L. (1998), "Alibis: The Poetics of Callimachus within the Multi-Ethnic and Expatriate Socio-Political and Cultural Context of Ptolemaic Alexandria", *Classical Antiquity* 12: 289–412.
Serafy, S. (2003), "Egypt in Hollywood: Pharaohs of the Fifties", in S. MacDonald and M. Rice (eds), *Consuming Ancient Egypt*, 77–86, London: Routledge.
Sethe, K. (1906), *Urkunden der 18. Dynastie*, Leipzig: J. C. Hinrichs.
Shanks, J. (2013), "Hyborian Age Archaeology: Unearthing Historical and Anthropological Foundations", in J. Prida (ed.), *Conan Meets the Academy: Multidisciplinary Essays on the Enduring Barbarian*, 13–34, Jefferson, NC: McFarland & Company.
Sharpe-Young, G. (2003), *A-Z of Doom, Gothic & Stoner Metal*, London: Cherry Red.
Sharpe-Young, G. (2007), *Metal: The Definitive Guide*, London: Jawbone Press.
Silent Dominion (2013), "Pest Webzine", *pestwebzine.com*, October. Available online at: http://pestwebzine.com/index/silent_dominion/0-791 (accessed July 5, 2018).
Simon (1977), *Necronomicon*, New York: Avon Books.
Sloat, L. J. (1998) "Incubus: Male Songwriter's Portrayal of Women's Sexuality in Pop Metal Music", in J. S. Epstein (ed.), *Youth Culture: Identity in a Postmodern World*, 286–301, Oxford: Blackwell Publishers.
Smith, M. (2017), *Following Osiris: Perspectives on the Osirian Afterlife From Four Millennia*, Oxford; New York: Oxford University Press.
Solomon, J. (2001), "The Sounds of Cinematic Antiquity", in M. M. Winkler (ed.), *Classical Myth and Culture in the Cinema*, 319–37, Oxford: Oxford University Press.
Souter, A. (1949), *A Glossary of Later Latin to 600 A.D.*, Oxford: Clarendon Press.
Southon, E. (2017), "Caligula and Drusilla in the Modern Imagination", in E. Almagor and L. Maurice (eds), *The Reception of Ancient Virtues and Vices in Modern Popular Culture: Beauty, Bravery, Blood and Glory*, 187–205, Leiden and Boston: Brill.
Spence, S. (1999), "*Varium et Mutabile*: Voices of Authority in *Aeneid* 4", in C. Perkell (ed.), *Reading Vergil's Aeneid: An Interpretive Guide*, 80–95, Norman: University of Oklahoma Press.
Spivak, G. C. (1994), "Can the Subaltern Speak?", in P. Williams and L. Chrisman (eds), *Colonial Discourse and Post-Colonial Theory: A Reader*, 66–111, New York: Columbia University Press.
Spracklen, K. (2015), "'To Holmgard . . . and Beyond': Folk Metal Fantasies and Hegemonic White Masculinities", *Metal Music Studies* 1: 354–77.

Bibliography

Spracklen, K., C. Lucas, and M. Deeks (2014), "The Construction of Heavy Metal Identity through Heritage Narratives: A Case Study of Extreme Metal Bands in the North of England", *Popular Music and Society* 37: 48–64.

Squires, N. (2011), "The Caligulan Court of Silvio Berlusconi Laid Bare", *The Telegraph*, January: 20.

St. Lawrence, J. S. and D. J. Joyner (1991), "The Effects of Sexually Violent Rock Music on Males' Acceptance of Violence Against Women", *Psychology of Women Quarterly* 15: 49–63.

Staff Writer (2017), "Mai dubitare del risveglio italiano: leggere Virgilio per ritrovare noi stessi", *Il Primato Nazionale*, October 15. Available online at: www.ilprimatonazionale.it/cultura/risveglio-italiano-leggere-virgilio-ritrovare-noi-stessi-74160/ (accessed February 27, 2019).

Stahl, H. P. (1998), "Editor's Introduction: Changing Views of the Political *Aeneid*", in H. P. Stahl (ed.), *Vergil's Aeneid: Augustan Epic and Political Context*, xv–xxxiii, London: Duckworth in association with The Classical Press of Wales.

Steadman, J. L. (2015), *H. P. Lovecraft & The Black Magickal Tradition: The Master of Horror's Influence on Modern Occultism*, San Francisco: Weiser Books.

Stefanis, J. (2006), "Interview: Byron (Bal-Sagoth)", *getreadytorock.com*, Available online at: www.getreadytorock.com/pure_metal/bal_sagoth_interview.htm (accessed April 1, 2018).

Stephens, S. A. (2003), *Seeing Double: Intercultural Poetics in Ptolemaic Alexandria*, Hellenistic Culture and Society 37, Berkeley; London: University of California Press.

Stephens, S. A. (2015), *Callimachus: The Hymns*, New York: Oxford University Press.

Stevens, C. E. (1938), "Magnus Maximus in British History", *Études Celtiques* 3: 86–94.

Stoffel, C. (2015), "Popsongs über Julius Caesar. Prolegomena zu einer popmusikalischen Antikerezeption", *thersites* 1: 123–55.

Strong, A. K. (2013), "Objects of Desire: Female Gazes and Male Bodies in Spartacus: Blood and Sand (2010)", in M. S. Cyrino (ed.), *Screening Love and Sex in the Ancient World*, 167–81, New York: Palgrave MacMillan.

Strunk, W. O. (1930), "Vergil in Music", *Musical Quarterly* 16: 482–97.

Suetonius (1914), *Lives of the Caesars, Volume I: Julius. Augustus. Tiberius. Gaius. Caligula*, trans. J. C. Rolfe, Loeb Classical Library 31, Cambridge, MA: Harvard University Press.

SuidAkrAOfficial (2013), "SuidAkrA—Eternal Defiance—Track by Track –", *YouTube.com*, May 20. Available online at: www.youtube.com/watch?v=bs4E6HDiOEM (accessed 28 July 2018).

Syed, Y. (2005), *Vergil's Aeneid and the Roman Self: Subject and Nation in Literary Discourse*, Ann Arbor: University of Michigan Press.

Syme, R. (1939), *The Roman Revolution*, Oxford: Oxford University Press.

Syson, A. (2013), *Fama and Fiction in Vergil's Aeneid*, Columbus: Ohio State University Press.

Tanaseanu-Döbler, I. (2013), *Theurgy in Late Antiquity: The Invention of a Ritual Tradition*, Göttingen: Vandenhoeck & Ruprecht.

Tatum, J. (1996), "Allusion and Interpretation in *Aeneid* 6.440-76", *American Journal of Philology* 105: 434–52.

Taylor, J. H. (2001), *Death and the Afterlife in Ancient Egypt*, London: British Museum Press.

Taylor, J. H. (2010), *Journey Through the Afterlife: Ancient Egyptian Book of the Dead*, London: British Museum Press.

thegothictale (2011), "Theatre of Tragedy—Cassandra (Live at Metalmania Fest. 2000, Katowice, Poland)", *YouTube.com*, August 30. Available online at: www.youtube.com/watch?v=Kf8CEhkT0D4 (accessed May 31, 2018).

Thin, D. (2002), *Shadows of Carcosa: Tales of Cosmic Horror by Lovecraft, Chambers, Machen, Poe, and Other Masters of the Weird*, New York: New York Review Books Classics.

Thomas, R. F. (2001), *Virgil and the Augustan Reception*, Cambridge: Cambridge University Press.

Thomas, R. F. (2007), "The Streets of Rome: The Classical Dylan", *Oral Tradition* 22: 30–56.

Thomasson, F. (2013), *The Life of J. D. Åkerblad: Egyptian Decipherment and Orientalism in Revolutionary Times*, Brill's Studies in Intellectual History 213, Leiden: Brill.

Bibliography

Thompson, J. (2010), *Edward William Lane, 1801–1876: The Life of the Pioneering Egyptologist and Orientalist*, London: Haus.
Toll, K. (1997), "Making Roman-ness and the *Aeneid*," *Classical Antiquity* 16: 34–56.
Tomlinson, J. (1999), *Globalization and Culture*, Chicago: University of Chicago Press.
Trafford, S. and A. Pluskowski (2007), "Antichrist Superstars: The Vikings in Hard Rock and Heavy Metal", in D. W. Marshall (ed.), *Mass Market Medieval. Essays on the Middle Ages in Popular Culture*, 57–73, Jefferson, NC: McFarland Publishing.
Trompf, G. W. (2013), "Theosophical Macrohistory", in O. Hammer and M. Rothstein (eds), *Handbook of the Theosophical Current*, 375–403, Leiden and Boston: Brill.
Tully, C. (2010), "Walk Like an Egyptian: Egypt as Authority in Aleister Crowley's Reception of The Book of the Law", *The Pomegranate* 12: 21–48.
Tuschinski, A. (2013), "Caligula. Reconstruction, Analysis and its Place in Tinto Brass' Oeuvre", Bachelor-Thesis, Stuttgart Media University, Stuttgart.
Tybjerg, C. (2016), "Devil-nets of Clues: *True Detective* and the Search for Meaning", *Northern Lights: Film & Media Studies Yearbook* 14: 103–21.
Umurhan, O. (2012), "Heavy Metal Music and the Appropriation of Greece and Rome", *Syllecta Classica* 23: 127–52.
Varisco, D. M. (2007), *Reading Orientalism: Said and the Unsaid*, Publications on the Near East, Seattle; London: University of Washington Press.
Vasunia, P. (2001), *The Gift of the Nile: Hellenizing Egypt from Aeschylus to Alexander*, Berkeley; London: University of California Press.
Vidal-Naquet, P. (2007), *The Atlantis Story: A Short History of Plato's Myth*, trans. J. Lloyd, Exeter: University of Exeter Press.
Vinson, S., and J. Gunn (2015), "Studies in Esoteric Syntax: The Enigmatic Friendship of Aleister Crowley and Battiscombe Gunn", in W. Carruthers (ed.), *Histories of Egyptology: Interdisciplinary Measures*, 96–112, New York; London: Routledge.
Vitali, D. and G. Kaenel (2000), "Un Helvète chez les Etrusques vers 300 av. J.-C.", *Archäologie der Schweiz* 23: 115–22.
von Helden, I. (2010a), "Barbarians and Literature: Viking Metal and its Links to Old Norse Mythology", in N. W. R. Scott (ed.), *The Metal Void: First Gatherings*, 257–64, Oxford: Inter-Disciplinary Press.
von Helden, I. (2010b), "Scandinavian Metal Attack: The Power of Northern Europe in Extreme Metal", in R. Hill and K. Spracklen (eds), *Heavy Fundametalisms: Music, Metal, and Politics*, 33–41, Oxford: Inter-Disciplinary Press.
von Helden, I. (2017), *Norwegian Native Art: Cultural Identity in Norwegian Metal Music*, Berlin: LIT Verlag.
Voulgarakis, E. (2014), "Mary, Athena, and Kuan-yin: What the Church, the Demos, and the Sangha Can Teach Us about Religious Pluralism and Doctrinal Conformity to Socio-cultural Standards", in D. M. Nault, B. Dawei, E. Voulgarakis, R. Paterson, and C. A.-M. Suva (eds), *Experiencing Globalization: Religion in Contemporary Contexts*, 81–108, London: Anthem Press.
Wagner, J. (2010), *Mean Deviation: Four Decades of Progressive Heavy Metal*, Brooklyn: Bazillion Point Books.
Waksman, S. (1999), *Instruments of Desire: The Electric Guitar and the Shaping of Musical Experience*, Cambridge, MA: Harvard University Press.
Waksman, S. (2009), *This Ain't the Summer of Love: Conflict and Crossover in Heavy Metal and Punk*, Berkeley: University of California Press.
Waksman, S. (2011), "War is Heavy Metal: Soundtracking the US War in Iraq", in J. P. Fisher and B. Flota (eds), *The Politics of Post-9/11 Music: Sound, Trauma, and the Music Industry in the Time of Terror*, 185–204, Farnham: Ashgate.

Bibliography

Wallach, J., H. M. Berger, and P. D. Greene, eds. (2011a), *Metal Rules the Globe: Heavy Metal Music Around the World*, Durham: Duke University Press.

Wallach, J., H. M. Berger, and P. D. Greene, eds. (2011b), "Affective Overdrive, Scene Dynamics, and Identity in the Global Metal Scene", in J. Wallach, H. M. Berger, and P. D. Greene (eds), *Metal Rules the Globe: Heavy Metal Music Around the World*, 3–33, Durham: Duke University Press.

Walser, R. (1993a), *Running with the Devil: Power, Gender, and Madness in Heavy Metal Music*, Hanover, NH: Wesleyan University Press.

Walser, R. (1993b), "Forging Masculinity: Heavy-Metal Sounds and Images of Gender", in S. Frith, A. Goodwin, and L. Grossberg (eds), *Sound and Vision: The Music Video Reader*, 131–58, New York and London: Routledge.

Wardle, D. (1994), "Suetonius' *Life of Caligula*: A Commentary", *Latomus* 225, Brussels.

Waswo, R. (1997), *The Founding Legend of Western Civilization: From Virgil to Vietnam*, Hanover, NH: Wesleyan University Press.

"We brought Nile's Karl Sanders, former Hate Eternal drummer Derek Roddy and Perversion's Mahmud Gecekusu to collaborate with Nader Sadek in Egypt. Part 1" (2018), *cairometal.net*, January 13. Available online at: http://cairometal.net/we-brought-niles-karl-sanders-former-hate-eternal-drummer-derek-roddy-and-perversions-mahmud-gecekusu-to-collaborate-with-nader-sadek-in-egypt-part-1/ (accessed February 28, 2019).

Weinstein, D. (2000), *Heavy Metal: The Music and its Culture*, revised edition, Boulder, CO: Da Capo Press.

Weinstein, D. (2011), "The Globalization of Metal", in J. Wallach, H. M. Berger, and P. D. Greene (eds), *Metal Rules the Globe: Heavy Metal Music Around the World*, 34–59, Durham: Duke University Press.

Weinstein, D. (2014a), "Just So Stories: How Heavy Metal Got its Name—A Cautionary Tale," *Rock Music Studies* 1: 36–51.

Weinstein, D. (2014b), "Pagan Metal", in D. Weston and A. Bennett (eds), *Pop Pagans: Paganism and Popular Music*, 58–75, New York: Routledge.

Weinstein, D. (2016a), "Playing with Gender in the Key of Metal", in F. Heesch and N. W. R. Scott (eds), *Heavy Metal, Gender and Sexuality: Interdisciplinary Approaches*, 11–25, London and New York: Routledge.

Weinstein, D. (2016b), "Reflections on Metal Studies", in A. R. Brown, K. Spracklen, K. Kahn-Harris and N. W. R. Scott (eds), *Global Metal Music and Culture: Current Directions in Metal Studies*, 22–31, New York and London: Routledge.

West, G. S. (1980), "Caeneus and Dido", *Transactions of the American Philological Association* 110: 315–24.

West, M. L. (1983), *The Orphic Poems*, Oxford: Clarendon Press.

Wharton, D. (2008), "*Sunt lacrimae rerum*: An Exploration in Meaning", *Classical Journal* 103: 259–79.

Whiteley, S. (1997), "Introduction", in S. Whiteley (ed.), *Sexing the Groove: Popular Music and Gender*, xiii–xxxvi, New York and London: Routledge.

Wiederhorn, J. and K. Turman (2013), *Louder Than Hell: The Definitive Oral History of Metal*, New York: It Books.

Wilcox, A. (2008), "Nature's Monster: Caligula as *Exemplum* in I. Sluiter and R. M. Rosen (eds), Seneca's *Dialogues*", in *Kakos: Badness and Anti-Value in Classical Antiquity*, 451–76, Leiden and Boston: Brill.

Wildung, D. (1977), *Egyptian Saints: Deification in Pharaonic Egypt*, Hagop Kevorkian Series on Near Eastern Art and Civilization, New York: New York University Press.

Wilkins, A. (2004), "'So Full of Myself as a Chick': Goth Women, Sexual Independence, and Gender Egalitarianism", *Gender and Society* 18: 328–49.

Wilson-Okamura, D. S. (2010), *Virgil in the Renaissance*, Cambridge: Cambridge University Press.

Bibliography

Wilson, B. ("n.d."), "*Arma virumque cano*: Singing Vergil's *Aeneid* in Early Modern Europe", *Dickinson College Commentaries*, Available online at: http://dcc.dickinson.edu/vergil-aeneid/musical-settings (accessed February 27, 2019).

Wilson, S. (2008), *Great Satan's Rage: American Negativity and Rap/Metal in the Age of Supercapitalism*, Manchester: University Press.

Winterling, A. (2011), *Caligula: A Biography*, Berkeley, Los Angeles and London: University of California Press.

Wolff-Mann, E. (2016), "Sorry James Joyce, the People Buying Ulysses Don't Actually Read It", *money.com*, June 16. Available online at: http://time.com/money/4369192/ulysses-james-joyce-unread-book/ (accessed February 22, 2019).

Wong, C. (2011), "'A Dream Return to Tang Dynasty': Masculinity, Male Camaraderie, and Chinese Heavy Metal in the 1990s", in J. Wallach, H. Berger, and P. D. Greene (eds), *Metal Rules the Globe: Heavy Metal Music Around the World*, 63–85, Durham, NC and London: Duke University Press.

Wyke, M. (1997), *Projecting the Past: Ancient Rome, Cinema and History*, London: Routledge.

Wyke, M. (2007), *Caesar: A Life in Western Culture*, Chicago: University Press.

Yiannis (2013), "Interview with Maurizio Iacono (Ex Deo)—10 September 2013", *getreadytorock.me.uk*, September 29. Available online at: http://getreadytorock.me.uk/blog/2013/09/interview-with-maurizio-iacono-ex-deo-10-september-2013/ (accessed August 30, 2018).

ysee.gr (2012a), "ΥΣΕΕ—ΤΕΛΕΤΗ ΘΑΡΓΗΛΙΩΝ '2012'", *YouTube.com*, June 3. Available online at: www.youtube.com/watch?v=vTxdHyDZelw (accessed July 5, 2018).

ysee.gr (2012b), "ΧΑΡΙΣΙΑ—ΑΦΡΟΔΙΣΙΑ '2012': ΥΜΝΟΣ ΣΤΟΝ ΘΕΟ ΑΠΟΛΛΩΝΑ", *YouTube.com*, May 28. Available Online at: www.youtube.com/watch?v=0O5BdJ0I8v0 (accessed July 1, 2018).

ysee.gr (2013), "ΑΦΡΟΔΙΣΙΑ '2013': ΥΜΝΟΣ ΘΕΟΥ ΑΠΟΛΛΩΝΟΣ", *YouTube.com*, April 28. Available online at: www.youtube.com/watch?v=KwL9Mj-0g9Y (accessed July 1, 2018).

Zandee, J. (1960), *Death as An Enemy: According to Ancient Egyptian Conceptions*, Studies in the History of Religions (Supplements to Numen) 5, Leiden: Brill.

Zetzel, J. E. G. (1989), "*Romane memento*: Justice and Judgment in *Aeneid* 6," *Transactions of the American Philological Association* 119: 263–84.

Ziolkowski, J. M. and M. C. J. Putnam, eds. (2008), *The Virgilian Tradition: The First Fifteen Hundred Years*, New Haven: Yale University Press.

Ziolkowski, T. (1993), *Virgil and the Moderns*, Princeton: Princeton University Press.

Zuckerberg, D. (2018), *Not All Dead White Men: Classics and Misogyny in the Digital Age*, Cambridge, MA: Harvard University Press.

Master discography

Acherontas (2015), *Ma-IoN (Formulas of Reptilian Unification)*, World Terror Committee.
Ade (2010), *Prooemivm Sangvine*, Casket Music.
Ade (2013), *Spartacus*, Blast Head Records.
Ade (2016), *Carthago Delenda Est*, Xtreem Music.
Aherusia (2017), *Prometheus: Seven Principles on How to Be Invincible*, Prime Eon Media Ltd.
Ancestral Rhymes (2008), *The Cosmic Law*, Self-released.
Ancient Rites (2001), *Dim Carcosa*, Hammerheart Record.
Ancient Rites (2006), *Rubicon*, Season of Mist.
Anthrax (1985), *Spreading the Disease*, Megaforce Records.
Archaeos (2016), *Archegono Miasma*, Celtic Fog Productions.
Archaeos (2016), *The Forgotten Art of Sacrifice*, Lower Silesian Stronghold.

Bibliography

At the Gates (1994), *Terminal Spirit Disease*, Peaceville Records.
Athos (2004), *Return to the Hellenic Lands*. Self-released.
Athos (2007), *The Awakening of Athos*, Candarian Demon Productions.
Athos (2008), *Crossing the River of Charon*, Candarian Demon Productions.
Bacchia Neraida (1998), *Εις τους δώδεκα θεούς του Ολύμπου*, Dionysion.
Βάκχειος (1998), *Μάκαρ Κερασφόρε*. Self-released.
Bal-Sagoth (1995), *A Black Moon Broods Over Lemuria*, Cacophonous Records.
Bal-Sagoth (1996), *Starfire Burning Upon the Ice-Veiled Throne of Ultima Thule*, Cacophonous Records.
Bal-Sagoth (1998), *Battle Magic*, Cacophonous Records.
Bal-Sagoth (1999), *The Power Cosmic*, Nuclear Blast Records.
Bal-Sagoth (2001), *Atlantis Ascendant*, Nuclear Blast Records.
Bal-Sagoth (2006), *The Chthonic Chronicles*, Nuclear Blast Records.
Bathory (1990), *Hammerheart*, Noise Records.
Bathory (1996), *Blood on Ice*, Black Mark Production.
Behemoth (2009), *Evangelion*, Nuclear Blast Records.
Black Sabbath (1970), *Black Sabbath*, Vertigo.
Black Sabbath (1970), *Paranoid*, Vertigo.
Bleeding Gods (2018), *Dodekathlon*, Nuclear Blast Records.
Blind Guardian (2002), *A Night at the Opera*, Virgin Records.
Caligula (2013), *Greatest Hits*, Independent.
Celtefog (2016), *Sounds of the Olden Days*, Self-released.
Celtic Frost (1985), *To Mega Therion*. Noise Records.
Celtic Frost (1987), *Into the Pandemonium*, Noise Records.
Celtic Frost (1992), *Parched with Thirst Am I and Dying*, Noise.
Centvrion (2002), *Non Plvs Vltra*, Scarlet Records.
Chuck Berry (1958), *Johnny B. Goode*, Chess Records.
Civil War (2013), *The Killer Angels*, Despotz Records.
Coffin Texts (2000), *Gods of Creation, Death and Afterlife*, Dwell Records.
Coffin Texts (2012), *The Tomb of the Infinite Ritual*, Dark Descent Records.
Cradle of Filth (1998), *Cruelty and the Beast*, Music for Nations.
Cradle of Filth (2008), *Godspeed of the Devil´s Thunder*, Roadrunner Records.
Cream (1967), *Disraeli Gears*, Reaction.
Diabolical Principles (2014), *Manifesto of Death,* Kristallblut Records.
Dio (1984), *The Last in Line*, Vertigo.
Dithyramvos (1998), *Pagan Perpetuation,* Self-released, 1998.
Dizziness (2013), *Offermort Heritage*, Apocalyptic Art.
Dominion Caligula (2000), *A New Era Rises*, No Fashion Records.
Edguy (2001), *Mandrake*, AFM Records.
Eluveitie (2010), *Everything Remains (As It Never Was)*, Nuclear Blast Records.
Eluveitie (2012), *Helvetios*, Nuclear Blast Records.
Enslaved (1994), *Vikingligr Veldi*, Deathlike Silence Productions.
Evil Scarecrow (2009), *Sixty-Six Minutes Past Six*, Independent.
Ex Deo (2009), *Romulus*, Nuclear Blast Records.
Ex Deo (2012), *Caligvla*, Napalm Records.
Ex Deo (2017), *Immortal Wars*, Napalm Records.
Freedom Call (2001), *Crystal Empire*, Steamhammer.
Giant Squid (2014), *Minoans*, Translation Loss Records.
Goat of Mendes (1997), *To Walk Upon the Wiccan Way*, Perverted Taste.
Grave Digger (2007), *Liberty or Death*, Locomotive Records.
Hades Adorned (2002), *Crata Repoa*, Tetragrammaton Records.

Bibliography

Halford (2000), *Resurrection*, Metal-Is Records.
Heimdall (2013), *Aeneid*, Scarlet Records.
Hesperia (2003), *Aeneidos Metalli Apotheosis Pt. I*, Ab Sibillinis Montibus Artificii.
Hesperia (2008), *In Honorem Herois—Aeneidos Metalli Apotheosis Pars II*, Forart.It.
Hesperia (2013), *Spiritvs Italicvs—Aeneidos Metalli Apotheosis Pars III*, Sleaszy Rider Records.
Hesperia (2015), *Metallvm Italicvm—Aeneidos Metalli Apotheosis Pars IV*, Sleaszy Rider Records.
Hesperia (2017), *Caesar [Roma vol. I]*, Sleaszy Rider Records.
High on Fire (2012), *De Vermis Mysteriis*, eOne.
Holy Martyr (2008), *Hellenic Warrior Spirit*, Dragonheart Records.
Iced Earth (2001), *Horror Show*, Century Media Records.
Illusion Suite (2013), *The Iron Cemetery*, Power Prog Records.
I Miti Eterni (2014), *Historia Cumae*, Jolly Roger Records.
Imperivm (2017), *Rome Burns*, Virus Records.
Imperium des Tenebras (2012), *Absconditus Umbrae*, Culminis.
In Flames (1995), *Subterranean*, Wrong Again Records.
Iron Maiden (1981), *Killers*, EMI.
Iron Maiden (1983), *Piece of Mind*, EMI.
Iron Maiden (1984), *Powerslave*, EMI/Capitol.
Iron Maiden (1986), *Somewhere in Time*, EMI.
Jose Beausejour (2014), *Monetized Pagan Gods IV*, Utrumque Paratus.
Kawir (1993), *Promo '93,* Self-released.
Kawir (1994), *Eumenides.* Dark Side Records.
Kawir (1997), *To Cavirs*, Nix Records.
Kawir (1999), *Epoptia*, Storm Records.
Kawir (2005), *Arai,* Solistitium Records.
Kawir (2008), *Ophiolatreia,* Those Opposed Records.
Kawir (2010), *To Uranus*, Those Opposed Records.
Kawir (2012), *Isotheos*, Deathrune Records.
Kawir (2014), *Νυχτός τελετήσιν: 20 Years of Recordings*, Those Opposed Records.
Kawir (2016), *ΑΜΥΗΤΟΝ ΜΗ ΕΙΣΙΕΝΑΙ*, Those Opposed Records.
Kawir (2016), *Πάτερ Ήλιε, Μήτερ Σελάνα*, Iron Bonehead Records.
Kawir and Scythian (2011), *Grunwald / Τιτανομαχία* (split), Nuclear Winter Records.
Kawir and Zemial (2003), *Δαίμων* (split), Apocalyptor Records.
Led Zeppelin (1969), *Led Zeppelin II*, Atlantic.
Led Zeppelin (1970), *Led Zeppelin III*, Atlantic.
Led Zeppelin (1976), *Presence*, Swan Song.
Lord Impaler (2011), *Admire the Cosmos Black*, Self-released.
Maat (2014), *As We Create the Hope from Above*, Aural Attack Productions.
Manowar (1983), *Into Glory Ride*, Megaforce Records.
Manowar (1992), *The Triumph of Steel*, Atlantic.
Marduk (1998), Nightwing, Osmose Productions.
Mercyful Fate (1983), *Melissa*, Roadrunner Records.
Metallica (1984), *Ride the Lightning*, Elektra Records.
Metallica (1991), *Metallica*, Elektra Records.
Morbid Fog (2012), *Αρχέγονο Σκότος*, Grim Reaper Records.
Morbid Fog (2014), *Daemones*, Self-released.
Naer Mataron (2000), *Skotos Aenaon*, Black Lotus Records.
Nåstrond and Acherontas (2016), *Chthonic Libations*, Zazen Sounds.
Nightwish (1997), *Angels Fall First*, Spinefarm Records.
Nile (1998), *Amongst the Catacombs of Nephren-Ka*, Relapse Records.
Nile (1999), *In the Beginning*, Relapse Records.

Bibliography

Nile (2000), *Black Seeds of Vengeance*, Relapse Records.
Nile (2002), *In Their Darkened Shrines*, Relapse Records.
Nile (2005), *Annihilation of the Wicked*, Relapse Records.
Nile (2007), *Ithyphallic*, Nuclear Blast Records.
Nile (2009), *Those Whom the Gods Detest*, Nuclear Blast Records.
Nile (2012), *At the Gate of Sethu*, Nuclear Blast Records.
Nile (2015), *What Should Not Be Unearthed*, Nuclear Blast Records.
Ozzy Osbourne (1980), *Blizzard of Ozz*, Jet Records Productions.
Protean (2015), *The Burning Centuries*, Beverina Productions.
Rebellion (2012), *Arminius—Furor Teutonicus*, Massacre Records.
Sabaton (2008), *The Art of War*, Black Lodge Records.
Sacred Blood (2015), *Argonautica*, Pitch Black Records.
Saltatio Mortis (2007), *Aus der Asche*, Napalm Records.
Scarab (2010), *Blinding the Masses*, Osmose Productions.
Scarab (2015), *Serpents of the Nile*, ViciSolum.
Septicflesh (2008), *Communion*, Season of Mist.
Serpentyne (2014), *Myths and Muses*, Serpentyne Music.
ShadowIcon (2011), *Empire in Ruins*, Independent.
Silent Dominion (2013), *Spiritual Flesh Around the Cycles of Inexistence*, Abyssic Black Cult Records.
Silent Dominion and Morbid Fog (2013), *Defending the Ancient Spirit* (split), Schattenkult Produktionen.
Skyclad (1991), *The Wayward Sons of Mother Earth*, Noise Records.
Sodom (2016), *Decision Day*, Steamhammer.
Son of Aurelius (2010), *The Farthest Reaches*, Good Fight.
Spinal Tap (1984), *Spinal Tap*, Polydor.
Stormlord (2001), *At the Gates of Utopia*, Scarlet Records.
Stormlord (2004), *The Gorgon Cult*, Scarlet Records.
Stormlord (2008), *Mare Nostrum*, Locomotive Records.
Stormlord (2013), *Hesperia*, Trollzorn Records.
SuidAkrA (2006), *Caledonia*, Armageddon Music.
SuidAkrA (2013), *Eternal Defiance*, AFM Records.
Symphony X (1997), *The Divine Wings of Tragedy*, InsideOut Music.
Symphony X (2000), *V: The New Mythology Suite*, InsideOut Music.
Symphony X (2002), *The Odyssey*, InsideOut Records.
Theatre of Tragedy (1998), *Aégis*, Massacre Records.
Therion (1993), *Symphony Masses: Ho Drakon Ho Megas*, Megarock Records.
Therion (1996), *Theli*, Nuclear Blast Records.
Therion (2004), *Lemuria/Sirius B*, Nuclear Blast Records.
Therion (2007), *Gothic Kabbalah*, Nuclear Blast Records.
Therion (2012), *Les Fleurs Du Mal*, End of the Light.
Therion (2018), *Beloved Antichrist*, Nuclear Blast Records.
Thy Catafalque (2001), *Microcosmos*, KaOtic.
Triptykon (2010), *Eparistera Daimones*, Century Media.
Triptykon (2014), *Melana Chasmata*, Century Media.
Turisas (2011), *Stand Up and Fight*, Century Media Records.
Unholy Archangel (2000), *Blessed by Aris*, Iron Fist Domain Productions.
Uranus (1998), *The Clang of Lances*, Self-released.
Various (1984), *Scandinavian Metal Attack*, RCA.
Venom (1982), *Black Metal*, Neat Records.
Verberis (2016), *Vexamen*, Iron Bonehead Productions.

VerSacrum (2009), *Tyrrenika*, Rock Over Records–Horus.
Virgin Steele (1999), *The House of Atreus: Act I*, T&T Records.
Virgin Steele (2000), *The House of Atreus: Act II*, T&T Records.
White Skull (2000), *Public Glory, Secret Agony*, Nuclear Blast Records.
Wotan (2000), *Under the Sign of Odin's Cross*, Independent.
Wotan (2004), *Carmina Barbarica*, Eat Metal.
Yngwie Malmsteen's Rising Force (1985), *Marching Out*, Polydor.

Filmography and TV

300 (2006), [Film] Dir. Zack Snyder, USA: Warner Brothers.
Caligula (1979), [Film] Dir. Tinto Brass and Rob Guccione, Italy: Penthouse Films International.
Gladiator (2000), [Film] Dir. Ridley Scott, USA: Dreamworks.
I, Claudius (1976), [TV program] BBC2.
Rome, Season 1 Episode 1, "The stolen eagle" (2005). Dir. By Michael Apted and Mikael Salomon. BBC, HBO and RAI.

INDEX

300 (film, graphic novel) 199 n.79

ABBA (band, Sweden) 10
Absu (band, USA) 169 n.65
Acherontas (band, Greece) 89, 93
Achilles 1, 7, 12, 17, 19 n.20, 19 n.29, 97, 128 n.36, 128 n.47, 191, 212
Ade (band, Italy) 1, 201, 204–6, 209, 211
aegis 100–1
   See also Athena
Aeneas 14, 23–52, 115–30, 212
   See also Aeneid, Heimdall, Stormlord
Aeneid 1, 3–4, 14, 15, 23–52, 112 n.31, 112 n.32, 115–30, 148
   See also Aeneas, Dido, Heimdall, Hesperia, Vergil
Aeschylus 101–2, 103, 107–8, 110, 112 n.32, 113 n.42
Africa 76 n.64, 118, 203, 207–8, 209, 215 n.30
   See also Carthage
Agamemnon 101, 107–8, 128 n.36
aggression
   in metal 132, 142, 146–7, 175, 184, 212–13
   Roman 58, 6
   See also brutality, violence
Aherusia (band, Greece) 93
Ajax, son of Oileus 101, 107
album artwork 157–8, 201, 209, 211
   Ade 204–5, 206
   Caligula 135
   Ex Deo 137–8
   Heimdall 126 n.16
   Hesperia 41
   Iron Maiden 185–6
   Kawir 81–2
   Manowar 10–11
   Nile 179, 180, 188, 193
   SuidAkrA 64
   See also booklets, liner notes
Alcaeus 79
Alesia, siege of 61–2, 136
   in Eluveitie 62–4
Alexander the Great 1, 12, 45, 125 n.6, 152 n.61
   See also under Iron Maiden
Alice Cooper (band, USA) 7, 131
"Alternative" Egyptology
   See under Nile

alt-right 89
   See also politics
Amalthea 84–5
American Philological Association (APA) 18 n.5
Amon Amarth (band, Sweden) 11, 152 n.62
Amorphis (band, Finland) 74 n.37
Ancestral Rhymes (band, Greece) 92
Ancient Rites (band, Belgium)
   Carcosa 155–56, 167 n.3
   esoteric interests 155–6, 169 n.65
Antony, Marc 25, 117, 136, 211, 212
Anthrax (band, USA) 8
"anti-conquest narrative" 59, 71
antiquity
   as familiar 16, 17, 31, 61, 66, 118, 136–7, 143–4, 156–66, 174, 203
   romanticized view of 27, 60–1, 71–2, 152 n.65, 192
anti-Semitism 208
   See also racism, white supremacy
Aphrodite 88, 91, 92, 161
   See also Venus
Apollo 83, 86–8, 91, 100–4, 107, 113 n.42
   See also "Hymn to Apollo"
Apollonius of Rhodes 1
Arabic
   See under languages
Arabs 164, 166, 182, 192, 193
arcane
   knowledge 177, 180, 182, 187, 193
   in metal 155–8, 161
   See also occult
Archaeos (band, Greece) 89, 93
archaizing English
   See under language
Ares 80, 91, 92
   See also Mars
Argonauts 1, 45
   See also Jason, Medea
Arminius 44–5, 155
Artemis 80, 81, 88, 91
Athena 80, 91–2, 100–1
   See also aegis
Athens 1, 77, 88, 125 n.6
Athos (band, Greece) 92
Atlantis 158, 163, 164, 165, 188
At the Gates (band, Sweden) 28, 54

Index

audience
  ancient 125
  Anglophone 33, 45, 60
  Classical scholars 2, 4
  desires of 135, 145–6, 149 n.4, 197 n.43
  general 17, 21 n.61, 33, 36, 77, 145–8, 201, 204, 206, 213
  global/international 14, 27, 33, 45, 201, 203, 207
  Greek 60, 89, 91
  heavy metal 14, 116, 124–5, 125 n.6, 132, 138, 203
  Italian 14, 23–4, 33–4
  listening 66, 99, 102–3, 109, 115, 143, 147–8
  live 147
  local 34, 99, 110
  local vs. international 33–6, 45–6
  Metal scholars 2, 4 (*see under* Metal Studies)
  participation 109–10
  Roman 36, 124
  scholars reaching multiple audiences 149
  TV 6, 134
  See also fans
Augustus Caesar 1, 25, 39, 55, 117, 136, 140
  See also Octavian
Avenged Sevenfold (band, USA) 10

Babylon 158, 165
Bacchia Neraida (band, Greece) 88–9, 91
Bacchus 80, 101
  See also Dionysus
Βάκχειος (band, Greece) 88–9, 91
ballad 15, 37, 70, 120
Bal-Sagoth (band, UK)
  Chthonic Chronicles 163–5
  and the invented/antediluvian world 162–3, 165–6
  style 162
Bannerwar (band, Greece) 89
Bathory (band, Sweden) 11, 20–1 n.50, 26–7, 28, 72 n.3, 94 n.14, 132
Bathory, Erzsebeth 132, 149 n.5, 149 n.7
"beauty and the beast"
  See under vocals
Behemoth (band, Poland) 88–9, 92
Berlioz, Hector 6, 18 n.14, 115
Bible 107, 197 n.48
  See also New Testament
black metal 8
  Christian 195 n.20
  conservatism of 78
  Greek 12, 207 (*see also* Kawir)
  and global appeal 9–10
  and nationalism 167 n.14
  National Socialist Black Metal 78, 89, 94 n.11, 153 n.66, 157, 208
  Norwegian 20 n.48, 21 n.50, 79, 86, 95 n.45, 212

origins 9, 19 n.34
Scandinavian 11
style 9, 20 n.41
Swedish 11, 26, 132
See also Ancient Rites, Bal-Sagoth, Hesperia
Black Sabbath (band, UK) 6–7, 8, 19 n.27, 131, 157–8
Bleeding Gods (band, Netherlands) 1
Blind Guardian (band, Germany) 10, 15
  homosocial bonding 106–10
  influences 107
  style 98, 107
  treatment of Cassandra 107–9
blood 27, 36, 39, 40, 42
blues 7, 19 n.26
booklets 35, 99–100, 185–6, 195 n.18
  See also album artwork, liner notes
Boreas 80
Boudicca 2, 169 n.72, 261 n.41
Britain 2, 7, 65, 163, 192, 203, 207
  in Bal-Sagoth 162–3
  in SuidAkrA 66–71
brutality 131, 132, 136, 147, 176, 188
  See also aggression, violence
Budge, E. A. 184, 189
Burzum (band, Norway) 11
Byzantine Empire 2
Byzantium 165, 171 n.96

Caesar 167 n.23
  See also Augustus Caesar, Caligula, Julius Caesar, Nero, Tiberius
Caledonia(ns) 64–5, 69–70, 74 n.38
Caligula 131–54
  ancient reception 132–4
  as evil 131–48
  in Ex Deo 135–42
  live performance 147–8
  in metal 135
  modern reception 133–5
  and "The Tiberius Cliff (Exile to Capri)", 142–6
Caligula (band, Belgium) 135
Caligula (film, 1979) 16, 134–5, 140, 144, 146
Caligula's Horse (band, Australia) 135
Callimachus 14–15, 79–81, 85, 96 n.54
Carcosa 155, 156
Carthage 24, 28, 31–2, 37, 38, 115–16, 118, 120–2, 124, 137, 158, 204
  See also Africa, Dido, Punic Wars
CasaPound 43–4
Cassandra 15, 110–11
  in Blind Guardian 107–9
  in Classical sources 101–2
  in Theatre of Tragedy 103–6
Cassius Dio 73 n.30, 113 n.52, 113 n.53, 149 n.10
Cato the Elder 204

Index

Catullus 42
Celtefog (band, Greece) 93
Celtic Frost (band, Switzerland) 16, 158
    and occult 161, 165-6
    style 158
    use of Greek 159-60
Celtic identity 14, 53-76
    in Eluveitie 54, 59, 64
    in SuidAkrA 54, 64, 71
Celtomania 53, 72 n.1
Celts (or Celticism) 55, 64, 158, 204
Centvrion (band, Italy) 41-2, 44
China 46
Christianity 86, 187, 209
    metal reaction against 11, 26-7, 79, 85-6, 91, 178
    and Nero 134-6
    and paganism 11, 79, 90, 209-10
    See also black metal, heavy metal
Chuck Berry (artist, US) 19 n.24
church burnings (in Norway) 77, 79, 86, 91, 95 n.45
Church of Satan 160
    See also Satanism
cinema
    See film
Circus Maximus 169 n.72
Civil War (band, Sweden) 2
civil wars (Rome) 25, 31, 126 n.18, 136, 211
Classical Association of the Middle West and South (CAMWS) x, 2
Classical music 5, 98, 120, 122-3, 127 n.27
Classical mythology 5, 23, 110
Classical Reception Studies 2-3, 201-4
    definition 5
    in opera 5, 115
    See also Reception Studies
Classical Studies 13, 156
    and Egypt 198 n.70
    and women 15, 17 (*see also under* women)
    definition of 3
    trends in 17, 57, 158, 202
    See also Classics
Classical tradition 3-4, 167 n.12
classic metal
    See traditional metal
Classics
    and Classical Studies 3
    compared to esotericism 155, 156
    definition 3
    and Metal Studies (*see under* Metal Studies)
    at odds with folk traditions 53
    and Reception Studies 3-5 (*see* Classical Reception Studies, Reception Studies)
    and the study of film 5-6
    and the study of heavy metal 2-3, 7, 13, 15, 17, 18 n.3
    See also Classical Studies

Claudius 134, 138, 142
Cleanthes 81, 95 n.38
Cleopatra 1, 117-18, 121, 211-12
Clytemnestra 101, 103, 109
Coffin Texts (band, USA) 175
colonization 59, 62, 192-3
Conan the Barbarian 16, 47 n.20, 162
    See also Howard, Robert E.
concept album 11, 14, 23, 28, 59, 65-6, 98, 107, 110, 116, 132, 161, 168 n.43
Coptic
    See under language
corpse-paint 9, 41, 78-9, 82
cover, album
    See album artwork
Cradle of Filth (band, UK) 132
Cream (band, UK) 7
Crete 84-6
Cronos (god) 132
Crowley, Aleister 157-8, 159, 160, 166, 189-90, 196 n.33
    See also occult
Cthulhu 162, 164, 170 n.89, 188
    See also Lovecraft, H. P.

damnatio memoriae 66-7
Dante 3-4, 6, 25, 28, 44, 47 n.14
Dark Funeral (band, Sweden) 132
Death (god) 80, 89, 92, 93
death metal 28, 131-48, 155-6, 173-94
    characteristics 8-9, 131, 142, 160-1, 166, 175, 176, 183, 186
    and folk metal 53
    and gender 142
    melodic 54, 64, 66, 136
    origins 8-9
    stage personas in 132
    symphonic 28, 136, 138, 155-6
    and transgression 175-6 (*see also under* transgression)
    versus power metal 36
    vocals/growls 8, 106, 139, 176
    See also aggression, Ex Deo, Nile, Scarab, Therion
decay 41, 176, 177, 179-80, 186
Deep Purple (band, UK) 7
Def Leppard (band, UK) 7
Demeter 80, 91, 95 n.32
Deviate Damaen (band, Italian) 49 n.54
Diabolical Principles (band, Greece) 89, 92
Diamond Head (band, UK) 7
Dido, queen of Carthage 15, 115-30
    and Aeneas 24, 31, 32, 34-5, 37, 48 n.35, 118-20
    ancient reception 124
    emotion 122-3

feminine and masculine qualities 116, 118, 120–2
and metal fans 124–5
and opera 115
as ruler 118, 120
See also Aeneas, *Aeneid*
Dike 80, 83
Dio (band, USA) 173–4, 183, 194 n.4
Dionysus 80, 81, 92
See also Bacchus
Dioscuri 81
Dithyramvos (band, Greece) 88, 91
Divico 57, 61
Dizziness (band, Greece) 89, 92
Dominion Caligula (band, Sweden) 135
Donatus 124
doom metal 11, 112 n.19
Dracula 132
dragon 70, 160, 163
Dragon Rouge 160–1
dress 8, 9, 45, 69, 78–9, 81, 103, 126 n.16, 141–2, 211, 212, 215 n.30
See also performance
Drusilla 134, 141–2
Dryden, John 31–2, 38
Dune (book) 8
Dungeons & Dragons 107
Dylan, Bob 25

eagle 40, 42, 64, 69–70, 147–8
Eddie the Head 8, 185
See also Iron Maiden
Edguy (band, Germany) 194 n.5
Egypt
Egyptomania 173–4
and esoteric metal 158, 160–1, 165, 209–10
as "Other", 16, 174, 177, 190–3
Tutankhamun 173
See also Cleopatra, Egyptology *and under* Nile
Egyptian language
See under language
Egyptology 173, 184, 187–9, 192, 193, 194, 198 n.70
See also under Nile
Elegabalus (band, USA) 132
Eleusinian
See under Mysteries
Eluveitie (band, Switzerland) 1, 14, 50 n.80, 58–64, 208, 209
Gallic Wars 54, 59–60 (*see also* Gallic Wars)
La Tène 54–5, 60, 64
name 55
origins 54–5
style 54–5, 72 n.11
See also postcolonialism *and under* Gaulish, identity, Julius Caesar

Emperor (band, Norway) 11, 21 n.52, 48 n.27, 74 n.37, 126 n.16
England
See Britain
English language
See under language
Enslaved (band, Norway) 11
epic
elements in metal 136
fits with metal 45
heavy metal as 27–8, 69, 136
metal 97
metal epics 106–7
poetry 81
themes in metal 117
Epica (band, Netherlands) 211, 215 n.24
Erinyes 80
esotericism 79, 174, 175–94
See also occult
esoteric metal 16, 155–8, 160–2, 166
ethnography 56, 61
Etruscans 1, 48 n.30
Euripides 101–2, 108, 110, 112 n.32, 128 n.36, 128 n.38
Europe 42–3, 98
Celtic 54–5
Eurocentrism 157, 174
identity 71–2
European Union 44
evil 163
and dark 102
metal's fascination with 15, 26–7, 131–2
women seen as evil 103, 104
See also under Caligula
Evil Scarecrow (band, UK) 1
Ex Deo (band, Canada) 1, 16, 62, 131–54, 201
Caligula (*see under* Caligula)
"I, Caligvla", 138–42 (*see also under* Caligula, music video)
influences on 133–4
live performance 147–8, 211
origins 136
and politics 51 n.82, 147, 208
Romulus (2009), 136–7
style 111 n.4, 135–6
"The Tiberius Cliff (Exile to Capri)", 1–2, 131, 136, 140, 142–6
See also under Latin language, music videos
extreme metal 8, 11, 131, 135, 176
anti-Christian stance 11, 27, 77, 91, 178
as learned 156
definition 8, 11
origins 12
and paganism 12
and Satanism 11
sounds 183–5

style 131–2, 135, 142, 156
and transgression(s), 176 (*see also* transgression(s))
See also black metal, death metal, doom metal

Falkenbach (band, Germany) 11
fan(s)
  of ancient world 4–5, 136–7, 156
  of Classics 2, 5
  female 9, 105, 116
  of Iron Maiden 185
  of metal 2, 4–5, 13, 45, 99–100, 125–6, 129 n.50, 135–6, 159–60, 210–13, 214 n.16
  of Nile (band, USA), 174–6, 186, 188
  of opera 122
  participation 97, 109
  of popular culture 4
  queer metal 124–5
  See also audience
fantasy 8, 51 n.83, 69, 97, 107, 162
  See also Conan the Barbarian
far-right
  See under politics in metal
Fascism/Fascist
  and ancient Rome 40–4
  and Classics 25, 47 n.13
  and Hesperia 41
  ideologies 90, 147–8, 208
  and Italy 25, 40–4
  See also Mussolini, nationalism, politics
female voice
  See under vocals
film
  and Classical reception 4, 5–6, 53, 138–9, 201, 203
  influence on metal 8, 16, 19 n.29, 138–9
  romanticizing Vikings 27
  reception of Egypt in 173
  See also Caligula *and under* Classics
folk metal 14, 53–76
  style 53
folk music 98
Ford, Lita 216 n.45
France 55–6, 57, 63
Freedom Call (band, Germany) 194 n.5
F.R.O.S.T. (band, Greece) 89

Gaia 86
Gaius
  See Caligula
Gallic Wars 14, 54, 59–60, 136, 155
  See also under Julius Caesar
Gaul(s) 53–64
Gaulish
  See under language

gender 15, 97–130
  dynamics 98
  expressed by Theatre of Tragedy 103, 105
  gender roles 99, 102
  in heavy metal 21 n.59, 97–111, 115–25, 128 n.41, 152 n.51, 207, 211–13
  and historical female figures 111
  instrumentation 109, 127 n.20
  LGBTQ 126 n.13
  in music 123–4
  power-relations 106, 110
  See also sex
genre
  See under heavy metal
Geoffrey of Monmouth 67–8, 71
German
  See under language
Germanicus 134, 140, 143–4, 145–6
Germany 44–5, 56
Giant Squid (band, USA) 1
Gladiator (film) 6, 204
gladiators 136, 169 n.72
glam rock 9
  See also hair metal
globalism 208
globalization
  as hybridization 210
  and immigration 41, 44
  and nationalism 208, 213
  and spread of metal 16–17, 203, 207, 210, 213
glocalization 46
glory
  and heroism 23, 117
  and honor 117, 124
  individual 175, 191
  and Italian heritage 25, 38, 41
  military 10
  of Rome 14, 23, 29, 35, 211
Gnosticism 161, 209–10
Goat of Mendes (band, Germany) 2, 216 n.41
Golden Dawn 42, 89
  in black metal 89–91
  and imprisonment 89
  and politics 208
Golden Dawn, Hermetic Order of the 189
gorgon 28, 100
  See also Medusa
gothic metal 15, 98, 132
  aesthetics 102, 111
  as feminine 105
  style 100
  See also Theatre of Tragedy
Grand Funk Railroad (band, USA) 7
Grave Digger (band, Germany) 2
Graves, Robert 134, 138
Greece, metal bands from 10, 12, 23, 27, 45–6, 77–93

251

Index

Greek hymns/hymnography 77–96
   characteristics 78
   in Greek black metal 91–3
   Greek politics 88–90
   Homeric Hymns 14–15, 79–81, 89, 91–3
   Orphic Hymns 14–15, 79–83, 84, 87, 89, 209
   tripartite structure in Kawir 83–8
   types 94 n.7
Greek language (ancient)
   in Bal-Sagoth 163–5
   in Celtic Frost 158–60, 163–5
   and Classics 3–4
   in Kawir 79, 86–8
   in other metal 208–10, 215 n.25
Greek language (modern) 81, 86–8, 92–3, 95 n.46
Greek magical papyri 79, 81, 95 n.49
Greek mythology
   See under mythology *and individual names*
grunge 9

Hades 37, 92, 204 (*see also* Pluto)
Hades Adorned (band, Netherlands) 88, 92
hair metal 9, 120
Halford (band, UK) 19 n.23
Hannibal 1, 24, 211 (*see also* Punic Wars)
Harmodius and Aristogeiton 1
heavy metal
   anti-Christian sentiments of 12, 207
   as cinematic 136, 142
   and Classical Reception 201–3
   different from other genres 46
   erudition of 12, 53
   image 8
   interest in history 10, 12, 132
   interest in war 37, 212
   musicians as part-time 45, 203
   name 7–8
   nationalistic turn 14, 26–7
   origins and history 6–12, 19 n.19, 19 n.21
   and power 61, 97, 110–11, 115–16, 128 n.40, 146, 150 n.37
   spread of 12, 16, 17, 20 n.46, 203–4, 209, 210
   stereotypes of 1, 5, 97, 105, 116, 173, 176, 185, 193
   subgenre affects choice and presentation of topic 53–4, 132–3, 135–6, 173–4, 97–111
   women in 211–13
   and violence 175–94
   See also black metal, death metal, doom metal, esoteric metal, extreme metal, folk metal, gothic metal, hair metal, Mediterranean metal, pagan metal, power metal, thrash metal, traditional metal, Vedic metal, Viking metal *and under* gender, Metal Studies, war
Hecate 80, 92
Hector 108, 212

Heimdall (band, Italy) 6, 14–15, 115–29
   and Aeneas 37–40, 42
   and *Aeneid* 29–33
   "Ballad of the Queen", 118–25
   and Dido (*see under* Dido)
   and nationalism 28, 40–3, 205
   origins 27, 116
   style 27–8
   themes 117
Helios 87–8, 144
   See also Sun
Helloween (band, Germany) 10, 215 n.24
Helvetians
   in Eluveitie 58–63
   and Julius Caesar 56–8, 66
   origins 54–5
Hephaestus 80, 9
   See also Vulcan
Hera 91
   See also Juno
Heracles 1, 81
Herbert, Frank 8
Hercules
   See Heracles
heritage
   Celtic 64
   Italian 206 (*see also under* glory)
   national 11, 207
   Roman, ancient 205
   Swiss 60
   See also identity, nationalism
Hermes 80, 91
   See also Mercury
Hermes Trismegistus 161
Hermeticism 187, 196 n.28
Herodotus 165
heroine(s) 67, 101–2, 123, 128 n.44
Hesiod 1, 79
Hesperia (band, Italy) 1, 23, 40–1, 48 n.28
Hesperia (place) 30, 34–5, 41
   See also Hesperia (band), Stormlord
Hestia 91
High on Fire (band, USA) 1
hip hop 9
historiography 53, 67, 69, 71
history
   See under heavy metal
Hitler, Adolf
   See Nazis
Hittites 191
hobbits
   See Tolkien, J. R. R.
Holy Martyr (band, Italy) 1, 42–4, 50 n.70
Homer 1, 3–4, 7, 24, 31, 79, 97, 100–1, 112 n.32, 155
Homeric Hymns
   See under Greek hymns/hymnography

Index

homosocial bonding 106–10
Horatius Cocles 1
horror 131, 146, 162, 187
Horus 190
Howard, Robert E. 16, 162–3, 165–6, 169 n.59, 169 n.61
hybridity 53, 68, 69, 71, 89, 210
hymns
    See Greek hymns/hymnography
Hyperborea 163, 164

Icarus 8, 17
Iced Earth (band, USA) 181, 194 n.6, 215 n.24
I, Claudius (novel) 134, 138
I, Claudius (television series) 134
identity
    British 66–7, 70–1
    Caledonian 65
    Celtic 14, 54, 59, 64, 71
    European 53–4, 72
    Germano-Celtic 65
    heavy metal and 97–8
    Helvetian 60, 62
    Italian 25, 29, 36
    national 12–13, 44
    Roman(ized), 70–1
    Scandinavian 27
    Swedish 27
    Swiss 54–64, 206
    Welsh 68
Illusion Suite (band, Norway) 2
Il primo re (film) 24
imaginary, the
    in folk metal 54
    in esoteric metal 162–3, 166, 188
Imhotep 181
I Miti Eterni (band, Italy) 206
immigration 41, 208
    see also refugee crisis
Imperivm (band, Italy) 206, 214 n.13
Imperium des Tenebras (band, Colombia) 201, 209–10
Indian mythology
    See Vedic metal *and under* mythology
In Flames (band, Sweden) 54
initiation 81, 187, 193
instruments 66, 69, 71, 82, 85, 87, 98, 120, 165
    ancient 84
    classical instruments in metal 158, 161, 184, 205
    folk 54, 64–5
    as gendered 15, 105, 109, 127 n.29
    non-metal 160–1
    synthesized 9, 28, 85, 100, 120, 162
Iran 161
Iron Maiden (band, UK) 8, 194 n.3
    "Alexander the Great", 1, 97, 142, 145, 181
    influence on metal 8–9, 19 n.27
    New Wave of British Heavy Metal (NWOBHM), 7
    performance 8, 10, 185–6
    "Powerslave" 173, 181, 183, 194 n.4
Isis (goddess) 180
Islam 207
Israel 177, 192
Italian language
    See under language
Italy
    education 25, 124
    metal bands from 10, 14, 23–46 *passim* 206, 215 n.23
    and the Roman Empire 14, 23, 29, 38, 44, 147–8
    synonymous with Rome 48 n.32
    See also under identity, nationalism

Janus 80
Jason 128 n.38
    See also Argonauts, Medea
Jett, Joan 126 n.13
John the Baptist 75 n.62
Jose Beausejour (band, France) 88–9, 92
Joyce, James 6, 204
Judas Priest (band, UK) 7–10, 11, 19 n.27
Julio-Claudian emperors 1–2, 138, 143
    See also Augustus Caesar, Caligula, Claudius, Nero, Tiberius
Julius Caesar 1, 4, 12, 25, 39, 126 n.18, 151 n.46, 155
    in Eluveitie 14, 55–64, 71, 206
    in Ex Deo 136–7, 150 n.31, 211
    Gallic Wars/Bellum Gallicum (BGall.), 14, 54–5, 65, 66, 74 n.36
Jupiter 24, 36, 40, 118, 138, 145, 150–1 n.38, 151 n.46
    See also Zeus

Kabeiroi 14, 77, 81, 93 n.2
ΚΑΒΕΙΡΟΣ (band, Greece) 82–3, 90
Kamelot (band, USA) 152 n.57
Kataklysm (band, Canada) 136, 147, 152 n.63
Kawir (band, Greece) 14–15, 77–91, 206, 208, 215 n.25
    and neo-paganism 83, 90–1, 93–4 n.3
Knights Templar 75 n.62, 155
Korn (band, USA) 9
Korybas/Korybantes 80, 83, 84, 85
Kouretes 80, 83, 85

landscape
    See under place
language
    ancient Egyptian 184–6, 191, 196 n.39
    Arabic 160, 164, 166, 170 n.90

Index

archaizing English 101, 105, 162
choice of 14, 20 n.43, 23, 29, 30, 33–6, 45, 54, 60, 61–2, 63, 68, 71, 86–8, 101, 105, 124, 159, 161, 184–5, 208–10
    Coptic 165, 184
    English 30, 33–6, 45
    Gaulish 54, 72 n.10, 209
    German 11, 64, 161, 188, 191
    Italian 23, 33–6, 38–9, 136
    mixing of 33–36, 210
    Old English 163
    Sanskrit 160
    See also Greek (ancient), Greek (modern), Latin language
La Tène
    See under Eluveitie
Latin language 17, 23, 28, 133–6, 105, 208–9, 215 n.24
    in Ade 204, 206
    in Bal-Sagoth 163–5
    in Eluveitie 61, 63
    in Ex Deo 136, 138, 150 n.32, 211, 215 n.25
    in Imperium des Tenebras 209–10
    in SuidAkrA 68
    in Theatre of Tragedy 98, 101, 105
    See also language *and see also under* Stormlord
LaVey, Anton Szandor 155
Led Zeppelin (band, UK) 6–8, 10, 189–90
legions, Roman 28, 41, 59, 64–5, 69, 136, 141, 145, 147, 149 n.8, 163, 211
Lemuria 158, 160, 163, 164
Limp Bizkit (band, USA) 9
liner notes
    Ancient Rites 155
    Bal-Sagoth 164–5, 170 n.78
    Bathory 26
    Heimdall 30–1, 33, 38, 116, 118–20, 124
    Nile 174–5, 184, 188–90, 194
    Stormlord 34, 39
    SuidAkrA 65, 74n39
    See also album artwork, booklets
Linkin Park (band, USA) 9
live performance 79, 97, 131, 206
    Blind Guardian 107–9
    Ex Deo 141, 145, 211
    Iron Maiden 185
    Kawir 79, 81–3, 88
    Nile 186
    Theatre of Tragedy 102–3
Livy 46 n.4, 205–6
Lizzy Borden (band) 131
Lordi (band, Finland) 131
Lord Impaler (band, Greece) 92
Lovecraft, H. P. 16, 28
    in esoteric metal 161–6, 188–9, 196 n.33, 198–9 n.74

and *Necronomicon* 164, 166, 170 n.83, 188
    See also Cthulhu
Lucan 50 n.66, 74 n.38
lyrics 174, 193, 201
    general disregard of in Metal Studies 13, 99, 177
    importance of 99–100, 138
    prominence in metal 3, 10–11, 13, 209
    See also under liner notes

Maat (band, Germany) 175
Mabinogion 67–71, 75 n.57
Macsen Wledig 2, 14, 66–71
madness 107–8, 122–3, 131, 146, 162
magic 16, 119, 123, 156, 157, 160, 166, 174, 175, 180–3, 189–90, 192, 194, 198 n.68
    See also Greek magical papyri
Magnus Maximus
    See Macsen Wledig
Malaysia 207–8
Manilla Road (band, USA) 169 n.65
Manowar (band, USA) 1, 10, 97, 191
Marduk (band, Sweden) 132
Mars 24
Martindale, Charles 3, 5–6, 190, 202, 204
Masada 2
masculinity
    in ancient literature 116
    in Blind Guardian 106–10
    in esoteric metal 162
    in Eluveitie 61
    in Ex Deo 142
    in Heimdall 116–18, 121, 123–4
    in metal 15, 17, 61, 97–9, 103, 111, 123, 142, 174, 211–13
    in Theatre of Tragedy 100–1, 103, 107–9
"mash-up" 210–11
"Masturbating the War God" 178–9, 188–9, 191
Maximian
    See Macsen Wledig
Mayans 165
MC5 (band, USA) 7
Medea 116, 128 n.36, 128 n.38
    See also Argonauts, Jason
Medieval
    See Middle Ages
Mediterranean metal
    characteristics 10–12, 208–9, 211
    and Classical antiquity 12, 17, 23–4, 28–9
    definition 2, 11, 44, 50 n.80, 174, 203
    and esoteric metal 157
    and nationalism 13, 17, 23–4, 44, 208
    origins 2, 9, 26–9, 44
    rise of 10–12, 23, 44, 45
    spread 11, 46, 208, 213
    and Viking metal 10–12, 26–9, 43–4

Index

Medusa 8, 100, 116
   See also gorgon
Megadeth (band, USA) 8
Megiddo 177–8
Mercury 118
   See also Hermes
Mercyful Fate (band, Denmark) 131, 162
Mesomedes 79, 81
Mesopotamia 191
metal
   See heavy metal
Metallica (band, USA) 8–10, 21 n.50, 162, 194 n.6
Metal Studies
   in academia 12–13
   and Classics 1–3
   fondness for black metal 9
   and global attention 207
Metastasio, Pietro 115
meter (dactylic hexameter) 34
Middle Ages 18 n.9, 25, 46 n.1, 48 n.40, 67, 97, 133, 155
Min 179
Minoans 1
Mithraic mysteries 81
modes
   See scales (musical)
Mongolia 46
monsters 15, 16, 133–5, 145–6
Montu 179
Morbid Fog (band, Greece) 88–9, 92
moshing 97, 186
Mötley Crüe (band, USA) 9
Motörhead (band, UK) 152 n.62
movies
   See film
MTV 9
mummies 173, 179–80, 181, 182–3, 185–6, 187, 192, 193
The Mummy (film) 196 n.28
musical traditions 54, 64
music videos 116, 131, 133–4, 150 n.31, 174, 201
   Eluveitie 59
   Ex Deo 135, 141–2, 145, 211
   Hesperia 41
   Nile 185–7
   Sacred Blood 216 n.34
   SuidAkrA 64, 69
Mussolini, Benito 25
   See also Fascism
Mysteries
   Eleusinian 81
   Greek 81
   of the Kabeiroi 93 n.2
   Mithraic 81
   Orphic 93

mysticism 16, 78, 177, 182
   See also occult
mythical narrative 78, 85–6
mythology 7
   Arabic 160
   British 69, 71
   Celtic 68, 205
   Classical 5, 23, 110, 115–16, 161, 174
   Egyptian 16, 160–1, 181–2, 186, 195 n.21
   European 101
   German 101
   Greek 1, 8, 12, 51 n.83, 101, 132
   Indian 160
   Italian 117
   and nationalism 14
   Norse 10–12, 27–9, 45, 46, 51 n.83, 116–17, 126 n.16, 160
   Orphic 85–6
   pagan 132
   Roman 12, 24, 43, 211
   Scandinavian 28
   Sumer 166
   Tolkien 211
   Viking 205
   Welsh 69

Naer Mataron (band, Greece) 89, 91–2
Nag Hammadi 209, 215 n.28
names
   of genres 7, 8, 9, 27, 100
   meaning of metal bands', 11–12, 14, 18 n.2, 18 n.3, 27–8, 54, 55, 77, 89, 102, 132, 136, 148 n.1, 155, 158, 159, 160, 162, 209, 212
   stage names 132, 205, 206, 212
Napalm Death (band, UK) 153 n.66
Narcissus 1
Nästrond (band, Sweden) 93
nationalism 12, 13–15, 17, 53, 67, 126 n.16, 182, 192, 206, 208, 213
   definitions of 13–14
   Italian 14, 23–46 *passim* 147–8, 205
   See also globalization, racism, white supremacy *and under* Europe, Heimdall, Hesperia, Mediterranean metal, mythology, politics
National Socialist Black Metal
   See under black metal
Necronomicon 164, 166, 170 n.83, 188
   See also Lovecraft, H. P.
Nekysia (band, Greece) 89
Nemesis 80, 83, 92
neoclassical 19 n.26
   See also Classical music *and under* instruments
neo-paganism
   See paganism *and under* Kawir
Nero 1–2, 106, 134, 136, 142
Neron Kaisar (band, Russia) 132

255

Index

New Testament 159, 210
   See also Bible
New Wave of American Heavy Metal 10
New Wave of British Heavy Metal (NWOBHM) 7–9
New York Dolls (band, USA) 9
Night (goddess) 92
Nightwish (band, Finland) 211, 216 n.37
Nile (band, USA) 16, 162
   and "Alternative" Egyptology 174–5, 187–9, 194
   and Egypt 173–200
   and Egyptology 181, 187
   metal narratives of 176–82
   and occult 187–90
   and Orientalism 190–4
   origins 175
   performance 185–7
   style 175–6
   and violence 177–9, 182–3, 186–7, 191–3
the 1990's 26, 131
   female presence 98–100, 111 (*see under* gender, sexuality, Theatre of Tragedy, vocals, women)
   heavy metal's development 3, 9, 11, 20 n.48
   and Scandinavian metal 28, 54, 77, 161, 212
Nirvana (band, USA) 9
Norse mythology
   See under mythology
Norwegian metal 20 n.49, 20–1 n.50, 77, 79, 86, 91
   See also church burnings
Notos 80
nu metal 9
Nymphs 92, 93

occult 8, 15, 26, 78–9, 89, 131, 156–61, 187–90, 209
   definition 156, 167 n.9
   Dragon Rouge 160–1
   and Egypt (*see under* Nile)
   perennial philosophy 158, 160
   See also Crowley, Aleister; Howard, Robert E.; Lovecraft, H. P.
Oceanus 93
Octavian 40, 121, 125 n.6, 126 n.18, 136
   See also Augustus Caesar
Odysseus 3–4, 128 n.47
   See also Homer, *Odyssey*, Ulysses
Odyssey 1, 3–4
opera 5, 18 n.13, 18 n.14, 25, 47 n.20, 115, 122
   See also Classical music *and under* vocals
Orientalism 124, 157, 183, 187
   See also Said, Edward *and under* Nile
Orpheus 94 n.21, 161
Orphic Hymns
   See under hymns
Orphic tablets 158, 161

Osbourne, Ozzy 198 n.65
   See also Black Sabbath
Osiris 180, 184
Ovid 1, 5, 115

Pacatus 66, 70, 75 n.62
Pagan(ism) 78–9, 86, 178, 186, 205, 209
   mythology 132, 205
   revival 15, 27, 77, 82, 83, 91, 215 n.19
   and Viking metal 11–12
   types of 93–4 n.3
pagan metal 40, 90, 94 n.17
   See also folk metal, Viking metal
Pan 81, 87, 93
Pandora 1
Pantera (band, USA) 9
Paradise Lost (band, UK) 100
Pausanias 95 n.32, 112 n.29
Pearl Jam (band, USA) 9
"perennial philosophy"
   See under occult
performance
   See under live performance
Pericles 125 n.6
Persephone 80, 92, 93
Persian Wars 1, 199 n.79
Phaedra 123
Phaethon 144
pharaoh 178, 181, 185, 188, 194 n.5, 194 n.7, 195 n.19, 210
Philo Judaeus 133, 141, 151 n.39
Phrygian mode
   See under scales (musical)
Physis 80, 83
place
   connection with topic 13
   influence of on metal 10, 11
   See also identity, nationalism
Plato 161, 163, 170 n.75
Pliny the Elder 73 n.16, 74 n.38, 113 n.53, 214 n.8
Plutarch 196 n.26
Pluto 80, 89, 92, 93
Poison (band, USA) 9
politics 8, 147–8, 182
   apolitical tendency in metal 157, 208
   right-wing political agendas 14, 15, 42, 42–5, 77, 88–91, 208
   See also alt-right, Fascism, nationalism
Polybius 206
Pompey 25, 126 n.18
pop culture 4
pop music 20 n.37, 21 n.61, 168 n.43
Poppaea Sabina 98, 101, 106
populism 208
Poseidon 80, 91
Posidonius 55, 59

Index

postcolonialism 14, 53–72, 206
   in Eluveitie 62–6 , 71, 206
   in SuidAkrA 69, 71, 206
Pound, Ezra 50 n.76
power
   See under heavy metal
power metal 97, 98, 99, 106–11, 111 n.8, 175
   characteristics 10, 15, 27, 111, 117
   definition of 15
Proclus 14–15, 79–81, 89, 92
progressive metal 135, 175
Protean (band, Latvia) 1
pulp fiction 15, 156, 157, 161–6
Punic Wars 1, 24, 28, 122, 137, 204–5, 206
   See also Carthage, Hannibal
punk rock 8, 9, 19 n.35
Purcell, Henry 6, 115
pyramids 179, 187, 192, 197 n.56
Pythagoras 161

Queen (band, UK) 107

racism 41, 208
   globalization 208
   and National Socialist Black Metal 78, 94 n.11, 215 n.21
   See also anti-Semitism, National Socialist Black Metal, white supremacy
Rebellion (band, Germany) 1, 44–5
Reception Studies 3–6, 190, 193
   See also under Classics
refugee crisis 43, 50 n.73
   See also immigration
religion
   in black metal 79, 86, 90–1
   Egyptian 190
   Greek 77, 79, 82, 88, 209
   Norse 11, 79
   of Thelema 189–90
   See also Christianity, paganism, ritual(s)
Religious Community Labrys 82, 90
Remus 1, 24, 136–7
Rhea 80, 83
ritual(s) 81, 159
   in Nile 177, 179–81, 184, 186
   performed by Dragon Rouge 160
   performed by Kawir 81, 87–8
romanticization
   See under antiquity
Rome
   as bloody 135, 137, 138, 148, 152 n.65
   emperors 67
   Empire 2, 10, 14, 65–72
   fall of 2
   founding of 1, 24, 46 n.5, 136, 137
   glory of 29
   as head of the world 41–2
   as idea 4, 17
   imperialism 164–5
   origins of 31–3, 39
   See also Italy, legions
Rome (television series) 151 n.41
Romulus
   in metal 136–8, 148
   and Rome's foundation 1, 24, 33, 35
   See also Remus
Rotting Christ (band, Greece) 12, 21 n.53

Sabaton (band, Sweden) 21 n.51, 98
Sacred Blood (band, Greece) 1, 45–6, 51 n.83, 211, 216 n.34
Said, Edward 16, 174, 191–2
   See also Orientalism *and under* Nile
Saltatio Mortis (band, Germany) 1
Samnites 28
Sanskrit
   See under language
Satanic Bible 155
   See also LaVey, Anton Szandor
Satanism
   and black metal 79, 89, 94 n.16, 195 n.20
   and Christianity 29, 79
   and extreme metal 11
   and heavy metal 5, 173
Saxon, (band, UK) 7
scales (musical)
   Mixolydian 107
   octatonic 183
   Phrygian mode 107, 110, 183
   quarter-tone 183 (*see also* tritone)
Scarab (band, Egypt) 175–6, 182, 192, 194 n.8
Schwarzenegger, Arnold 162
Scotland 64–5
Sejanus 142–3
Selene 80
Seneca the Younger 133, 142, 150 n.38, 151 n.44
Septicflesh (band, Greece) 1, 138
Serpentyne (band, UK) 216 n.41
Severus, Septimius 165
sex
   in metal 102, 106, 212, 216 n.36
   as subject matter 9, 26
   and violence 195 n.23
   See also gender
Scandinavia(n) 11–12, 27–8, 98, 205
ShadowIcon (band, Slovenia) 1, 211
Silent Dominion (band, Greece) 89, 92
singing
   See vocals
Siren 101, 105
Sirenia (band, Norway) 211
Skyclad (band, UK) 72 n.3

Index

Slayer (band, USA) 8, 19 n.27
Social Wars 25
Society for Classical Studies (SCS) 18 n.5
Sodom (band, Germany) 1, 135
Son of Aurelius (band, USA) 1
Soundgarden (band, USA) 9
Spain 66, 69
Sparta 125 n.6
Spartacus 1, 136
Spinal Tap (band, UK) 158
S.P.Q.R. 61, 73 n.24, 211
stage names
    See under names
Stargate (film) 198 n.61
Stoicism 133
Stooges, The (band, USA) 7
Stormlord (band, Italy) 1, 6, 14, 23
    and *Aeneid* 29–31, 33–6, 42
    influences 28
    Italian history 28, 205, 208
    origins 28
    style 28–9
    use of Latin, Italian, and English 32–6, 38, 215 n.25
Stosstrupp (band, Greece) 89
Strabo 55
Strauss, Nita 212
Stutthof (band, Greece) 89
subgenre
    See under heavy metal
Suetonius
    on Caligula 133, 134, 139, 140, 144, 150–1 n.38, 151 n.39, 152 n.60
    and Ex Deo 141, 143, 146
    on Tiberius 142–7
SuidAkrA (band, Germany) 2, 14, 208
    British identity 66–71 (*see also* Macsen Wledig)
    Celtic identity 64–5
    identity formation, Romano-Celtic, Germano-Celtic 65–7
    instrumentation 65
    style 64
    and Tacitus 65, 71
Sun 80, 81, 83, 87, 92, 93, 95 n.49
    See also Helios
Sweden 8, 11, 20 n.48, 27, 54
    See also under identity
Switzerland 16, 54–7, 158
    See also under identity
Symphony X (band, USA) 1, 188, 194 n.7, 196 n.31, 204
syncretism 83, 87–8, 103

Tacitus 4, 65, 71, 113 n.52, 143, 151 n.44, 152 n.55, 152 n.61

Templar Knights
    See Knights Templar
Tennyson, Alfred Lord 3–4, 8
Teutoburg Forest 1, 44, 136, 155
Theatre of Tragedy (band, Norway)
    and female icons 98, 101–4
    and gender construction 15, 98–9, 101, 105–6, 110–11
    style 98, 100, 102, 109, 169 n.70
theatricality 98, 100, 103, 131, 145, 152 n.63, 185, 186, 208
The Gathering (band, Netherlands) 100
Themis 92
Theodosius I 66, 67
Therion (band, Sweden) 16
    eclecticism of 161, 165–6
    occult influences 158, 160, 168 n.41, 169 n.57
    style 158, 161
Thermopylae 12, 45
Thor 45, 126 n.16
Thor Ragnarok (film) 10
thrash metal 8, 175
    and antiquity 8, 135, 175
    characteristics 8, 19 n.35, 195 n.13
    and folk metal 53
    influence on black metal 77–8
Thy Catafalque (band, Hungary) 1
Tiamat (band, Sweden) 100
Tiberius
    in ancient sources 133, 140, 142–5, 151 n.42
    See also under Ex Deo
Tiberius Project (band, Brazil) 132
Titans 93
Tolkien, J. R. R. 10, 107, 211
traditional metal 20 n.45, 41–2, 105, 122 n.19, 175
    style 9–10
tragedy 107–8, 110, 123, 126 n.14
transculturation 62–3, 68, 71
    See also folk metal
transgression(s) 118, 122, 131–2, 147, 176–87, 190
translation 31–6, 38
tritone 165, 176
    See also scales (musical)
Triptykon (band, Switzerland) 159
Trivium (band, USA) 10
Troy/Trojan War 19 n.29, 24, 31–2, 37–8, 40, 101, 107–10, 117–18, 120, 122
True Detective (television series) 155
Trump, Donald J. 208
t-shirts 75 n.62, 195 n.23
    See also dress
Turisas (band, Finland) 2
Turkey 50 n.75
Turnus 24, 36, 42–3, 48–9, 129
Týr (band, Faroe Islands) 11

Index

Ultima Thule 163, 164
Ulysses 3
    See also Homer, Joyce, Odysseus
Ulysses 6, 204
Underworld
    in *Aeneid* 24, 35, 40
    in black metal 89
    in Heimdall 38, 117–18, 123
    and Lovecraft 164
    in Nile 184, 186
    in Stormlord 35
Unholy Archangel (band, Greece) 92
United Nations 43
Ύπατο Συμβούλιο των Ελλήνων Εθνικών (ΥΣΕΕ) 77, 82–3, 86, 96 n.62, 208
    and Greek religious festivals 88, 90–1, 96 n.56, 96 n.57
Uranus 80, 84, 92
Uranus (band, Greece) 88, 92

Van Halen (band, USA) 9
Varangian Guard 2
Vedic metal 21 n.54
Venom (band, UK) 7, 9, 132, 149 n.5
Venus
    in antiquity 40, 117
    in heavy metal 37, 98, 101, 105, 117–18, 161
    See also Aphrodite
Verberis (band, New Zealand) 89, 93
Vercingetorix 12, 61–4
Vergil 3, 23–52, 115–30
    See also Aeneid
VerSacrum (band, Italy) 1, 48 n.30
Vikernes, Varg 79
Viking metal
    compared with Mediterranean metal 12, 26, 43
    connection with Scandinavian countries 11
    definition of 11
    and growth of Mediterranean metal 11–12, 45
    influence on Mediterranean metal 26–9, 207
    masculinity in 142
    origins 9–12, 26–7, 47 n.19, 132
    spread of 11–12, 27
violence 147, 183
    See also aggression
Virgil
    See Vergil
Virgin Steele (band, USA) 194 n.3
virtus 56–8, 61–2, 65
visuals 8, 99
    See also album covers, dress, live performance
vocals 19 n.32, 36, 117
    backing 107
    "beauty and the beast", 100, 102–3, 105–6, 109
    booming 117–18
    choice of style 63, 86, 105–6, 121, 122, 162, 191–2
    choral 109, 121, 158, 160–1, 167 n.22
    "cookie monster", 8
    female 15, 37, 61, 63, 100, 103, 106, 216 n.41
    "growling", 28, 63, 105, 139
    male-female 15, 105, 109, 124
    operatic 100, 123
    screaming 78, 162, 165
    See also under death metal
Vulcan 40
    See also Hephaestus

Wagner, Richard 47 n.20
war 21 n.60, 126 n.6, 174, 195 n.13, 211
    in Ade 205
    black metal and 78
    in Ex Deo 136
    in Heimdall 117–18
    in Nile 177–9
    tragedy of 108–9
    See also civil wars (Rome), Punic Wars, Troy/Trojan War *and under* heavy metal
Warrant (band, USA) 9
W.A.S.P. (band, USA) 131
Weird Tales 156–7, 161–2
Welsh mythology
    See under mythology
We Start Wars (band, USA) 212
"Western Civilization" 43
    See also nationalism, politics
White Skull (band, Italy) 1, 211, 216 n.41
white supremacy 50 n.70, 208
    See also anti-Semitism, nationalism, racism *and under* politics
Wolfnacht (band, Greece) 89
women
    of antiquity 15, 30, 57, 63, 108, 127 n.33, 141, 212
    and Classics 17
    in Ex Deo 141–2
    in heavy metal 15, 17, 63, 102–4, 108, 123, 185, 212
    heavy metal musicians 61, 103–6, 126 n.13, 212
    marginalization of 63, 116, 126 n.7, 128 n.40
    in Mediterranean metal 12
    in Viking metal 12
    See also Dido, gender, heroine(s) *and under* Heimdall, Theatre of Tragedy, vocals
worship
    devil 78
    of Olympian gods 15, 77–9, 82, 86–8, 90
    pagan 77

259

Index

of Tiberius 143
See also paganism, religion, ritual(s)
Wotan (band, Italy) 11–12

Yngwie Malmsteen's Rising Force (band, Sweden) 11

Zarathustra 161
Zephyr 80, 92
Zeus 80, 83–6, 87, 88, 91, 93, 132, 198 n.6
  See also Jupiter
Zombie, Rob 131
Zosimus 66, 70

www.ingramcontent.com/pod-product-compliance
Lightning Source LLC
Chambersburg PA
CBHW050324020526
44117CB00031B/1702